Conquering the maharajas

Manchester University Press

STUDIES IN IMPERIALISM

General editors: Andrew S. Thompson and Alan Lester
Founding editor: John M. MacKenzie

When the 'Studies in Imperialism' series was founded by Professor John M. MacKenzie more than thirty years ago, emphasis was laid upon the conviction that 'imperialism as a cultural phenomenon had as significant an effect on the dominant as on the subordinate societies.' With well over a hundred titles now published, this remains the prime concern of the series. Cross-disciplinary work has indeed appeared covering the full spectrum of cultural phenomena, as well as examining aspects of gender and sex, frontiers and law, science and the environment, language and literature, migration and patriotic societies, and much else. Moreover, the series has always wished to present comparative work on European and American imperialism, and particularly welcomes the submission of books in these areas. The fascination with imperialism, in all its aspects, shows no sign of abating, and this series will continue to lead the way in encouraging the widest possible range of studies in the field. 'Studies in Imperialism' is fully organic in its development, always seeking to be at the cutting edge, responding to the latest interests of scholars and the needs of this ever-expanding area of scholarship.

To buy or to find out more about the books currently available in this series, please go to: https://manchesteruniversitypress.co.uk/series/studies-in-imperialism/

Conquering the maharajas

India's princely states and the end of
empire, 1930–50

Harrison Akins

MANCHESTER UNIVERSITY PRESS

Published by Manchester University Press
Oxford Road, Manchester M13 9PL

www.manchesteruniversitypress.co.uk

British Library Cataloguing-in-Publication Data
A catalogue record for this book is available from the British Library

ISBN 978 1 5261 6785 9 hardback

First published 2023

Typeset
by Cheshire Typesetting Ltd, Cuddington, Cheshire

Contents

Maps

Introduction: Conquering the maharajas

'15 August 1947, India became free. But up until now some princely states remain subjugated by a raja.' So runs the opening narration of the 1969 Bollywood film *The Prince*, a story of the erstwhile princely order of India—the maharajas, rajas, nawabs and khans—forced to navigate the rapid political changes brought on by the British withdrawal from the Indian Subcontinent. Following the film's opening credits, the audience is greeted by the visage of the famed actor of Bollywood's golden age, Shammi Kapoor, as he lazily gazes with disinterest at a dancing girl. A bevy of turbaned servants tend to his every need—lighting his cigarette, fixing him drinks and feeding him pills. 'It's crap,' he slurs as he orders the dancing girl to stop. Kapoor plays the film's eponymous protagonist Prince Shamsher Singh, the spoiled son of the maharaja of the fictional state of Ramnagar who still rules his princely domain in the early years of India's independence. The heavily mustachioed maharaja is later introduced in the film reclining on a chaise longue in a lush palace garden as groveling servants brush his moustache and trim his toenails, all while he unsuccessfully attempts to convince his wayward playboy of a son to marry the daughter of a reputable local landowner. Yet, the irresponsible Prince Shamsher dismisses his father's suggestion. 'I am not interested in marriage … I am not interested in anything,' he retorts, as he slowly sips his morning brandy.

Prince Shamsher is portrayed as a comic and buffoonish figure, one played to great effect by the inimitable Shammi Kapoor. Early in the film, he spends his listless days drinking and sleeping as his irrational whims are attended to by perpetually hovering servants. During a drunken fit, he even whips a priest over the perceived insult of comparing the prince to an ordinary man. Immediately afterwards, the drunk prince repents over the beating, and the priest advises him that the only way for him to find true happiness is to learn to be an ordinary man by giving up his princely duties for six months, hiding his true identity and working as an ordinary laborer. What follows is a series of misadventures and mistaken identities. The prince fakes his own death, has run-ins with dacoits, poses as a peasant woman's son, becomes the aide-de-camp of another local maharaja and ultimately finds himself forced to pretend to be himself after catching the attention of a pair of corrupt palace officials who notice his resemblance to the missing prince—along with the requisite romance, songs and spectacle of Bollywood.

The Prince depicts India's princely order as cruel and corrupt masters living extravagant and pampered lives. Their days are full of polo, cricket and hunting expeditions. Their evenings are spent attending lavish parties in verdant gardens and marbled palaces, with no indication of any real administrative work being done or any thought spared for their subjects. This fictional representation reflects not only the traditions of colonial-era British literature but the views of many British officials who served within India and saw the princes as oriental despots reveling in sin and extravagance.[1] Indeed, the bard of British Empire, Rudyard Kipling, once quipped, 'God created the maharajas so that mankind could have the spectacle of jewels and marble palaces.' These popular stereotypes of India's princely states as curious remnants of the British Raj persist even today, as embodied in the East India Company artwork of the seventeenth and eighteenth centuries, the fantasies of Bollywood and the numerous tourist sites dotting the Indian landscape; these include Jaipur's Amber Palace and Hawa Mahal with their famous facades of pink sandstone, the expansive Bara Imambara in Lucknow, the ornate Mysore Palace in southern Karnataka and the iconic Charminar in Hyderabad. The lavish lifestyles of several former princely families continue to serve as fodder for India's gossip columns and further feed this perception. These royals without states have been an aristocratic class of wealthy playboys and socialites lacking any political authority but continuing to carry their traditional titles. Their numbers include business tycoons, polo players, cricketers, hoteliers and Bollywood stars. A January 2020 magazine spread in *GQ India* presented these princely families as 'fairy tales in modern times.'[2]

Yet, such caricatures gloss over the very serious and consequential political role the princely states played in the formation of India and Pakistan and the potential they had in undermining the political and territorial unity of both countries in their early years. At independence from British colonial rule, India and Pakistan confronted a vast mosaic of different political divisions in which the central government exercised uneven control: the British-administered provinces, largely unadministered tribal areas on British India's northwestern and northeastern frontiers, enclaves ruled by different European powers such as Portuguese Goa and French-ruled Pondicherry and the hundreds of princely states. India's over 560 autonomous princely states were no minor or inconsequential feature of the British Raj. They constituted a significant proportion of its territory and population. By the 1940s, the combined territory of the princely states added up to approximately six hundred thousand square miles, around 40 percent of India's total territory, and contained nearly one hundred million people.

The princely states were politically and administratively distinct from the rest of the British Raj. Each sovereign prince possessed internal political autonomy within their states, with a number of them maintaining a direct treaty relationship with the British Crown that served as the basis for the princes' sovereignty. Given their distinct political status, the princely states were not included in British plans for Partition, which only affected the provinces. Therefore, the princely states did not automatically join either India or Pakistan at the transfer of power in August 1947, with Indian and Pakistani authorities left with the monumental task of convincing each individual prince to accede to the appropriate postcolonial state. This was made all the more difficult as many princes were resistant to relinquish their

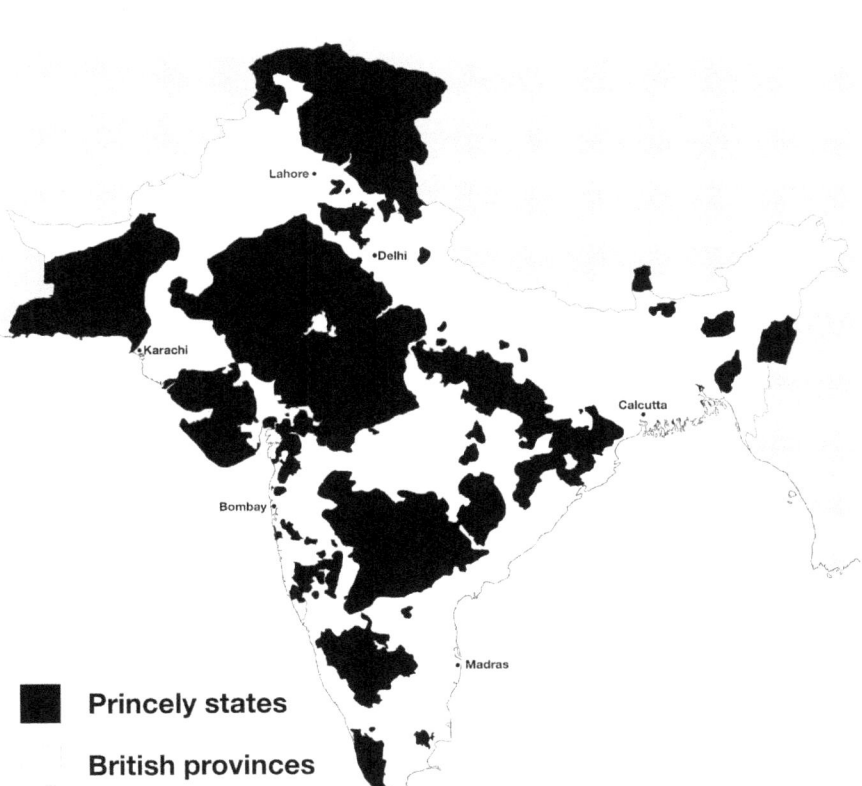

Map 1.1 Map of the princely states under the British Raj

sovereignty and accede to either successor government, with the status of several princely states left unsettled after the transfer of power. Given the princes' resistance, the accession and integration of the princely states posed perhaps one of the greatest challenges India and Pakistan faced in the weeks and months after independence and helped bring the two countries to the brink of war on multiple occasions.

In August 1947, the borders of India and Pakistan did not suddenly take shape as we imagine them today. Historian Norman Davies argued in his study of vanished European kingdoms varyingly broken up or absorbed into present-day countries:

> Our mental maps are thus inevitably deformed. Our brains can only form a picture from the data that circulates at any given time; and the available data is created by present-day powers, by prevailing fashions and by accepted wisdom. If we continue to neglect other areas of the past, the blank spaces in our minds are reinforced, and we pile more and more knowledge into those compartments of which we are already aware.[3]

When imagining countries of the past, many inevitably superimpose present-day borders, geographies and political identities back into history. They view the state-building process teleologically, already knowing what would emerge and frequently overlooking the process in between that constructed and produced the boundaries that we see today. Within South Asia, there is a tendency to implicitly portray India and Pakistan as emerging fully formed out of the violence of Partition. (Pakistan's borders were again revised in 1971 when East Pakistan successfully broke away to form Bangladesh.) Yet, in the weeks and months after independence, the maps of India and Pakistan were far from settled and the ultimate outcome far from certain as several princely states had not yet acceded to either India or Pakistan and remained essentially independent states.

Today, we know the ending of the story. During the final days of the British Raj, the princely states inched closer and closer to the dustbins of history. Ian Copland, a leading historian of India's princely states, noted the rapid decline of the princely order between the end of the First World War, when the Indian princes were at the peak of their power and prestige, and the transfer of power three decades later, when the princely states would soon disappear from the map of South Asia.[4] For the many people living through the end of empire in India, however, it was difficult to tell where the chips would fall. Officials in New Delhi and Karachi (Pakistan's first capital) were faced with the challenge of convincing, cajoling and, in some cases, forcing the numerous princes who were committed to preserving their sovereignty to accede to either India or Pakistan. This was an exhaustive process full of many twists, turns, missteps and even violence left unresolved at independence. This book unpacks the process of the princely states' eventual integration into India and Pakistan as the political actors involved would have seen it—with all the heated debates, numerous false starts, personality clashes and conflicts without a certain outcome. The noted Indian diplomat K.M. Panikkar, who served in prominent positions within several princely states before 1947, once remarked, 'Any account of the last days of princely rule will sound incredible today.'[5]

Clashing ideas of state sovereignty

'The period of Indian history since 1947,' political theorist Sunil Khilnani wrote, 'might be seen as the adventure of a political idea: democracy.'[6] With the transfer of power in August 1947, the British government passed its political authority to Indian hands who sought to construct a government based in the ideals of a modern democratic state in which political authority and legitimacy derived from the will and consent of a unified Indian people. The state was further defined by the universality of its laws and the uncontested and exclusive sovereignty of the central government. In December 1946, India's first Prime Minister Jawaharlal Nehru unequivocally announced in the newly established Constituent Assembly that 'a free India can be nothing but a republic.'[7]

This conception of state sovereignty—centralized state authority with its legitimacy rooted in democratic institutions and the consent of the people—was in stark contrast to the political order under the British Raj. In their volume on postcolonial states' sovereignty, Thomas Blom Hansen and Finn Stepputat argued: 'Colonial sovereignty was constructed slowly and piecemeal and oscillated between confrontation and alignment, between spectacular representations of European might and culture, and incorporation of local idioms and methods of rule.'[8] They further observed that the pragmatic construction of European sovereignty over distant colonial possessions had a distinct purpose to the forms of political power that emerged within Europe itself, stating:

> European states never aimed at governing the colonial territories with the same uniformity and intensity as were applied to their own populations. The emphasis was rarely on forging consent and the creation of a nation-people, and almost exclusively on securing subjection, order, and obedience through performance of paramount sovereign power and suppression of competing authorities ... As a result, the configurations of *de facto* [*sic*] sovereign power, justice, and order in the postcolonial states were from the outset partial, competing, and unsettled.[9]

In a study of frontier governance in several British colonies in Africa and Asia, historian Benjamin Hopkins also explained:

> By the latter half of the nineteenth century the issues of communication, transportation, and finance that previously limited the ability of early modern suzerains to assert claims of exclusive authority had largely been overcome, though by no means totally eradicated. Nonetheless, the colonial state abjured uninhibited claims of sovereignty. Instead, it created a universe of sovereign pluralism, where the exclusivity associated with the idea of sovereignty was present, as paradoxically was the space for multiple political allegiances.'[10]

In building up their political authority, the Indian and Pakistani governments confronted the legacy of the layered and fragmented sovereignty of British colonial rule—not just the political, social and legal institutions left behind by the departing British but the many elites whose entrenched political and economic interests were shaped by these institutions and whose goals were to retain them in some form. The foundations laid by a century of British Crown rule in India, even with all its paradoxes, did not fall overnight. To build up and consolidate new ideas of sovereignty and nationalism within their claimed territory, Indian and Pakistani authorities had to conquer the colonial legacy of layered sovereignty to which many princes and other political elites clung. Leading up to and following the transfer of power, one of the foremost challenges Indian and Pakistani political leaders faced was to overcome and integrate the hundreds of princely states whose rulers contested the sovereignty of the new governments and sought to protect their political autonomy following the British departure, even if that meant seeking outright independence for their princely state. Khilnani observed, 'Thus was the Indian state embattled in contests over rights to territory from its inception.'[11]

As I argue here, India and Pakistan's struggles to assert the writ of the postcolonial state over Princely India, including the use of military force against the most recalcitrant princely states, was a product of these clashing ideas of state sovereignty. On one side of this conflict were numerous princes, urged on by several British officials, who sought to protect their sovereignty as enjoyed under the umbrella of British paramountcy. On the other side, the Indian nationalist movement and the political movements representing the princely states' subjects (such as Jammu and Kashmir's National Conference, the Hyderabad State Congress and the Provisional Government of Junagadh) challenged the princes' sovereignty, pushed for political reforms within the princely states and generally sought to support the sovereignty of the postcolonial central government. The intersection of these different perspectives on the issue of sovereignty within the princely states—British paramountcy, the princely order, the nationalist movement and the states' subjects—helps to explain the political debates and resulting conflicts involving the princely states leading up to and following the transfer of power. Therefore, this book follows the interactions between these differing perspectives over the issue of state sovereignty through the narrative of events surrounding the princely states' status through the end of British empire in South Asia. It demonstrates the changing understanding of sovereignty and political power in India and how the process of dismantling colonial-era institutions continued through the early years of independence.

Through the late 1930s and 1940s, the princes and their supporters largely opposed the political reforms sought by the Indian nationalist movement, which increasingly worked in tandem with the states' subjects, and instead sought to maintain the sovereignty of the princely states as it existed under British paramountcy. As a clear demonstration of their position, the princes consistently opposed any efforts to alter the political status of the princely states, such as British plans to introduce an All-India Federation consisting of both the British Indian provinces and Princely India during the 1930s. Princely opposition to the federation scheme was based on fears of a new federal government within New Delhi eroding the princes' sovereignty as recognized by the British Crown. During the debates about India's constitutional future in the 1940s, the princes continued to cling to the layered sovereignty of the British colonial order in India to protect their status and privileges, often under the encouragement of departing British officials. Furthermore, the ambiguity of British policy toward the princely states at this time provided the princely order both the space and legal justification to assert their sovereignty following the British withdrawal from the Subcontinent.

The princes' position was strengthened by the British authorities' long-standing recognition of the princes' sovereignty. The upshot of British policy toward the princely states ultimately was to prop up and perpetuate the rule of India's princely order even in the face of the misrule and, at times, political repression by the princes. Several British viceroys, from Lord Canning to Lord Mountbatten, asserted to the princes that the British government respected the political sovereignty of the princes within the umbrella of British paramountcy. They further provided assurances that their treaties with the British Crown were binding, and the rights and privileges contained within them would be respected, especially amid broader political changes in the Subcontinent. However, there was an inherent tension between the British government supporting the princes' sovereignty and British officials frequently interfering in the internal affairs of the states in the interests of promoting good governance and efficient administration, both of which were ambiguously defined. The relationship between the British government and the princely states was inherently fluid and the line between these two opposing positions frequently shifted according to changes in British political interests or turnover in government personnel.

In the early twentieth century, Viceroy Lord Minto introduced a general policy of nonintervention toward the internal affairs of the princely states, an approach that generally held into the 1940s. This laissez-faire approach left the princely states in an ambiguous position as India moved toward independence, ambiguity that was exasperated by the conflicting views and debates among British officials. The British government continued to assert that the princely states' sovereignty would be respected, and no political outcome would be forced on the princes as officials in London and New Delhi began to plan for the British withdrawal. Yet, the princely states' relations with an independent India and Pakistan remained unclear with the British government essentially leaving the matter to be settled by the two successor governments.

With the princely states untethered from their Crown treaties, it became the responsibility of the princes and Indian and Pakistani authorities to enter negotiations and decide the future position of the princely states within both countries. In these negotiations, the princes' commitment to protecting their sovereignty remained firm, and many repeatedly pointed to the policies of the British government as giving them the legal right to abstain from acceding to either an Indian National Congress-dominated India or a Muslim League-controlled Pakistan and enter alternative political arrangements with New Delhi and Karachi other than accession, based in British recognition of their unique sovereign status. The princes were generally a conservative lot who opposed the more socialist and populist policies of the Indian National Congress, especially as the nationalist movement increasingly found common cause with states' subjects who actively opposed the princes' continued rule. The princes were soon facing both top-down and bottom-up pressure to relinquish their political authority and grant responsible government to their subjects. As a result, many princes feared for their rule within an independent and democratic Indian government under the control of the Congress. The princely states represented a more traditional and monarchical form of state formation that did not sit well with the nationalism espoused by Indian authorities and their conception of state sovereignty.

The announcement of Partition in June 1947 only further complicated the situation as some princely states had a majority Muslim population and Hindu ruler, and vice versa. Their path remained unclear. While the British government felt that the partition of the British Indian provinces was unavoidable, they failed to make a similar determination about the division of the princely states between India and Pakistan given their sovereign status. This omission helped to engender the territorial disputes and early military clashes between the two postcolonial states. While Partition would exacerbate the problem of the princely states, however, the underpinning catalyst for the princes' clashes with the successor states to British rule was fundamentally the clash between the different conceptions of sovereignty and where political power rested. Even before Partition was announced, many princes were committed to protecting their sovereignty and opposed integration into an independent Indian Union. To protect their political authority from interference from the postcolonial governments, many princes asserted that British policy, reflecting the laissez-faire approach to the princely states' internal affairs, not only recognized their right to maintain their sovereignty but also the right to become independent states.[12] Some British colonial officials even encouraged this perspective and argued that the princes held every legal right to pursue the path of independence, while other officials were adamant that the princely states should accede to the appropriate dominion government.

Amid the ambiguity over the princely states' status and the perceived threat to their sovereignty from anticipated political reforms under a Congress-controlled government, several princes began 'to luxuriate in wild dreams of independent power' following the British withdrawal, especially those states with large populations, expansive territory and high state revenues, or if they held strategic positions within the Subcontinent—which they felt lent credence to their capacity to sustain an independent political existence following the lapse of British paramountcy.[13] As the British hastened their exit in the summer of 1947, Indian authorities scrambled to convince the princes of the merits of accession with New Delhi, fearing that the princes' efforts to preserve the layered sovereignty of British colonial rule would threaten the security and sovereignty of the postcolonial state. Following the transfer of power, ensuring the accession and political integration of the many princely states quickly became one of the major challenges facing the Indian and Pakistani governments as part of their efforts to decolonize the Subcontinent's political institutions and build up their territorial integrity. While Indian and Pakistani authorities mostly succeeded in convincing the princes to accede in the run up to independence, with some princes proactive in their support of the nationalist movement and integration into the Indian Union, numerous problems remained after 15 August 1947—foremost among them were those presented by the princely states of Jammu and Kashmir, Hyderabad and Junagadh in India, and Kalat in Pakistan, all of which resulted in the use of the military in some form to pressure the rulers to accede. Thus, the layered sovereignty of British colonial rule and British policies toward the princely states set the stage for the political and military clashes between the princely states and the successor governments to British colonial rule.

In his magnum opus, *India After Gandhi: The History of the World's Largest Democracy*, historian Ramachandra Guha outlines four key axes of conflict within India that have driven much of its politics following independence: caste, language, religion and class. The divisions of Indian society along these fault lines have operated 'both singly and in combination' to threaten the territorial and political integrity of his 'unnatural' country. Guha also points to a number of factors that have counteracted the potential for these forces to divide India and 'helped transcend or contain the cleavages of class and culture, that—so far at least—have nullified the many predictions that India would not stay united and not stay democratic': the pluralistic approach to religion and language serving as the cornerstone of a unified political order, the shared respect for the country's political and economic institutions and Bollywood movies and song acting as a shared culture across these various fault lines.[14] But we can add another item to Guha's list of fault lines—the political tensions and conflict over spaces of contested sovereignty, a legacy of British indirect rule in South Asia.

The British Raj and indirect rule

The princely states were emblematic of the British policy of indirect rule. This was an administrative approach employed not only in India but across the British Empire as a pragmatic solution to a pressing problem—the British government simply did not have the resources at hand, or at times the political will or strategic interests, to directly rule the entirety of its vast colonial possessions. Indirect rule relied on coopting, building up or recognizing local leaders who were granted political, administrative and judicial authority within defined geographic, legal or social limits. These were areas of shared sovereignty in which the sovereignty of the recognized local authorities overlapped with and was nested within that of the imperial power.[15] Frederick Lugard, the first Governor of the British colony of Nigeria who spent the early years of his career in India and was a noted champion of indirect rule, argued that building up local authorities 'with a recognized and legal standing,' as opposed to the implementation of direct rule by external actors, was important for averting 'social chaos' as the legal borders of the British Empire were expanded, disrupting existing political, economic and social structures.[16] For the financially conscious British officials responsible for wide swathes of territory, this administrative approach became a more expedient and cost-effective alternative to introducing new political institutions that frequently required costly military deployments to support them, especially within frontier areas that offered little economic benefits in return. Other European colonial powers intermittently relied on indirect rule in their colonies, such as France in Tunisia and Morocco and the Netherlands in the Dutch East Indies' Aceh region, but, for the most part, they instituted direct administrative control to replace both traditional political structures and local political and social identities.[17] Indirect rule was most associated with the rule of the British Empire given its wide use by British colonial authorities in both Asia and Africa.

Yet, indirect rule was not a single, monolithic or static system. It was a governance approach that encompassed a variety of legal frameworks and styles of administration influenced and shaped by local political, economic and social contexts within which they were established over time—from tribal areas and distant frontiers to the wealthy princely states in the heart of India.[18] Political scientists Adnan Naseemullah and Paul Staniland identified three primary forms of indirect rule implemented by British colonial authorities within South Asia: suzerain, hybrid and *de jure*.[19] Hybrid governance involved sharing political and legal authority with local elites, often under explicit legal frameworks that defined the boundaries of authority and coercive force practiced by both colonial and local officials. In particular, a hybrid system was employed in frontier areas where the establishment of direct rule was prohibitively expensive with little promise of revenue generation for the colonial government. One often-cited example of this form of governance was the northwestern frontier's Tribal Areas along the border between Afghanistan and British India, where a hybrid administration was established with the 1901 Frontier Crimes Regulation (FCR) that governed the region through the recognition of local tribal elders (and remained in effect in Pakistan until 2018). Within such areas, the British Indian government recognized the authority of local tribal elders and frequently relied upon them to deploy coercive force while also maintaining the right for its own military interventions, as the British frequently did within the Tribal Areas. *De jure* governance was an arrangement in which the state asserted its legal sovereignty over a defined territory, but de facto authority and the use of coercive force was practiced by local intermediaries acting on behalf of the state. This included various parts of the Punjab following its annexation by the British in 1849 where British authorities relied on a feudal relationship with large-scale landowners.[20]

Within India's princely states, the British colonial government instituted a suzerain system of governance under which local princes held nominal sovereignty and internal political autonomy but maintained allegiance to an overarching imperial power that recognized their political authority to rule. In his analysis of Hyderabad's position in the varied political landscape of the late-colonial period of South Asia, historian Eric Lewis Beverley argued that the princely states occupied 'a vast legal gray area.' In contrast to the emerging international system based in states' uncontested territorial sovereignty throughout their borders along the line of the Westphalian ideal type of states, he asserts that the position of the princely states demonstrated that political sovereignty within British India under the suzerain system was essentially fragmented and heterogenous, which would form the basis of the ambiguity of the princely states' position through the transfer of power in 1947.[21]

Through recognizing the princes' authority within a system of layered sovereignty, the British government hoped to weld the political interests of the princes and other political elites within the princely states to imperial rule. The princely elites' political interests were shaped and defined by the political system that granted them access to power and privileges, and, thus, they became committed to its perpetuation, especially in the face of the states' subjects challenging the political status quo from which they derived few benefits. Given the intimate connection between their political authority and the British Raj, the princes were resistant to any broader political reforms that could undermine their authority, a position that was frequently supported and encouraged by the British government's policies and rhetoric.

Scholars have recognized how the institutional and political legacy of indirect rule in South Asia shaped and defined the interests of political actors and laid the foundation for conflicts over asymmetric access to political power, especially as postcolonial states retained various colonial institutions. Following independence, for instance, Pakistan maintained the undemocratic system of semi-control under the FCR in the Federally Administered Tribal Areas (FATA) until 2018, when it was repealed, and the region merged with the neighboring Khyber Pakhtunkhwa Province. The recognized tribal elders under the FCR consistently pushed back against any attempts to reform or repeal this legal framework to protect their status and privileges, especially during periods of broader political turmoil such as the transfer of power in 1947. Anthropologist Akbar Ahmed observed within FATA:

> Independence came to mean different things to the center and the periphery. The center's main priority was to consolidate and establish its authority in all its parts. The periphery assumed that its state of semi-independence would be preserved, and that its own unique identity would be left untouched. From the birth of the nation, the divergence in the two points of view began to show, and before long the relationship between the center and periphery fluctuated between a working, if not entirely amicable, partnership and a rupture with attendant conflict.[22]

During Pakistan's initial efforts to repeal the FCR in 2016, as I earlier argued, the Pakistani government's FATA Reforms Committee confronted the entrenched political interests of tribal elders as a barrier to the further political integration of the region. The tribal elders, the committee explained, 'have many privileges and benefits from the existing semi governed system' and sought to preserve the system of indirect rule held over from British colonial rule.[23] In opposition to the position of the elders, the younger generation within FATA, known as the kashar, was disadvantaged by the FCR as political authority was concentrated in the hands of the recognized elders with civil and political rights denied to all FATA residents. Throughout the twentieth century, this younger generation consistently challenged the FCR, including forming various political movements to push for broader political reform, and violently clashed with the tribal elders in their attempts to undermine the colonial system of governance. During debates about repealing the FCR, representatives of the kashar pushed for the government to repeal the law and extend access to the regular judicial system and constitutional rights to all FATA residents.

As I further demonstrate in this book, violence not only provided the context for the formation of both South Asian countries, given the communal turmoil sparked by Partition, but was used as a strategic tool by political leaders in extending the sovereignty and reach of the central government into spaces of contested sovereignty, such as the princely states. Scholars have long connected violence and political legitimacy. At the turn of the twentieth century, Max Weber placed a government's use of force as the core feature of the modern state with his oft-cited dictum: 'A state is a human community that (successfully) claims the *monopoly of the legitimate use of physical force* [sic] within a given territory.'[24] The use of force was often deployed as governments sought to construct their sovereignty and protect it against political rivals—both internal and external—that challenged the writ of the modern state, including over competing visions of what sovereignty and independence meant to different political actors vying to protect their political interests and assert their authority. Charles Tilly even compared the state-building process to a criminal protection racket in which coercive force is used to assert a state's legitimacy and sovereignty: 'quintessential protection rackets with the advantage of legitimacy.'[25]

Violence also lay at the heart of British colonial rule in South Asia. Despite British proclamations that they were bringing European civilization to what they perceived as the 'backward'—and at times 'barbarous'—communities of the Subcontinent, historian Kim Wagner demonstrated that British colonial authorities' use of violence was not an aberration but an integral part of their assertion of political control within India. This was rooted in British officials' colonial mentality shaped by the violence of the 1857 uprising and a response to the growing Indian opposition to British rule in India beginning in the early twentieth century.[26] Mark Condos similarly argued that the British reliance on graphic displays of violence, such as the 1919 Jallianwala Bagh massacre, was born out of 'an enduring and pervasive sense of anxiety, insecurity, and fear' in response to challenges to the British government's sovereignty and political control within India.[27]

Despite the frequent democratic appeals of India's founding fathers, this inclination toward force as the ultimate arbiter of various disputes, a means of establishing political control and an assertion of state sovereignty continued into South Asia's postcolonial era—from Operation Polo (India's military action in Hyderabad in September 1948) to Operation Vijay (India's military annexation of Portuguese-ruled Goa in December 1961), as well as the deployment of Indian security forces into Jammu and Kashmir and Assam to secure and consolidate its political control over the country's northern and northeastern frontiers. India's and Pakistan's leaders frequently proved willing to sacrifice their democratic principles for the cause of integrating the princely states and asserting the sovereignty of the state. In his study of the transformation of India from a British colony to a democratic republic through the lens of the violence in Hyderabad and the Punjab, Sunil Purushotham argues: 'A regime of sovereignty conceptualizes the legal, territorial, and institutional dimensions of sovereignty as arising out of historically contingent power relations between state and society. Violence and coercive force were constitutive of the contractual and negotiated dimensions of sovereign power at the founding moment of the Indian Republic.'[28]

As a means of asserting uncontested political control, India and Pakistan deployed their militaries to ensure the accession of the princely states whose rulers sought to preserve the layered sovereignty of British rule against the claims of the newly independent governments. Even in a democracy, V.P. Menon observed in the context of India's 1948 police action in Hyderabad, 'It is axiomatic that no nation can afford to be generous at the cost of its integrity, and India has no reason to be afraid of her own shadow.'[29] This particularly has been the case within territory in which sovereignty is contested, as both the Indian and Pakistani government exercised varying levels of political control within their borders at independence and had to deal with the legacies and competing political interests held over from the system of British indirect rule—from unadministered frontier areas to the unsettled status of the princely states.

The study of the princely states

Conquering the maharajas looks to the unique position of the princely states as part of the state-building process during the years leading up to and following Indian and Pakistani independence, and tells their often-overlooked history. This is a relatively understudied aspect of the transfer of power and decolonization process in both India and Pakistan. Even contemporary accounts often misrepresented the political dynamics in the Subcontinent, giving it the appearance of a struggle between the British government and the Indian National Congress with a powerful Muslim minority clamoring for a separate state, while ignoring the hundreds of princes and millions of princely states' subjects who had their own distinct political interests and exerted a sizable influence in the trajectory of events during the 1930s and 1940s.[30] Far from playing second fiddle to the political parties in British India, the princely states were an integral part of the many debates and struggles over the constitutional future of the British Raj, the circumstances of the transfer of power, the contentious aftermath of Partition and the resulting political tensions, rivalry and conflict between the two successor states to British rule. This book lays out the historical narrative of the princely states and their political relationship with the British, Indian and Pakistani governments and helps provide a better understanding of the often messy and unsettled legacy of British colonial rule in South Asia.

Scholars have increasingly integrated aspects of the princely states into broader discussions and debates on South Asian history, focusing on such areas as economic and social development, the politics of religion, the status of women, public health and influences on art and architecture.[31] These studies have engaged with various aspects of the Indian princes' rule during the colonial era without grappling with the broader sovereignty issues that pushed Princely India toward its ultimate demise following the transfer of power. Dedicated studies of the broader princely states in the final years of the British Raj tend to focus on the princes' relations with colonial authorities and end their analysis with the transfer of power in August 1947. Therefore, these studies also do not address the clashing ideas of sovereignty at play in the early years of Indian and Pakistani independence and the postcolonial governments' efforts to undo the layered sovereignty of British rule to which the princes clung.

The standard scholarly work on the princely states through the final years of the British Empire is Ian Copland's *The Princes of India in the Endgame of Empire, 1917–1947*. Yet, Copland's analysis ends with the transfer of power and largely focuses on interactions between the princely order and British authorities to explain the decline of the princely states. He does not address the political activism of the princely states' subjects or fully engage with the debate over the states' sovereignty in respect to the Indian nationalist movement. Copland explicitly describes his book as 'a study in the diplomacy of the princely courts' that focuses on 'high politics' and 'the most privileged of elites.'[32] By not engaging with the role of the states' subjects and the nationalist movement in challenging the princes' rule at the grassroots level, his analysis does not provide a full picture of the various political pressures that the princes faced through the 1930s and 1940s and that influenced their actions in seeking to protect their sovereignty in the early months and years of Indian and Pakistani independence.

Other scholars have studied the construction and limitations of princely states' sovereignty under British rule without addressing the question of their demise after August 1947. For instance, John McLeod's study of the Western India States Agency from 1916–47 examines the triangular relationship between the princes who sought to assert their sovereignty, the nationalist politicians who sought political power and British colonial authorities who sought to demonstrate their control. He envisions the trajectory of events during this period (with his analysis ending with the transfer of power and only focusing on a single region) as bound by the 'three-way dialogue' and shifting alliances between princes, politicians and the paramount power.[33] Caroline Keen studies the scope of British engagement and influence within the princely states from 1858 to 1909, including the limits of the princes' sovereignty under the British system of indirect rule during this period.[34] Milinda Banerjee further examines how the sovereignty of the princely states served as a model of indigenous political authority for the nationalist movement and helped shape political debates around Indian sovereignty during the late nineteenth and early twentieth centuries.[35]

On the other hand, studies of the end of British colonial rule in South Asia and the early years of Indian and Pakistani independence usually relegate the princely states to mere passing mentions, perhaps dedicating a handful of pages amid the hundreds of pages focused on events within the British Indian provinces. The scant attention the princely states have received within existing scholarship on the early years of independence in South Asia leads to an incomplete picture of the Indian and Pakistani governments' efforts to assert their vision of state sovereignty and undo the layered sovereignty of the British Raj through the decolonization process.

There have been studies of individual princely states that have addressed these issues, but without the historical context of Princely India's relations with British colonial authorities or an analysis of the broader scope of the clashing ideas of sovereignty and the implications for the state-building process in South Asia. Sunil Purushotham's *From Raj to Republic: Sovereignty, Violence, and Democracy in India* discusses the Nizam of Hyderabad's efforts to consolidate his state's sovereignty within the British imperial framework while simultaneously seeking to modernize his state, which set up the resulting clashes with Indian authorities after the transfer of power.[36] Margrit Pernau and Eric Lewis Beverley similarly examine Hyderabad as an example of the fluidity of state sovereignty at the height of European imperialism by focusing on the intersection of patrimonialism (the loyalty of officials to the personal authority of the prince) with the increasing bureaucratization and professionalization of the state administration.[37] Taylor Sherman's *Muslim Belonging in Secular India* further examines the transition from princely rule to democratic and secular government within postcolonial Hyderabad through the framework of communal politics, focusing on how India's Muslim population engaged with the broader efforts to establish democratic rule in the country's early years.[38] Mridu Rai similarly examines these themes in the construction of the political legitimacy and sovereignty of Jammu and Kashmir's Dogra Rajput rulers from 1846–1947 and the role of religion in bolstering political mobilization against their rule.[39] Within postcolonial Jammu and Kashmir, Shahla Hussain analyzes the emergence of a distinct Kashmiri political identity rooted in and reinforced by resistance to India's 'territory of sovereignty' in which Indian political leaders asserted uncontested control throughout India's claimed territory.[40] Srinath Raghavan's study, *War and Peace in Modern India*, discusses Indian military actions in Jammu and Kashmir, Hyderabad and Junagadh, but frames them in the context of Nehru's foreign policy and India's early relations with Pakistan.[41] His analysis begins at Indian independence and only focuses on the immediate crisis facing Indian political leaders as they deployed the Indian military into these three princely states, alongside other case studies analyzing ongoing international tensions with Pakistan and China. Raghavan does not engage with the historical context of Princely India and the broader issues of contested sovereignty within India's newly delineated borders.

By combining the broad scope of Princely India's engagement on issues of sovereignty before and after Indian and Pakistani independence with detailed case studies of the most intractable princely states in both successor states, *Conquering the maharajas* offers a more complete understanding of the transfer of power and state-building process within South Asia, Indian and Pakistani authorities' efforts at dismantling the layered sovereignty of British colonial rule to which many princes remained committed and the resulting military clashes that this process provoked. While postcolonial political leaders sought to promote their vision of a modern democratic state, the case studies help to show their willingness to resort to decidedly undemocratic measures to assert their conception of state sovereignty, underlying the importance of understanding the sovereignty question at play in the years surrounding the transfer of power.

In examining the historical narrative of the princely states' political relationship with authorities in New Delhi and Karachi through the end of

the British Empire, the timeframe of this study roughly spans from 1930 to 1950, during which the process of the political integration of the princely states played out. This period is bookended on one side by the first Round Table Conference, held in London in November 1930, which launched the failed effort of the British government to form an Indian federation with the princely states as members; and, on the other side, by India's annexation of the princely states of Junagadh and Hyderabad and the establishment of a political status quo in Jammu and Kashmir, events which played out in the lead up to 1950—the year in which India's constitution went into effect and the Republic of India was formally established.

In analyzing the princely states' integration, the analysis focuses not only on the conflicts and debates that occurred between the princes, Indian and Pakistani political leaders and British colonial authorities, but also the struggles and disagreements within the princely states, especially between the princes and their subjects, among the various British officials over the most appropriate means of handling the princely states amid the British withdrawal and among Indian and Pakistani political leaders over what the best approach to the princely states should be. Therefore, my research strategy was to focus on primary sources that not only provide a detailed account of the policies and decisions taken in respect to the princely states but also elucidate individuals' motivations behind these actions and the various conflicts that motivated the ultimate outcome, with reference to the four distinct perspectives to the process of integrating the princely states—British officials, the princely order, the nationalist movement and the princely states' subjects. These sources include a wide range of British, Indian and Pakistani government documents from the period under study, including government treaties, fortnightly reports from British residents within the princely states, intelligence reporting from the Home Department, diplomatic cables, internal memorandum and notes, meeting minutes, public statements, speeches and official letters, as well as a wide range of nongovernmental sources, such as private letters, journals and political pamphlets. These primary sources were supplemented by contemporary media reporting, published memoirs and relevant secondary sources.

Amid the far-reaching political movements and conflicts that rocked the Subcontinent during these two decades, the integration of the princely states in South Asia frequently circled around a war of personalities— the British officials who worked to redraw the political map of the Subcontinent; various princes who wielded autocratic political authority within their states and dreamed of independence; Indian and Pakistani leaders who pushed against these dreams; and representatives of the states' subjects that consistently challenged the princes' right to rule. This book's

analysis focuses on key individuals involved in this process and the decisions and debates they had with one another around the issue of the
princely states' sovereignty: the two Viceroys during the late 1930s and
1940s, Lord Linlithgow and Lord Wavell, who left the princely states
in an ambiguous position amid broader debates on India's future; Lord
Mountbatten, the last Viceroy of British India and first Governor General
of an independent India who was appointed to oversee the transfer of
power and played a leading role in convincing the princes of the merits of
accession to India; Sardar Vallabhbhai Patel, the ironman of India who
helmed Indian efforts to integrate the princely states as States Minister;
V.P. Menon, the capable bureaucrat who served as the secretary of India's
States Ministry and personally shepherded countless princes to signing the
Instrument of Accession; the Indian National Congress leader and first
Prime Minister of India, Jawaharlal Nehru, who frequently clashed with
Patel over the matter of the princely states and resisted the use of force
to compel them to accede to India; the leaders of Pakistan, Mohammad
Ali Jinnah and Liaquat Ali Khan, who persistently had the issue of the
princely states as one of their foremost concerns; Maharaja Hari Singh
of Jammu and Kashmir, the Nizam of Hyderabad Mir Osman Ali Khan
and Khan Ahmad Yar Khan of Kalat, who reveled in dreams of independence; Nawab Mahabat Khan of Junagadh, who fell under the sway of his
pro-Pakistan diwan Shah Nawaz Bhutto and sought to preserve his own
sovereignty and the privileged position of Muslims within his state; the
populist leaders Sheikh Abdullah of Jammu and Kashmir and Kasim Razvi
of Hyderabad, who stymied and supported, respectively, their princes'
plans for independence; Samaldas Gandhi, Mahatma Gandhi's nephew,
who led a popular uprising against the Nawab of Junagadh; the Nawab of
Bhopal Hamidullah Khan, the Chancellor of the Chamber of Princes on the
eve of the transfer of power who took the British withdrawal from India as
a personal affront; Sir Conrad Corfield, the political adviser to the Viceroy
and member of the Indian Political Service, who encouraged the princes'
ambitions for independence; Walter Monckton, the English counsel who
attempted, unsuccessfully, to bridge the divide between Hyderabad and
New Delhi; and countless other princes, politicians, bureaucrats and states'
activists who each played their own role, both major and minor, in the
drama of the princely states during this time frame. It was the debates,
disagreements and clashes among these individuals over the status of the
princely states, and their appropriate trajectory following the transfer of
power, that engendered many of the problems and conflicts surrounding
them.

   This book's analysis can largely be divided into two parts. The first part
details the princely states' broader engagement with British authorities and

the Indian nationalist movement during the 1930s and 1940s as the princes sought to protect their sovereignty amid broader political changes in the Subcontinent. Chapter 1 provides an overview of the relationship between the princely states and British paramountcy and how it shifted over time. Chapter 2 details the Indian nationalist movement's engagement with the princely states, including their interactions with the political organizations representing the states' subjects. Chapters 3 through 5 examine the princes' efforts to protect their sovereignty through the broader political changes of the 1930s and 1940s, including British plans for an All-India Federation, debates in the 1940s surrounding India's constitutional future and the resulting transfer of power in 1947.

The second part presents four detailed case studies of the most intractable princely states whose accession and integration into India and Pakistan proved the greatest challenge: Jammu and Kashmir, Hyderabad, Junagadh and Kalat. It was in these four princely states, whose status remained unsettled following the transfer of power, where the layered sovereignty of British colonial rule directly clashed with the sovereign nationalism of India and Pakistan and provoked a military response. The Indian and Pakistani authorities saw the princes' efforts to evade accession as a direct threat to the integrity of the newly independent states, producing political tensions that resulted in the use of military force as the two governments sought to expand and consolidate their political control and assert their sovereignty over the princely states. Each case study examines the trajectory of events during the 1930s and 1940s, including the princes' efforts to protect their sovereignty and Indian political leaders' and states' subjects' efforts to introduce various political reforms as independence neared, resulting in later clashes with the Indian and Pakistani governments.

Any discussion of princely states in India must begin with Jammu and Kashmir on India's northern frontier. It has been the most studied and analyzed former princely state given its role as a flashpoint of conflict between two nuclear states and the ongoing separatist insurgency that erupted in the 1980s. The struggle over this territory originated with the ambiguous position of the princely states in the context of Partition. While the state was ruled by a Hindu Maharaja, its population was overwhelmingly Muslim. There was a clear divide between those favoring accession to India and those favoring Pakistan, with both governments laying claim to the territory. Yet, the Maharaja dreamed of an independent Kashmir neutral to both successor governments and serving as a sort of 'Switzerland of the East.' These dreams quickly came crashing down with an invasion of Pashtun tribesmen from Pakistan's North-West Frontier Province in October 1947, which soon drew in both Indian and Pakistan militaries. The mediation efforts of the United Nations helped result in the present division of the former princely state between Indian- and Pakistani-administered territories as defined by the Line of Control.

Second only to Jammu and Kashmir, scholars have increasingly examined the history of Hyderabad and India's military annexation of this princely state in September 1948. Hyderabad, one of the largest and wealthiest of the princely states, was Kashmir in reverse—a Muslim prince, known as the Nizam, ruling over a largely Hindu population. Given the princely state's size and resources, it had generally stayed aloof from the broader politics of the princely order under British colonial rule. When the British withdrawal was announced, the Nizam felt his state had both the capacity and the legal right to maintain its independence by virtue of its sovereign status and economic strength. However, Indian political leaders viewed the existence of an independent Hyderabad in the heart of India as a grave threat to the country's security with the potential to virtually cut off south India from the north. For over a year, New Delhi and Hyderabad were locked in tense negotiations until the Indian government dispatched its military into the princely state in a 'police action' to assert Indian sovereignty.

Before the situations in Jammu and Kashmir and Hyderabad flared up, the small princely state of Junagadh in Gujarat's Kathiawar region first threatened to force India and Pakistan into a military clash. Even though the princely state was not contiguous with Pakistan and had a majority Hindu population, its Muslim Nawab and Muslim-dominated state government acceded to Pakistan in a bid to protect their political status. While the princely state held little broader political, economic or strategic importance, like Jammu and Kashmir and Hyderabad did, India's political leadership feared the potential of Junagadh's actions setting a dangerous precedent for other princely states. New Delhi quickly instituted a blockade of Junagadh, positioned the Indian military around the princely state's borders and forced its subsidiary states to accede to India to exert further pressure on Junagadh's leadership. As security conditions deteriorated within the princely state, the Nawab and his family fled to Pakistan with the government officials left behind soon inviting Indian military forces to temporarily enter the state to restore law and order. Yet, with the Indian government taking control in November 1947, Junagadh's integration into the Indian Union became a fait accompli.

Finally, this book examines the frontier state of Kalat in Pakistan's Balochistan Province lying near the border with Iran and Afghanistan. The Khan of Kalat asserted that his state located far from the imperial capital had a different status than other princely states within India and was more akin to Nepal or Afghanistan, an assertion denied by British authorities. Nevertheless, the Khan claimed that Kalat would revert to a fully

independent status following the British withdrawal and the lapse of paramountcy. While Pakistan's leadership had previously taken a noninterference approach to the princely states within its sphere of influence, they now
faced the struggles of establishing the writ of the Pakistani state throughout the territory awarded to it by Partition. If Kalat was able to assert its
independence, this would have created dangerous implications for Pakistani
sovereignty elsewhere, such as within the distant, Bengali-populated East
Pakistan. Under pressure from the Pakistani government, the Khan finally
acceded to Pakistan in March 1948, a move which provoked the Khan's
brother to launch an anti-Pakistan rebellion requiring the deployment of the
Pakistani military to the region.

Combined with a broad overview of the princely states' position leading
up to and following the transfer of power, *Conquering the maharajas*
places each of these princely states in the broader context of the challenges stemming from the uncertain status of the princely states and the
clashes over state sovereignty, a framework through which British, Indian
and Pakistani officials would have understood them at the time. As made
clear through numerous primary sources, officials at the time did not view
each princely state in isolation but understood them as part of a broader
context with the potential to set dangerous precedents in respect to the
protection of the sovereignty of the newly independent state, frequently
drawing references between princely states and making clear that their
actions toward one princely state were taken with the potential impact on
relations with another in mind. The final chapter concludes with a discussion of the fate of the princes and the final integration of the princely states
into India and Pakistan following independence, ultimately leading to the
demise of the layered sovereignty of the colonial era as the princely states
were broken up or absorbed into other political units in both India and
Pakistan.

Notes

1 Indrani Sen, '"Oriental despots": Representations in nineteenth-century British
   colonial fiction, 1858–1900,' in Waltraud Ernst and Biswamoy Pati (eds),
   India's Princely States: People, princes and colonialism (Abingdon: Routledge,
   2007), pp. 30–48; Manu Pillai, 'India's misunderstood maharajahs,' *BBC* (27
   September 2021).
2 Vrutika Shah, '9 existing royal families, their source of income and how they live
   their lavish lifestyles,' *GQ India* (25 January 2020).
3 Norman Davies, *Vanished Kingdoms: The Rise and Fall of States and Nations*
   (London: Penguin Books, 2011), p. 4.

4 Ian Copland, *The Princes of India in the Endgame of Empire, 1917–1947* (Cambridge: Cambridge University Press, 1997).

5 K.M. Panikkar, *An Autobiography*, trans. K. Krishnamurthy (Madras: Oxford University Press, 1977), p. 189.

6 Sunil Khilnani, *The Idea of India* (New York: Farrar, Straus, Giroux, 1997), p. 4.

7 'Constituent Assembly Debates on 13 December, 1946,' Constituent Assembly of India Debates (Proceedings) – Volume 1, 13 December 1946, accessed at: http://loksabhaph.nic.in/writereaddata/cadebatefiles/C13121946.html [accessed 20 December 2022].

8 Thomas Blom Hansen and Finn Stepputat (eds), *Sovereign Bodies: Citizens, Migrants, and States in the Postcolonial World* (Princeton, NJ: Princeton University Press, 2005), p. 19.

9 Hansen and Stepputat, *Sovereign Bodies*, p. 4.

10 Benjamin D. Hopkins, *Ruling the Savage Periphery: Frontier Governance and the Making of the Modern State* (Cambridge, MA: Harvard University Press, 2020), p. 19.

11 Khilnani, *The Idea of India*, p. 31.

12 W.H. Morris-Jones, 'The Transfer of Power, 1947: A View from the Sidelines,' *Modern Asian Studies* 16:1 (1982), 17–18.

13 Morris-Jones, 'The Transfer of Power, 1947,' pp. 17–18.

14 Ramachandra Guha, *India After Gandhi: The History of the World's Largest Democracy* (New York: Ecco, 2007), pp. 8–9, 11, 740–55.

15 Hopkins, *Ruling the Savage Periphery*, pp. 13–26.

16 Frederick Lugard, *The Dual Mandate in British Tropical Africa* (London: William Blackwood and Sons, 1922), p. 217.

17 Jean-Loup Amselle, *Affirmative Exclusion: Cultural Pluralism and the Rule of Custom in France*, trans. Jane Marie Todd (Ithaca, NY: Cornell University Press, 2003); Adam Guerin, 'Racial myth, colonial reform, and the invention of customary law in Morocco, 1912–1930,' *Journal of North African Studies* 16:3 (2011), 361–80; Mary Dewhurst Lewis, *Divided Rule: Sovereignty and Empire in French Tunisia, 1881–1938* (Berkeley, CA: University of California Press, 2014); Anthony Reid, 'Colonial Transformation: A Bitter Legacy,' in Anthony Reid (ed.), *Verandah of Violence: The Background to the Aceh Problem* (Singapore: University of Singapore Press, 2006), pp. 96–108.

18 Lauren Benton, 'Colonial Law and Cultural Differences: Jurisdictional Politics and the Formation of the Colonial State,' *Comparative Studies in Society and History* 41:3 (1999): 563–88.

19 Adnan Naseemullah and Paul Staniland, 'Indirect Rule and Varieties of Governance,' *Governance* 29:1 (2016), 13–30.

20 Ian Talbot, 'The Punjab Under Colonialism: Order and Transformation in British India,' *Journal of Punjab Studies* 14:1 (2007), 3–10.

21 Eric Lewis Beverley, *Hyderabad, British India, and the World, c. 1850–1950* (Cambridge: Cambridge University Press, 2015), p. 5; Eric Lewis Beverley, 'Frontier as Resource: Law, Crime, and Sovereignty on the Margins of Empire,' *Comparative Studies in Society and History* 55:2 (2013), 241–72.

22 Akbar Ahmed, *The Thistle and the Drone: How America's War on Terror Became a Global War on Tribal Islam* (Washington, DC: Brookings Institution Press, 2013), p. 64.

23 Harrison Akins, 'Mashar versus Kashar in Pakistan's FATA: Intra-tribal Conflict and the Obstacles to Reform,' *Asian Survey* 58:6 (2018), 1136–59; *Report of the Committee on FATA Reforms* (Islamabad: Ministry of States and Frontier Regions, Government of Pakistan, 2016), p. 33.

24 H.H. Gerth and C. Wright Mills (eds), *From Max Weber: Essays in Sociology* (Abingdon: Routledge, 1991), p. 78.

25 Charles Tilly, 'War Making and State Making as Organized Crime,' in Peter Evans, Dietrich Rueschemeyer, and Theda Skocpol (eds), *Bringing the State Back In* (Cambridge: Cambridge University Press, 1985), pp. 169–87.

26 Kim A. Wagner, *Amritsar 1919: An Empire of Fear and the Making of a Massacre* (New Haven, CT: Yale University Press, 2019).

27 Mark Condos, *The Insecurity State: Punjab and the Making of Colonial Power in British India* (Cambridge: Cambridge University Press, 2017), p. 3.

28 Sunil Purushotham, *From Raj to Republic: Sovereignty, Violence, and Democracy in India* (Palo Alto, CA: Stanford University Press, 2021), p. 2.

29 V.P. Menon, *The Story of the Integration of the Indian States* (Bombay: Orient Longmans Ltd., 1956), p. 389.

30 Note by Sir F. Wylie, undated, *TOP Volume VII*, p. 68.

31 Manu Bhagavan, 'Princely States and the Hindu Imaginary: Exploring the Cartography of Hindu Nationalism in Colonial India,' *The Journal of Asian Studies* 67:3 (2008), 881–915; Ian Copland, *State, Community and Neighbourhood in Princely North India, c. 1900–1950* (Basingstoke: Palgrave Macmillan, 2005); Ian Copland, 'Crucibles of *Hindutva*? V.D. Savarkar, the Hindu Mahasabha, and the Indian princely states,' *South Asia: Journal of South Asian Studies* 25:3 (2002), 211–34; Waltraud Ernst, Biswamoy Pati, and T.V. Sekher, *Health and Medicine in the Indian Princely States, 1850–1950* (Abingdon: Routledge, 2017); Vibhuti Sachdev, 'Negotiating Modernity in the Princely State of Jaipur,' *South Asian Studies* 28:2 (2012), 171–81; Chitralekha Zutshi, 'Re-visioning princely states in South Asian historiography: A review,' *The Indian Economic and Social History Review* 46:3 (2009), 301–13.

32 Copland, *The Princes of India in the Endgame of Empire*, pp. 2, 8.

33 John McLeod, *Sovereignty, Power, Control: Politics in the States of Western India* (Leiden: Brill, 1999), p. 6.

34 Caroline Keen, *Princely India and the British: Political Development and the Operation of Empire* (London: Bloomsbury Academic, 2012), pp. 128–72.

35 Milinda Banerjee, *The Mortal God: Imagining the Sovereign in Colonial India* (Cambridge: Cambridge University Press, 2018), pp. 108–61.

36 Purushotham, *From Raj to Republic*, pp. 35–46.

37 Beverley, *Hyderabad, British India, and the World*, p. 7; Margrit Pernau, *The Passing of Patrimonialism: Politics and Political Culture in Hyderabad, 1911–1948* (Delhi: Manohar, 2000).

38 Taylor Sherman, *Muslim Belonging in Secular India: Negotiating Citizenship in Postcolonial Hyderabad* (Cambridge: Cambridge University Press, 2015).

39 Mridu Rai, *Hindu Rulers, Muslim Subjects: Islam, Rights, and the History of Kashmir* (Princeton, NJ: Princeton University Press, 2004).

40 Shahla Hussain, *Kashmir in the Aftermath of Partition* (Cambridge: Cambridge University Press, 2021).

41 Srinath Raghavan, *War and Peace in Modern India* (Basingstoke: Palgrave Macmillan, 2010).

1

British paramountcy and the princely states

The notion of Princely India is not as clear cut as it may seem and often proved difficult for British colonial authorities to categorize with any consistency. The princely states were scattered across the Indian Subcontinent—in both present-day India and Pakistan—and added up to as many as 565 different states. There were variations with the actual count of distinct princely states as some small states were mere estates or villages and considered subsidiaries to other states—and not all agreed on the exact definition of what qualified as a princely state in the first place. Nevertheless, the princely states were a varied lot. Some were no larger than a sizeable urban park. The state of Bilbari in eastern Gujarat covered only 1.65 square miles, around the total area of New York City's Central Park, and had a population barely exceeding eighty by the 1940s. Vejanoness in Gujarat's Kathiawar region was even smaller, coming in at a mere 0.29 square miles with a population of around two hundred and annual revenues adding up to a paltry five hundred rupees a year. At the other extreme, a handful of the major princely states had territories, populations and revenues that rivaled European countries. Jammu and Kashmir and Hyderabad, for instance, were each nearly the size of Great Britain with populations counting into the millions.

The princes themselves were likewise varied. There were, in fact, sadists, murderers and crooks among their ranks who cleaned out their state treasuries and left their subjects in a state of oppression and destitution. At the other end of the spectrum, there were princes who were capable administrators, intellectuals and dedicated rulers who cared deeply for their subjects and introduced progressive political reforms that placed their states ahead of the British Indian provinces in many economic and social development categories. This included the Maharaja of Mysore at the turn of the twentieth century who was frequently lauded as one of the most progressive rulers among the princely order with his state earning a reputation within colonial India as a model state.[1] However, following the law of averages, most of the thousands of princes over time were middling at best—not particularly brilliant nor particularly cruel. They did just enough to keep their states running and maintain their personal status and privileges, or remained entirely aloof of politics and left the state's administration to trusted British and Indian ministers, advisers and mid-level bureaucrats.

Many of India's princely states were remnants of alliances between Indian rulers and the East India Company, the erstwhile power in the Indian Subcontinent before the establishment of British Crown rule in 1858. Following the rapid expansion of the Mughal Empire under Emperor Aurangzeb in the seventeenth century, which overextended its military resources, and Nadir Shah's sacking of Delhi in 1739, the Mughals began to lose their tight grasp over the Subcontinent. Regional challengers quickly emerged to contest the Mughal Emperor's waning political authority. These rulers established a series of successor states to Mughal rule throughout India—most notably the former Mughal provinces of Awadh, Bengal and Hyderabad. While many of these states' rulers continued to nominally pledge allegiance to the Mughal Emperor in Delhi, they remained autonomous as they wielded independent political authority within their regional courts.

In the mid-eighteenth century, as the political landscape of the Subcontinent increasingly descended into anarchy, the East India Company began to consolidate and extend its political and commercial reach over Indian territory.[2] Beginning with Bengal's fertile agricultural lands fed by the Ganges Delta, the Company asserted direct political control over the most economically productive areas and sought the cooperation of neighboring princes to protect their economic interests. The controversial first British governor of the Bengal Presidency, Robert Clive, established ad hoc treaty relations between the Company and various individual Indian rulers as a matter of expediency, whether in facilitating commerce within their territory, supporting various aspects of internal administration such as revenue collection, controlling states' foreign affairs and trade, refraining from attacking any Company ally or using the princely states' military forces against the Company's regional rivals.[3] Company officials saw the array of surrounding Indian rulers as strategic allies to stymie the influence of the competing French forces and help form a protective ring of friendly buffer states around Company territory. Moreover, many of these princes were in less economically productive areas and therefore lacked the lure of easy profit and loot.

These alliances with Indian princes, which were primarily military in nature, not only allowed the East India Company to expand its available military strength without bearing the costs of building up its own forces, but also to curb the political power and independence of surrounding kingdoms who Company officials saw as too apt to engage in internecine warfare harmful to their bottom line. Of course, they did so without considering their own role in the violence during the previous century as the Company established an economic and political foothold in India. In February 1804, the Company's Governor General Richard Wellesley argued that the primary principle in establishing British alliances with the surrounding princely states within India

> is to place those states in such a degree of dependence on the British power as may deprive them of the means of prosecuting any measures or of forming any confederacy hazardous to the security of the British Empire ... This object can alone be accomplished by the operation of a general control over the principal states of India established in the hands of a superior power, and exercised with equity and moderation through the medium of alliances contracted with those states on the basis of the security and protection of their respective rights.[4]

As Governor General at the turn of the nineteenth century, Wellesley was the primary architect of Princely India under British control. During his tenure, he instituted a central policy of pursuing subsidiary alliances with Indian rulers, both with princes who either voluntarily aligned themselves with a powerful ally or required military pressure to do so. The treaties defined the specific terms of their relationship, in particular laying out the conditions in which military assistance would be extended and to what extent. Through this approach, the East India Company established itself as the paramount power over nominally independent Indian states. Yet, the British did not attempt to provide a precise, legal definition to paramountcy given the wide variety of provisions that were unique to each princely states' treaty.[5] In this way, the East India Company gradually subverted and replaced the Mughal Empire's nominal status as the suzerain power over the various successor states across India. By adopting this role, Company officials asserted that its dominance over the princely states was a means of avoiding the anarchy that had prevailed in the previous century following the decline of Mughal power and maintaining peaceful conditions in India—which were of course conditions allowing for the Company to generate maximum profit for its officials and shareholders back in London.

The 1857 Sepoy Rebellion and its aftermath helped to further institutionalize the relationship between the British government and the Indian princes. Some princes joined the uprising, but others came to the aid of their British allies, most notably the Nizam of Hyderabad and several Maratha and Rajput rulers who helped to contain the anti-British violence. The Company's Governor General at the time, Earl Canning, remarked that the 'patches' of princely states within India who supported the British forces were 'breakwaters in the storm which would otherwise have swept over us in one great wave' and underlined the importance of maintaining and bolstering the princes' position.[6]

This rebellion highlighted the limitations and problems of Company rule and prompted the British government to assert Crown rule with the Government of India Act of 1858, which transferred control of India from the East India Company to the British Crown. While introducing a new political structure over the Subcontinent, the British government maintained the legal status of the princely states. The final clause of the Act stated that 'all treaties made by the Company shall be binding upon her Majesty.' Additionally, Lord Canning, who was appointed the first Viceroy (or Crown Representative) of India, made sure that Queen Victoria's proclamation of 1 November 1858 announcing the imposition of Crown rule reiterated that all existing treaties and engagements the East India Company made with various Indian princes would be recognized and 'scrupulously maintained' by the new governing structure. The Queen asserted that under Crown rule the princely states would retain their sovereignty, and the British government would 'respect the rights, dignity and honour of the native princes as our own.'[7]

Thus, a number of princely states entered into a direct treaty relationship with the British Crown, which served as the basis for their engagement with the British Indian government in Calcutta, and later New Delhi. During the nineteenth and twentieth centuries, British officials continually alluded to the binding nature of the treaties with the princely states and the obligations they entailed for both parties. Yet, these treaties were not all-encompassing documents, underlying the difficulty in defining and codifying the inherently political, rather than simply legal, relationship between the paramount power and the princely states, which the British government never attempted to systematize. The British relationship with the princely states was 'embodied in no constitution,' in the words of the Viceroy at the turn of the twentieth century Lord Curzon, and relied heavily on traditions, political practices and obligations which emerged informally, in addition to those outlined in various legal documents, with often multiple and competing ideas of the princely states' sovereignty and the extent of British influence and control over them.[8]

Therefore, paramountcy was 'a thing of gradual growth; it has been established partly by conquest; partly by treaty; partly by usage,' as the Viceroy Lord Lytton explained in 1877.[9] In the late 1920s, the Indian States Committee further reflected: 'The relationship of the Paramount Power with the states is not a merely contractual relationship, resting on treaties made more than a century ago. It is a living, growing relationship shaped by circumstances and policy, resting … on a mixture of history, theory and modern fact.'[10] With the passage of time, a number of archaic stipulations in the treaties frequently became inapplicable or obsolete, but nevertheless their practices persisted. One example was article ten of the 1846 Treaty of Amritsar with the Maharaja of Jammu and Kashmir. It dictated that the Maharaja would send Kashmiri shawls every year to the British monarch as a symbol of British paramountcy over the state. Despite making little sense within the context of modern politics, this symbolic practice continued into the 1940s, with the final treaty shawls (two shawls along with three romals) dispatched from New Delhi to King-Emperor George VI in London on 25 March 1947.[11]

Though not all princely states had treaties with the British Crown; only forty did. Many princes instead relied on a legal document known as a sanad (a certificate or grant) as the basis of British recognition of their political sovereignty; the first one was awarded in 1862. A sanad not only recognized a princes' authority to rule within his state but also his ability to pass that political authority to a designated heir, necessary for British recognition of the succession. Sanads also extended to adoption, allowing the princes the right to select an heir. Adoption sanads were formally awarded based on 'the merits of loyal and faithful services,' though prevailing political interests often played a role.[12]

The British government oversaw the administration of India's princely states through the Political Department (known as the Foreign and Political Department from 1914–37), which was formalized into the Indian Political Service (IPS) in 1937. The IPS was a distinct service from the Indian Civil Service (ICS). The ICS was formed by the Government of India Act of 1858, and its officers were responsible for administering districts under direct British rule. On the other hand, members of the IPS, popularly known as 'politicals,' represented British interests at the courts of the princely states, on the frontier and in other areas outside of direct British control where they served as political agents, agents to the governor general or residents within areas of shared sovereignty. Its members were largely recruited from military ranks, as well as from the ICS and Indian Medical Service. Given that the politicals were drawn from existing members of other colonial services, they were often described with the Brahmin appellation 'twice-born.'

Unlike the other services, the Political Department was designed simply as a channel for political relations with the princes and possessed no technical experts of its own. It instead relied on other government departments when technical advice was needed on issues such as customs and excise, railways, the postal service or communications.[13] Yet, the residents serving within the princely courts, or durbars, carried the responsibility of being the man on the spot in close touch with local politics and steeped in the complicated protocol of courtly culture. Thus, they were in the best position to 'detect and correct any tendency towards maladministration' by closely monitoring developments and offering timely advice and interventions.[14] The unique rigors of working within the princely courts often required extroverted personalities, charisma and an aristocratic bearing, not to mention the requisite skills in sporting and hunting given the princes' pre-dilections for both pursuits. The politicals required an intricate knowledge of local customs and the idiosyncrasies of local personalities. 'Very often things will be important in his eyes—and justly important,' Lord Curzon remarked, 'which to a Civilian might appear insignificant or ridiculous.'[15] Many politicals' lengthy associations with the princely order during their Indian career was such that they frequently played a dual role—both representing British interests at the princely states' courts and representing the princes' interests in New Delhi and London.

Despite colorful caricatures of British officers who spent their days dressing for court and sporting with royals (caricatures often based in reality), the politicals did not always have a leisurely life among compliant princes. Many faced the anxieties and hardship of combining tact with the forceful assertion of British influence, especially when dealing with princes who were either apt to ignore their regal duties or went overboard in asserting their autocratic authority. These issues could be compounded by tensions between the princes and political officers dispatched to their courts. Some princes were so dissatisfied by the residents' behavior and frequent intrusions that they appealed to the British government to have them removed. Lord Lytton, the Viceroy from 1876–80, observed: 'I have long thought that the British Resident at Native Courts is on the whole a political mistake. I am certain that he is regarded by those courts as an intolerable nuisance, and that, instead of facilitating our relations with them, or increasing our influence over them, he is either a chronic source of irritation to them, or else, for all practical purposes, their agent and advocate in every matter of dispute with the British Government.'[16] Nevertheless, the politicals remained a key aspect of the system of British paramountcy up to 1947 as they worked behind the scenes to protect British interests within the princely states while maintaining the facade of aloofness and noninterference; not all were able to effectively strike this balance.

The shifting nature of British paramountcy

Through the late nineteenth and early twentieth centuries, British paramountcy and its relationship to the princely states' sovereignty gradually took on the shape that it would hold to the end of British rule. With the British government's position as the paramount power, British colonial authorities held the right to interfere in the princely states' internal affairs, recognize princely succession, manage relations between different states, serve in an advisory capacity to improve the states' administrations and, if necessary, depose a prince and take over the administration of his state. While the princely states were treated as sovereign states with internal autonomy, the British government treated them as distinct from truly independent states that have an internationally recognized political status. The sovereignty of the British Crown ultimately reigned supreme above the princes. An Indian government notification issued on 21 August 1891 declared that 'the principles of international law have no bearing upon the relations between itself and the native States under the suzerainty of the Queen Empress.'[17] With the princely states having no international life, it was the responsibility and the right of the British Crown to represent the states in international affairs, giving the princely states and their subjects the same legal status as British India in regard to foreign relations. In 1926, the Viceroy Lord Reading dispatched a letter to the Nizam of Hyderabad responding to long-standing territorial disputes with the British government, with a definitive statement on the rights of the paramount power in relation to the princely states. Without diplomatic nuance, he asserted, 'The right of the British Government to intervene in internal affairs of Indian States is another instance of the consequences necessarily involved in the supremacy of the British Crown … The varying degrees of internal sovereignty which the rulers enjoy are all subject to the due exercise by the Paramount Power of this responsibility.'[18]

Nevertheless, colonial officials continued to highlight the princely states' sovereign status and their importance within the empire, rhetoric that frequently went to the head of the princes. In 1899, Lord Curzon portrayed the princely order as a key part of the British imperial project, stating: 'The native Chief has become by our policy an integral factor in the imperial organisation of India. He is concerned not less than the Viceroy or the Lieutenant-Governor in the administration of the country. I claim him as my colleague and partner.'[19] In 1904, he further stated: 'I have always been a devoted believer in the continued existence of the Native States in India, and an ardent well-wisher of the Native Princes. But I believe in them not as relics, but as rulers; not as puppets, but as living factors in the administration.' Yet, Curzon also felt that in this role the princes had a responsibility to practice good governance within their states. 'If the Native States are to accept this standard, it is obvious that they must keep pace with the age,' he stated in Rajkot State in 1900. 'They cannot dawdle behind, and act as a drag upon an inevitable progress. They are a link in the chain of Imperial administration. It would never do for the British links to be strong and the Native links weak, or *vice versa* [*sic*].'[20]

Despite colonial authorities alluding to the states' sovereignty and the inviolability of the treaties, British policy toward the princely states contained an inherent tension between the preservation and protection of the states' sovereignty with the British government exercising its rights as the paramount power. This included interfering in states' internal affairs to press for various political and administrative reforms, including stamping out 'barbaric' practices such as slavery, female infanticide, and sati (widow burning).[21] As early as 1832, John Malcolm, the Governor of Bombay and long-serving soldier and administrator for the East India Company, pointed to 'the general impression that our sovereignty is incompatible with the maintenance of Native Princes and Chiefs.'[22] Though some bad practices were at times permitted to continue in the interests of preserving the princely states' sovereignty and in the broader political interests of the British government. Indeed, from the perspective of many British officials, princes who were too progressive and capable also had the potential to work against British political interests by demonstrating the Indians' capacity to govern, which could then be used as a tool of propaganda by the growing nationalist movement within the British Indian provinces.[23]

Given the ambiguity in the relationship between the British government and the princely states, and the lack of legal definitions of misrule, the line between these two positions—the maintenance of the princely states' sovereignty versus the assertion of British paramountcy—was largely settled on an ad hoc basis. It frequently shifted depending on the inclinations of the key individuals holding the reins of political power in India, the government's prevailing political interests and the nature of the scandal provoking British authorities to react. Nevertheless, this was an ever-present point of contention between colonial authorities and the princes; the princes ruled their states with the threat of a British intervention always at the back of their minds.

Before his assassination in 1872, Lord Mayo was the first Viceroy to embark on a comprehensive tour of the princely states. He was shocked with what he saw. In several of the princely states he visited, such as Jodhpur, Alwar and Udaipur, he observed that 'a state of chronic anarchy prevails—that corruption and intrigue is as rife in several courts as it was in the days of the Emperors.' He argued that 'an Entire Change of Policy must be adopted, the present mixture of *Laissez-Faire* [sic] and niggling interference must be abandoned, and the Chiefs must be told what they will not be allowed to do.' In an October 1870 gathering of Rajput princes in Jaipur, Lord Mayo warned: 'If we respect your rights and privileges, you must also respect the rights and regard the privileges of those who are placed beneath your care. If we support you in your power, we expect in return good government.' If 'chronic misrule' within a princely state persisted, he stressed that the British government reserved the right to intervene and take what steps they thought were needed for administrative reform and 'the redress of the grievances from which the people of the State are suffering.'[24]

While many politicals enthusiastically shared this view, Lord Mayo's approach did not always find willing supporters among the officers in the field, who feared the broader ramifications of taking too keen an interest in the internal affairs of the princely states. In March 1889, as British officials debated the removal of the Maharaja of Jammu and Kashmir over his mismanagement of the frontier state's finances and administration, the Resident in Srinagar, R. Parry Nisbet, initially opposed such a move. He reasoned:

> No Native State that I know of has good officials. In Kashmir the class is probably worse than in most other States, but we cannot continue to administer the country through foreigners; and I feel sure that there as elsewhere we can in time get men who will be good enough for practical purposes. It is important to avoid as far as possible the appearance of annexing Kashmir. We have often been accused of a desire to do so. If the Native States came to believe that we were practically annexing the country their confidence should be shaken, and the effect upon their loyalty would be very serious indeed.[25]

Despite these warnings, Calcutta still found it warranted having the Maharaja relinquish his authority to Jammu and Kashmir's State Council under the authority of the state's Prime Minister Raja Amer Singh for a period of five years. During this period, the caretaker government would enact needed reforms, though the Maharaja would continue to receive a personal income and enjoy the honorary rights and privileges as ruler of the state. In this way, they hoped to send a warning to other princes 'not to neglect the frequent admonition of the paramount power ... to perform the duties of high position and establish just, impartial, and good administration within his jurisdictions.'[26]

In other instances, princes' maladministration was to such an extreme that British authorities felt that nothing less than full abdication was necessary. In 1875, British authorities received reports that Maharaja Mulharao Gaekwad of Gujarat's Baroda State was severely mismanaging his state's finances, engaging in various other abuses of power, and ultimately neglecting his responsibilities as head of state. While misrule and corruption within the state government had been a chronic issue for several years, it reached a point under Maharaja Mulharao beyond which the British would tolerate. According to British authorities, he displayed 'an utter extinction of a sense of responsibility to God and man, undisguised spoliation, tyranny of almost every kind and degree, boundless folly, reckless extravagance and intolerable venality, pervading all the departments of the State.'[27] The Maharaja even attempted to poison the British Resident at the Baroda Court, Colonel R. Rahyre, to cover up his misdeeds.[28]

In response, the Secretary of State for India, Lord Salisbury, ordered the Maharaja deposed and British officials to temporarily assume control of the state's administration. While this measure did not alter the treaty relationship between Baroda and the British Crown, the dispatched officials worked on reforming the administration. The British government also selected a new line of succession from among the dynasty's extended family. Maharaja Mulharao was exiled to Madras, where he died in 1882, and the British installed a new Maharaja, the 13-year-old Sayaji Rao Gaekwad III, who was invested with full powers in December 1881 after he turned 19. Maharaja Sayaji Rao would go on to earn a reputation as one of the most enlightened and progressive princes in India. During his 63-year reign, he expanded access to education for female students, introduced free primary school for children in his state and banned child marriages and untouchability.[29]

In Rajputana's Alwar State during the early 1930s, the British government faced similar problems. On 22 May 1933, Alwar's Maharaja was forced to leave the state over British concerns with his mismanagement of the state's administration. Prior to his departure, Alwar had been experiencing communal agitation due to the Maharaja's misrule. This created several difficulties, particularly with administrative structures staffed with 'untrained and incompetent' personnel whose priorities were the personal needs of the Maharaja rather than the responsibilities of governing the state. Alwar's financial condition was described as 'chaotic' owing to the Maharaja's lavish expenditures that emptied the state treasury and complete neglect of his subjects, who were 'ruined by oppression and misrule.' The primary focus of the administration seemed to have been solely focused on extracting greater and greater revenue from the princely state's subjects, irrespective of the diminishing resources of the taxpayers from whom the revenues were wrung. It was even reported that state officials resorted to torture to meet revenue demands. British authorities expressed concern that the growing disorder within the state could spread to neighboring areas of British India, made worse by the Maharaja's perceived unwillingness to follow British advice to improve the situation.[30]

Due to the untenable situation, British authorities took over Alwar's administration in light of their responsibility for 'the safety and tranquility of India as a whole and in order to prevent the possibility of serious bloodshed.' The Viceroy placed the IPS officer Francis Wylie in charge of the state's administration while the Maharaja was in exile. British officials deputed to the state sought to rehabilitate its finances, overhaul its administrative structures, improve its governance and ensure its population returned to 'a measure of prosperity,' reforms which they felt would be hindered by the Maharaja's presence. They were especially concerned with the state's administration given that the British government advanced it huge loans and were thus anxious to see the state's finances stabilized before the Maharaja was able to return. The Maharaja initially left for Europe but returned to India after a few months, remaining in residence outside of Alwar. While his period of exile was intended to be for two years, the British felt this was not a sufficient period to turn the administration around and, in August 1934, the Maharaja's exile was extended indefinitely. The following year, British officials concluded that its planned scheme for reforming the finances and administration of the princely state would necessitate New Delhi maintaining control for at least another fifteen years with no possibility of the Maharaja returning to Alwar during that period. In 1937, however, the Maharaja died in exile without naming an heir, and the Viceroy selected a new Maharaja, the 24-year-old Thakur Tej Singh.[31]

While there was a long history of such interventions in the princely states, British officials remained sensitive to appearances of princely autonomy to bolster the authority of the princes. They largely engaged with them behind the scenes and worked to ensure that decisions or actions taken by the princes appeared to be autonomous decisions rather than the result of British pressure or demands. This consideration even influenced the timing of their visits and meetings with the princes, careful to avoid sensitive times that could give the impression of British officials coming to 'dictate terms.'[32]

While the British government remained prepared to intervene if the situation dictated it, internal debates continued over the extent to which the British should be engaged in the princely states' internal affairs, particularly amid changes in the broader political conditions within the Subcontinent. In 1909, in contrast to Lord Mayo's and Lord Curzon's positions, the Viceroy at the time, Lord Minto, established a laissez-faire approach to the princely states' internal administration. He believed there was far too much petty interference with the internal administration of the princely states and was growing frustrated with the 'constant pin-pricks inflicted upon Chiefs and Durbars.' Lord Minto complained to the Undersecretary of State for India that he would be 'astonished' if he knew of 'the departmental decisions sent up to me for approval in respect to [the princely states], which I have over-ruled.'[33] At the same time, some British residents also felt that Lord Curzon had previously 'pushed things much too far' in his 'tutelage' of the princes, with their Indian counterparts expressing their 'exceedingly strong' views against 'the petty and humiliating interferences' into the internal affairs of the princely states.[34]

Under this new approach, Lord Minto hoped to cultivate the loyalty of the princes as a counterweight to the increasing problems of communalism following the partition of Bengal in 1905, and to forestall the possibility of the princely states being used as bases for political agitation against British rule.[35] He advised the residents to err on the side of latitude and understanding in their engagement with the princes. In a November 1909 speech in the state of Udaipur, the Viceroy argued:

> The foundation-stone of the whole system is the recognition of identity of interests between the Imperial Government and the Durbars and the minimum of interference with the latter in their own affairs. I have always been opposed to anything like pressure on Durbars with a view to introducing British methods of administration. I have preferred that reforms should emanate from Durbars themselves and grow up in harmony with the traditions of the State ... I cannot but think that Political Officers will do wisely to accept the general system of administration to which the Chief and his people have been accustomed. The methods sanctioned by tradition in States are usually well adapted to the needs and relations of the ruler and his people. The loyalty of the latter to the former is generally a personal loyalty which administrative efficiency, if carried out on lines unsuited to local conditions, would lessen or impair.[36]

In a new *Manual of Instructions to Officers of the Political Department* issued the following year, residents were advised against frequent and excessive offers of advice or 'overt action for enforcing reform' and always to keep in mind the interests and perspective of the princes. According to the manual, unilateral interference in the states' affairs was reserved only for instances in which 'misrule reaches a pitch which violates the elementary laws of civilisation.'[37]

It took time for Lord Minto's policy to take hold among the political officers serving within the princely states. However, this approach, which was helped along by the princes' support for the British war effort in the First World War, slowly became the modus operandi among the residents. In 1925, for instance, the British Resident in Hyderabad, Sir Lennox Russell (who would soon be dismissed for sharing secret government correspondences with the Nizam), received numerous complaints about the Nizam's recent 'oppressions' against the state's Hindu population, including the dismissal of the only Hindu member of the state's Executive Council and taking control of the administration of a vassal estate of a Hindu family following the death of its Raja. As public sentiment against the Nizam grew stronger, many leading Hindus in the state blamed the Residency and the British Indian government for failing to intervene to address the Nizam's misrule. During a meeting with a leading lawyer in Hyderabad, Russell explained:

> [T]he Nizam's Treaties expressly dealt with interference in the internal affairs of the State, that in the long run the salvation of Hyderabad must be worked

out by its own people, that the Residency would do anything that was practicable to help the Nizam and the people of Hyderabad but that indiscriminate interference would do more harm than good.[38]

While the line of interference shifted over time, given the predilection of various officials and the demands of different political situations, the princes' internal autonomy and actions were persistently held in check by British willingness to intervene in extraordinary circumstances, along with the princes' awareness of their willingness to do so. In 1938, the Secretary of State of India expressed the government's official position on the relationship between the British government and the princely states, stating: 'It is not the policy of the Paramount Power in ordinary circumstances to intervene in the internal administration of full-powered States ... The Paramount Power would in ordinary circumstances confine itself to tendering advice when consulted.'[39] While balancing these two positions, British authorities' ultimate aim was to bolster and perpetuate the system of princely rule, fearing too much intervention would degrade the princes' authority while also recognizing that committing to a policy of complete noninterference could allow princes to degrade their own authority through unchecked misrule and corruption and undermine the British role as paramount power.

Much as the British government sought to alleviate the adverse effects of mismanagement, it also sought to protect the administration of princely states from political activities within both Princely and British India that might undermine their authority. During the 1920s and 1930s, several political groups emerged within the princely states in opposition to the autocratic rule of the princes and advocating for representative government (see Chapter 2). Such groups often pushed for British interference into the internal affairs of the states in cases of perceived misgovernment and criticized princes' claims of autonomy from British control. The Working Committee of the Indian States' People's Conference (whose name was later amended to the All-India States' People's Conference) argued that the princes' assertions were 'untenable and fallacious.' In defense of a request for British interference, one of the group's pamphlets stated: 'Indian States have been in subordinate alliance with the Government of India. They are under the control of the Foreign and Political Department of the Government of India. They are maintained in their positions by the power of the Government of India. How can they, therefore, pretend to claim any independence of this Government of India?'[40]

In the face of this upsurge in political activity among the states' subjects, the British government remained committed to the overall protection of the princely order and the princely states' sovereignty. In September 1922, for example, the British government introduced the Princes' Protection Act, an act enthusiastically welcomed by the princes, and, twelve years later, expanded it with the Indian States (Protection) Act for the purpose of protecting the princely states' governments from any activities that threatened to 'subvert, or to excite disaffection towards, or to obstruct such Administrations,' including limiting attacks within the press and other kinds of political activism.[41] While some legislators recognized this as an official form of censorship for legitimate grievances against the princes, New Delhi was adamant that the act did no such thing and, by mirroring press laws existing in British India, was only intended to halt the publication of material that could 'excite hatred, contempt or disaffection against the State.'[42] The Home Department further reasoned that the princely states 'speaking as a whole, have no hesitation whatever in promptly suppressing within their territories any agitation directed against the Government of India or Provincial Governments. It would seem desirable in the interests of India in general that this attitude should be encouraged by as great a measure of reciprocity as it is practicable to attain.'[43]

Beginning with Lord Minto's policy of general noninterference, British officials hoped that these measures would strengthen the bond between the British government and the princely order, as well as improving the states' standards of administration on their own terms. To the contrary, they ultimately helped to bolster the princes' sense of political autonomy and the illusion that they could govern independent of British intervention and British control. After Lord Minto's 1909 speech, the Nawab of Palanpur stated that 'like schoolboys we got a holiday when Lord Minto at Udaipur declared the non-intervention policy.'[44] Because of British rhetoric and policy in the early twentieth century, often premised on the assumption of continued British dominance in South Asia, many princes embraced the illusion of political autonomy and were increasingly committed to protecting the political status quo, especially in the face of broader political changes through the 1930s and 1940s. British authorities' hesitance to become too involved within the princely states to force any political decisions extended to the constitutional debates of the 1940s about their future political status, leaving them in an increasingly ambiguous position in respect to the successor governments to British colonial rule.

Ultimately, the British government would leave the matter of the princely states' status following the transfer of power to be decided by the Indian and Pakistani governments and the princes, who remained committed to protecting the layered sovereignty of the British Raj. British policy toward the princely states planted a seed in the minds of many princes that their territories could continue as independent states as a means of protecting their sovereignty. British authorities in New Delhi and London were initially only too happy to let this fiction play out to their own benefit, unaware of the ultimate consequences of their approach as political turmoil boiled up across India and eventually led to the British withdrawal from the Subcontinent. This set up inevitable clashes between the political interests of the princely states and the governments of India and Pakistan. As early as 1922, the Political Secretary Sir John Thompson, an opponent of Lord Minto's reforms, remarked, '[W]e have carried the policy of non-interference too far,' though Thompson's successors would be committed supporters of this approach.[45]

Notes

1 Aya Ikegame, *Princely India Re-imagined: A Historical Anthropology of Mysore from 1799 to the Present* (Abingdon: Routledge, 2013).
2 William Dalrymple, *The Anarchy: The East India Company, Corporate Violence, and the Pillage of an Empire* (New York: Bloomsbury, 2019).
3 British Library, London, IOR/A/2/22, Treaties, &c. between the East-India Company and the states bordering on the Presidency of Bombay, 1838.
4 Barbara N. Ramusack, *The New Cambridge History of India: The Indian Princes and Their States, Volume III, No. 6* (Cambridge: Cambridge University Press, 2004), p. 62.
5 Keen, *Princely India and the British*, pp. 9–10.
6 Copland, *The Princes of India in the Endgame of Empire*, p. 16.
7 A. Berriedale Keith, *Speeches & Documents on Indian Policy, 1750–1921, Volume I* (London: Oxford University Press, 1929), pp. 382–3.
8 National Library of Scotland, Edinburgh (NLS), 72627b-01, Summary of the Proceedings of the Government of India in the Foreign Department During the Viceroyalty of Lord Curzon of Kedleston, Part 1. General Review, Indian Papers of the Fourth Earl of Minto, 1908, p. 5; Priyasha Saksena, 'Jousting Over Jurisdiction: Sovereignty and International Law in Late Nineteenth-Century South Asia,' *Law and History Review* 38:2 (2020), 409–57.
9 Charles Umpherston Aitchison, *The Native States of India: An Attempt to Elucidate a Few of the Principles which Underlie Their Relations with the British Government* (Calcutta: Office of the Superintendent of Government Printing, 1881), p. 12.
10 *Report of the Indian States Committee, 1928–1929* (London: His Majesty's Stationery Office, 1929), p. 23.
11 National Archives of India, Delhi (NAI), File No. 135-P/47, PR_000004002001, Kashmir treaty shawls for the year 1946, Political Department, Government of India, 1947, pp. 3–4.
12 NAI, File No. 86-P/44, PR_000005014538, Request of His Highness the Maharaja of Ratlam for grant of an Adoption Sanad to the Ruler of the State, Political Department, Government of India, 4 April 1944, pp. 2–3; Keen, *Princely India and the British*, pp. 25–45.

13 Sir C. Corfield to Mr. Abell, 27 March 1947, *TOP Volume X*, p. 30.
14 NAI, File No. 32-X, PR_000004001990, Administration of Najer, on death of Sir Sikandari Khan, Mir of Nagir, External Affairs Department, Government of India, 1940, p. 102.
15 NLS, 72627b-01, Summary of the Proceedings of the Government of India in the Foreign Department During the Viceroyalty of Lord Curzon of Kedleston, Part 1. General Review, Indian Papers of the Fourth Earl of Minto, 1908, p. 53.
16 Keen, *Princely India and the British*, pp. 135–6.
17 NAI, File No. 498-P, PR_000004010091, Muslim agitation against the Kashmir Darbar. Decision not to take action against the Muslim Jathas under sections 125 and 126 of the Indian Penal Code as the State is not a 'Power,' Foreign and Political Department, Government of India, 1931, p. 4.
18 G.R. Abhyankar, *Problem of Indian States* (Poona: Aryabhushan Press, 1928), pp. 183–4.
19 NAI, PP_000000005926, Kathiawar state (Junagadh) 1947–1948, Private Papers of Sardar Patel, 1948, p. 18.
20 NLS, 72627b-01, Summary of the Proceedings of the Government of India in the Foreign Department During the Viceroyalty of Lord Curzon of Kedleston, Part 1. General Review, Indian Papers of the Fourth Earl of Minto, 1908, pp. 1, 20.
21 Sir William Lee-Warner, *The Native States of India* (London: Macmillan and Co.: 1910), p. 40; Sakuntala Narasimhan, *Sati: Widow Burning in India* (New York: Anchor Books, 1990), pp. 71–2; 'No More Slavery in Kalat. The Khan Follows the Example of Burma and Nepal,' *New York Times* (30 December 1926).
22 Lee-Warner, *The Native States of India*, pp. 27–8.
23 Manu Bhagavan, *Sovereign Spheres: Princes, Education and Empire in Colonial India* (New Delhi: Oxford University Press, 2004); Manu Bhagavan, 'Demystifying the "Ideal Progressive": Resistance through Mimicked Modernity in Princely Baroda, 1900–1913,' *Modern Asian Studies* 35:2 (2001), 385–409; Fiona Groenhout, 'Loyal feudatories or depraved despots?: The deposition of princes in the Central India Agency, *c.* 1880–1947,' in Ernst and Pati (eds), *India's Princely States: People, princes, and colonialism*, pp. 99–117.
24 Keen, *Princely India and the British*, pp. 129–30, 142.
25 NAI, File No. 80–98, PR_000004002063, Affairs of the Kashmir State. Discovery of treasonable letters. Maharaja's resignation of power. Reorganization of the Government, Foreign Department, Government of India, 1889, p. 5.
26 NAI, File No. 80–98, PR_000004002063, Affairs of the Kashmir State. Discovery of treasonable letters. Maharaja's resignation of power. Reorganization of the Government, p. 25; NAI, File No. 162-203, Kashmir Affairs, Foreign Department, Government of India, 1889, p. 24.
27 NAI, File No. 356-359, PR_000005013913, Present Administration of Baroda State, Foreign Department, Government of India, 1875, p. 9.
28 'Deposition of the Gaekwar of Baroda,' *Times of India* (26 April 1875).
29 Uma Balasubramaniam, *Sayajirao Gaekwad III: The Maharaja of Baroda* (New Delhi: Rupa Publications, 2019).

30 NAI, PP_000000010106, Alwar- Correspondence re. Engaging of Mr. Jayakar as counsel in various state affairs and also papers re. the exile of Maharaja from the state for the rehabilitation of the administration, Private Papers of M.R. Jayakar, 1933, pp. 22, 48, 51, 57–8.

31 NAI, PP_000000010106, Alwar- Correspondence re. Engaging of Mr. Jayakar as counsel in various state affairs and also papers re. the exile of Maharaja from the state for the rehabilitation of the administration, Private Papers of M.R. Jayakar, 1933, pp. 43–5, 48, 86, 95.

32 NAI, File No. A_1920_JUL_95, PR_000003004832, Fortnightly Reports on the Internal Political Situation for the Second Half of May 1920, Home Department, Government of India, 1920, p. 28.

33 NLS, MS. 12736, Lord Minto to John Morley, 29 August 1906, Correspondence, July–Dec 1906, Indian Papers of the Fourth Earl of Minto, 1906; NLS, MS. 12736, Lord Minto to Sir Arthur Godley, 9 August 1906, Correspondence, July–Dec 1906, Indian Papers of the Fourth Earl of Minto, 1906.

34 NLS, MS. 12736, John Morley to Lord Minto, 27 July 1906, Correspondence, July–Dec 1906, Indian Papers of the Fourth Earl of Minto, 1906; NLS, MS. 12736, John Morley to Lord Minto, 30 November 1906, Correspondence, July–Dec 1906, Indian Papers of the Fourth Earl of Minto, 1906.

35 NLS, MS. 12739, Lord Minto to Viscount Morley of Blackburn, 17 June 1909, Correspondence, Indian Papers of the Fourth Earl of Minto, 1909.

36 Mary Minto, *India: Minto and Morley, 1905–1910, Compiled from the Correspondence Between the Viceroy and the Secretary of State* (London: Macmillan and Co., 1934), p. 344.

37 Sir Kenneth Fitze, *Twilight of the Maharajas* (London: John Murray, 1956), p. 173.

38 NAI, File No. F112_Apr_P-2, PR_000003031238, Fortnightly Reports on the Internal Political Situation in India for April 1925, Home Department, Government of India, 1925, p. 23.

39 NAI, File No. 407-P(S)/42, PR_000005002680, Position of Depressed classes vis-à-vis constitutional reforms in Indian States, Political Department, Government of India, 1942, p. 1.

40 NAI, PP_000000010098, Indian States—activities of the various Indian States' People's Conference relating to the problem of the future of the Native States in India, Private Papers of M.R. Jayakar, 1926, pp. 4, 18.

41 Indian States (Protection) Act, 1934, accessed at: https://legislative.gov.in/sites/default/files/legislative_references/1934.pdf [accessed 20 December 2022].

42 NAI, File No. F_42–1_34, PR_000003037531, Question of Enacting Legislation to Afford Protection to Ruling Princes and Chiefs Against Press Attacks and Agitations Organised in British India Against Them and Their Administrations, Home Department, Government of India, 1934, p. 141.

43 Ibid., p. 5.

44 Copland, *The Princes of India in the Endgame of Empire*, p. 31.

45 Ibid., pp. 50, 61.

2

The nationalist movement
and the princely states

By the 1920s, British authorities were largely content to maintain a laissez-faire approach to the princely states' internal politics, only interfering in instances of the most egregious abuses of power. At the same time, India's political scene was becoming dominated by the leading parties of the Indian nationalist movement—the Indian National Congress and the Muslim League. This movement pushed for increased representation for Indians within government and the eventual withdrawal of British rule from the Subcontinent. As Indian nationalists increased their campaign of civil disobedience, British authorities saw the more conservative princely order, whose sovereignty was tied to the maintenance of British colonial rule, as allies in stemming the tide of popular mobilization and broader anti-British sentiment.

With the princes' general antipathy to meaningful political reforms within their states or significant changes to the broader political order in India that could undermine their authority, there were growing tensions between the nationalist movement and the princely order. While the nationalist movement had initially seen the princely states as an exemplar of Indian capacity for governance, leading nationalist figures in the twentieth century, including Jawaharlal Nehru and Mahatma Gandhi, soon saw the princes' continued rule as an impediment to the implementation and expansion of a modern democratic government ruled by Indians. With the nationalist movement increasingly hostile toward the rule of the princely order, the princely states' subjects were more and more active in demonstrating their opposition to the princes' continued rule. In the late 1930s, the Congress leadership saw this as 'a mighty awakening' among the states' subjects and sought to coopt this momentum to undermine British colonial rule.[1]

While Congress and the political groups representing the states' subjects were distinct movements and not always in sync with one another, the increasing coordination between them fed into a broader apprehension among the princely order about an independent Indian government controlled by Congress and the implications for their sovereignty, based on recognition by British authorities and hereditary rule. Many princes feared that this path could lead to the implementation of democratic institutions within their states, which would undermine their political control and further degrade their sovereignty. In the face of growing political agitation from among their subjects, a number of princes did implement political reforms within their governments, but states' subjects frequently criticized them as mere eyewash, with Congress leadership growing more and more insistent in their political stance that the princes must make way for popular government through the late 1930s and 1940s. The princes' antagonistic position toward the nationalist movement demonstrated their general resistance to any internal political reforms that would increase their subjects' civil and political rights and impinge on their sovereignty.

While many Indian nationalists would come to criticize the autocracy and political oppression prevalent within the princely states, the nationalist movement did not initially hold this view. During the late nineteenth and early twentieth centuries, as Indian nationalism took its early steps, leading members of the movement pointed to the internal political autonomy enjoyed by the princely states as 'undeniable evidence of the aptitude of the Native races for Government,' as described by Surendra Nath Roy, a High Court lawyer in Calcutta. Unlike the British Indian provinces at the time, the princely states offered Indians the opportunity to gain experience and display practical knowledge in governing the affairs of state. While Roy reasoned that Indians living under direct British rule may 'boast of a better education and a higher culture than under the native states,' British India was 'hardly a proper field for the display of native statesmanship ... for reasons not far to seek.' Its residents could 'soar high into the cloudy region of political speculation, they can discourse eloquently on the vague generalities and stilted abstractions of political science, but, when it is action and not speculation, practice and not theory, that is in question, they must yield the palm to the men under the native regime.'[2]

In fact, many educated Indians had a history of service as senior ministers, advisers and bureaucrats within the administrations of various princely states given the lack of comparable opportunities within British India at the time.[3] During the formative years of Indian nationalism, historian Milinda Banerjee argues that the princely states played a key role in the emergence of new visions of Indian sovereignty and rulership. He writes:

Many Indian nationalists were attracted by the possibility of indigenous sovereignty that the princely states seemingly promised; they often desired alliances with the rulers so that they could implement their programmes of national uplift. The states could (potentially) offer lucrative jobs to independent-minded nationalists, implement nationalist educational agendas, promote social reforms and welfare-oriented public works and serve as stark reminders that Indians could govern themselves without British interference.[4]

At the turn of the twentieth century, the president of the Indian National Congress, Romesh Chunder Dutt, similarly pointed to the princely states as evidence of Indian ability to govern and used their example to bolster the group's goals of eventual Indian self-sufficiency and home rule. To push this political agenda, Dutt argued that 'no part of India is better governed to-day than these States, ruled by their own Princes.'[5] Partially because of this perspective, the Congress largely maintained a hands-off approach to political activism within the princely states at this time, formally prohibiting the setting up of local Congress branches within the states. Due to legal restrictions on political organizing and limited resources, Congress leaders also did not see the princely states as a promising field of political activity and deferred to the Indian princes' right to rule their subjects. The group initially kept their focus on the provinces and challenging British colonial rule. In fact, through the late nineteenth and early twentieth centuries, British interferences in the internal affairs of princely states often provoked public outcries from Indian nationalists.

Such rosy views soon faded. Beginning in the early twentieth century, Congress leaders increasingly criticized the princes' autocracy but maintained a pragmatic approach to engagement with the princely states. Mahatma Gandhi, for instance, took an ambiguous political position toward the princely states. Through his family connections and upbringing (his father and grandfather had both served as diwan of Porbandar State within Gujarat), Gandhi was intimately familiar with conditions prevalent under the princes' rule and personally knew several members of the princely order. Nevertheless, he was a sharp critic of the princes, referring to their autocracy as 'a powerful cause of our miserable plight.' In a 1917 lecture at Banares Hindu University, Gandhi lambasted 'the richly bedecked noblemen' who directed so much public wealth for their personal benefit at the expense of the poor peasants who labored under their stifling rule. He stressed that swaraj (self-rule) was not possible so long as the princely class was able 'to take away from them almost the whole of the results of their labour' and argued that the princes' jewelry should be taken and held in trust for their subjects. His message was a harsh and offending tonic to the many princes who happened to be in the audience. The moderator was forced to bring Gandhi's lecture to an abrupt halt and adjourn the meeting.[6]

In the coming years, Gandhi continued to oppose the exploitative nature of princely rule in India. However, he was hesitant to directly challenge the princes through direct action and pointed his animus and agitations toward the broader colonial system that created and supported their political rule. He stated, 'The present Princes are puppets created or tolerated for the upkeep and prestige of the British power. The unchecked powers exercised by them over their people is probably the worst blot on the

British Crown.' He argued that the states' subjects were 'backward' not because they were different from those residing within British India but because they had been 'groaning under a double yoke'—both British and princely oppression.[7] Upon his return to India from South Africa in 1915, he advocated for a continuation of the Congress policy of noninterference in the princely states. He explained that his attitude toward the Indian princes was one of 'perfect friendship' and felt that the autocratic conditions prevalent in the states, while 'most deplorable,' must be reformed from within through direct engagement and negotiation between the rulers and the subjects. He initially felt that outside pressure should be limited to 'the expression of enlightened public opinion in their neighborhood.'[8] Yet, Gandhi advocated for the princes to 'march with the times' and join the Congress cause for Indian independence, arguing to the princely order that 'they need not feel so helpless if they could consider themselves as an integral part of the nation instead of being, as they are, an integral part of the Imperial machine. If the machine topples, they may disappear unless they become part of, and depend upon, the nation.'[9] Though, in the face of many princes' intransigence to any political reforms through the 1930s, he later took a more active approach in engaging with internal political conditions within the princely states, such as undertaking a fast in Rajkot State in 1939.

Like Gandhi, Nehru was personally opposed to the hereditary, monarchical rule of the princely states, where 'the autocracy of the medieval age is still going on in full blast.'[10] Moreover, he feared the future prospect of the many princes, under the urging of departing British officials, attempting to set themselves up as independent states following the transfer of power and creating a chaotic and divisive political landscape within the Subcontinent that undermined the cohesion and self-sufficiency of an independent India. In engaging with British officials over the constitutional future of India, he argued that any debates about the future status of the princely states must be about the status of their people and not the princes.[11] However, echoing Gandhi's exhortations, he pointed to the role played by the British in propping up and perpetuating the princely order. In 1939, Nehru stated to a gathering of states' representatives in Ludhiana that most princely states:

> are sinks of reaction and incompetence and unrestrained autocratic power sometimes exercised by vicious and degraded individuals. But whether the Ruler happens to be good or bad, or his Ministers competent or incompetent, the evil lies in the system. This system has vanished from the rest of the world, and left to itself, it would have vanished from India also long ago. But in spite of its manifest decay and stagnation, it has been propped up and artificially maintained by British Imperialism.[12]

To undo the autocracy of the princes, he argued that British colonial rule needed first to come to an end.

While many individual Congress members had been active within the princely states and states' subjects had been active in Congress activities, the Indian National Congress as an organization had remained aloof from the princely states through the early twentieth century, particularly as it struggled with limited funds, internal dissension and poor morale.[13] This began to change in the late 1930s. After the Congress rose to power in seven (out of eleven) provincial legislatures during the 1937 elections in the British Indian provinces, the group began to shift away from its earlier approach. While some Congress members remained hesitant to commit the group's resources to intervening in the princely states' internal affairs, they increasingly saw the perpetuation of the princely order, whose status was so intimately tied to the continuation of imperial rule, as an additional obstacle to furthering their political agenda and establishing representative government throughout India. Moreover, the Congress now held a firmer political position following the provincial elections to expand their activities into Princely India.

In February 1938, Congress passed the Haripura Resolution declaring the princely states to be 'an integral part of India' and laying out the need to pursue the same political, social and economic freedoms within the princely states as in the British Indian provinces.[14] This was the first step toward reversing its earlier policy by authorizing Congress members to engage in political struggles within princely states, leading to a number of local Congress committees to be set up within the princely states and the eruption of widespread protests and satyagrahas against the states' governments. At this time, it was also becoming increasingly difficult for Congress to ignore the political activism of the states' subjects: 'a mighty awakening among the people of the states,' as Nehru described it in early 1939.[15]

During the 1920s, states' subjects began to increase their political activism against the princes and launched new political organizing efforts. Political groups known as Praja Mandals (The People's Organization) began to emerge in several princely states to advocate for the introduction of responsible government. This movement sought to make the state governments more democratic and increase the states' subjects' political and civil rights, as well as agitating to develop local self-government and stamp out corruption.[16] Such political activists were at times careful to express their loyalty to the person of the prince while focusing their grievances against corrupt officials within the state administration, given the various restrictions on their political activities. They also criticized the practice of employing retired British officials within state governments, such as in Bharatpur State where they alleged that the British officials employed by the Maharaja cared little for the well-being of the states' people and further contributed to the repression of the broader population as they supported the interests of their Maharaja alone.[17] The widespread practice of employing outsiders, both British and Indian, within the state governments, had been a long-standing critique by the states' elites and the broader public.[18]

Even in the face of legitimate grievances against their rule, princes often found scapegoats to explain away such opposition, especially pointing to outside instigation by Congress. In October 1938, a British adviser, Sir Patrick Cadell, informed the ruler of Rajkot State, Shri Dharmendrasinhji Lakhajiraj, that recent political agitations and complaints against his government involving the Praja Mandal were 'based on your behavior' and not the product of outside influence as he had asserted. Many believed that Lakhajiraj spent too large a share of the state's revenues on 'unworthy objects' while ignoring the administration of the princely state. Lakhajiraj waived away such criticism and claimed that 'the present agitation is only a wave spread by the Congress for the initiation of responsible government in the State.'[19] In an effort to further discourage agitation and deflect blame onto the British, the Diwan of Travancore, C.P. Ramaswamy Iyer, suggested that it was legally impossible for the princes to unilaterally make constitutional changes within their states to establish responsible government without the approval of the British government.[20]

In December 1927, the Indian States' People's Conference was formed in Bombay as a coordinating body for the increased political activism within the princely states and to help forge closer connections between states' organizations and the Indian National Congress. In the late 1930s, Congress leaders took control of this movement largely to ensure it stayed in line with their broader objectives, with Nehru becoming its presiding president in 1939. Following the Haripura Resolution in 1938 and the increasing support from Congress, political agitation within the princely states became more widespread. Some princes acquiesced to the pressure by introducing various political and constitutional reforms, such as the rulers of Rajkot, Aundh and Narsinghgarh. Officials in Hyderabad, Travancore and Jammu and Kashmir even reached out to Congress seeking advice for dealing with the spreading unrest. The kneejerk reaction of a concerned Bertrand Glancy, a member of the IPS, was that these events presaged 'a general collapse' of the princely states.[21]

These fears proved to be overblown at the time, particularly with major princely states much more effective in handling the disturbances and British authorities providing guarantees of security to the princes' rule, even dispatching troops to quell any unrest. British officials also recognized that each state's sovereignty placed limitations on the ability of the British government to confront Congress and their various civil disobedience activities

within the princely states. Officials were at pains to prevent various agitators from taking advantage of the internal boundaries between British-ruled
districts and princely states to avoid being arrested, as British Indian police
did not have jurisdiction within the princely states. This necessitated British
officials gaining the cooperation of the states' governments and bolstering
their capacity in combating subversive activities, even as they increasingly
faced internal protests and political agitation.[22]

With little experience in organizing nonviolent protests and political
demonstrations, the protests that emerged in the princely states in 1938
often escalated into violence. Faced with worsening unrest that threatened
to spiral out of control, the Congress Working Committee passed a resolution calling for a cessation of the violence within the princely states as
'it did great injury to the cause of freedom in the States.' Gandhi likewise
denounced the violence and called for the agitations to cease.[23] Conditions
settled down by the following year, with many of the princely states enacting bans against Praja Mandal activities. Yet, this growing activism caught
the attention of Congress. Congress leaders began to travel to the princely
states as part of their campaigns across India, engaging with states' subjects
and finding support for their cause. They encouraged the states' subjects
to politically organize, including forming local Congress committees, and
expressed sympathy and overall support to their struggle for representative government. They also raised needed funds. During the 1930s, British
officials reported that considerable financial contributions for the Congress
were raised within the princely states (including in some instances from
princes themselves before many princes grew disillusioned with Congress
through their increased activism against princely rule), which prompted
requests from the British Indian government to the states' durbars to bring
pressure on their subjects to block such contributions.[24]

However, the message delivered by Congress officials amid this new
activism was not always what the states' subjects—whose focus frequently
remained confined to events within their individual states—hoped to hear.
While recognizing that the problems of Princely India were distinct from
British India, they urged the gathered audiences to cooperate with their
rulers in the broader, primary struggle to establish an independent India
free from British colonial rule. During a May 1938 speech in Mysore State,
for instance, Sardar Patel, who played a leading role in Congress engagement with the princely states, stated: 'You must remember that in this fight
for freedom, we fight for the freedom of Indian Princes also. Once the
Princes are free we shall settle our accounts with them without the intervention of a third party.' Later that month, at the Deccan States' Peoples'
Conference, Patel told those present that Congress was unable to devote its
limited energy and resources with the problems of the princely states as it

struggled for Indian independence. He instead exhorted them to unite and continue to work to wrest power from the princes for themselves.[25] Once the British departed India, Congress officials stressed, the princes would lose their support structure that perpetuated their political rule, allowing for various political reforms and the introduction of democratic government within the princely states to take place. In a July 1946 speech at Jhansi in the United Provinces, Nehru further argued: 'The mainstay of the autocracy of the Indian princes is the British power and with the British off the scene, the edifice of the autocratic princely structure will also crumble and the princes will have to come to some arrangement with revolutionary and progressive forces.'[26]

Congress' increased engagement in the princely states underlay the princes' growing concern with the nationalist movement, which not only had the potential to stoke further unrest among their subjects but had implications for British rule in the Subcontinent that buttressed their own political authority. In early October 1942, the Maharaja of Patiala told the Viceroy Lord Linlithgow: 'We, the States, are surrounded by enemies, and when the intentions of [His Majesty's Government] and their policy was far from clear or reassuring, it was all the more important that we should have some warning in advance.' Soon after this conversation, Linlithgow wrote to the Secretary of State for India in London:

> In the old days, when we had been here with every prospect of remaining here indefinitely and were prepared ourselves to look after and safeguard the interests of the States, that state of things was all right and perfectly understandable. But that was not the position now. Every day we advertised our impending departure, and every day we weakened our grip over India as a whole and more especially over British India. At the same time we depended greatly on the Princes: the Princes, as we had publicly admitted had done an immense amount for us in the war, both directly and indirectly; they had kept their States quiet; they had prevented a dangerous situation from developing in those States; they had helped us with money and with men, and done everything they could to encourage war effort; and they were entitled to claim in these circumstances, particularly where an anti-British movement in British India was concerned, that they ought to be taken into greater confidence.[27]

Nevertheless, British authorities eventually hoped to leave the matter of the princely states' status following independence to be decided by these two opposing sides, setting the stage for clashes over their competing visions of state sovereignty.

While Congress became increasingly engaged in the princely states through the late 1930s and 1940s, the more conservative Muslim League was much less active in its engagement. The League's leadership feared that too much interference in the princely states' internal affairs could provoke retaliatory actions from its political opponents—not to mention the fact that the group struggled with internal dissensions and lack of funds during the 1930s and did not wish to pile onto their problems by undertaking a potentially costly political campaign among the many princely states.[28] Despite this overall approach, the Muslim League formed the All-India States Muslim League in October 1939 to shoulder the responsibility of representing its interest among the princely states. This organization was the initiative of Bahadur Yar Jung from the Muslim-ruled state of Hyderabad. So dominant was Jung's role in the organization that India's Intelligence Bureau described the group as a 'one-man show.' Its first session was held in Lahore on 23 March 1940, where Jung was unanimously elected its president. The All-India States Muslim League's principal object was 'the safe-guarding of Muslim interests in Indian States in various ways such as ensuring proper representation of Muslims in State Services and Legislatures.'[29] It was intended to be an allied body of the Muslim League rather than a formal constituent of it, with Jinnah remaining almost solely focused on Muslim League activities within British India. Following the death of Jung in 1944, the group slipped into relative inactivity until February 1947, with the establishment of the Central Office of the States Muslim League in Delhi under the leadership of Rasool Khan. Nevertheless, the Muslim League largely maintained an official policy of nonintervention in the affairs of the princely states up to the date of the transfer of power.[30]

Jinnah's general approach to the princely states was legalistic in nature, rather than political. Prior to the transfer of power, he recognized the princes' legal right as sovereign rulers to accede to either dominion or choose to remain independent. While the Muslim League did recommend that Muslim-majority princely states join the Pakistani Constituent Assembly in the lead up to Pakistani independence, its leadership recognized states' rights to pursue independence and pushed for princes not inclined to join either dominion to maintain harmonious relations with both. Before the decision to create Pakistan had been made, Jinnah was also generally of the opinion that any questions of political or constitutional reforms within the princely states were internal matters between the princes and their subjects. Yet, he believed that political progress was inevitable given the influence of political developments within the provinces. 'In course of time,' Jinnah surmised in a November 1946 press conference, 'I think there will be complete self-Government in the States, quicker than we imagine because of events in British India.'[31]

Following the announcement of Partition in June 1947, Jinnah reiterated his view that the princes' decision on accession was their own and maintained his recognition of their legal right to remain independent. Either way, he had no intention of interfering with that process at the time.

'We have made it clear that we are not going to coerce, intimidate, or put any pressure on any State making its choice,' he explained in an 11 July press statement. 'But those States who wish to join the Pakistan Constituent Assembly will find us ready and willing to negotiate with them [on an] agreement for the mutual advantage of both. Those who wish to declare their complete independence may do so. Pakistan is willing to come to such terms with them as may be beneficial for both and secure mutual and reciprocal interest.'[32] The All-India States Muslim League's working committee also announced its support for the declarations of independence by the Nizam of Hyderabad and Maharaja of Travancore as well as the All-Jammu and Kashmir Muslim Conference's efforts to secure independence for Jammu and Kashmir. The Muslim League's noninterference approach to the princely states even attracted the interest of Hindu princes, such as the Hindu Maharaja of Jodhpur who believed that his state's internal political autonomy and sovereignty would be better protected within Pakistan than in a Congress-controlled India, despite his state's Hindu majority (see Chapter 5).

Jinnah's noninterference policy prior to the transfer of power was partly driven by the unsettled nature of Pakistan. At the time, Jinnah was deep in negotiations over the future of the Muslim state and was largely unwilling to engage with princely states interested in acceding to it until the creation and structure of the state had been definitively settled. His attitude toward the princely states was essentially, 'Let us first put our own house in order in British India and then it will be time enough to bother about the States,' as recounted by Jammu and Kashmir's Prime Minister B.N. Rau following a conversation with Jinnah in 1946.[33] In July 1947, for instance, the ruler of Las Bela, a subsidiary state of Kalat, reached out to Jinnah to discuss its future status within Pakistan following independence. Jinnah responded: 'I was very glad to see you and thanked you for your good wishes for Pakistan. Beyond that I am not in a position to say anything at present.'[34] There were a number of complaints among Muslim political leaders and activists over this policy at the time. Muslim leaders in Jammu and Kashmir, for example, complained that Jinnah's approach, in stark contrast to Congress' activist approach and engagement with pro-India political movements within the princely states, left them without guidance and support from the Muslim League and tipped the scales of political influence toward Congress.[35] It wasn't until after the transfer of power that Jinnah and the Pakistani leadership began to take a more active interest in the status and internal affairs of the princely states within Pakistan's sphere of influence (see Chapter 9).

With the widespread arrests of Congress members as the group launched the Quit India movement in 1942, British preoccupation with the Second World War and the Muslim League maintaining a hands-off approach to the princely states, the immense pressure on the princes was lifted for the time being, not to mention that wartime demands for domestically manufactured goods provided an economic boost to the states. Many princes also used the war to demonstrate their loyalty to the paramount power by contributing supplies, men and money to the British war effort, which earned high praise from the Viceroy and political leadership in London.[36] This respite for the princes would be short-lived. At the war's conclusion, British plans for the withdrawal from India would be put on the fast track and the position of the princely states in India and Pakistan would once again take center stage.

The princes' antagonistic position toward the nationalist movement and its vision of Indian nationalism demonstrated their resistance to any internal political reforms that could increase their subjects' civil and political rights. With Congress becoming increasingly hostile to the princes' rule as an impediment to political progress in the Subcontinent and growing more and more engaged with the political activism of the princely states' subjects, the princes were under both top-down and bottom-up political pressure to introduce political reforms. Yet, they feared that this path could lead to the implementation of representative government within their states and undermine the princes' sovereignty as the nationalist movement pressed their new vision of state sovereignty, especially following the transfer of power when the safety net of British paramountcy would be severed. As the princes worked to maintain the political status quo of British rule, with some even beginning to dream about outright independence with the impending British withdrawal, the coming debates on India's constitutional future in the 1940s would soon challenge the sustainability of the princely system and the layered sovereignty of the British Raj following the transfer of power.

Notes

1 Purushotham, *From Raj to Republic,* p. 33.
2 Surendra Nath Roy, *A History of the Native States of India, Volume 1, Gwalior* (Calcutta: Thacker Spink & Co., 1888), pp. 3–5.
3 John R. McLane, *Indian Nationalism and the Early Congress* (Princeton, NJ: Princeton University Press, 1978), pp. 193–5; Ramusack, *The Indian Princes and Their States*, pp. 182–6; Susanne Hoeber Rudolph, Lloyd I. Rudolph, and Mohan Singh, 'A Bureaucratic Lineage in Princely India: Elite Formation and Conflict in a Patrimonial System,' *Journal of Asian Studies* 34:3 (1975), 717–53.
4 Banerjee, *The Mortal God*, pp. 112.
5 Romesh Dutt, *The Economic History of India in the Victorian Age, From the Accession of Queen Victoria in 1837 to the Commencement of the Twentieth Century* (London: Kegan Paul, Trench and Trubner, 1903), p. 32.

6 Anthony J. Parel (ed.), *Gandhi: Hind Swaraj and Other Writings* (Cambridge: Cambridge University Press, 1997), p. 76.
7 Mr. Gandhi to Lord Pethick-Lawrence, 20 May 1946, *TOP Volume VII*, p. 636.
8 S.H. Patil, *The Congress Party and the Princely States* (Bombay: Himalaya Publishing House, 1981), p. 32.
9 Anand Hingorani (ed.), *Gandhi Series: To the Princes and Their People, Volume IV* (Karachi: Anand T. Hingorani, 1942), p. 1.
10 NAI, File No. F-51-2, PR_000003017378, Political Situation Reports Supplied by I & B Department, Political Department, Government of India, 1946, p. 235.
11 Note by Sir S. Cripps, Interview with Maulana Azad and Jawaharlal Nehru, 2 April 1942, *TOP Volume I*, p. 609.
12 Copland, *State, Community and Neighbourhood in Princely North India*, p. 101.
13 Ian Copland, 'The Princely States, the Muslim League and the Partition of India in 1947,' *International History Review* 13:1 (1991), 38–69, at 44.
14 Purushotham, *From Raj to Republic*, p. 95.
15 Ibid., p. 33.
16 NAI, File No. F112_I, PR_000003031242, Fortnightly Reports on the Internal Political Situation in India for February 1925, Home Department, Government of India, 1925, p. 20.
17 NAI, File No. F-18–16, PR_000003016367, Fortnightly Report Received from the Residents—From July to Dec 1945, Home Department, Government of India, 1945, p. 218.
18 Ramusack, *The Indian Princes and Their States*, pp. 184–6.
19 NAI, PP_000000005423, Rajkot communication with Maharaja 35–39, Private Papers of Sardar Patel, 1939, pp. 5, 7.
20 Copland, *The Princes of India in the Endgame of Empire*, p. 165.
21 Ibid., p. 169.
22 NAI, File No. F-5-4_32, PR_000003033325, Co-Operation of Indian States in Dealing With the Civil Disobedience Movement, Home Department, Government of India, 1932, p. 3.
23 Copland, *The Princes of India in the Endgame of Empire*, p. 170.
24 NAI, File No. F-5-4_32, PR_000003033325, Co-Operation of Indian States in Dealing With the Civil Disobedience Movement, Home Department, Government of India, 1932, p. 4.
25 NAI, File No. F-17-5_38, PR_000003036850, Fortnightly Report for the First Half of May 1938, Home Department, Government of India, 1938, pp. 72, 141.
26 NAI, File No. F-51-2, PR_000003017378, Political Situation Reports Supplied by I & B Department, Political Department, Government of India, 1946, p. 235.
27 NAI, File No. F-34-3, PR_000003013810, Point Raised by the Maharaja of Patiala with H.E. the Viceroy, Home Department, Government of India, 1942, pp. 14–15.
28 Copland, 'The Princely States, the Muslim League, and the Partition of India in 1947.'

29 NAI, File No. F-17–2_43, PR_000003015465, Organisation and Constitution of the All-India States Muslim League, its Activities and Programme, Home Department, Government of India, 1943, pp. 3–5.
30 Note by All-Jammu & Kashmir Muslim Conference, 25 August 1947, *Jinnah Papers Volume V*, p. 568; Copland, 'The Princely States, the Muslim League, and the Partition of India in 1947.'
31 Mr. Abell to Mr. Turnbul, 15 November 1946, *TOP Volume IX*, p. 76.
32 Press Statement by M.A. Jinnah, 11 July 1947, *Jinnah Papers Volume IX*, p. 179.
33 Sir B.N. Rau to Mr. Abell, 1 June 1946, *TOP Volume VII*, p. 762.
34 M.A. Jinnah to Ruler of Las Bela, 28 July 1947, *Jinnah Papers Volume VIII*, p. 237.
35 Muslim Princes Asked to Join Pakistan Constituent Assembly, 12 July 1947, *Jinnah Papers Volume IX*, pp. 179–80.
36 Copland, *The Princes of India in the Endgame of Empire*, p. 187.

3

The All-India Federation, or the first failed accession

The various constitutional developments and gradual progression toward limited representative government during the interwar years helped to lay the foundation and legal framework for the increased calls for Indian self-government and the eventual transfer of power in 1947.[1] Beginning with the August 1917 declaration of the Liberal Secretary of State for India Edwin Montagu, the policy of the British government had been to support 'the increasing association of Indians in every branch of the administration and the gradual development of self-governing institutions with a view to the progressive realization of responsible government in India as an integral part of the British Empire.'[2] However, the limited franchise granted to Indians under the Government of India Act of 1919, which reflected this new policy, was only applicable to the British Indian provinces.

At this time, no definitive objective for the princely states was laid out within British policy, which instead offered the princes and the states' subjects more ambiguity. The 1929 report of the Indian States Enquiry Committee, known as the Butler Committee after its chairman Sir Harcourt Butler, admitted that paramountcy was 'impossible to define.' Its tautological declaration that 'Paramountcy must remain paramount' also offered little clarity. Nevertheless, the Butler Committee recommended that the British government maintain its treaty relationship with the princely states, thereby protecting their sovereignty and political status (which the princes welcomed), while also arguing that intervention into the states' internal administration was justified if changing circumstances and popular demand dictated such an action (which the princes rejected). The Committee report noted: 'Conditions alter rapidly in a changing world. Imperial necessity and evolving conditions may at any time raise unexpected situations. Paramountcy must remain paramount; it must fulfill its obligations, defining or adapting itself according to the shifting necessities of the time and the progressive development of the states.'[3]

During the interwar period, British engagement with the princely states would not remain static, and their efforts to reform the overarching governing structures within India would eventually extend to Princely India. In the 1930s, British plans to create an All-India Federation encompassing both British and Princely India, as authorized under the Government of India Act of 1935, dominated the British government's relationship with the princely states.[4] This altered the broader political context within India amid which the princes increasingly acted to protect their sovereignty and political status, all while British officials worked to convince them of the merits of acceding to the federation. Rapid political and constitutional changes further entrenched many princes into resisting any disruptions to the political status quo, as demonstrated by the princes' concerted opposition to both the federation scheme.

The princes' opposition to plans for an All-India Federation foreshadowed key obstacles that British, Indian and Pakistani authorities would later face in their efforts to integrate the princely states leading up to and following the transfer of power in 1947. The princes' refusal to accede to the federation scheme shows their resistance to any external constitutional changes that might threaten their sovereign status and direct relationship with the British Crown, whose recognition as the paramount power in India served as the source of the princes' sovereignty. The layered sovereignty of the British system of indirect rule created entrenched political interests that opposed such reforms, even British-led efforts. The princes held grave concerns about the future strength of any federal government in India and the extent of its authority over the princely states that acceded to it. Thus, the federation, controlled by the political parties within British India, would become an intermediary between the princely states and the British government and would weaken and infringe upon their political autonomy and sovereignty. Finding ways to overcome such princely opposition to various political and constitutional reforms would occupy British and Indian political leaders' attention throughout the decade. Indeed, princely opposition to the All-India Federation would directly inform how Indian leaders envisioned the scope of accession to the Indian Union and their engagement with the princes on this issue in 1947 (see Chapter 5).

The federation scheme and the first failed accession

By the late 1920s and early 1930s, demands for self-rule in India were growing increasingly strident. As a result, British politicians saw the necessity of framing an Indian constitution and putting India on the path toward dominion status. Several commissions were formed to study this question. While the 1928 Nehru Report (named after the chair of the committee that prepared it, Motilal Nehru, Jawaharlal Nehru's father) advocated for

the framing of an Indian constitution for British India without reference
to the princely states, there was a growing acknowledgement that any
future constitutional reforms would need to encompass both British and
Princely India in some form. The Indian Statutory Commission, known
as the Simon Commission after its chairman Sir John Simon, was also
dispatched to India in 1928 to study the question of India's constitutional progress. This commission noted the economic interdependence of
the two political realms of the British Raj and argued in its 1930 report,
'Economic forces are such that the States and British India must stand or
fall together.'[5]

Between November 1930 and December 1932, the British government
held three Round Table Conferences in London, during which British
officials, Indian political leaders and representatives of the princely states
discussed the constitutional future of India and the potential devolution
of power that could put India on the path toward dominion status, then
seen as the logical goal begun with Montagu's reforms. Many princes
initially saw the landmark meetings as an opportunity to reassert their
sovereign status and clear up any ambiguities about their relationship with
the paramount power. Ahead of the first conference in 1930, the Maharaja
of Bikaner, Ganga Singh, then serving as Chancellor of the newly formed
Chamber of Princes,[6] proclaimed: 'Far from feeling any apprehensions, the
Princes ... welcome the proposed Round Table Conference as it will finally
set at rest all doubts [about their sovereignty] and ... clarify the position of
the States within the Empire.'[7]

As princes debated what their practical objectives should be in London,
the idea of an Indian federation was introduced by two officials on the
princely states' side: Kailash Haksar, a minister for Gwalior State, and
former journalist K.M. Panikkar, then working with the Chamber of
Princes as the secretary of the princes' delegation. British authorities were
apprehensive about Haksar and Panikkar's efforts to attempt a rapprochement between the princes and Indian nationalists as a united front against
the British. To get ahead of potential British interference, the two states
officials formed a plan for an autonomous All-India Federation combining
British and Princely India under a single federal structure with the hope
that this would free princely states from British meddling in their internal
affairs while strengthening the princely order's overall political role within
India.[8] While ideas for an Indian federation had been circulated a decade
prior to this, they were never taken seriously. The Round Table Conference
provided the opportunity for Haksar and Panikkar to repackage the idea
and sell it to the princes as a viable path forward to settle and institutionalize their political position. Several leading British officials, including the
Resident to Hyderabad Sir Terence Keyes and Sir George Schuster of the

India Office, soon became ardent supporters of the federation scheme and on their own initiative sought to build support for the plan.

Ahead of the first Round Table Conference, the broad position of the princes on any federal structure, as expressed by the Maharaja Sayaji Rao Gaekwad III of Baroda State, was:

1. The need for the complete autonomy of the States in internal affairs.
2. The strict observance of our Treaties, both in the letter and in the spirit.
3. The establishment of an independent court of arbitration to which both sides can appeal, as of right.
4. The devising of some means whereby the States will be able to speak with weight in all matters that are common between them and the rest of India.[9]

Under these conditions, many princes at the first Round Table Conference initially warmed to the idea of an All-India Federation as it would replace the vaguely defined paramountcy with a clearly delineated division of political authority between the federal government and its constituent political units. Various princely states' ministers and British officials walked the princes through the plan, making sure to emphasize 'all the sweets and omit … [all] the sacrifices.' The British Indian government's special observer at the conference in November 1930, Harry Haig, reported shortly before the start of the proceedings: 'States as a whole are considering seriously the possibilities of some immediate federal union with British India.' During the opening speeches of the conference, rulers and representatives from Jammu and Kashmir, Hyderabad, Baroda, Mysore and Bikaner announced their states' willingness to join the federation in 'a position of honour and equality in the British Commonwealth of Nations.' British officials were stunned, with Keyes calling the day's outcome a 'miracle.' With the princes' announcement, the British government now directed their efforts to make the federation scheme a reality, despite opposition from some British officials within India.[10]

While the idea of an All-India Federation was still an ill-defined concept following the first Round Table Conference, it began to take a more defined form in subsequent conferences. Not all were pleased with how the federation scheme was taking shape, with princely attitudes cooling to the idea through the second and third conferences. The Chamber of Princes passed a resolution signaling their commitment to an All-India Federation provided that the British Crown guaranteed legal and political protections for the princely states' internal autonomy.[11] Even though the princes showed a marked shift in their support for a federation, the British government remained committed to pursuing it, seemingly due to a lack of realistic alternatives. In February 1932, Richard Glancy of the India Office observed a common view among his colleagues: 'We are none of us, I should imagine, convinced that [federation] ... will work, but we ... are pledged to try the experiment.'[12] And if they were moving forward with establishing the federation, British authorities understood that participation of the princely states was necessary for its success, especially with the princes serving as a conservative bulwark against the Indian nationalist parties within British India.

Ultimately, it was the fine print that tripped up the implementation of the federation scheme. It largely failed to win broad support among the princely order in the coming years due to quibbling over the particulars of states' representation within the federal government, the extent of the federal government's jurisdiction, the impact on states' revenues and the terms of accession—all of which carried implications for the princely states' sovereignty. Initially, there were divisions among the princely states regarding their representation in the federal legislature. The major states, such as Hyderabad, Mysore and Baroda, argued for proportional representation in the legislature in deference to their political importance and population size; other states pushed for 50 percent representation in the legislature reserved for the princely states with each member of the Chamber of Princes being allotted a seat. Maharaja Bhupinder Singh of Patiala State also advocated for a confederation of all the princely states as a preliminary step toward accession to an Indian federation. There were further sticking points between the representatives of the princely order and the Indian National Congress (which refused to attend the first Round Table Conference but attended later conferences). Within the proposed federal structure, the Congress and All-India States' People's Conference advocated for elected representatives of the princely states, while the princes pushed for the states' representatives to be nominated by them. The Congress representatives argued that the prospect of having the princes nominate their representatives within a federal legislature was 'repugnant to and vitiates responsible government and is not conducive to best interests of people or states.'[13]

Political movements representing the states' subjects also voiced concerns over being excluded from the federation's political structures, especially as the British government often deferred to the views of the princes to ensure their participation and support. In early June 1933, the Central India States' People's Conference was convened in Jhansi in the United Provinces by the Servants of the Indian States' People's Society with the intention of presenting to the Political Department a list of grievances against the princes. The speakers at the conference stressed that the princes' only interest was to maintain their autocratic rule. As a result, they stressed, '[T]here was no responsible government in the States; the municipalities were not free, there were no district boards and the rulers govern as they please.' On the second day of the conference, a resolution was adopted that stated:

The Indian States must join the Federal Government of India and they must endeavour to secure adequate representation for their subjects. Disregard of the peoples representation is very much detrimental to the interests of our States ... While holding that the Federal form of government is a proper one this conference regards it unsatisfactory from the point of view of the people of the Native States and requests the Paramount power to have adequate representation for the subjects of the Native States in the Federal Government.[14]

During a November 1933 public meeting in Rajkot to discuss the proposed plan for federation, one speaker denounced the scheme as 'defective and detrimental to the interests of the general public, especially the States' subjects, as it would not give proper representation to them.' He was convinced that the representatives appointed by the princes would always be on their side and encouraged the 300 people in attendance to protest the implementation of the federation scheme as currently envisioned.[15] Both the Muslim League and Congress also opposed the federation scheme, fearing it would only serve to empower the princes' rule and hinder progress toward the establishment of democratic governance within India, as well as undermining the momentum of their own efforts in pushing for Indian self-rule.[16]

Following the distribution of a draft bill for the Government of India Act in early 1935, several princes reached out to the British residents in their states to express their considerable apprehension about their future safety within the federation scheme as the bill did not contain protections for the states' sovereignty as the princes had hoped.[17] As he leafed through the act, V.P. Menon, then serving as the Undersecretary of the Reforms Department in New Delhi, was pessimistic about the princes' willingness to go along with its provisions. He remarked: 'The princes will never give up their privileges or power. They were already showing signs of dismissing a federation at the Round Tables. It is not likely they will concede now.'[18] As the Chamber of Princes debated a resolution in opposition to the bill in Bombay, the Maharaja of Patiala, Bhupinder Singh, denounced it as a 'counterfeit' scheme with 'nothing in common, except in name, to the general outline we accepted at the first Round Table Conference.' The Nawab of Bhopal argued that it fell 'far short of many of our vital demands.'[19]

Even in the face of princely opposition, the British parliament easily passed the bill, which received royal assent on 2 August 1935. Its passage authorized the creation of an All-India Federation but did not result in its immediate formation. While the British-ruled provinces would automatically join the federation under the act, the entry of the princely states was voluntary. The British parliament's Joint Select Committee, appointed in April 1933 to consider the future government of India, explained in its 1934 report that Princely India had a distinct status and characteristics that necessitated distinct terms for accession to any federal structure.

The committee, in particular, pointed to the states' sovereignty under a system of 'personal government' unlike the provinces, which were ruled directly by British authorities.[20] Moreover, the federation would not go into effect unless a majority of states agreed to join it. Therefore, the federation scheme essentially included a princely veto. As one princely delegate to the Round Table Conferences noted, the princely states 'held the future of India … in the hollow of their hand.'[21] Nevertheless, with plans for an All-India Federation now law, British officials were optimistic that getting the requisite number of states to join would not pose an insurmountable hurdle. Lord Linlithgow, appointed Viceroy in 1936, adopted a slow approach to convincing the princes, but was sure that he would be able to get the federation up and running within two years.

Even after the passage of the Government of India Act in 1935, the exact details and scope of the princely states' accession were not yet settled. In late March and early April 1936, the India Office in London was busy preparing the document laying out the terms of the states' accession to the federation—the Instrument of Accession—for transmittal to the princes. To protect the interests of the princely states within the proposed federation scheme, the princes leaned on an American lawyer, Judge William Wadhams, as the lead counsel for the Chamber of Princes to negotiate directly with British authorities. As the instrument was being prepared, Wadhams arrived in London to press the Secretary of State for India Lord Zetland and Sir Maurice Gwyer, the First Parliamentary Counsel in charge of preparing the document, to consider the interests of the princes in establishing its terms and form. In particular, he highlighted the importance of restating the princes' sovereign rights, including clauses specifying financial obligations and referring to any future obligations. He reminded them that the goodwill and support of the princes was the 'vital force of the Federation' underpinning its success. The proposed scheme would only be possible if the princely order was 'satisfied with the terms and form of the Instrument of Accession.' Until the details of the instrument were finalized, Wadhams explained he could not advise any of the princes on whether it would be to their benefit to join the federation. When Gwyer shared a draft instrument with Wadhams in late April 1936, his initial response was that it was 'better than expected but requires amendment and additions without commitment to safeguard States' interests.'[22]

Wadhams worked tirelessly through the summer months of 1936 to lobby the India Office on amendments and edits to the instrument to ensure the full protection of the princes' sovereignty. By mid-August 1936, the India Office released an updated draft instrument. However, Wadhams advised the Chamber of Princes that this draft was still incomplete in clearly delineating the political relationship between the federal government and the princely states, and required further revisions.[23] During the winter of 1936, as negotiations with the princely states' legal team went nowhere, the Viceroy dispatched three senior officials from the Political Department—Courtenay Latimer, Francis Wylie and Arthur Lothian—on a tour of the princely states to consult with the princes on the terms of accession in order to move the federation scheme forward without further delay. As recounted in their report submitted to the Viceroy in early 1937, they found the princes in the mood for negotiation.[24]

Over the next two years, the princes and their representatives continued to consult and negotiate with British authorities on a range of broad and state-specific issues connected with the details of their existing treaties with the British Crown. The unsettled nature of these questions formed the basis of many princes' hesitation to accede to the federation. There were concerns over the financial basis of the federation and the strain this would put on the states' revenues, including states' inability under the proposed federation scheme to levy, collect and appropriate excise duties on state resources. In December 1936, the Diwan of Phaltan State, whose administration was heavily reliant on revenue generated from duties collected on sugar production, argued, 'The proceeds of the duty collected in the Phaltan State being an integral part of Phaltan State's revenue it cannot afford to take any chance with it by federating on this point.' The following month, the Raja of Phaltan, while offering broad support for the federation scheme, reiterated to the British Resident at Kolhapur the impossibility of his small state giving up the significant revenues generated by the state's sugar excise duty.[25] During a February 1937 Durbar, Sir Kishen Pershad, the president of Hyderabad's Executive Council, similarly stated: 'It is a matter of profound satisfaction to Your Exalted Highness's loyal subjects to know that the aim resolutely pursued by our Government has been that our State shall not join the Federation unless and until it is satisfied that by joining the Federation, it will not forfeit a particle of its present source of revenue and that internal autonomy and the special privileges hitherto enjoyed by it will remain absolutely unimpaired.'[26]

The princely states also questioned the specific jurisdiction of the new federation government over such matters as the management of railways, handling of business licensing and the reach of the Central Intelligence Bureau (CIB). The princes treated the proposed arrangements for expanding the CIB's presence in states' territory with 'considerable suspicion,' particularly over concerns with the British authorities' intentions as 'some States have rather formidable skeletons in their cupboards,' according to a senior Indian Civil Service officer in the Home Department. The fear of having their secrets exposed to New Delhi or having intelligence agents freely roaming through their territory was palpable enough that representatives of the princely states openly asserted to British officials in London that the imposition of a super Inspector General of Police or any suggestions for reciprocal arrangements for information sharing would be a roadblock to the federation scheme.[27] Given concerns over such issues, some princes argued that the princely states should 'bide their time' before joining the federation in order to assess how it functioned, the impact on the princely states that entered into it and the implications for their sovereignty.[28]

At a November 1938 session of the Chamber of Princes in Bombay, the princes requested the inclusion of the following passage in the Instrument of Accession: 'Nothing in this instrument affects my sovereignty in and over the State and save as otherwise herein provided all powers, authority and rights of the Ruler in and over this State and the exercise thereof are reserved to the Ruler of this State.' To even be considered, let alone accepted, by the princes, the Nizam of Hyderabad's Prime Minister, Sir Akbar Hydari, likewise demanded that the Instrument of Accession must be amended to include a clause protecting princes' sovereignty over their states. The British government, however, argued that any such clause addressing princes' sovereignty was unacceptable as it could create undesirable pressure or limitations on the position of the British Crown in its future relation with the princely states, especially regarding matters outside the scope of their terms of accession to the federation.[29]

Representatives of the Deccan States also sought to extensively modify the Instrument of Accession to further limit the authority of the federation government and to ensure the protection of their administrative, financial and legal autonomy to its fullest extent.[30] The Viceroy's representative explained that the Instrument of Accession 'cannot cut down the powers which the Federation would have possessed if the State had not federated at all.'[31] Other state governments pushed for wide-ranging limitations on the political authority exercised by the federation government over the princely states, even delving into minor issues such as the extent of state control over individuals entering state territory or landing at state ports, various property rights of the states' residents, the ability to employ a specific number of foreigners within state forces and other issues of particular concern to different princes. At each step of the way, the British authorities pushed back against the princes' modifications and additions to the instrument, believing their demands were simply their desire to provide an overt manifestation of their sovereignty and political influence. British officials were also hesitant to allow any limitations on specific authorities of the central government as it could be construed as a broader limitation on the executive authority of the federation in relation to the princely states.[32]

The British refusal to negotiate on the terms of accession stoked increased princely opposition. So unpopular was the idea of an Indian federation among the princes by this time that the Maharaja of Patiala resigned his post as the Chancellor of the Chamber of Princes rather than continue to serve as 'Britain's whip over his fellow princes.' The princes' primary concern was the upending of the political status quo and increased interventions by central government authorities into their internal affairs undermining their political authority, a recurring theme in their political engagement over the next decade. Underlying their obsession over the details, several princes feared that the new federal government replacing the current treaty-based political structure would alter the defining features of paramountcy. As early as June 1931, the Maharaja of Patiala forewarned of 'inevitable interferences by the federal legislature and the federal executive not only in respect of federalised subjects but also in matters outside the scope of the federal constitution.'[33] The Nizam of Hyderabad further asserted in his rejection of the federation scheme:

> If, tomorrow, there are to be in all parts of my State, in addition to my own officers, Federal officers who are not my servants and owe me no allegiance, it is not difficult to see how far my authority and even the good order of my State may be prejudiced. Villagers do not understand abstruse questions of political theory; but, from the actual presence throughout my State of officers who do not acknowledge my authority, they would draw the inevitable conclusion that I am no longer master in my own house.[34]

Panikkar, who had taken up the post of Foreign Minister to the Maharaja of Patiala but continued to champion the cause of federation, argued that the scheme was essentially 'still-born' given the absence of a powerful enough prince to sponsor it to overcome the strong opposition within the princely order. Nevertheless, he continued to point to the growth of popular forces within British India as threatening the long-term sustainability of the princely order and saw the federation scheme as their only means to protect their sovereignty in the long run. The only alternative to the Indian federation, Panikkar felt, was the eventual collapse of princely rule in India. He remarked, 'While I knew it was a personal defeat, it was even more the folly of the princes, cutting their nose to spite their face, as it were, that made me despair.'[35]

After years of exhaustive engagement, the British government made little progress in the negotiations and was unable to produce an instrument that satisfied the princes' many demands. In 1939, Lord Linlithgow ordered an outreach campaign to convince the princes of the merits of joining the federation, particularly pointing out that it offered them 'the most efficacious, if not the only, means of defending themselves' from the growing threat posed by the Indian National Congress' civil disobedience movement. These arguments did not find many receptive ears.[36] Facing an impasse,

Linlithgow finally drew a line in the sand. In reference to the Instrument of Accession shared with the princes in 1936, he wrote to them: 'In conclusion I must again emphasize that there is no prospect of any substantial variation of the terms now indicated in the direction of allowing a less measure of accession than what is shown therein or of modifying or adding to the limitations specified.'[37]

Despite some rank-and-file princes reaching out to the Viceroy expressing their interest in acceding to the federation, the Chamber of Princes passed a resolution in June 1939 rejecting the instrument. Yet, the resolution also alluded to the princes' willingness to not close the door to continued negotiations and the potential for a future federation more in line with their demands.[38] Over the summer months, Linlithgow hatched various schemes to try and reverse the Chamber of Princes' opposition and directed the residents to continue to apply pressure on uncommitted or malleable princes. He even secured approval from Lord Zetland for an extension of the deadline for replies to his letter until 1 September, giving him additional time to change princes' minds. In the end, only 101 princely states replied with fifty-one agreeing to accede, though some only agreed with conditions attached. This was below the required number of states needed to move the federation scheme forward under the Government of India Act.[39]

With war clouds forming in Europe, British plans for an All-India Federation were soon derailed after a decade of work. On the very day of the deadline for responding to the Viceroy's letter, Adolf Hitler's army invaded Poland and, two days later, the United Kingdom declared war on Nazi Germany. Following the outbreak of hostilities in Europe, British officials recognized that war preparations would occupy their full attention, with Lord Zetland stating that the federation scheme was 'now in cold storage.'[40] Political officers in the field were informed that the British Indian government would not be able to give 'active attention to Federal problems at the present juncture and that no developments as regards Federation are therefore to be looked for at present.'[41] While the federation remained a long-term goal of the British government, even in the face of opposition from Congress, the Muslim League and the princely order, Linlithgow announced that 'the compulsion of the present international situation and the fact that, given the necessity for concentrating on the emergency that confronts us, we have no choice but to hold in suspense the work in connection with preparations for federation.'[42] At this point, the federation scheme in India was effectively dead and would not be resurrected in any meaningful way before the British government made the decision to depart the Subcontinent following the conclusion of the Second World War. While the princes managed to temporarily preserve their sovereignty under the umbrella of British paramountcy, the British decision to leave India would open serious debates and clashes over the future of the princely states, with the princes' opposition to the federation scheme shaping how British and Indian officials would engage on the integration of the princely states into a future Indian Union.

Notes

1 Sunil Purushotham, 'Sovereignty, Federation, and Constituent Power in Interwar India, ca. 1917–39,' *Comparative Studies of South Asia, Africa and the Middle East* 40:3 (2020), 421–33.
2 The Montagu Declaration, 20 August 1917, *TOP Volume V*, p. 328.
3 *Report of the Indian States Committee, 1928–1929*, p. 31.
4 Andrew Muldoon, *Empire, Politics and the Creation of the 1935 India Act: Last Act of the Raj* (Surrey: Ashgate, 2009).
5 War Cabinet, India Committee, Memorandum by the Secretary of State for India, 5 January 1945, *TOP Volume V*, p. 368.
6 The Chamber of Princes was a 120-seat deliberative body representing the princely order, but without legal authority, formed in 1921. It was intended to serve in an advisory role to the Viceroy on issues related to Princely India and represent the interests of the princely states as a whole to the British Indian government.
7 Copland, *The Princes of India in the Endgame of Empire*, p. 72.
8 Ibid., pp. 79–80.
9 NAI, PP_000000010098, Indian States—activities of the various Indian States' People's Conference relating to the problem of the future of the Native States in India, Private Papers of M.R. Jayakar, 1926, p. 101.
10 Copland, *The Princes of India in the Endgame of Empire*, pp. 88–9, 97.
11 Ibid., pp. 108–11.
12 Ibid., p. 111.
13 NAI, File No. 474, PP_000000010500, Delhi Negotiations regarding Round Table conference—Correspondence with S.C. Mitra, T.B. Sapru, A. Latifi, R.G. Pradhan, M.B. Kolaskar, etc., Private Papers of M.R. Jayakar, 1931, pp. 19, 118.
14 NAI, File No. F-115, PR_000003034079, Proceedings of the Central India States' People's Conference Held at Jhansi in June 1933, Home Department, Government of India, 1933, pp. 15, 17.
15 NAI, File No. F-18-13_33, PR_000003033741, Fortnightly Report on the Political Situation in India for the Month of November 1933, Home Department, Government of India, 1933, p. 39.
16 Purushotham, *From Raj to Republic*, pp. 29–31.
17 NAI, File No. F-18-2, PR_000003035004, Fortnightly Reports from Local Governments and Administrations on the Political Situation in India, for the Month of February 1935, Home Department, Government of India, 1935, p. 36.

18 Narayani Basu, *V.P. Menon: The Unsung Architect of Modern India* (New Delhi: Simon & Schuster, 2020), p. 94.
19 Copland, *The Princes of India in the Endgame of Empire*, p. 137.
20 Menon, *The Story of the Integration of the Indian States*, p. 34.
21 Copland, *The Princes of India in the Endgame of Empire*, p. 91.
22 NAI, File No. 29-G/39, PR_000005013814, Accession of Indian States to federation, Sikkim Agency, 1939, pp. 37, 40, 43.
23 Ibid., pp. 52, 89.
24 Menon, *The Story of the Integration of the Indian States*, p. 37.
25 NAI, PP_000000010682, M.R. Jayakar's correspondence and other papers re: Indian states and the Question of Indian Federation, Private Papers of M.R. Jayakar, 1936, pp. 28–9, 183.
26 NAI, File No. 18/2/37, PR_000005014525, Fortnightly reports from Local Governments and Administrations on the Political Situation in India for the month of February 1937, Home Department, Government of India, 1937, p. 57.
27 NAI, File No. F-159_38, PR_000003037388, Accession of States to Entry Into the Federal Legislative List—Central Intelligence Bureau and Preventive Detention in British India Only Decision of the Crown Representative and the Govt of India on the Limitations Put Forward by States on the Acceptance of the Entry, Home Department, Government of India, 1938, p. 6.
28 NAI, File No. 12(13)-S.R.II, PR_000004001275, Papers relating to the accession of Mayurbhanj State to the Federation and the notes of discussions held with that State, Foreign and Political Department, Government of India, 1937, pp. 25, 73–5; NAI, File No. F-18-12, PR_000003035941, Fortnightly Reports from Local Governments and Administrations on the Political Situation in India for the Month of December 1936, Home Department, Government of India, 1936, p. 84.
29 NAI, PP_000000010682, M.R. Jayakar's correspondence and other papers re: Indian states and the Question of Indian Federation, Private Papers of M.R. Jayakar, 1936, pp. 94, 96–7; 'The Nizam of Hyderabad,' *Time* magazine, Volume XXIX, No. 8 (22 February 1937).
30 NAI, PP_000000010682, M.R. Jayakar's correspondence and other papers re: Indian states and the Question of Indian Federation, Private Papers of M.R. Jayakar, 1936, p. 94.
31 Ibid., pp. 96–7.
32 NAI, File No. F-102_338, PR_000003037343, Accession of State to Entry 17 of the Federal Legislative List, Home Department, Government of India, 1938, p. 5; NAI, File No. F-159_38, PR_000003037388, Accession of States to Entry Into the Federal Legislative List—Central Intelligence Bureau and Preventive Detention in British India Only Decision of the Crown Representative and the Govt of India on the Limitations Put Forward by States on the Acceptance of the Entry, Home Department, Government of India, 1938, p. 8.
33 Copland, *The Princes of India in the Endgame of Empire*, p. 96.
34 A.G. Noorani, *The Destruction of Hyderabad* (New Delhi: Tulika Books, 2013), p. 49.

35 Panikkar, *An Autobiography*, p. 119.
36 Copland, *The Princes of India in the Endgame of Empire*, p. 176.
37 NAI, File No. 29-G/39, PR_000005013814, Accession of Indian States to federation, Sikkim Agency, 1939, p. 122.
38 Copland, *The Princes of India in the Endgame of Empire*, pp. 176–8; Menon, *The Story of the Integration of the Indian States*, pp. 40–1.
39 Copland, *The Princes of India in the Endgame of Empire*, pp. 179, 279.
40 Ibid., p. 181.
41 NAI, File No. 29-G/39, PR_000005013814, Accession of Indian States to federation, Sikkim Agency, 1939, p. 163.
42 Menon, *The Story of the Integration of the Indian States*, p. 45.

4

The debates over India's constitutional future

The Second World War was a watershed for British rule in India. As the United Kingdom emerged from six long and costly years of war with the Axis powers across Europe, Africa and Asia, the once mighty British Empire upon which the sun never set had lost its draw for an exhausted British public. With the many demands of the war effort, British recruitment for the Indian Civil Service had effectively stopped by mid-war, and with the mass demobilization at the war's conclusion, it was difficult to find men willing to serve the Empire thousands of miles away when new business opportunities in the postwar economy were popping up closer to home. The British government had likewise lost the political will to continue to hold onto a colony that increasingly agitated for their colonial masters to leave as the demands of rebuilding the country occupied its attention and resources.[1]

The war transformed the broader political context of and British attitudes toward colonial rule in the Subcontinent, ultimately leading to Partition and the transfer of power to the Indian and Pakistani governments in August 1947. Yet, British officials had already signaled Britain's interest in putting India on the path toward increased political autonomy and dominion status. In November 1929, the government authorized the Viceroy, Lord Irwin, to explicitly announce for the first time that the attainment of dominion status was 'the natural issue of India's constitutional progress,' which British authorities recognized as implicit to Montagu's 1917 declaration.[2] But the necessities of the war drastically sped up this process. In early 1942, British authorities announced the decision to support the formation of an autonomous constitutional government in India as part of the British Commonwealth at the successful conclusion of the war in return for Indian cooperation with the war effort. At the war's end, it was ready to put this into effect.

With many princes committed to preserving their sovereignty, and opposition to meaningful democratic reforms within their states, Princely India did not fit easily into this political picture. Debates quickly emerged among British officials, Indian political leaders and the princes themselves about the most appropriate future path for the princely states, with the princes pushing for the protection of their sovereignty as their fate was decided. As British officials debated India's constitutional future through the Second World War, the position of the princely states remained unclear. While many British officials understood that it would be in the best interests of India for the princely states to join a future Indian Union, they also felt bound by the Crown treaties with various states, a point continuously stressed by the princes themselves. In early discussions, many ideas were put forth about how to integrate the princely states within any future federal structure and handle princely opposition as the princes sought to preserve their sovereignty. But what most officials agreed on was that the princes must enter any new political arrangements voluntarily.

In the early 1940s, the British Cabinet was sensitive to the position of the princely states within an independent India and argued that the government would need to plan for 'the fulfilment of the obligations of the Crown toward the States (which will remain unimpaired except in so far as they may have voluntarily transferred powers to the new Indian Union).' Cabinet members also argued that the princely states' representatives should be on an equal footing with representatives from British India in any constitution-making body and hold the freedom to decide whether to adhere to a new constitution.[3] At this time, British officials in London even entertained the idea that they would maintain their treaty relationship with the princely states after an Indian constitution went into effect on any matters outside the explicit terms on which they joined the Indian Union. Given past failures to convince enough princes to join the federation scheme, the 1942 announcement also tacitly dropped the requirement for a minimum number of princely states to inaugurate any new federal government.[4] British officials accepted the fact that some princes might choose not to join the Indian Union and would continue their direct relationship with the British Crown, despite the many administrative and political challenges this would pose.

During Sir Stafford Cripps's 1942 trip to India to win full cooperation for the British war effort, cooperation that he failed to attain, he further communicated the view that the British government could not relinquish its paramountcy over the princely states to a new Indian constitutional government except through the consent of the sovereign princes, nor could it force them to join the future Union. For princely states that rejected the new constitution, he argued that the continuation of the British government's present obligations under the Crown treaties would be inevitable. Doing otherwise would be a breach of these treaties, and the government, Cripps asserted, 'did not propose to commit such breaches.' Cripps, however, was cognizant of the inherent contradiction in the British government simultaneously supporting the continuation of the princely states' status and expressing support for India's democratic development. He warned Prime Minister Winston Churchill that the perpetuation of the princely states' autocratic rule was 'a negation of democracy and self-determination' and 'may become barriers to growth of Indian freedom.'[5]

Despite his recognition of the binding nature of the princely states' treaties with the British Crown, Cripps's mission raised doubts within the minds of the princes over the attitude and policies of the British government and the Crown's future relationship with the princely states, particularly with his focus on engaging with Congress and the Muslim League as the dominant political forces in India and not recognizing the princely states as a sort of political minority requiring explicit legal protections in the same way as Muslims or Sikhs.[6] The Chamber of Princes made it clear that the princes' aim was to protect their rights and status contained within their treaties and ensure the continued recognition of their sovereignty, in particular preventing any interference in their internal affairs by a future constitutional government in India. Representatives of the princely order even advocated that if a number of princely states chose to remain outside of the Indian Union, they would have the right to band together to form their own union with full sovereign status equal to that of an independent India.[7] While the idea of a separate states' union was not considered a serious or practical objective, Lord Linlithgow floated the idea with the India Office that the British government should privately encourage such a proposal to be used as leverage to secure improved terms for the princely states' accession to the Indian Union.[8]

Nevertheless, with the Second World War continuing to rage, British officials at the time were hesitant to push for any major political reforms within the princely states for fear of disturbing the princes' support of the war effort.[9] Midway through the war, the India Office established a policy confining itself to pushing for the minimum necessary administrative reforms to avoid open insurrection against the princes' rule and maintain law and order. Any reform measures beyond this, including any efforts at democratization in preparation for joining the Indian Union, was a matter between the princes and their subjects. Bound by treaty obligations to recognize and preserve the princes' sovereignty, the India Office had no intention of imposing any form of government within the princely states opposed by the princes, arguing that in this regard the states were in the same position as any foreign country with the ability to choose their own form of government.[10]

Yet, debates emerged between the India Office in London and New Delhi concerning how best to handle the princely states amid future political and constitutional developments in India. By October 1944, Secretary of State for India, Leo Amery, began to have doubts about the India Office's hands-off approach toward the princely states. He felt that the princes would be unable 'to work out their own salvation' if left to themselves, and the princely states could not survive independently, either economically or politically, following the withdrawal of British support, especially the numerous smaller states. With any potential separation of British and Princely India creating a variety of practical difficulties, he reasoned that the British government could not 'safely leave to chance the destiny of so large a part of India which it is not possible to dispose of either by parliamentary enactment or by the bestowal on its inhabitants of freedom to exercise an option under democratic forms of procedure.' Amery, therefore, advocated for a more active approach for integrating the princely states while the British still had the machinery of the Political Department in place.[11] 'In any case,' he lamented, 'I wish it were possible to encourage the States to think a little more of the general constitutional future of India and a little less about their own position.'[12]

On the other hand, Lord Wavell, the former Commander-in-Chief in India, who succeeded Lord Linlithgow as Viceroy in September 1943, advocated a wait-and-see approach. While he recognized that the intention to give self-government to India was incompatible with the preservation of princely rule, he argued that the princes' political isolation would be organically undermined by economic pressure. Economic considerations, Wavell argued, would be more successful than any political pressure as New Delhi and provincial authorities would largely be in control of the Indian economy and industry. 'Thus it seems to me that time is on our side,' he responded to Amery's suggestions, 'and that the approach of the Indian Princes to the next proposal for a Federal union with British India is perhaps being determined for them in advance, by economic considerations ... we should let time and events work for us, postponing any definite move until the constitutional position becomes clearer with the end of the war.'[13] These views were shared by his predecessor who believed that any attempt at coercing the princes, who were 'not always long-sighted,' would only lead to further political difficulties. Even with the princely states' many deficiencies, Linlithgow also felt that some consideration should be given to the princes' contributions to the war effort and the fact that the princes had consistently been 'a conservative and reliable element in Indian polity'; one ICS member remarked that the princely states were 'our sheet anchor in India.'[14]

On the eve of the war's conclusion in the Pacific, the British government's approach toward India's political future shifted with the Conservative Party's losses to Clement Attlee's Labour Party in the July 1945 election. Many within India, in particular members of the Indian National Congress, celebrated Labour's victory. They viewed the formation of Prime

Minister Attlee's government as a means of expediting India's political progress toward constitutional reform and self-governance, with Lord Wavell convinced that he would be the last Viceroy of India. During a visit to the princely state of Swat in India's North-West Frontier Province, he explained this to the ruler of the state, known as the Wali, and asked, 'And is there anything I can do for the state, or for Badshah Sahib personally?' The Wali's son translated this into Pashto for his father, who brusquely responded, 'A moment ago he told me that he is the last Viceroy and the British are leaving—then how could *he* do anything for *me* [*sic*]?' So as not to offend the Viceroy, the Wali's son politely translated this as, 'My father is very thankful and grateful to Your Excellency, but there is no problem for the present.'[15]

The princes were not so jubilant over this news from London. They saw the loss of Conservative Prime Minister Winston Churchill, whose personal antipathy toward Gandhi and Congress was well known, as the loss of a key ally. With the election of a stable Labour government, the princes feared the prospect of the British government allying with Congress leadership and encouraging the formation of 'an exaggerated and unsuitable democracy ... run by irresponsible and half educated political agitators.'[16] In one sense, they were right to be worried. Based on advice from the India Office, Attlee and members of his Cabinet felt that the princely states did not have the sufficient economic and political capacity to maintain an independent existence apart from a future Indian Union and would simply serve as barriers to India's democratic development. More importantly, the Labour government saw no means of continuing the treaty relationship between the British Crown and the princely states or to exercise the functions of paramountcy following the establishment of a self-governing Indian Union.[17]

Though the new government was sensitive to the terms of the treaties, the India Office now presented the British Prime Minister with a legal argument that nullified the Crown's obligations to the princely states. Given the fact that many of the treaties were at least a century old, the India Office argued, they ceased to be appropriate regarding present political conditions given 'the efflux of time and change of circumstances.' British officials now felt they could safely abrogate the treaties amid broader constitutional reforms in India. 'Thus paramountcy itself essentially derived from the fact that we were the paramount power in British India,' Cripps explained to the British Cabinet in September 1945. 'If ... India acquired an independent status, certain of our obligations which we had undertaken, in quite different conditions, would clearly not admit ... [of] being discharged.'[18] As British authorities continued to debate India's future, they nevertheless sought to assure the princes of their support in finding a secure position within the Indian Union respecting their sovereign status. While the British announced that they would not transfer paramountcy to a successor government, which they felt could provoke violent opposition within the princely states, they made it clear that the princely states had no future outside of the Indian Union.[19]

During 1946, two British delegations arrived in India to study further the question of India's constitutional development. In early 1946, a Parliamentary Delegation embarked on a fact-finding mission. During their travels, the delegation members visited several princely states to discuss states' issues in the context of the framing of an Indian constitution. While communal issues and the question of the potential creation of Pakistan occupied most of their attention, one member of the delegation stated that the matter of the princely states was 'obviously only second to that.'[20] Of more consequence was the subsequent Cabinet Mission that departed London in March 1946, which laid the foundation for the British government's Indian policy. The members of this mission had marching orders to press the advantages of accession to the princes.

In meetings with the Cabinet Mission, several princes assured its members that they were 'ready and willing to co-operate in the new development of India.'[21] On 2 April 1946, the Nawab of Bhopal, Hamidullah Khan, then serving as the Chancellor of the Chamber of Princes, met with Lord Wavell and the Cabinet Mission in New Delhi to discuss the future of the princely states. He assured the gathered British officials that the princes had no intention of standing in the way of the realization of an independent India. 'But naturally,' the Nawab stressed, 'the Indian States wish to survive and to continue their existence if this was possible consistently with the progress of India and the world as a whole.' He hoped that Princely India would be treated on a basis of political equality during deliberations on the future of India as a whole, as the princely states were independent and sovereign under the terms of their treaties. He also asked that the princely states maintain their close alliance and friendly relationship with the British government. When pressed for specifics on how he envisaged the princely states fitting into the general picture of an independent India, he demurred, explaining he could not answer such a question until the general structure of the Indian government was decided between the British government and the two leading Indian parties, which at that point remained unresolved. If the ultimate outcome was the partition of the Subcontinent, the Nawab explained that the princes held the general view that there was 'no reason why a third India composed of the Indian States should not be recognized,' which could then join a loose federation with the other two states like earlier plans for an Indian federation.[22]

In a 16 May 1946 statement, the Cabinet Mission recommended that the future Indian Union should embrace both the British Indian provinces and the princely states, with the states retaining 'all subjects and powers other than those ceded to the Union.'[23] The Cabinet Mission ultimately said little regarding the specifics of the princely states' position within the proposed union. Instead, it announced that 'the precise form which their co-operation will take must be a matter for negotiation during the building up of the new constitutional structure, and it by no means follows that it will be identical for all the States,' leaving them in a somewhat ambiguous position amid future constitutional developments.[24] Cripps, who participated in the Cabinet Mission, added that the princely states would become completely independent as the continuation of paramountcy would not be possible following the British withdrawal nor could paramountcy be transferred to a successor government. The means by which the princely states would enter the Indian Union would be a matter left to negotiations between the princely states and the Indian authorities without interference from British authorities.[25] This position was embodied in a memorandum on the princely states' treaties and paramountcy released by the mission members on 22 May 1946, which read:

> When a new fully self-governing or independent Government or Governments come into being in British India … the rights of the States which flow from their relationship to the Crown will no longer exist and … all the rights surrendered by the States to the paramount power will return to the States … The void will have to be filled either by the States entering into a federal relationship with the successor Government or Governments in British India, or, failing this, entering into particular political arrangements with it or them.[26]

In drafting their recommendations, the members of the Cabinet Mission hoped to avoid in any way committing the princes in advance to specific conditions under which they would join India's constitution-making body, the Constituent Assembly, which would have ninety-three seats allotted for the princely states. In discussions with Congress leaders, they feared this could weaken the position of the States Negotiating Committee, which had been set up by the Chamber of Princes in June 1946 to represent the princely states' interest in negotiations with Congress.[27] Speaking in the House of Lords in July 1946, the Secretary of State for India, Lord Pethick-Lawrence, who replaced Amery the previous year following Labour's election win, reiterated the conclusions of the Cabinet Mission. He stressed, 'As to the States, they need have no anxiety since it is for them to decide freely to come in or not, as they choose.'[28] It was the position of the British government that it would not force the princely states to come to an agreement with any successor government within the Subcontinent.[29] Taking the princes' word at face value, the members of the Cabinet Mission expressed their rather naive confidence to Attlee and the India Office that the princely states would join in negotiations for the drafting of an Indian constitution and voluntarily participate in the new constitutional framework 'in the interests of India as a whole,' without reference to the princes' parochial interests and the past challenges British officials faced in bringing the princely states into the proposed federation. In the interim, the members of the Cabinet Mission were also certain that the princes would do everything possible to improve their administrations 'up to the highest possible standard.'[30]

The princes welcomed the Cabinet Mission's pronouncements, in particular latching onto the argument that the princely states would become independent states following the transfer of power. In June 1946, the Chamber of Princes unanimously adopted a resolution in support of the Mission's views regarding the lapse of paramountcy and states' sovereign rights. Yet, it also recognized that many points required further elucidation in negotiation with the Constituent Assembly, which was first convened on 9 December of that year to begin debates on India's future constitution. Some princes' optimism at the time was palpable, goaded on by British assurances for the preservation of their sovereign rights and the potential for them to assert their independence. Following a visit to Rampur State, Francis Wylie came away thinking that the princes were in a 'dreamland.'[31] Philip Mason, then serving as the tutor to the Nizam's grandchildren in Hyderabad, later observed that the Nizam and his supporters were living in a fantasy realm. 'The rabbit had lived so long in so secure a hutch that it did not know it was a rabbit.' He further wrote, 'It was like the spring of 1789 at Versailles,' with 'only five months till the end of nearly two centuries of stability.'[32]

The Mission also had its critics who pointed to the fact that rather than attempt to find a resolution for the issue of the princely states it was merely sidestepping it. In September 1946, P.J. Griffiths, a former ICS member, wrote to Lord Pethick-Lawrence that the Mission was essentially leaving the future of the princely states within the Indian Union 'to chance,' which was 'difficult to defend on logical grounds.'[33] Nehru further complained that in some princely states that the Mission visited there was 'considerable irritation at the fact that no representatives of the States people were interviewed by the Cabinet Mission,' with no record of any meeting between the members of the mission and representatives of states' subjects.[34] From this perspective, the Mission members failed to fully grasp the myriad challenges facing the princely states, underpinning its ambiguous position. All the while, a groundswell was being prepared as political organizations representing the states' subjects continued agitating against the princes and in support of various political reforms. After the war, Congress members expanded their efforts to open local branches within the princely states and directed Praja Mandals to challenge the princes' rule; the fomenting of political agitation became the Congress' principal method to undermine the political authority of the princely order.[35]

Many of these organizations' demands related to the conditions under which the princely states would join the Indian Union. In October 1945, Mysore Congress leaders sent a memorandum to the All-India Congress Committee advocating for elected representation of the states' subjects within the proposed Constituent Assembly. They argued that the broader political problems within India could not be fully solved until the issue of the princely states was addressed and the aspirations of the states' people were satisfied. The Travancore State Congress likewise passed a resolution demanding adult franchise and responsible government within the state and approving affiliation with the All-India States' People's Conference. During a 2 October 1945 meeting of the Praja Mandal in Dungarpur State, the speakers ridiculed the princely order, saying that the Indian princes were 'dancing like monkeys at the behest of the "Madari" [juggler] – the British Government.' While the British and Allied forces had defeated Hitler and the Nazis, they further argued, the British government 'kept India under 562 Hitlers.'[36] In November of the following year, the President of the Gwalior State Congress, Shri Liladhar Joshi, further stressed that princes should give up 'their evasive, makeshift, and dilatory tactics' and emphasized the need for the immediate establishment of interim governments within the princely states as a first step toward true representative government. He criticized existing reform efforts within the states as 'mostly meant for window dressing and propaganda outside and they are far from satisfactory.'[37] By early 1947, Nehru warned the Viceroy of 'a progressive deterioration' of conditions within the princely states. '[W]hen the people of the States were looking forward to the introduction of a democratic form of government,' he wrote, 'they have to face instead repressive action by the authorities.'[38]

The question of who would represent the princely states in the Constituent Assembly—the states' subjects or the princes—became a key point of contention, like previous debates about representation within the political structures of the All-India Federation during the 1930s. Congress leaders felt that the states should be represented by elected representatives, while the princes argued they held the power to nominate the states' representatives. Nehru recognized, 'The real difficulty is that apart from the rulers' position the governments in the Indian States are so unrepresentative that a proper procedure must be adopted to make them representative,' a process that some British authorities felt would be impossible given the complete lack democratic precedent in the states.[39] Faced with such difficulties, some Congress members even expressed the view that representatives of the provinces should move forward with the framing of a new constitution without the participation of the princely states. Only after the task of drafting a constitution was complete should they then consider the question of admitting the princely states into the Indian Union.[40]

On 9 July 1946, the Standing Committee of the All-India States' People's Conference met to discuss this problem, with Nehru presiding over the meeting at Congress House in Bombay. The Committee noted their displeasure with how both the British government and the princes were ignoring the states' subjects and resolved that 'the people of the states will not recognise any decision taken without their approval and consent and that representation from the states must come from the people by way of election.'[41] Nehru also increasingly pushed for the scrapping of the Crown treaties to make way for representative government and referred to anyone speaking of the importance of treaty rights as 'lunatics, knaves or fools.'[42] In the months before the transfer of power, Nehru became even bolder in his stance against the princes, threatening British authorities that he would encourage rebellion in any of the princely states that went against the Congress and its priorities.[43]

During the first session of the Constituent Assembly in December 1946, with representatives of the princely states absent, Nehru introduced a resolution asserting that all territories comprising the British Raj, including the princely states, would be constituted into an independent and sovereign India. Even though he assured the princes that the Indian government had no intention of imposing any form of government over the princely states against their will, he asserted that 'no State can have an administration which goes against our fundamental principles or gives less freedom than obtaining in other parts of India,' and future decisions on the structure of the princely states' governments would wholly reside with the people.[44] During a conference of states' representatives the following month, Hamidullah Khan argued that Nehru's resolution conflicted with the Cabinet Mission's plan, which had been broadly accepted by the princes. His speech took a tone of defiance. 'We are asked to quit or exist on sufferance only,' the Nawab stated. '[I]t would be unworthy on our part to succumb to these threats … We have been the spearhead of progress in many a field. Are we to disappear simply because we fail to subscribe to certain dogmas?'[45]

With Congress positioning itself in 1946 as the logical inheritor of political power in India and its policy toward the princely states becoming clearer, the princes grew ever more anxious about what their position would be following the transfer of power. As Lord Wavell reported back to London: 'The Rulers of States are perplexed and anxious; they realise that their former protectors, the British, are going, that they will be subject to the agitation of Congress, and that the end of their autocracy and easy living is in sight.'[46] Reflective of Lord Wavell's assessment of the princes' outlook, Hamidullah Khan was incredulous that the British government would leave the princely states 'as a sort of no man's child without any effort on the part of the Crown to protect their legitimate and reasonable demands and their established and accepted rights as Sovereign bodies.'[47]

By early 1947, with the Constituent Assembly in place and other preparations underway, the British government was prepared to move forward with its withdrawal and the transfer of political power to Indian hands. On 20 February 1947, Prime Minister Attlee announced in the House of Commons the end of nearly a century of British Crown rule over India. The British government intended to transfer political control to Indian authorities no later than June 1948 in the hopes that setting a definite date for withdrawal would increase the prospects for Congress and the Muslim League to reach a settlement.[48] He also informed Parliament that Lord Wavell had resigned as Viceroy—which provoked a number of 'barbed questions' from Churchill—and Lord Louis Mountbatten, King George VI's second cousin who had served as Supreme Allied Commander of South East Asia Command during the Second World War, had been appointed as his replacement to oversee the transfer of power. Regarding the princely states, the Prime Minister reiterated the position taken by the Cabinet Mission the previous year: 'His Majesty's Government do not intend to hand over their powers and obligations under paramountcy to any Government of British India.' Instead, the system of paramountcy and the Crown's treaty relationships with the princely states would cease to exist at the final transfer of power, with the princely states in a position to negotiate their future relations with the Indian government.[49] During the drafting of this momentous announcement, Lord Wavell stressed to the Secretary of State for India that it should be worded in such a way to avoid any speculation that the British government 'would contemplate maintaining alliances with certain States after repeat after the final transfer of power.'[50]

While the decision not to transfer paramountcy to a successor government was in some ways a victory for the princes, it still left unsettled future relations between the princely states and the Indian Union. In early 1947, Congress representatives were engaged with the States Negotiating Committee to convince its members of the importance of joining the Constituent Assembly and playing a role in the drafting of the Indian constitution. In these discussions, Patel assured the committee members that Congress had 'no desire on our side to encroach upon your rights' nor 'the slightest intention to interfere with [the territorial integrity of the states].' During a 9 February 1947 meeting, the Diwan of Hyderabad directly asked Patel, 'Is there any objection to the existence of the monarchy?' To which Patel responded, 'No responsible person, no Congress man has said "We do not want you". Don't have any unnecessary suspicion, which creates unnecessary difficulties.'[51]

Even following Attlee's announcement, negotiations made little headway. By early 1947, a split emerged among the princes' ranks as they debated the most efficacious way of protecting their sovereign status—some advocated full cooperation with the princely states joining India's Constituent Assembly at the earliest possible stage, while others pushed for the princely states to join at the last possible moment.[52] As negotiations continued, the Nawab of Bhopal nevertheless bristled at the criticism that the princes were sitting on the fence. In an April 1947 circular for the Chamber of Princes, he reiterated: 'The Indian States feel, and feel very strongly, that they have a right to survive and to retain their autonomy and independence. They are, therefore, anxious to safeguard their integrity and autonomy and their cherished and inherent rights.'[53]

On 18 April 1947, Nehru offered an ultimatum during the annual session of the All-India States' People's Conference. In a clear rejection of the states' sovereign status under the layered sovereignty of British rule, he stated that any state that did not join the Constituent Assembly would be treated as hostile to India and would bear the consequences of their actions. This remark created some consternation among the princes. British authorities even pressed Nehru not to put this ultimatum into effect, to which he replied that he was speaking only in his role as president of the States' People's Conference and his remarks did not represent an official Congress position; Nehru later asserted the press had misquoted him.[54] However, Nehru's speech provoked a response. Representatives of several princely states, including Baroda, Bikaner, Cochin, Jaipur, Jodhpur, Patiala and Rewa, joined the Constituent Assembly ten days after Nehru's speech, with other princely states soon following their example.[55]

The Maharaja of Bikaner was an early supporter of Congress efforts to integrate the states. He made an appeal to his fellow princes to support the inevitable forces of Indian nationalism and join the Constituent Assembly, helping to pull in several states. The princes' inclusion in the Constituent Assembly, Bikaner's Diwan K.M. Panikkar argued, would make it clear to everyone that the princes were 'not only working for the good of their States and for their mother country but are above all patriotic and worthy sons of India.'[56] Panikkar later explained to the Viceroy that these states joined the assembly less to ingratiate themselves with Congress and more for 'the absolute need to stand in well with their own people and make them feel that they had a voice in affairs,' not to mention his and the Maharaja's belief that the princely states could not stand apart from the Indian Union and their willing participation would ensure that the body was not entirely controlled by Congress. He further argued that the princes who continued to stand apart from India were only strengthening the forces of communalism and would further feed unrest both within the princely states and the provinces.[57]

Panikkar was joined by the Diwan of Udaipur, Thiruvalayangudi Vijayaraghavacharya, in his support for the princely states' participation in the Constituent Assembly. In opposition to the Nawab of Bhopal and his supporters' efforts to impede the princes from joining the assembly, Udaipur's Diwan stated in an early 1947 conference of princes in Delhi: 'Whether you obstruct it or not, whether you oppose or support, freedom is coming to India. What you now contemplate is like the action of the foolish woman who tried to dam the Atlantic Ocean with a broom; I have no hesitation in saying that if you adopt this resolution it will be your own death warrant.'[58] By June 1947, at least forty princely states had joined the constitution-making body.[59] The Nawab of Bhopal, on the other hand, felt that the Maharaja of Bikaner and the 'dissident' princes that supported his position were fast 'becoming the tools of Congress.' He asserted that their willingness to join the assembly undermined the entire bargaining position of the princely order as the Nawab and his backers sought to ensure the security of the princes' sovereignty and succession rights, which flew in the face of the democratic principles espoused by Congress.[60]

As debates continued among the princes through the spring of 1947, Indian politics was becoming increasingly volatile. Anti-British and inter-communal violence was rapidly spreading, and the Muslim League became further entrenched in their demands for a separate Muslim state, first announced in the Lahore Resolution of March 1940.[61] In February 1947, Jinnah announced that the Muslim League 'will not yield an inch in their demand for Pakistan' and privately remarked that the unified Constituent Assembly was now dead.[62] With British authorities unable to break the impasse between Congress and the Muslim League and broader turmoil in India quickly growing beyond British control, the British government decided it could no longer wait another year to allow for a gradual transfer of power. On 3 June 1947, Mountbatten announced an accelerated time-line for the British withdrawal. India would now be granted independence on 15 August of that year, a mere ten weeks later. He also announced that British India would be partitioned into India and Pakistan (consisting of the Muslim-majority regions of British India) with both states holding domin-ion status within the British Commonwealth, which would maintain admin-istrative continuity based on the Government of India Act, 1935. However, this plan, which came to be known as the Mountbatten Plan, related only to British India, with the British government's policy toward the princely states remaining unchanged.[63]

Following this momentous announcement, the Viceroy's staff found the princes 'divided and uncertain, baffled by the pace of events.'[64] The princely states were now implicitly left with the option to accede to either domin-ion. Though he received no detailed directives from London about how to handle the princely states and existing British policy offered little guidance, Mountbatten asserted that the princes' decision should be guided by the principle of geographic contiguity and the cultural affinity of the states' populations. On 14 June 1947, anticipating potential difficulties in getting all the princes to decide on accession to India or Pakistan before the transfer of power, the Political Department wrote to the various residents authorizing them to enter into standstill agreements with the princely states to cover any interim period between the lapse of paramountcy and accession in order to avoid a breakdown in the states' administration.[65] The standstill agreements maintained existing political and administrative arrangements between the princely states and the Indian government following the British departure until the states entered into a new relationship with either of the two dominion governments.

Partition placed the princely states in an even more difficult position, especially those states with Muslim rulers and majority Hindu populations, and vice versa, such as Bhopal, Hyderabad and Jammu and Kashmir. Their path remained uncertain with opinions divided among both the British and the Indians. Some even argued for a third path—the right to claim full independence following the lapse of paramountcy. The Viceroy's political adviser Conrad Corfield, who Mountbatten had inherited from Lord Wavell, felt that princely states should have the right to become independent and even argued 'with some bitterness' that the efforts of the Maharaja of Bikaner to push the princes to join the Constituent Assembly were weakening the bargaining position of the princes.[66] The 'excessively conservative' Corfield had been a member of the Political Department since the 1920s and served in several princely states. His close association with the princely order over the previous two decades had elicited in him a sincere belief in the idea of 'Indian India' and a respect for the princely states' courtly culture. Among senior British officials, he was known as a princes' man. Francis Wylie, the Viceroy's former political adviser, stated, 'He has been all his life in Indian States and has imbibed, perhaps too successfully, the Princely point of view.'[67] Corfield would clash with Mountbatten on the issue of the princely states, with tensions between the two reflective of a broader anti-Mountbatten sentiment among the British in India. Many of them saw the new Viceroy and his staff as coming to the position knowing nothing about India and labeled Mountbatten a mere 'play-boy.' Topping this off was misplaced anger over the 'abominable' treatment of Lord Wavell.[68]

Demonstrating his bias toward the princes' interests, Corfield argued that the Cabinet Mission's recommendations from the previous year permitted the sovereign princes to choose independence as an option once paramountcy lapsed. In defense of his position, he pointed to the passage in the mission's memorandum stating, 'The void will have to be filled, either by the States entering into a federal relationship with the successor Government or Governments in British India, or failing this, entering into particular political arrangements with it or them.' Corfield interpreted the phrase 'particular political arrangements' as implying the possibility of the princely states entering treaty relationships with the Indian or Pakistani governments as co-equal independent states.[69] His position reflected the views of several high-ranking British officials from earlier in the decade. In his 1940 August offer, Lord Linlithgow stressed that the princely states held the right to remain outside of any Indian Union formed as the result of postwar constitutional reforms. During the war and amid outpouring of support from the princes for the British war effort, Churchill's government made it clear that it too intended to protect 'the interests of those who have proved themselves our friends and loyal supporters.'[70]

In contrast to the views of his political adviser, Mountbatten felt it necessary for the princely states to avoid pursuing full independence and accede to the appropriate dominion, reflecting the perspective of the Labour government in London and the Congress leadership (especially Nehru who he first met during his South East Asia Command and with whom he and his wife would grow increasingly close). Any alternative arrangement, Mountbatten soon became convinced, would result in nothing less than the disintegration of India.[71] He was of the opinion that the princely states would be unable to stand on their own; shortly after his appointment he even suggested that the British government look to Napoleon's consolidation of smaller German kingdoms as a 'valuable precedent' for dealing with the princely states.[72] Nehru later remarked to Mountbatten's Chief of Staff, Lord Ismay, that if the princely states were allowed to remain outside of India, this would lead to the outbreak of conflict until 'some suitable equilibrium was arrived at,' which he feared would set the country back more than a hundred years.[73] Attlee directed Mountbatten to assist the princes in making 'fair and just arrangements' with the Indian nationalist leaders to facilitate their merger into the Indian Union and avoid a potentially catastrophic outcome. In support of this goal, he was authorized to engage in direct negotiations with individual princely states.[74]

Many princes remained apprehensive about British plans for Partition and Mountbatten's position toward the princely states. During a 3 June 1947, meeting at the Viceroy's House in New Delhi, the Raja of Bilaspur asked Mountbatten what would happen to the princely states that decided against joining either Constituent Assembly. The Viceroy rejected the question, calling such a scenario hypothetical until the shape of the two dominion governments was finalized.[75] Regardless, he felt that it would be impossible due to geographic and economic reasons for the states to have a fully independent existence. At the same time, the Nawab of Bhopal wrote to Jinnah complaining of the Viceroy's indirect pressure on the princely states to join India and requested the Muslim League leader to 'lodge a strong protest.' The princely states, the Nawab argued, 'should be left absolutely free to take what action they like. It should be purely voluntary for them to join the one Constituent Assembly or the other. If they want to be independent, they can do so. No pressure should be brought to bear on them to join any one or the other Constituent Assembly.'[76]

Hamidullah Khan also complained directly to the Viceroy. As the British government finalized the plan for the division of the Subcontinent along communal lines, he argued that the princely states' interests and views were essentially omitted from the deliberation process. Partition cut 'right across the principles to which the States have throughout adhered' and placed them in 'a very delicate position.' In fact, the Nawab stated:

> [A]fter the lapse of Paramountcy the States would be completely sovereign and independent in every respect. If the States cannot be admitted as members of the Commonwealth without associating themselves with Hindu India or Muslim India, such of them as may desire to keep aloof from both communal sections of British India, would have to proclaim their independence as has already been done by Hyderabad and Travancore, and would have to adopt suitable measures to safeguard their independence and integrity. This state of affairs would indeed amount to Balkanisation of the country but it would be the direct consequence of the Mountbatten Plan as interpreted by his Excellency the Viceroy.

He further argued that if Muslims and Hindus were afforded the right to form their own dominion governments within the Commonwealth, then so too should the princely states.[77] Otherwise, the princely states would be forced to merge under an Indian government controlled by Congress and would be represented 'by rabid, half educated, ignorant men owing allegiance to Congressmen with ultra communistic tendencies,' with the conservative princes no longer able to serve as a check on Congress activities.[78]

Following the announcement of Partition, Nehru and Jinnah also directly clashed over the princely states' future status. In a discussion between Mountbatten, Corfield, Nehru and Jinnah on 13 June 1947, Nehru rejected Corfield's arguments and was adamant that in no way did the Cabinet Mission allow for princely states to claim independence, a public position Congress had already taken. Nehru further argued that the states possessed at best only semi-sovereignty and had no capacity for international relations, a key test for recognition of a state's sovereignty. Jinnah, on the other hand, pushed back against Nehru's arguments. Stressing that he spoke as a lawyer, he countered that each state was sovereign in every way, except in so far as they had signed treaties with the British Crown. As sovereign states, they held the legal right to choose their own path—whether to join India or Pakistan or remain independent—once they were freed from their Crown treaties. Neither the British nor the future Indian and Pakistani governments could force their decisions.[79]

Two days after the tense meeting between Jinnah and Nehru, the All-India Congress Committee (AICC) formally announced that it

> cannot admit the right of any State in India to declare its independence and to live in isolation from the rest of India. That would be a denial of the course of Indian history and of the objectives of the Indian people today. The A.I.C.C. trusts that the Rulers of the States will appreciate fully the situation as it exists today and will, in full cooperation with their people, enter as democratic units in the Indian Union thereby serving the cause of their own people as well as of India as a whole.[80]

Nehru argued that any princely state that declared its independence—and therefore was able to control their own external relations, form alliances with countries hostile to India, raise their own armies and declare war or peace—would be a direct challenge to India's security.[81]

On 17 June 1947, Jinnah released his own public statement clarifying the Muslim League's position. In it, he made clear that the princely states, both constitutionally and legally, will be 'independent Sovereign States on the termination of Paramountcy and they will be free to decide for themselves to adopt any course they like: it is open to them to join the Hindustan Constituent Assembly, or the Pakistan Constituent Assembly, or decide to remain independent.' In contrast to the position laid out in Congress' resolution, Jinnah stated that 'the Cabinet Mission's Memorandum of May 12, defining the policy of His Majesty's Government towards the Indian States, does not in any way limit them, as it is often wrongly repeated, that they have no option except to join one or the other Constituent Assembly. In my opinion, they are free to remain independent, if they so desire.' He added: 'We do not wish to interfere with the internal affairs of any State, for that is a matter primarily to be resolved between the rulers and the peoples of the States.'[82] Even as late as July 1947, the Muslim League's leadership was unsure exactly how they would handle the princely states after the British withdrawal, informing Mountbatten that they were even prepared to enter into treaty relationships with states rather than having them sign the Instrument of Accession if the princes preferred this route (see Chapter 9 for Pakistan's position toward the princely states).[83]

Throughout the many debates over the constitutional future of India between and within the different sides to the issue, Indian authorities struggled to convince the broader princely order to acquiesce to what they saw as India's inevitable political progress. On the whole, the princes remained committed to preserving their political autonomy and sovereignty in some form, even following potential accession to the Indian Union. The ambiguity of the British position regarding the status of the princely states led to an inevitable clash between competing ideas of state sovereignty—the nationalist movement's commitment to the uncontested sovereignty of a modern and democratic Indian state and the princes' commitment to the perpetuation of the layered sovereignty of British indirect rule. As the transfer of power neared, the tension over these competing ideas persisted and laid the foundation for some princes' commitment to pursuing independence as a means of protecting their sovereignty against the top-down and bottom-up pressures they were facing to democratize their states within an independent India.

Notes

1 Yasmin Khan, *India at War: The Subcontinent and the Second World War* (New York: Oxford University Press, 2015); Srinath Raghavan, *India's War: World War II and the Making of Modern South Asia* (New York: Basic Books, 2016).
2 U.K. Parliament, India (Viceroy's Statement), 1 November 1929, accessed at: https://api.parliament.uk/historic-hansard/commons/1929/nov/01/india-vice roys-statement [accessed 20 December 2022].
3 War Cabinet Committee on India, Paper I (42) 5, Draft Declaration Circulated by the Secretary of State for India, 28 February 1942, *TOP Volume I*, p. 265; Mr. Amery to the Marquess of Linlithgow, 1 March 1942, *TOP Volume I*, p. 273.
4 Note by Mr. Amery, Notes for Discussion on an Interim Constitution, 19 March 1945, *TOP Volume V*, p. 709.
5 Note by Sir S. Cripps, My Interview with Congress Members, 29 March 1942, *TOP Volume I*, p. 528; Sir S. Cripps to Mr. Churchill, 2 April 1942, *TOP Volume I*, p. 617; Sir S. Cripps to Viscount Halifax, 5 April 1942, *TOP Volume I*, p. 641.
6 The Marquess of Linlithgow to Mr. Amery, 25 May 1942, *TOP Volume II*, p. 123; The Marquess of Linlithgow to Mr. Amery, 13 September 1943, *TOP Volume IV*, p. 236–7.
7 Maharaja Jam Saheb of Nawanagar to Sir S. Cripps, 10 April 1942, *TOP Volume I*, p. 734; Maharaja Jam Saheb of Nawanagar to Sir H. Craik, 1 June 1942, *TOP Volume II*, p. 172.
8 War Cabinet Paper, Indian States: Request by Chamber of Princes for Statement of Policy by His Majesty's Government, Memorandum by the Secretary of State for India, 4 September 1942, *TOP Volume II*, p. 895.
9 The Marquess of Linlithgow to Mr. Amery, 30 June 1942, *TOP Volume II*, p. 295.
10 Notes by the India Office, Notes on Sir S. Cripps' Memorandum, undated, *TOP Volume III*, p. 7.

11 Mr. Amery to Field Marshall Viscount Wavell, 26 October 1944, *TOP Volume V*, p. 144; War Cabinet, India Committee, Memorandum by the Secretary of State for India, 17 February 1945, *TOP Volume V*, p. 565.

12 Mr. Amery to Field Marshall Viscount Wavell, 18 May 1944, *TOP Volume IV*, p. 977.

13 Field Marshall Viscount Wavell to Mr. Amery, 28 November 1944, *TOP Volume V*, pp. 241, 245; Field Marshall Viscount Wavell to Mr. Amery, 20 April 1944, *TOP Volume IV*, p. 901.

14 The Marquess of Linlithgow to Mr. Amery, 13 September 1943, *TOP Volume IV*, p. 244; Copland, *The Princes of India in the Endgame of Empire*, p. 269.

15 Fredrik Barth, *The Last Wali of Swat: An Autobiography as told to Fredrik Barth* (New York: Columbia University Press, 1985), p. 101.

16 NAI, File No. F-18–16, PR_000003016367, Fortnightly Report Received from the Residents—From July to Dec 1945, Home Department, Government of India, 1945, pp. 47, 59.

17 Copland, *The Princes of India in the Endgame of Empire*, pp. 218–19.

18 Minutes of India and Burma Committee meeting, 11 September 1945, *TOP Volume VI*, p. 253.

19 Lord Pethick-Lawrence to Field Marshall Viscount Wavell, 25 September 1945, *TOP Volume VI*, p. 298; National Archives, U.K., FO/371/63567, Transfer of power in India—relations of India with the United Kingdom (Folder 3), August–September 1947.

20 NAI, File No. F-51-2, PR_000003017378, Political Situation Reports Supplied by I & B Department, Political Department, Government of India, 1946, p. 59.

21 Copland, *The Princes of India in the Endgame of Empire*, p. 222.

22 Note of an Interview between Cabinet Mission, Field Marshall Viscount Wavell and the Nawab of Bhopal, 2 April 1946, *TOP Volume VII*, pp. 83–7.

23 NAI, File No. F-48, PR_000003015331, British Declaration on India, Home Department, Government of India, 1946, p. 10.

24 Copland, *The Princes of India in the Endgame of Empire*, p. 222.

25 NAI, File No. F-48, PR_000003015331, British Declaration on India, Home Department, Government of India, 1946, p. 28.

26 Menon, *The Story of the Integration of the Indian States*, pp. 475–6.

27 Field Marshall Viscount Wavell to Lord Pethick-Lawrence, 3 August 1946, *TOP Volume VIII*, p. 179; Sir Sultan Ahmed to Sir C. Corfield, 21 November 1946, *TOP Volume IX*, p. 121.

28 Field Marshall Viscount Wavell to the Nawab of Bhopal, 20/21 July 1946, *TOP Volume VIII*, pp. 96–7.

29 National Archives, U.K., FO/371/63567, Transfer of power in India—relations of India with the United Kingdom (Folder 3), August–September 1947.

30 Cabinet Delegation to Mr. Attlee and India Office, 30 March 1946, *TOP Volume VII*, p. 61.

31 Wylie to Wavell, 7 February 1947, *TOP Volume IX*, p. 640.

32 Philip Mason, *A Shaft of Sunlight: Memories of a Varied Life* (London: Andre Deutsch, 1978), pp. 200, 212.

33 Mr. Griffiths to Lord Pethick-Lawrence, 3 September 1946, *TOP Volume VIII*, p. 408.

34 A Note on Kashmir, 17 June 1947, *Jinnah Papers Volume IX*, p. 164; Record of Meeting of Cabinet Delegation and Field Marshall Viscount Wavell, 28 March 1946, *TOP Volume VII*, p. 29, n. 4.

35 NAI, File No. F-18-16, PR_000003016367, Fortnightly Report Received from the Residents—From July to Dec 1945, Home Department, Government of India, 1945, p. 309; Cabinet, India and Burma Committee, Policy In India, Memorandum by the Secretary of State for India, 18 December 1946, *TOP Volume IX*, p. 374.

36 NAI, File No. F-18-16, PR_000003016367, Fortnightly Report Received from the Residents—From July to Dec 1945, Home Department, Government of India, 1945, pp. 205, 235, 250.

37 'Establish Interim Governments in Indian States,' *Bombay Chronicle* (5 November 1946).

38 Pandit Nehru to Field Marshall Viscount Wavell, 25 January 1947, *TOP Volume IX*, p. 540.

39 Cabinet, India and Burma Committee, Memorandum by the Secretary of State for India, 9 September 1945, *TOP Volume VI*, p. 234; NAI, File No. F-51-2, PR_000003017378, Political Situation Reports Supplied by I & B Department, Political Department, Government of India, 1946, p. 241.

40 Shiva Rao to Sir S. Cripps, 15 December 1945, *TOP Volume VI*, p. 706.

41 NAI, File No. F-51-2, PR_000003017378, Political Situation Reports Supplied by I & B Department, Political Department, Government of India, 1946, p. 252.

42 Menon, *The Story of the Integration of the Indian States*, p. 52.

43 Record of Interview No. 146, 10 June 1947, *TOP Volume XI*, p. 232.

44 Constituent Assembly Debates On 13 December 1946, accessed at: https://indiankanoon.org/doc/548244/ [accessed 20 December 2022].

45 '"Campaign Against Princely Order" Regretted, Bhopal Ruler on Nehru Resolution,' *Times of India* (30 January 1947).

46 Memorandum by Field Marshall Viscount Wavell, 30 May 1946, *TOP Volume VII*, p. 732.

47 The Nawab of Bhopal to Field Marshall Viscount Wavell, 2 June 1946, *TOP Volume VII*, p. 780.

48 National Archives, U.K., FO/371/63529, Situation in India—preparations for the transfer of power (Folder 2), February–March 1947.

49 U.K. Parliament, Change of Viceroy, 20 February 1947, accessed at: https://hansard.parliament.uk/Commons/1947-02-10/debates/29adbd34-b107-47ba-bc88-1ceb74065aa2/ChangeOfViceroy [accessed 20 December 2022]; 'British give date for Indian independence,' *United Press International* (20 February 1947): www.upi.com/Archives/1947/02/20/British-give-date-for-Indian-independence/3317410585124/ [accessed 20 December 2022]; Alan Campbell-Johnson, *Mission with Mountbatten* (Bombay: Aico Publishing House, 1951), p. 24.

50 Field Marshal Viscount Wavell to Lord Pethick-Lawrence, 13 February 1947, *TOP Volume IX*, p. 687.

51 NAI, PP_000000006658, States Negotiating Committee 9-2-47 and 3-6-47, Private Papers of Sardar Patel, 1947, pp. 61, 67.

52 The Maharaja of Bikaner to Rear-Admiral Viscount Mountbatten of Burma, 3 April 1947, *TOP Volume X*, pp. 110–11.

53 '"Princes Not Sitting on The Fence"—Bhopal Ruler,' *Statesman* (27 April 1947).

54 Minutes of Viceroy's Nineteenth Staff Meeting, 21 April 1947, *TOP Volume X*, pp. 352–3; Record of Interview between Rear-Admiral Viscount Mountbatten of Burma and Pandit Nehru, 22 April 1947, *TOP Volume X*, p. 362.

55 Menon, *The Story of the Integration of the Indian States*, p. 78.

56 Guha, *India After Gandhi*, p. 55.

57 Record of Interview between Rear-Admiral Viscount Mountbatten of Burma and Sardar K.M. Panikkar, 5 May 1947, *TOP Volume X*, p. 624; Campbell-Johnson, *Mission with Mountbatten*, pp. 45–6.

58 Panikkar, *An Autobiography*, p. 154.

59 'More States Come Into the Assembly,' *Indian Daily Mail* (28 June 1947).

60 National Archives, U.K., FO/371/63532, Situation in India—preparations for the transfer of power (Folder 5), April–May 1947; Campbell-Johnson, *Mission with Mountbatten*, p. 45.

61 Yasmin Khan, *The Great Partition: The Making of India and Pakistan* (New Haven, CT: Yale University Press, 2007), pp. 81–103.

62 Mr. Abell to Mr. Harris, 25 February 1947, *TOP Volume IX*, p. 813.

63 National Archives, U.K., FO/371/63535, Situation in India—preparations for the transfer of power (Folder 8), May 1947.

64 Campbell-Johnson, *Mission with Mountbatten*, p. 163.

65 NAI, File No. 46, PR_000005002283, Formula for Standstill agreements on the lapse of paramountcy, Political Department, Government of India, 1947, p. 5.

66 Campbell-Johnson, *Mission with Mountbatten*, p. 49.

67 Sir F. Wylie (United Provinces) to Rear-Admiral Viscount Mountbatten of Burma, 12 August 1947, *TOP Volume XII*, p. 682.

68 Campbell-Johnson, *Mission with Mountbatten*, p. 40.

69 Minutes of Viceroy's meeting with Congress and Muslim League Leaders, 13 June 1947, *Jinnah Papers Volume VIII*, p. 14.

70 Copland, *The Princes of India in the Endgame of Empire*, pp. 188–9.

71 Abell to Mieville, 20 May 1947, *TOP Volume X*, p. 922.

72 National Archives, U.K., FO/371/63531, Situation in India—preparations for the transfer of power (Folder 4), April 1947.

73 Pandit Nehru to Lord Ismay, 19 June 1947, *TOP Volume XI*, p. 510.

74 Attlee to Mountbatten, 18 March 1947, *TOP Volume IX*, pp. 972–3.

75 Meeting of the Viceroy with Members of the States Negotiating Committee, 3 June 1947, *TOP Volume XI*, pp. 84–5.

76 Note by Nawab of Bhopal, 6 June 1947, *Jinnah Papers Volume VIII*, p. 11.

77 Note on H.M.G.'s Policy toward States, 14 June 1947, *Jinnah Papers Volume VIII*, pp. 21–7.

78 The Nawab of Bhopal to Rear-Admiral Viscount Mountbatten of Burma, 7 July 1947, *TOP Volume XI*, p. 970.

79 Minutes of Viceroy's meeting with Congress and Muslim League Leaders, 13 June 1947, *Jinnah Papers Volume VIII*, pp. 14–15; Menon, *The Story of the Integration of the Indian States*, p. 87.

80 Resolution of the All India Congress Committee (A.I.C.C.) on the States, 15 June 1947, *Jinnah Papers Volume VIII*, p. 29.

81 Pandit Nehru to Lord Ismay, 19 June 1947, *TOP Volume XI*, p. 510.

82 'Mr. Jinnah Concedes States' Right to Independence,' *Times of India* (17 June 1947).

83 Record of Interview Between Louis Mountbatten and Sardar Abdur Rab Nishtar and Akhtar Hussain, 18 July 1947, *Jinnah Papers Volume VIII*, p. 39.

5

The princes' resistance to accession

On 18 July 1947, the British parliament passed the Indian Independence Act, legally paving the way for the establishment of India and Pakistan as independent dominion governments on 15 August of that year. Rather than transfer paramountcy functions to the successor governments, the law officially ended the British Crown's role as paramount power and nullified 'all treaties and agreements in force at the date of the passing of this Act between His Majesty and the rulers of Indian states.'[1] Even though British authorities had earlier provided assurances that the princes' treaties and the rights and privileges contained within them were 'inviolate and inviolable,' the British government now unilaterally scrapped them, leaving the problem of the princely states' status to Indian and Pakistani authorities to figure out.[2] With the lapse of paramountcy, the princely states' legal status would essentially be that of independent states.

As the transfer of power neared, the princely states' status remained unsettled; neither Attlee's statement on 20 February 1947 announcing the end of British rule in India nor Mountbatten's 3 June announcement of the date of the British withdrawal definitively settled the issue. In the ambiguity of their position, some princes began 'to luxuriate in wild dreams of independent power in an India of many partitions,' as one British observer of the events of 1947 recalled.[3] For the Indian National Congress, however, its position was never in question—the princes must recognize the sovereignty of the new Indian government and politically integrate their states with no option to remain independent.

Yet, the continued coordination between Congress and the states' subjects and Indian authorities' refusal to concede to the princes' demands convinced many within the princely order that their sovereignty would be threatened under an independent Indian government, regardless of past verbal assurances from Congress leadership. Several princes saw independence as the only path to preserving their sovereignty, a choice that they felt they had the right to pursue within the scope of British policy. In the weeks before the transfer of power, Mountbatten, Congress leadership and the newly formed States Department dedicated their attention to finding a political arrangement amenable to the princes and pressuring them to give up their dreams of independence, with Indian leaders fearing the political repercussions if they failed to convince them to accede.

The States Department and the princely states

With the urging of Nehru, the British government recognized the necessity of a new department to handle princely affairs through the transfer of power—an idea that had already been discussed over the previous year—and established the States Department (later India's States Ministry) on 27 June 1947. This department was to be the successor organization to the Political Department, which had been shutting down since April, to handle India's engagement with the princely states (a parallel administrative structure was set up for Pakistan). For the sake of continuity, Sardar Patel, who had already been handling Congress outreach to the princely states, was appointed as the department's minister in charge with the bureaucratically capable Vappala Pangunni Menon, who had served as the constitutional adviser and political reforms commissioner to the last three viceroys, selected as the department's secretary.

As Patel and Menon took the helm of the States Department, they confronted the reality that some princely states within India might opt for independence, or even choose Pakistan, rather than accede to India to preserve their sovereignty. Such scenarios created much anxiety among India's political leaders. Patel asserted to Menon that 'the situation held dangerous potentialities and that if we did not handle it promptly and effectively, our hard-earned freedom might disappear through the States' door.'[4] Even with the princes' uncompromising position on protecting their sovereignty, similar to the princes' opposition to the Indian federation in the 1930s, Menon saw a silver lining in the British government ending its status as the paramount power, as this abrogated the Crown's treaties with the princely states. 'The biggest advantage was that we would be writing on a clean slate, unhampered by treaties,' he told Patel. 'I reminded him how the federal negotiations with the rulers had foundered on the rock of treaty rights.'[5]

With the uncompromising attitude of the princes toward the federation scheme during the 1930s at the forefront of his mind, Menon presented to Patel an alternative plan for federation that he had originally drawn up in 1942 as a means of resolving the political deadlock over accession. As Menon had attempted to explain to the Viceroy at the time, Lord Linlithgow, the federation scheme was not practical given the numerous, and often conflicting, demands of the princes, along with the attention and resources consumed by the war effort. This precluded the possibility of continuing the difficult negotiations with individual princes on adjusting the political and fiscal relations as defined by each states' treaties with the British Crown. As an alternative and interim arrangement, Menon had suggested that British authorities ask the princes to accede only on defense and external affairs. The British Indian government already bore responsibility for these matters and, therefore, Menon argued, this move would not diminish in any way the princes' internal autonomy. If the states would agree to join the federation on these terms, Menon felt that this could help build trust and unity with the princes and facilitate conditions for successfully negotiating a future constitution. Linlithgow had summarily dismissed this new scheme, not even bothering to glance at the file Menon had presented him to review.[6] Menon later opined, 'When the partition of the country was decided upon, I could not rid myself of the regretful doubt whether this vivisection would have been necessary had my scheme of December 1942 been implemented.'[7]

Menon now advocated that an analogous scheme be pursued to ensure the princely states' integration into the India Union, with communications added alongside defense and external affairs as the terms of an Instrument of Accession. He explained to Patel: '"Defence" was obviously a matter which no State could conduct by itself; "external affairs" was a subject inextricably linked with "defence" and, as the States had never handled it before, even the largest State could not hope to do so effectively; "communications" was a means of maintaining the very life-lines of the country and without our co-operation, the States could do nothing in this matter.' These three areas were already de facto controlled by New Delhi, and, in all other matters of government, the princes would retain their political autonomy. This minimalist plan was intended to prevent the immediate 'Balkanization' of India and, regarding many of the other political problems connected with the princely states, simply kicked the can down the road. Yet, as a short-term solution, Patel agreed to the approach as outlined by Menon and, the following day, Nehru provided his official approval. Menon also secured the support of Mountbatten, whose active cooperation they felt would help influence the princes. Despite Mountbatten's support, Nehru remained skeptical about its chances of success, a view shared by Corfield who 'threw up his hands in surprise' when briefed on the new policy. He considered it 'far too ambitious and recalled the tortuous and infructuous negotiations with the rulers between 1934 and 1939.'[8]

On 5 July, the day that Patel officially assumed charge of the States Department, he distributed a statement drafted by Menon the previous night urging the princes to accede to India on the three subjects of defense, external affairs and communications. In all other matters, Patel assured the princes that the Indian government would 'scrupulously respect their autonomous existence.' It was only by an accident, the statement further read, that 'some live in the States and some in British India, but all alike partake of its culture and character ... None can segregate us into segments; no impassable barriers can be set up between us. I suggest that it is therefore better for us to make laws sitting together as friends than to make treaties as aliens.' It further assured them that the Congress leaders were 'no enemies of the Princely Order.' With India on the threshold of independence, the statement concluded by reminding the princes that the 'alternative to co-operation in the general interest is anarchy and chaos which will overwhelm great and small in common ruin.'[9] This statement was generally well received among the princes, helping to allay their concerns. The Maharaja of Alwar wrote to Patel: 'Your recent statement regarding the States is most welcome at this juncture ... There can be no manner of doubt that the hand of friendship and cooperation extended by you will be grasped firmly by the states.'[10] However, several princes remained apprehensive about joining the Constituent Assembly or signing the Instrument of Accession, which they dismissively referred to as the 'Instrument of Execution.'

With many princes continuing to sit on the fence, Indian leaders were wary of potential support from departing British officials for the princes that chose to pursue independence. Menon wrote to the Undersecretary of State for India in London: 'Even an inkling that [His Majesty's Government] would accord independent recognition would make infinitely difficult all attempts to bring the States and the new Dominions together on all vital matters of common concern.'[11] While the India Office in London was careful to avoid giving this impression, some officials within the Political Department, in particular Corfield, who frequently butted heads with Menon and the States Department, continued to encourage the idea that the princely states had the right to remain outside of the Indian Union. Corfield openly advised the princes to join ranks behind the Nawab of Bhopal and strengthen his hand in negotiations with Indian authorities.[12] India's political leadership was concerned that the Political Department's meddling could convince some princes not to accede, obstruct the peaceful integration of the princely states and ultimately weaken India.[13] Reflecting a general distrust of the motives and actions of the department's officials, Nehru argued that 'the Political Department works in secret and no one know what it does,' and even requested to be kept informed of all important communications between officials in the department and the princely states, a request that British authorities rejected. He further argued that the Political Department consistently pushed back against any progressive tendencies within the princely states that could lead to internal political reforms and perhaps even encouraged 'repression of the people in the States,' resulting in an ever-widening gap between British and Princely India. 'I doubt if there is any one in India, whether among the Rulers of the States or the people of the States,' Nehru presumed, 'who has any faith in the present set-up of the Political Department.'[14]

Corfield later rationalized his support for the princely states' right to remain independent by explaining: 'I have never been able to appreciate why Nehru was so afraid of India disintegrating, if the Rulers had *technical* [*sic*] independence when paramountcy lapsed. No State could have preserved *actual* [*sic*] independence for very long. The country had been welded by the exercise of paramountcy into too firm a structure.' If his advice had been followed, he argued that further negotiations between New Delhi and the princely states could have been pursued at a more leisurely pace and ultimately arrived at more satisfactory permanent arrangements for the states' accession and 'preserve more good will,' as opposed to the rushed approach that was ultimately taken.[15]

With such encouragement coming from departing British officials, Patel, Nehru and Menon felt that they needed a British voice as a counterweight to convince the princes that support from the British government would not be forthcoming and accession was their only option. They now went to work on Mountbatten to push him on what he would do to assist with India's 'most pressing problem—relations with the States.' With the Indian leaders making heavy and frequent appeals to his vanity, Mountbatten promised to make this issue his primary consideration moving forward.[16] In early July, Gandhi likewise called on the Viceroy and urged him to ensure that the British government did not leave 'a legacy of Balkanisation and disruption on the 15th August by encouraging the States to declare their independence, or by leaving the arrangements between the States and the Dominions of India and Pakistan in a state of chaos.'[17] Mountbatten resolved that the princely states' aspiration to independence 'would not be worth a moment's purchase' without the support of at least one of the new dominion governments, and assured Congress leadership he would in no way support a continuing relationship between the British government and any non-acceding princely states.[18] London concurred with Mountbatten's sentiment and felt it 'undesirable to take any action which might lead to the "Balkanisation" of India or which might encourage the Indian States to feel that they can stand on their own.'[19] The challenge now was to convince the princes.

On the afternoon of 25 July 1947, Mountbatten addressed a special session of the Chamber of Princes, which kicked off a series of meetings between representatives of the princely states and the States Department to deal with several outstanding issues on accession, including circulating a draft Instrument of Accession based on the terms set by Menon. Dressed in all-white military finery with rows of medals across his chest, an outfit befitting a formal address to fellow royals, Mountbatten drew upon all his oratory skills and spoke at the lectern for more than an hour without notes to sway the arrayed princes before him. Mountbatten started by announcing that the Indian Independence Act passed by the British parliament the previous week released the princes 'from all their obligations to the Crown.' While he acknowledged that the princely states would be technically independent with the end of paramountcy, he also explained that 'if nothing can be put in its place, only chaos can result,' which 'will hit the States first.' Under the terms of accession, he assured them, 'My scheme leaves you with all practical independence you can possibly use.' He further advised them to accede to their appropriate dominion, plainly stating, 'you cannot run away from the Dominion Government which is your neighbour any more than you can run away from the subjects for whose welfare you are responsible.'[20]

Following his speech, Mountbatten undertook a leading role in convincing the princes to sign the Instrument of Accession for India, promising Congress leaders that he would deliver 'a full basket of apples.'[21] To ensure peaceful relations between the princely states and the Indian Union, he understood the importance of the princes acceding voluntarily without resorting to threats or force. 'You always talk about wooing people, and yet in the case of the States, you threaten,' Mountbatten once joked with Gandhi. 'Would you woo a girl you wanted to marry with a stick and expect her to accept?'[22] The Viceroy's House soon became a revolving door of chaotic meetings; it was an endless array of politicians and princes pulled into rooms for impromptu conversations as they appeared, regardless of the original purpose of their visit and back-to-back side chats at receptions and luncheons in which Mountbatten worked tirelessly alongside Patel and Menon to urge and cajole the princes to sign the Instrument of Accession. Mountbatten complained that the pressure on him at the time was so great that he often had two or even three meetings running simultaneously in different rooms as he juggled the various complaints of numerous princes alongside the pressing problems associated with Partition. He later wrote, 'I had been given no inkling that this [states problem] was going to be so hard, if not harder to solve, as that of British India.'[23]

Acting in concert with Mountbatten, Indian leaders didn't shy away from seemingly petty actions that helped put social pressure on the princes to fall in line. During a 28 July reception at the Viceroy's House, for instance, Mountbatten invited over fifty princes and another hundred representatives of the princely states to wine and dine them. This was, in effect, 'a last-minute canvassing of voters near the polling booth' with all the imperial grandeur that the Viceroy could muster—liveried attendants draped in crimson lining the marbled walls and butlers silently displaying endless trays of whiskeys, gins and champagne. For the princes who had not yet signified their intention to accede to India, they were escorted one by one over to Mountbatten by his aides-de-camp for a friendly chat. Afterwards, Mountbatten passed them over to Menon for further discussion about the issue of accession who then brought them across the room to Patel for the same purpose, in full view of everyone. The princes were 'three-deep in a semi-circle' watching the process play out and who was being worked on. Menon felt this combined effort had 'a good psychological effect on the rulers who were present.'[24]

Not all were pleased with Mountbatten's role in the negotiations with the princes. Not only did several princes bristle at the pressure the Viceroy placed on them, but the India Office was also sharply critical. Even though Attlee had directed Mountbatten to aid the princes in finding 'fair and just arrangements' with Indian leaders, Cabinet officials in London, who Mountbatten had not informed of what he agreed to with Congress leadership, felt his recent actions went beyond his official position and responsibilities as the Crown Representative.[25] In response to Mountbatten's 25 July speech in the Chamber of Princes, Secretary of State for India Lord Listowel (the last Secretary of State for India appointed to the position in April 1947) informed Attlee: 'It has to be remembered that in his discussions with States' representative the Viceroy is acting as mediator in his personal capacity and not on the advice of his Ministers either in form or in fact. We, are therefore, answerable in a special way for what he may do and it would seem advisable to warn him of the dangers, particularly in view of the importance which the Opposition attaches to no pressure being put on the Princes *by us* [sic].'[26] Mountbatten, of course, framed his actions as ultimately supporting British interests in India. He informed the Secretary of State: 'I am trying my very best to create an integrated India which while securing stability will ensure friendship with Great Britain. If I am allowed to play my own hand without interference I have no doubt that I will succeed.'[27]

By early August 1947, the British government was clear that it was not willing to recognize the independence of any princely states should the negotiations fail to bring all the princely states into the new dominion government, even though British policy in theory allowed for the possibility of the states to pursue recognition of their independence.[28] In a 6 August dispatch, the Foreign Office asserted: 'His Majesty's Government are not prepared to define what in the event of these negotiations failing their attitude would be toward any Indian States which claim to be independent. In any case His Majesty's Government do not propose to recognise any Indian State as a separate international entity on 15th August.'[29] At this time, however, the British government remained open to the possibility of engaging with any princely states that successfully kept out of the Indian Union and asserted independence at some indeterminate point in the future.[30] Nevertheless, in early August 1947, one former member of the IPS observed, 'The Princes have been abandoned to their fate.'[31]

The princes' resistance to accession

Patel, Menon, Mountbatten and countless others within India worked tirelessly through the summer of 1947 to ensure that the hundreds of princely states acceded to the Indian Union before the British withdrawal, with most princes signing the Instrument of Accession by the 14 August deadline. The day after the transfer of power ceremony in New Delhi, Mountbatten complained:

> We have been working longer hours and under more trying conditions, and with crises of differing magnitudes arising every day, and sometimes two or three times a day. The problem of the States continued to occupy most of my time, particularly of those Rulers who have kept changing their mind up to the last moment, whether to accede to India, to Pakistan, or to neither.[32]

However, not all princes came into the Indian fold quickly, willingly or peacefully for a variety of reasons, such as delaying accession as a negotiating tactic or facing bureaucratic hiccups.

In the days leading up to the transfer of power, the Maharaja of Indore, Yashwant Rao Holkar II, had been sending telegrams to his fellow princes encouraging them to wait until the last possible moment to sign the Instrument of Accession in a bid to improve the terms of accession. Several princes showed the telegram to Indian political leaders, with Mountbatten even remarking, 'It may not be a bad thing to have a thoroughly unsatisfactory State like Indore remaining outside the Dominion, as an example of what happens to states that try and stand on their own.'[33] Still, he felt that the unpopular Maharaja's 'ridiculous behavior' would be so widely detested among his subjects that they would rise up against him if he failed to accede. While the Maharaja failed to provide a signed Instrument of Accession by the 14 August deadline, he sent the signed paperwork to Mountbatten on 15 August but backdated to 14 August. The problems with Indore did not end there. Even after acceding, the Maharaja still wanted to explore matters of mutual interest with Pakistan. An infuriated Patel was reportedly in the mood to refuse Indore's accession but, nevertheless, went to discuss this with the Maharaja in person. On 1 September, the Maharaja sent a telegram informing Mountbatten, now serving as India's Governor General, that the matter had been 'ironed out to the entire mutual satisfaction of Sardar Patel and myself.'[34]

Even among willing princes, there were unforeseen challenges delaying their accession, including something as trivial as slow mail. On the eve of the transfer of power, the governments of several princely states reached out to the States Department informing them that they had not yet received the Instrument of Accession paperwork. Nevertheless, they assured the States Department of their intention to accede to the Indian Union and asked for an extension of the deadline to submit the signed instrument. On 21 August 1947, additional copies of the Instrument of Accession were dispatched to the rulers of Jashpur, Nandgaon, Sonepur, Rajgarh and Mandi states who shortly returned the instruments with their signatures affixed to the document.[35] The princes of other states, such as Dholpur, Bharatpur, Bilaspur and Nabha, required much arguing and cajoling by Menon before they agreed to sign the Instrument of Accession. And, when they did, they attached covering letters laying out the conditions under which they had signed the document, requiring Menon to gently remind them that with their accession they were no longer able to lay down any conditions beyond those contained in the instrument.[36]

While the circumstances surrounding the British departure created much confusion about the political status of the princely states, Nehru observed, 'Fortunately, in regard to nearly all the States matters were settled peacefully and cooperatively.' Barring the tumultuous events in Jammu and Kashmir, Hyderabad and Junagadh in the coming months, he also recognized that in a handful of other princely states 'there was the will to create trouble though not the capacity to do it.'[37] In the face of pressure from Indian authorities, several princes made concerted efforts to push back against Indian sovereignty and assert their independence as a means of preserving their sovereignty in the final weeks and days before the transfer of power, most notably Travancore, Bhopal and Jodhpur, but ultimately proved unable to follow through under political pressure from New Delhi.

One of the first princely states to push back against accession and assert the right to pursue independence was Travancore, located on India's southwestern coast in present-day Kerala. The state's Diwan, Sir C.P. Ramaswamy Iyer—who Lord Wavell referred to as 'one of the most capable politicians and administrators in the country' and held great sway over the compliant Maharaja—firmly believed that Travancore, with its highly educated population and access to a thriving maritime trade, would be a viable independent state once the British departed.[38] With the lapse of paramountcy, he argued that Travancore would regain its independent sovereign status held before signing its 1795 treaty with the East India Company.

Iyer insisted that Travancore intended to remain 'aloof from controversies in British India' and was preparing to assert its independence in the interests of 'preserving the homogeneity of the State.'[39] Travancore was only willing to sign treaties with the governments of India and Pakistan as a co-equal sovereign state.

On 18 June 1947, the Maharaja officially announced Travancore's independence once paramountcy lapsed. He later informed the British Resident for the Madras states that, as there was no question of accession, his government had no intention of participating in the formation of an Advisory Council for the States Department or attending the 25 July conference of princes in New Delhi. Given his assertion of the state's independence, the Maharaja regarded the problems between New Delhi and Travancore 'as special and individual.'[40] Shortly after this declaration and compounding the Congress leaders' concerns, Jinnah reached out to the Travancore government, which announced it had agreed to send a representative to Pakistan to establish a relationship of mutual advantage, particularly over fears that India would implement an economic boycott of the state and it would need to rely on foodstuffs from Pakistan.[41]

In late July 1947, Iyer traveled to New Delhi to meet with Mountbatten and senior British officials in the hopes of securing British recognition of Travancore's independence and promises for a trading relationship if India refused to economically engage with the state. The Diwan also went into the two-hour meeting 'determined to reject any such proposal outright' on the issue of accession. After a lengthy back and forth in which Iyar excoriated Congress and its leaders, Mountbatten finally got him to at least consider a treaty relationship with India, knowing that Patel would never accept anything short of accession. Afterwards, Mountbatten sent Menon 'to work on him.'[42] Many of the state's subjects, however, cared little for whether the Maharaja decided to pursue independence or join the Indian Union, if it meant that autocratic rule persisted in the state. One Travancore resident remarked: 'We're not interested in whether or not the State joins the Dominion. Give us representative Government and we will decide such things for ourselves.'[43]

Some British officials back in London had been encouraging Travancore's flirtation with independence for ease of access to the state's raw materials. In particular, they eyed its monazite deposits, with Travancore reportedly possessing one of the richest known deposits of monazite sand. Monazite was first discovered along Travancore's coastline in 1909, with mining activities beginning two years later.[44] The radioactive rare earth metal was initially used in the production of incandescent mantles. After 1945, monazite became a key source material for thorium, which was extracted from the ore and used in the production of fissile material for Britain's nuclear weapons and nuclear power plants. On 2 April 1947, the British Supply Ministry entered into a direct agreement with the Travancore government for the export of monazite to the United Kingdom for their nuclear industry in exchange for setting up a plant in the state for processing monazite. The supply minister observed, 'It would be an advantage if Travancore retained political and economic independence, at least for the time being' and advised that the British government 'should avoid any fresh action ... which would give the Indian Dominions leverage in combating Travancore's claim for independence.'[45] However, the Secretary of State for India disagreed with this view, arguing that it was necessary 'to avoid any statement which would give this State leverage in asserting its independence or economic autonomy,' while leaving open the possibility of reconsidering such a policy if Travancore successfully asserted its independence.[46]

During this time, the Travancore government had been dealing with ongoing communist activities within its borders, which would prove the undoing of the state's nascent bid for independence. In October of the previous year, Travancore experienced a communist uprising against the Maharaja's government, in which several thousand communists attacked police stations and government officials in Punnapra and Vayalar. The state government declared martial law and dispatched its military forces to put down the uprising, resulting in hundreds of deaths. In Menon's efforts to push the Travancore government to accede to India, he had even advised Mountbatten to 'play on the communist menace' as Iyer was 'rather frightened about it.'[47] On 25 July 1947, shortly after returning from Delhi, Iyer was heading to a music concert in the state's capital of Trivandrum when K.C.S. Mani, a member of a regional communist party, attacked the Diwan with a knife, stabbing him in the face and body. He narrowly escaped death and was rushed off for emergency surgery. In his vulnerable state, the States' People's Conference 'turned the heat full on' to press the issue of accession, highlighting the dangers of continuing to pursue the path of independence.[48] Laying in his hospital bed, the Diwan finally changed his mind and wrote to the Maharaja, 'If you want my earnest and sincere advise, you must let me go and all things considered, follow the path of conciliation and compromise.'[49] On 30 July, mere days after the Diwan's near fatal attack, the Maharaja informed the Viceroy that he had decided to accede to the Indian Union.

Travancore's reluctance to sign the Instrument of Accession was shared by Bhopal, a Muslim-ruled state in central India with a largely Hindu population. The Nawab of Bhopal, Hamidullah Khan, had served as Chancellor of the Chamber of Princes since 1944, and, in this role, worked closely with the leadership of the British Raj. He was also a bitter opponent of Gandhi, Nehru and the Congress leadership, but, as a leading Muslim voice in India, was close with Jinnah and the Muslim League. The Nawab's relationship with the highest echelons of power in the Subcontinent was strengthened with the arrival of Mountbatten as Viceroy, with whom he had enjoyed a close, personal friendship for over two decades. When the British government made it clear it intended to depart India, he took this as a personal betrayal. He melodramatically referred to this decision as 'one of the greatest, if not the greatest tragedies, that has ever befallen mankind' and feared the repercussions for both the princely states and India's Muslim population. 'I am unhappy about everything in this country,' the Nawab wrote to Corfield in November 1946. 'The States, the Moslems, and the entire mass of people who relied on British justice, and their sense of fair play, suddenly find themselves totally helpless, unorganised and unsupported ... The Princes betrayed by the British are already a lost cause and I feel I am wasting my energies and my humble resources in trying to protect their case ... I have no hope of any support for the States from the British and without this support the Princes cannot survive.'[50]

Following Mountbatten's announcement on 3 June 1947, the Nawab resigned his position in the Chamber of Princes. In his letter of resignation, he affirmed that his state would, '*as soon as paramountcy is withdrawn, be assuming an independent status* [sic].'[51] While Mountbatten wrote to the Nawab on 14 July encouraging him to accede to India, the Nawab responded a week later and refused his old polo-playing buddy's suggestion. He expressed his dismay that any princely state that acceded to the Indian Union would simply become part of a 'permanent powerless minority at the mercy of the Congress party,' not to mention the 'very awkward position' of Muslim-ruled states in India due to Partition. The Nawab instead reiterated to his 'dear Dickie' his intention to declare independence, but was still prepared to negotiate with both dominion governments 'on a basis of complete equality and reciprocity' so long as there was 'no discrimination against us and no interference with our internal affairs.' He additionally argued that the British were leaving the country vulnerable to the 'rising tide of Communism' by acquiescing to the demands of the Congress. If the Congress leadership wiped out the princely order and liquidated the zamindari (landlord) system, so prevalent among the princely states, they would be removing the country's defense against the Communist Party, which was gaining greater and greater influence. Nawab Hamidullah warned, 'I tell you straight that unless you and His Majesty's Government support the States and prevent them from disappearing from the Indian political map, you will very shortly have an India dominated by Communists.' He added, with a touch of sentiment for his old friend peeking through his anger, 'If the United Nations one day find themselves with 450 million extra people under the heel of Communist domination they will be quite justified in blaming Great Britain for this disaster, and I naturally would not like your name associated with it.'[52]

When the Nawab failed to show up for Mountbatten's 25 July address in the Chamber of Princes, the Viceroy once again reached out to him to urge him to sign the Instrument of Accession, repeating what he had said to the gathered princes in New Delhi. While he acknowledged the threat of communism in his letter, he countered that the best means of challenging its spread would be for the princely states to work with Congress leadership as they were 'as frightened of communism as you yourself are. If only they had support from all other stable influences such as that of the Princely Order, it might be possible for them to ward off the communist danger.' To further allay his old friend's suspicions, he stressed, with a touch of flattery, that the Instrument of Accession did not commit the princes to a future Indian Constitution. 'So you get a second choice at this time,' he wrote, 'and then, my dear Hamidullah, will come the chance of a leader like you among the Princes to hold them together to take a firm line if the new constitution turns out after all to be inacceptable to the States. What a tragedy if at this time they were deprived of their most outstanding leader by your own actions.'[53]

Under pressure from his old friend, and with the news that his fellow princes responded so positively to the Viceroy's speech, Nawab Hamidullah finally switched his position and agreed to accede to India. In his letter to Patel announcing his decision, he affirmed: 'I do not disguise the fact that while the struggle was on, I used every means in my power to preserve the independence and neutrality of my State. Now that I have conceded defeat, I hope that you will find that I can be as staunch a friend as I have been an inveterate opponent.'[54] His one request was that the deadline be extended by ten days so that Bhopal's accession would be announced after the transfer of power. While Patel stated that he would make no such exception for any individual state regarding the deadline, Mountbatten promised that if the Nawab would sign the instrument by 14 August he would keep the paperwork locked away in a sealed envelope and only hand it over to the States Department after 25 August.[55]

A more unexpected scenario played out in the princely state of Jodhpur, a Hindu-ruled state with a largely Hindu population within the Rajputana Agency (present-day Rajasthan). In July 1947, the 24-year-old Maharaja of Jodhpur, Hanwant Singh Rathore, who had only been installed the previous month, expressed to Mountbatten his willingness to accede to India at a luncheon held for several Rajput princes. Soon after, with Jodhpur lying astride the newly demarcated international border with Pakistan, the Maharaja began to flirt with the idea of acceding to Pakistan despite being a Hindu-majority state. He hoped to secure more amenable conditions from the Pakistani government than were being offered by India, while protecting his state's autonomy. At the insistence of the Maharaja, the Nawab of Bhopal arranged a meeting between the Jodhpur ruler and Jinnah, in which Jinnah extended the full use of Karachi's port facilities for the landlocked state, unrestricted arms imports and grain shipments from Sindh. He also assured the Maharaja that Pakistan would treat the princely states as independent and sovereign. Another version of events that circulated among Indian political leaders had Jinnah laying a blank sheet of paper before the young Maharaja and telling him, 'Here's my fountain pen; write your terms and I will sign it.' After Mountbatten heard that Nawab Hamidullah had arranged this meeting, the Viceroy informed him that 'no amount of friendship' would enable him to offer any protection if India's leadership believed that he was acting 'in a manner hostile to that Government by trying to induce an all-Hindu State to join Pakistan.'[56]

When the States Department caught wind of this, Patel was prepared to go to almost any lengths to prevent it from occurring, fearing such a move would create a dangerous precedent for other princely states near the international border with Pakistan, such as Jaipur and Udaipur.[57] On 8 August, Mountbatten sent for the Maharaja who immediately flew up to New Delhi, arriving later that night. The following morning, during a tense meeting with the Viceroy, he finally came clean that he had been 'flirting' with Jinnah on the issue of accession. Patel also met with the Maharaja and laid out an array of benefits to convince him to accede to India, matching and exceeding what Jinnah had offered: unrestricted import of arms, additional food supplies for famine-stricken districts and the completion of railway lines between Jodhpur and the ports of Cutch in Gujarat. The Maharaja was also pressured by members of his own government, village headmen within his state and neighboring princes. The ruler of Jaisalmer State, for instance, pressed him with the question that if he acceded to Pakistan as a Hindu ruler, which side would he take if communal rioting erupted between Hindus and Muslims.[58]

Under incessant pressure from all sides, the Maharaja acquiesced to demands that he accede to India, but not without a tense display of youthful defiance. During the week of 15 August, he came to New Delhi to sign the paperwork for accession. When the Maharaja arrived at the Viceroy's office on the appointed day, Mountbatten left Menon to secure the necessary signature as he dealt with a delegation from Hyderabad in his wife's study next door. When presented with the Instrument of Accession, the Maharaja began at once to make a series of impossible demands, to which Menon retorted, 'If you want to sign on false hopes, I will agree to your demands.' The Maharaja then drew his revolver, pointed it at Menon, and declared, 'I refuse to accept your dictation.' He further threatened that he would shoot him down like a dog if he betrayed the starving people of Jodhpur. After flaring tempers cooled, with Mountbatten returning to the room and treating the incident in jest, the Maharaja silently passed his revolver over to Menon and signed his name on the dotted line, affixing the future of his state with that of the Indian Union.[59]

These roadblocks were able to be resolved before the transfer of power on 15 August 1947. India's political leaders were not so fortunate in every case, with Mountbatten remarking that engagement with the princely states following the transfer of power was 'almost as hectic as it was before the 15th August.'[60] The status of the princely states of Jammu and Kashmir, Hyderabad and Junagadh remained unsettled following the lapse of paramountcy as its princes rejected accession to India in a bid to preserve their sovereignty—whether by pursuing independence or choosing to accede to Pakistan whose leadership expressed a laissez-faire approach to the princely states. These three states would soon pose some of the most pressing political and security challenges the new Indian government would face in the days, months and even years after independence. These crises pushed Indian political leaders to rely on military force and alliances with undemocratic elements within the states no less than political persuasion to assert the sovereignty of the Indian government and ensure the territorial integrity of the newly independent country, despite their stated commitment to democratic ideals of governance. Moreover, the delayed accession of these three princely states beyond the transfer of power served as focal points of increased political tensions, hostilities and even outright conflict between India and Pakistan.

Notes

1 Section 7(b), Indian Independence Act, 18 July 1947, accessed at: www.leg islation.gov.uk/ukpga/1947/30/pdfs/ukpga_19470030_en.pdf [accessed 20 December 2022].
2 U.K. Parliament, Indian Constitutional Reform, House of Common Debate, 11 December 1934, accessed at: https://api.parliament.uk/historic-hansard/commons/1934/dec/11/indian-constitutional-reform [accessed 20 December 2022].
3 Morris-Jones, 'The Transfer of Power, 1947,' pp. 17–18.
4 Menon, *The Story of the Integration of the Indian States*, p. 94.
5 Ibid., p. 95.
6 Basu, *V.P. Menon*, p. 164.
7 Menon, *The Story of the Integration of the Indian States*, p. 96.
8 Ibid., pp. 96–9.
9 Text of Statement by Sardar Patel, 5 July 1947, *TOP Volume XI*, pp. 928–30; Minutes of Viceroy's Fifty-Third Staff Meeting, 7 July 1947, *TOP Volume XI*, pp. 948–9.

10 Basu, *V.P. Menon*, p. 307.
11 Guha, *India After Gandhi*, p. 56.
12 Panikkar, *An Autobiography*, p. 148.
13 Menon, *The Story of the Integration of the Indian States*, p. 113.
14 Field Marshall Viscount Wavell to Lord Pethick-Lawrence, 25 September 1946, *TOP Volume VIII*, p. 586; Pandit Nehru to Rear-Admiral Viscount Mountbatten of Burma, 9 April 1947, *TOP Volume X*, pp. 160–1; Cabinet, India and Burma Committee, Attitude of Interim Government of India Towards Paramountcy, Memorandum by the Secretary of State for India, undated, *TOP Volume IX*, p. 369.
15 Sir Conrad Corfield, *The Princely India I Knew: From Reading to Mountbatten* (Madras: Indo-British Historical Society, 1975), p. 157.
16 Basu, *V.P. Menon*, p. 294; Minutes of Viceroy's Fifty-Fifth Staff Meeting, 9 July 1947, *TOP Volume XII*, p. 36.
17 Record of Interview between Rear-Admiral Viscount Mountbatten of Burma and Mr. Gandhi, Viceroy's Interview No. 159, 9 July 1947, *TOP Volume XII*, p. 51.
18 Rear-Admiral Viscount Mountbatten of Burma Mountbatten to the Earl of Listowel, 8 August 1947, *TOP Volume XII*, p. 585.
19 Ministry of Defence Chiefs of Staff Committee, Joint Planning Staff Paper, 1 July 1947, *TOP Volume XII*, p. 175.
20 Press Communique of an Address by Rear-Admiral Viscount Mountbatten of Burma to a Conference of the Rulers and Representatives of Indian States, 25 July 1947, *TOP Volume XII*, pp. 347–8.
21 Copland, *The Princes of India in the Endgame of Empire*, p. 255.
22 Record of Interview between Rear-Admiral Viscount Mountbatten of Burma and Mr. Gandhi, Viceroy's Interview No. 159, 9 July 1947, *TOP Volume XII*, p. 51.
23 Viceroy's Personal Report No. 17, 16 August 1947, *TOP Volume XII*, p. 767; Copland, *The Princes of India in the Endgame of Empire*, p. 247.
24 Campbell-Johnson, *Mission with Mountbatten*, p. 168; Menon, *The Story of the Integration of the Indian States*, p. 113.
25 Mr. Attlee to Rear-Admiral Viscount Mountbatten of Burma, 8 February 1947, *TOP Volume IX*, p. 653; Copland, *The Princes of India in the Endgame of Empire*, p. 255.
26 The Earl of Listowel to Mr. Attlee, 29 July 1947, *TOP Volume XII*, p. 403.
27 Rear-Admiral Viscount Mountbatten of Burma to the Earl of Listowel, 4 August 1947, *TOP Volume XII*, p. 530.
28 National Archives, U.K., FO/371/63572, Transfer of power in India—relations of India with the United Kingdom (Folder 8), November 1947–January 1948.
29 National Archives, U.K., FO/371/63567, Transfer of power in India—relations of India with the United Kingdom (Folder 3), August–September 1947.
30 National Archives, U.K., FO/371/63568, Transfer of power in India—relations of India with the United Kingdom (Folder 4), August–September 1947.
31 Sir William Barton, 'India's Princes When British Paramountcy Passes,' *Daily Telegraph* (7 August 1947).

32 Louis Mountbatten to the Earl of Listowel, 16 August 1947, *Jinnah Papers Volume V*, p. 622.
33 Viceroy's Personal Report No. 15, 1 August 1947, *TOP Volume XII*, p. 454.
34 Viceroy's Personal Report No. 16, 8 August 1947, *TOP Volume XII*, p. 593; Louis Mountbatten to the Earl of Listowel, 16 August 1947, *Jinnah Papers Volume V*, pp. 627, 630.
35 NAI, File No. 8(52)-PR/47, PR_000005002287, Supply of further copies of Instrument of Accession, Indian Ministry of States, 1947, p. 10.
36 Basu, *V.P. Menon*, p. 320.
37 NAI, PP_000000005819, Fortnightly letters of the hon'ble Prime minister to the Provincial Premiers from 1948 to 1949, Private Papers of Sardar Patel, 1948, p. 95.
38 Field Marshall Viscount Wavell to Mr. Amery, 15 November 1944, *TOP Volume V*, p. 206.
39 'Iyer's Reply to Gandhi,' *Dawn* (2 June 1947).
40 Resident for the Madras States to the Secretary to the Crown Representative, 13 July 1947, *TOP Volume XII*, pp. 138–9.
41 Memorandum by the Secretary of State for India, 14 July 1947, *TOP Volume XII*, p. 151; Record of Interview between Mr. Symon and Sir C.P. Ramaswarni Aiyar, 21 July 1947, *TOP Volume XII*, p. 281.
42 Record of Interview between Mr. Symon and Sir C.P. Ramaswarni Aiyar, 21 July 1947, *TOP Volume XII*, p. 281; Viceroy's Personal Report No. 14, 23 July 1947, *TOP Volume XII*, p. 336.
43 R.E.B. Bower to George Marshall, 23 August 1947, *Jinnah Papers Volume V*, pp. 560–1.
44 William C. Overstreet, *The Geologic Occurrence of Monazite* (Washington, DC: U.S. Government Printing Office, 1967), pp. 67–8.
45 Memorandum by the Minister of Supply, 18 July 1947, *TOP Volume XII*, p. 232.
46 Memorandum by the Secretary of State for India, 14 July 1947, *TOP Volume XII*, p. 153.
47 Mr. V.P. Menon to Sir G. Abell, 20 July 1947, *TOP Volume XII*, p. 275.
48 Viceroy's Personal Report No. 15, 1 August 1947, *TOP Volume XII*, p. 453.
49 A. Sreedhara Menon, *Triumph and Tragedy in Travancore: Annals of Sir CP's Sixteen Years* (Kottayam: Current Books, 2001), p. 253.
50 The Nawab of Bhopal to Sir C. Corfield, 23 November 1946, *TOP Volume IX*, pp. 156–7.
51 Menon, *The Story of the Integration of the Indian States*, p. 84.
52 The Nawab of Bhopal to Rear-Admiral Viscount Mountbatten of Burma, 22 July 1947, *TOP Volume XII,* pp. 291–7.
53 Rear-Admiral Viscount Mountbatten of Burma to the Nawab of Bhopal, 31 July 1947, *TOP Volume XII*, pp. 437–8.
54 Menon, *The Story of the Integration of the Indian States*, pp. 118–19.
55 Rear-Admiral Viscount Mountbatten of Burma to the Nawab of Bhopal, 11 August 1947, *TOP Volume XII*, p. 672.

56 NAI, PP_000000006119, Bhopal 1949–50, Private Papers of Sardar Patel, 1950, p. 82.

57 Viceroy's Personal Report No. 17, 16 August 1947, *TOP Volume XII*, p. 767.

58 Guha, *India After Gandhi,* p. 63.

59 Louis Mountbatten to the Earl of Listowel, Viceroy's Personal Report No. 17, 16 August 1947, *Jinnah Papers Volume V*, p. 627; Menon, *The Story of the Integration of the Indian States*, p. 117.

60 Campbell-Johnson, *Mission with Mountbatten*, p. 202.

6

Jammu and Kashmir: 'The Switzerland of the East'

Among India's princely states, Jammu and Kashmir sitting among the mountains of India's northern frontier presented one of the most difficult situations following the transfer of power and served as a focal point for the enduring interstate rivalry between India and Pakistan. The South Asian countries have fought three wars over the disputed territory and, since the 1980s, Indian-administered Kashmir has been rocked by an anti-government separatist insurgency. As a result, Jammu and Kashmir has attracted the most attention and study among the former princely states. Yet, the violence emanating from the region in recent decades and the internationalization of the conflict frequently overshadow the roots of the conflict, dating back to the circumstances of the transfer of power and the competing ideas of sovereignty at play within the state.

During the 1930s, Jammu and Kashmir's subjects were increasingly active in opposing the Maharaja's rule similar to other princely states, especially following the formation of Kashmir's National Conference whose leadership found common cause with the Indian National Congress. They advocated for an expansion of civil rights and for the accession and full integration of Jammu and Kashmir into the Indian Union, reflecting the ideas of state sovereignty pushed by Indian nationalists. On the other hand, the Maharaja clung to his sovereignty as enjoyed under the umbrella of British paramountcy, especially as the state's politics were becoming increasingly volatile and violent in the 1940s, including the launching of a rebellion against the Maharaja's rule from the Poonch region in 1947. At the transfer of power, the political status of the state remained unsettled. The Maharaja's refusal to accede to either India or Pakistan and his pursuit of independence as a means of protecting the state's sovereignty was soon challenged by the invasion of Pashtun tribesmen from northern Pakistan in October 1947, providing an opportunity for the Indian government to force the issue of accession. This set the stage for the violence that has long plagued the region.

While Kashmir today is closely associated with bloodshed, in centuries past it was famed for its natural beauty—snowcapped mountains, lush

Map 6.1 Map of Jammu and Kashmir (in black) in British India

forests and valleys and deep blue lakes crisscrossing the region. Its more temperate climate drew many Indian and British dignitaries on holiday seeking to escape India's brutal summer heat; seventeenth-century Mughal Emperor Jahangir once called Kashmir 'paradise on earth.' However, this rose-tinted description by political elites treated the region as essentially a landscape devoid of people and frequently overlooked the region's extreme poverty and political repression. Two British explorers, William Moorcraft and George Trebeck, observed in the 1820s, when Kashmir was still under the control of the Sikh Empire based in the Punjab, 'Everywhere, however, the people are in the most abject condition; exorbitantly taxed by the Sikh government, and subjected to every kind of extortion and oppression by its officers.' In the Kashmiri city of Islamabad, they further noted, 'It was as filthy a place as can well be imagined, and swarmed with beggars, some of whom were idle vagabonds, but the greater number were in real distress.'[1]

In 1846, following the British defeat of the Sikh Maharaja Duleep Singh, the Lahore Durbar was unable to pay a war indemnity of one crore rupees and, in lieu of this payment, ceded the territories of Jammu and Kashmir to British control. Yet, the British Governor General at the time, Lord Hardinge, considered the occupation of this vast frontier region inadvisable for several reasons, including the high costs of establishing direct British control and the inability for the mountainous terrain to generate sufficient revenues. A solution was found when Ghulab Singh, the Raja of Jammu who had served as a mediator between the British and the Sikh Empire, offered to pay a significant portion of the war indemnity if he was recognized as the independent ruler of Jammu and Kashmir. Despite facing opposition from the final Sikh governor and a group of Muslim political leaders, Ghulab Singh was installed as Maharaja of Jammu and Kashmir in 1846 with the aid of British troops. By establishing a treaty relationship with Maharaja Ghulab Singh, the British avoided the high costs of a direct military occupation, materially weakened Sikh power in the Punjab, recovered the war indemnity and helped secure the frontier through the principle of indirect rule.[2] Under British rule, the mountainous frontier region held a strategic importance that far outweighed its population, as it shared borders with Afghanistan, Xinjiang and Tibet—the various playgrounds of the Great Game with Imperial Russia.[3] The princely state's strategic position on the frontier helped establish its influence throughout the broader region and later contributed to the belief that the princely state could maintain an independent and neutral existence apart from both India and Pakistan as the British withdrawal inched closer and closer.

Hari Singh versus Sheikh Abdullah

The events leading up to and surrounding Jammu and Kashmir's accession to India were largely shaped by the orbits of two men: Maharaja Hari Singh, who had inherited the throne in September 1925 from his uncle Pratap Singh (Maharaja Ghulab Singh's grandson), and the leader of the National Conference Sheikh Mohammed Abdullah, who worked closely with Congress leadership. As tensions emerged between the Hindu Maharaja and the largely Muslim states' subjects during the 1930s, Hari Singh and Sheikh Abdullah held clashing ideas about state sovereignty— whether based in recognition of the Maharaja's sovereignty and hereditary right to rule, as defined by the state's treaty with the British Crown, or through the will and consent of the Kashmiri people.

During the 1910s and 1920s, Kashmiris faced a number of local economic and political grievances like high food prices and an absence of civil rights that contributed to unrest and increased political mobilization among the states' subjects.[4] In particular, representatives of the majority Muslim population made frequent demands of the Maharaja for the expansion of their civil and political rights and religious freedom to a level they saw as commensurate with British India—demands that were just as frequently ignored by the Maharaja fearing the implications for his rule.[5] At the time, Muslim grievances were connected to an ordinance against cow killing, the prohibition of the khutbah, the stoppage of azan and other measures restricting Muslim religious practices. While officially there were no legal restrictions on the khutbah and azan, with the azan heard daily in Srinagar and Gulmarg, there were reports of official interference in these practices in areas where Hindu influence predominated, such as Jammu. Under the Hindu-dominated government, there was also a general sense of unfairness in officials' treatment of Muslims as compared to Hindus. Kashmiri Muslims had been petitioning for an increase in Muslim representation in the state government since the early 1900s.[6]

In 1925, Hari Singh inherited a restless state. Nevertheless, he played the part of a princely playboy with seemingly little interest in governing his state. He spent his days at racetracks in Bombay or hunting game in the vast and wooded estates of his domain, expending little effort to remain in touch with his subjects and their concerns. His wife remarked that her husband 'never meets the people—that's the trouble. He just sits surrounded by fawning courtiers and favourites, and never really gets to know what is going on outside.'[7] Within Jammu and Kashmir, described one British journalist, 'abject destitution' lives side by side with 'excessive riches.' While the Maharaja and his courtiers 'laze in shikara on fairytale lakes' and engage in hunting, fishing and trekking 'amid scenery of breath-taking beauty,' Kashmiris of old Srinagar live in 'noisome dens in which stunted children and pallid women are condemned to exist on pay that barely keeps them alive.'[8]

While a number of Muslims held long-standing grievances against the Hindu-dominated government, flooding and a crop disease resulted in sky-rocketing food prices in the late 1920s and provided fertile ground for mass agitation to erupt.[9] In 1931, rumors that a Hindu policeman in Jammu had desecrated the Quran was the spark needed for protests to spread throughout the state, especially in the Kashmir valley, which provoked a crackdown by the state government. On 13 July, thousands gathered outside of the Central Jail in Srinagar to witness a sedition trial against one of the leading protestors, Abdul Qadir. As tensions rose within the crowd, the Kashmiri security forces opened fire, killing twenty-one protestors.[10]

This shooting sparked widespread agitation that was encouraged by outside supporters, such as the Muslim political party Majlis-i-Ahrar-i-Islam, founded in Lahore in 1929, which demanded an investigation into the treatment of Muslims in Kashmir. The group even dispatched jathas, or bands, of supporters into Jammu territory. In Jammu and Mirpur, clashes erupted between state forces and members of armed groups seeking to pressure the Durbar to redress alleged grievances from the Muslim population. At the time, the Maharaja entrusted two Kashmiri Pandit brothers—Hari Krishna Kaul and Dya Krishna Kaul—to handle the unrest. Many were outraged by this appointment. One British officer in Srinagar described the former as 'weak and lacked initiative' and the latter 'as crooked as a cork-screw.' The real challenge was their belief in the continued Brahmin domination in the state and support for a policy of repression to handle any unrest.[11] Despite the attention of the government, communal rioting and deadly clashes between protestors and state security forces persisted during the coming years, with British troops even dispatched to the state at one point to help restore order.

In October 1931, New Delhi detailed Bertrand Glancy, a senior officer in the Political Department, to head a commission tasked with conducting an impartial inquiry into Muslim demands and offer recommendations for administrative reforms in response to recent rioting. Glancy had experience working within the state and, during his service there in the early 1920s, had the confidence of both the Maharaja at the time and Hari Singh.[12] Nevertheless, Hari Singh was anxious that Glancy's efforts would be only in an advisory role and would not involve 'any dictation' from the Indian government.[13] The Glancy Commission report was released in March 1932, with several recommendations for reforming the state government. Many Pandits were dissatisfied with the commission's recommendations, fearing it would result in a higher proportion of Muslims within state services that had traditionally been a Pandit reserve. They urged the Maharaja to delay the introduction of representative government and other planned reforms until the British Indian government framed a federal constitution, which was currently being discussing at the Round Table Conferences in London. Once a new federal structure was implemented in India, it would be known whether protection of minorities would be the responsibility of New Delhi or the ruling princes.[14] Nevertheless, the Maharaja introduced some reforms in line with the Glancy Commission, including lifting prohibitions against overt political activities and introducing freedom of the press.[15] Yet, the political opposition argued that the state government failed to fully implement the commission's recommendations, particularly regarding the employment of Muslims within the administration, with political agitation against the Maharaja's government persisting.[16]

Amid the turmoil of the early 1930s, Sheikh Abdullah, the son of a shawl merchant in Srinagar and graduate of Aligarh Muslim University, emerged as the leader of the All-Jammu and Kashmir Muslim Conference and quickly became a prominent but controversial figure. Nehru later described him as 'amazingly popular among the masses and numerous songs and legends grew up about him.'[17] In 1939, Abdullah helped to transform the All-Jammu and Kashmir Muslim Conference into the National Conference and made a concerted effort to reach out to non-Muslim communities within the state, expanding its membership to include Hindus and Sikhs within Jammu. The now rebranded group remained opposed to the Maharaja's rule and the vast economic inequalities between the landed elite and the peasantry, which helped to bolster its broad popularity among working-class Muslims and nationalist-minded Hindus and Sikhs as the group agitated for a more representative form of government.

Under Abdullah's leadership, the National Conference increasingly became aligned with the Indian National Congress through the late 1930s and early 1940s, espousing the same ideals of interreligious cooperation, democracy and socialism as the bedrocks of Indian independence. In particular, Abdullah and Nehru grew close as they pushed for Jammu and Kashmir's accession to India. In March 1946, Nehru even advocated for Abdullah to be elected as the president of the All-India States' People's Conference. In his endorsement, he stated: 'Sheikh Abdullah has become the symbol of freedom not only for the people of Kashmir, but also for the people of other States ... I have no doubt in my mind that it is proper and fitting for the conference and its regional councils to elect Sheikh Mohammad Abdullah as the President for the next session and the coming year.'[18] This secular shift alienated some of the movement's members, most notably Ghulam Abbas who departed the group to re-establish the Muslim Conference to advocate specifically for the rights of Kashmiri Muslims.

Following the widespread disturbances in the early 1930s, the Maharaja, under advice from the British government, appointed a British official to serve as the state's Prime Minister, Lieutenant Colonel Elliot Colvin of the IPS. He was succeeded in 1935 by the highly effective Sir Gopalaswami Ayyangar of the Madras Provincial Civil Service, who served in the position for seven years before retiring. A quick succession of short-lived prime ministers followed Ayyangar before R.C. Kak, a Kashmiri Pandit and former minister of the army, was finally appointed to the role in the summer of 1945. Through these leadership changes, the political situation remained tense between the state's subjects and the Maharaja's government. In 1944, Jinnah visited Kashmir and, the following year, communicated to the Viceroy, Lord Wavell, that he saw with his own eyes that there was 'unimpeachable, material, cogent and overwhelming evidence of the way in which the people of Kashmir are treated.' He argued that, as the representative of the paramount power, the Viceroy had a responsibility 'to put an end to their misery, oppression and suppression which are reported to in a most vicious and rigorous form.'[19] During his visit, Jinnah also attempted to facilitate a rapprochement between the Muslim Conference and the National Conference. He failed with relations between the two parties becoming 'once again as bitter as ever before.'[20]

When Kak was made Prime Minister in 1945, the National Conference initially supported him by virtue of him being a Kashmiri. The Muslim Conference, on the other hand, was quick to speak against him as naturally anti-Muslim given his Pandit roots.[21] However, National Conference support for Kak was short-lived. In 1946, Kak had Abdullah, along with other National Conference leaders, arrested after launching the Quit Kashmir movement against the Maharaja and advocating for a representative government. The arrest of the hugely popular Abdullah sparked unrest across the state, during which over twenty people were killed. On 21 May, the military shot and killed five men in Srinagar, along with the police killing two more men in nearby Pampur. Two days later, a woman was shot, and six men were wounded by police after a mob threw stones at police and wounded thirty-six constables.[22] In response, the Maharaja declared martial law. Many within the state believed that the actions of the government had the backing of the Political Department, with the All-India States' People's Conference soon making Kashmir a test case for their political activities.[23]

With Abdullah in prison awaiting trial, Nehru, then in the middle of constitutional negotiations, dropped everything to rush to the princely state. The Kashmiri government denied Nehru—whom Kak and Singh bitterly hated—permission to visit the state under any circumstances amid increasing agitation in the state. The British Resident even suggested that Abdullah's trial be adjourned to remove the immediate reason for Nehru's visit. Nehru subsequently wrote a letter telling people to stop the agitation and to release Abdullah, which was broadcast on 14 June. He then telegraphed the Maharaja stating his intention to arrive in Srinagar on 19 June. When he arrived at the border on the appointed day, Kashmir authorities would not let him cross. Nehru's actions created a sensation, not least because the Indian press published a (quite false) story that he had been bayoneted as he attempted to enter the state.[24]

With Nehru's efforts drawing negative attention, the Congress Working Committee pressured him to give up his efforts to enter Kashmir. Maulana Azad ordered Nehru to return to Delhi in a 21 June telegram, which was released to the press. Nehru complied, but was unapologetic for the upheaval his visit generated. He argued that his actions helped to focus all of India's attention on 'the autocratic ways and vagaries of the princes and repression, suppression and oppression to which the States' people are subjected at the hands of the miniature dictators whose authority and powers are unlimited.'[25] However, under pressure from Lord Wavell, the Maharaja lifted the ban on Nehru's entry into the state the following month so long as his visit was confined to work related to Abdullah's legal defense. He reached Srinagar on 24 July without much public interest or controversy. Five days later, Abdullah was sentenced to nine years imprisonment for seditious activities.[26]

Amid these rising tensions with the Congress leadership, the Maharaja began to warm to the idea of Kashmiri independence under the influence of Kak, as it became increasingly clear the British would soon depart India. With the most strident and popular opposition to his rule so closely associated with Congress, he could not fathom the possibility of acceding to the Indian Union under a Congress-dominated government and retaining his sovereignty. Joining a Congress-ruled India, in his mind, necessarily meant abrogating his vested political authority and interests. Likewise, once the decision to establish Pakistan was made, accession to the Muslim state was not a path the Hindu ruler would consider. Nehru pointed to Kak as influencing the Maharaja's thinking and contributing to the numerous problems within the state, arguing that he had fomented communal friction to weaken the National Conference and keep Kashmir out of India. In June 1947, he advised Mountbatten that Kak, who had 'succeeded in antagonising every decent element in Kashmir and in India as a whole,' needed to be removed from his position with Abdullah and other political prisoners immediately released.[27]

After announcing Partition, Mountbatten departed for Jammu and Kashmir to assess the political inclinations of the state. During this visit, the Maharaja was 'very elusive,' and the only times Mountbatten was able to converse with him at any length were on car rides together. The Viceroy pressured him to decide to accede to either Pakistan or India, which state was a matter of a choice for the Maharaja. Mountbatten assured him that if he ultimately chose Pakistan the States Department would not view this as an 'unfriendly act' toward India.[28] In the meantime, the Maharaja should enter into a standstill agreement with both states. Kashmiri independence, Mountbatten counseled, was not a realistic option. On the final day of the visit, Mountbatten hoped to meet once more with the indecisive Hari Singh and urge him to a make a quick decision on accession. However, the Maharaja missed his scheduled meeting with the Viceroy by feigning an illness, even though the Maharaja himself had suggested the timing of their final meeting; he used the same ploy to avoid an earlier meeting with Nehru. After his visit, Mountbatten informed Nehru that it was the Maharaja's desire that no Congress or Muslim League members should visit Jammu and Kashmir until his final decision had been announced, fearing such a visit could foment unrest among the state's subjects. Nehru reluctantly agreed.[29]

Mountbatten's visit was followed by a flurry of letters from Indian political leaders pushing for the princely state to accede to India. In early July 1947, Patel wrote to the Maharaja advocating for Abdullah's release from prison and stressed that he and the other Congress leaders had no quarrel with the princely states. The Congress, he assured Singh, was 'not only not your enemy, as you happen to believe, but there are in the Congress many strong supporters of your State.' He stressed that Kashmir's interests lay 'in joining in Indian Union and its Constituent Assembly without any delay. Its past history and traditions demand it, and all India looks up to you and expects you to take that decision.'[30] On the same day, Patel wrote to Kak pushing the same message. Menon, on the other hand, felt that the matter of Kashmir's accession shouldn't be pushed by either India or Pakistan. He recognized that it was possible that a majority Muslim state like Kashmir would not be able to be kept out of Pakistan for long and argued that the situation should 'find its natural solution.'[31] Menon was sensitive to the Maharaja's frustrations with the frequent lobbying of Indian leaders and thought that such pressure might backfire.

Despite Mountbatten's and Patel's urgings, Kashmir's leadership would not budge. In an attempt to dissuade the mounting political pressure, the Maharaja told Mountbatten that he would make up his mind on accession when he could ascertain what the dominions' respective constitutions would be like in relation to the princely states' sovereignty and could gauge public sentiment.[32] Prime Minister Kak, however, continued to push the Maharaja to pursue the path of independence, while also advising him that autocracy must eventually give way to democracy in the state. This position was at first supported by Ghulam Abbas, who told the Congress leaders, 'Hands off Kashmir.' However, during a 21 July convention, the Muslim Conference passed a unanimous resolution urging the Maharaja to accede to Pakistan. They argued that in view of Jammu and Kashmir's geographical position, lines of communication, trade networks, racial and cultural affinities and the contiguity of its frontiers, not to mention the fact that Muslims comprised approximately 85 percent of the population, the 'only proper course' was for accession to Pakistan.[33] Nevertheless, as the transfer of power quickly approached, Menon found the Maharaja 'in a Micawberish frame of mind, hoping for the best while continuing to do nothing. Besides he was toying with the notion of an "Independent Jammu and Kashmir."'[34]

'The Switzerland of the East'

Maharaja Hari Singh, who hoped to maintain his sovereign rule, remained hesitant to commit to any course of action landing his princely state in either India or Pakistan. By the appointed day of the transfer of power, he had failed to sign the Instrument of Accession for either country, effectively leaving Jammu and Kashmir an independent state with the lapse of paramountcy. Instead, Kashmir's political leaders signaled their intention to enter into standstill agreements with both successor governments. While the standstill agreement with Pakistan was signed on 26 August, India wanted time to further examine the situation and implications of this action. Kashmir's government intended to establish a policy of 'strict neutrality' between the two dominions, as argued by Kashmir's Deputy Prime Minister R.L. Batra.[35] Many within the state were opposed to this move. There were several incidents in which the Pakistani flag or the Indian and National Conference flags were hoisted over several buildings, despite directives to the contrary. On 26 August, state forces opened fire on a crowd of people gathered to witness the raising of the Pakistani flag at Bagh, near Muzaffarabad.[36] The tribes on the border between Gilgit and Chitral and between Poonch and the North-West Frontier Province (NWFP) also warned the Maharaja of their opposition to his accession to India.[37]

With the Maharaja failing to accede to either successor government, Pakistani officials were increasingly worried that India's States Ministry was doing its utmost to pressure the Maharaja to accede to India. Throughout August 1947, Jinnah and Pakistan's political leadership in Karachi received frantic letters that Hari Singh was falling under the sway of the National Conference and intended to join India, in addition to reports of increasing violence against the Muslim population.[38] The Pakistani press at the time reported Kashmir's eventual accession to India as 'a foregone conclusion.'[39] Pakistani leaders were also concerned with the new Kashmiri Prime Minister and his relationship with India's political leadership. Only four days before the transfer of power, Kak was removed from office. Serious differences had emerged between the Maharaja and the Prime Minister over the future direction of the state, and there was increasing pressure from the Congress leadership to have him removed. Kak was placed under house arrest and later sentenced to two years imprisonment on corruption charges. However, after the intervention of Nehru and Patel, his sentence was kept in abeyance, and he was allowed to leave the state.[40] Following Kak's dismissal, the Maharaja appointed Major General Janak Singh as Prime Minister before replacing him six weeks later with Mehr Chand Mahajan, a former judge of the Punjab High Court who had good relations with Nehru and Patel and whose appointment was welcomed by the Indian leaders.[41]

Nehru, himself a Kashmiri Pandit, was adamant that the Maharaja should accede to India and feared a Pakistani military intervention to force a resolution of the situation should the Maharaja continue to delay making a definitive decision on the future of the state. On 27 September 1947,

Nehru wrote to Patel of the 'dangerous and deteriorating' conditions within the princely states and that he had caught wind of a potential invasion from Pakistan. He stressed that Kashmir's government was unequipped to handle the onslaught of an invasion on its own, especially 'if their own people go against them.' Nehru argued that the Maharaja should 'make friends with the National Conference so that there might be this popular support against Pakistan,' beginning with the release of Abdullah who was 'very anxious to keep out of Pakistan and relies upon us a great deal for advice.' This move would have the added benefit of speeding up the princely state's accession to India, which would make it 'very difficult for Pakistan to invade it officially or unofficially without coming into conflict with the Indian Union.' He feared any delays would lead to Pakistani military action 'without much fear of consequences.' With pressure from the Pakistani side mounting, Nehru pushed Patel 'to take some action in this matter to force the pace and to turn events in the right direction.'[42]

Two days later, Kashmir's government released Abdullah from prison, alongside other jailed National Conference members. While Abdullah had written to the Maharaja a few days before his release expressing his 'steadfast loyalty,' he immediately resumed his calls for a representative form of government representing all Kashmiris, whether Muslim, Hindu or Sikh, which would then 'decide whether the State should join India or Pakistan.'[43] Despite making concessions to the Indian position by releasing Abdullah, the Maharaja did not budge from his dream of an independent Jammu and Kashmir, convinced that the conditions of the British withdrawal from India afforded him this right. On 12 October 1947, Kashmir's Deputy Prime Minister stated to Indian officials in New Delhi:

> We intend to keep on friendly relations with both Pakistan and the Indian Union. Despite constant rumours we have no intention of joining either India or Pakistan … The only thing that will change this decision is if one side or the other decides to use force against us … The Maharaja has told me that his ambition is to make Kashmir the Switzerland of the East—a State that is completely neutral.[44]

Nevertheless, rumblings from Pakistan's North-West Frontier Province foreshadowed a coming conflict. In early October 1947, the Mehtar of Chitral warned Hari Singh: 'Chitral and your other neighbouring Frontier States strongly urge you to join Pakistan. Your joining Indian Union in teeth of opposition from vast majority of your Muslim subjects will be deeply resented and force hands of your neighbouring States to take steps to undo the great wrong.'[45] Amid the Maharaja's 'almost fatal indecisiveness,' Indian authorities were growing concerned that Pakistan would militarily intervene in the princely states. At this point, Patel pushed Defense Minister

Baldev Singh to arrange for available supplies of arms and ammunition to be sent to Kashmir to support its state forces.[46] On 17 October, Deputy Prime Minister Batra informed Patel that unfortunately no military supplies had yet arrived, which were needed immediately for ongoing operations in Poonch, and requested that the Defense Minister release stocks of arms and ammunition without delay.[47] It would only be a matter of days before these supplies would be desperately needed.

The tribal invasion of Kashmir

On 22 October 1947, thousands of Pashtun tribesmen from Pakistan's NWFP poured across the border into Kashmir. To this day, the circumstances surrounding this invasion are clouded by the politics of the interstate rivalry between India and Pakistan. Indians argue that the Pakistani government covertly supported the tribal fighters, many of whom would later hold up their participation in the fighting as service to the Pakistani state. On the other hand, Pakistan has denied any role in supporting the invasion, claiming that it was a spontaneous show of support by the Pashtun tribesmen who rushed to the defense of their fellow Muslims being oppressed by an autocratic Hindu ruler. Nevertheless, certain basic facts of the invasion are uncontested.

The eruption of violence against the Maharaja's government had its roots in discontentment within the largely Muslim-populated Poonch area of western Kashmir. Poonch was a subsidiary principality of Jammu and Kashmir, but had enjoyed internal autonomy under the leadership of a local Raja. However, there were prevailing tensions and debates between the Maharaja and the Raja over the extent of this autonomy and the nature of the relationship between the two governments. During the 1920s, the Raja complained of undue interference by the Kashmir Durbar into Poonch's internal administration. In an August 1923 conversation with the British Resident in Srinagar, he argued that the Durbar was 'thrusting their own officials on me, while I have better and cheaper men who have experience of local circumstances.' He also complained that officials in Srinagar 'seem to have been bent upon degrading me in the eyes of my subjects,' as rumors circulated about an impending curtailment of the Raja's powers. He asserted that the Durbar 'should have no interference in the internal affairs of my country.'[48]

In 1940, following the death of the Raja of Poonch, Jagat Dev Singh, the Maharaja installed a guardian for the Raja's minor son and further integrated the region into the Kashmir state, effectively removing its political autonomy. The region now found itself under the direct control of the

Maharaja, whose rule came with a slew of new taxes. Combined with complaints over the general lack of development and persistently high grain prices, this helped to engender broad discontentment against the Kashmir government in the coming years.[49] It was only after the Second World War and the return of many demobilized Muslim soldiers from Poonch, which had been a key recruiting ground for the British Indian army (60,402 of the 71,667 men from Jammu and Kashmir who served in the army during the Second World War were Muslims from Poonch and neighboring Mirpur), that these grievances were translated into political agitation and violent action. In June 1947, a protest campaign was launched against the Maharaja. Fearing the eruption of a rebellion, the Maharaja ordered all Muslims in the area to hand over their weapons the following month and refused to meet with a delegation of ex-servicemen to discuss their rehabilitation.[50]

On 14 August 1947, Pakistan's Independence Day, Muslims in Poonch raised the Pakistani flag over several shops and offices, with reports of clashes between pro-Pakistani protestors and Kashmiri troops. Several groups in Kashmir soon reached out to Pakistan's leaders with reports of harassment and attacks against Muslims as state forces were increasingly deployed to Poonch to handle the unrest. The first call for open revolt against the Maharaja's government was made on 23 August 1947, in the Poonch city of Rawalkot. By September, reports circulated in India that Poonch Muslims were receiving smuggled arms from informal sources in Pakistan, but with the approval of the Pakistani Prime Minister Liaquat Ali Khan and their distribution overseen by senior members of the Pakistani army.[51] The following month, India's Intelligence Bureau also noted a buildup of tribal forces along the Kashmir border, observing that they 'were not concentrated there for nothing.'[52] With conflict beginning to brew in October and unrest spreading into neighboring areas, a number of Kashmiri Muslims opposed to the Maharaja were suspected of crossing into Poonch to join the amassing rebels, including former Muslim officials of the state government.

When the Pashtun tribesmen poured across the border in support of the Poonch rebels on 22 October, they made quick progress in the face of the state forces' inadequate defenses, which were further weakened by large numbers of Muslim troops deserting their units and joining the invaders.[53] The invading tribesmen, accustomed to guerilla fighting in the mountainous terrain of the northwestern frontier, reached Mahuta within only two days. Upon taking Mahuta, which provided power to the Kashmir valley and Srinagar, the raiders shut off electricity production and turned toward the state capital. A British manager of a local timber firm located on the road between Mahuta and Srinagar observed that the invading tribesmen were well supplied with trucks, arms and ammunition, in addition to two- and three-inch mortars.[54] As the raiders moved toward Srinagar, there were reports of the tribesmen plundering the homes of both non-Muslims and Muslims that they passed, delaying their advance.[55]

The invasion whipped up extreme animosity between religious communities. Dalip Singh, the agent to the Indian government in Jammu and Kashmir, observed an extreme bitterness among refugees in the princely state, with many non-Muslims expressing their desire to take revenge against the Muslim population. Aware of the potential for violence, Muslim residents in Jammu city, who were concentrated into two mohallas, refused to come out and reopen their shops over fear of being attacked by Hindus and Sikhs, despite assurances that state forces would protect them. To avoid any communal discord, the government decided to evacuate the city's Muslims to Pakistan. Singh explained some difficulties with this decision: 'I went to their camp today and one man came up to me and said that he, a member of the National Conference and a loyal subject of His Highness, was being treated the same as a [Muslim] leaguer. I believe he was telling the truth. But I can think of no method of keeping back selected persons and giving them protection from Hindus and Sikhs in the city.'[56]

As the tribal raiders continued their advance, both British Prime Minister Clement Attlee and Nehru encouraged Liaquat Ali Khan to do everything possible to stop them.[57] Nehru and other Indian officials were adamant that the Pakistani government was responsible for the tribal invasion and providing encouragement and material support to the raiders, pointing to their motorized transport, modern arms and clear military training as indisputable evidence. Menon explained to the British High Commissioner in New Delhi that Pakistan's original plan had been for the Pashtun tribesmen to capture Srinagar by Eid al-Adha (26 October) and set up a new provisional government that would then announce Kashmir's accession to Pakistan. He argued that the Pakistani troops near the border were being held there in preparation for entering the princely state after such an announcement to help restore law and order.[58]

Despite reports coming from India's political leaders to the contrary, Pakistani leadership informed the British High Commission in Karachi that far from encouraging the incursion of tribesmen into Kashmir they had in fact opposed it and actively exerted political pressure to stop it. Nevertheless, the Pakistani government explained it did not have the capacity, resources or the political will to take any significant actions to stop the tribesmen from crossing into Kashmir for fear of provoking a major frontier war. Jinnah told the British High Commissioner in Pakistan that local authorities in NWFP could only have halted the tribal invasion by firing on them, which would have started 'a conflagration of incalculable consequences on the Frontier.'[59] Given the limited capacity of the Pakistani government at the time, the U.S. Ambassador in India, Henry Grady, inferred that if Jinnah had in fact planned the invasion, the violence against fellow Muslims would not have been so prevalent, violence which was alienating Kashmiri Muslims.[60] The NWFP Governor, George Cunningham, further explained that, if his government had encouraged the tribesmen in any way, at least forty thousand Pashtun would have overwhelmed Kashmir as opposed to the two thousand that had joined the invasion. Instead, he had been impressing upon tribal elders that they should not intervene in Kashmir at this time but would be called upon 'for the defence of Islam' if necessary. Despite the orders of the government, he nevertheless was certain that members of the Muslim League had instigated the tribesmen and aided them in their invasion.[61] A British journalist who traveled through NWFP in late October and early November 1947 gathered the impression that the tribesmen essentially operated independently and were completely out of the control of everybody within the Pakistani government. Decisions were being made by a council of tribal leaders based in Abbottabad, 'which appeared to be entirely autonomous and independent of any authority … since the Provincial Government were unable, or afraid, or perhaps just unwilling, to take them on.'[62]

While the circumstance of the tribal invasion were (and still are) hotly contested, Pakistani officials warned the British High Commission that if India deployed its military to the princely state or forced the Maharaja to accede, 'it will be impossible for anyone to control the trouble since the whole of Kashmir would then flare up.'[63] At any rate, Prime Minister Khan maintained that the problems all started with the mass massacres of innocent Muslims in Poonch and Jammu by Kashmir state forces and Kashmiri raids into Pakistani territory targeting Muslim villages in the border area, citing one attack in which he claimed that 1,760 dead bodies of Muslims were discovered afterward. It was these actions, the Pakistani Prime Minister argued, that provoked a response from revenge-seeking Pashtun who hoped to prevent a repetition of the massacres in the Punjab.[64] India's leadership, on the other hand, maintained that the tribal raiders enjoyed free transit through Pakistani territory and their modern military equipment and training could only have come from Pakistani sources; thus, their actions represented an act of war against India.

As the tribal raiders pushed past Kashmir's forces and inched closer to Srinagar, Maharaja Hari Singh sent a telegram to New Delhi in the evening of 24 October requesting immediate military assistance from the Indian government to repel the invasion of his state, which he argued could not have been done without the knowledge of the Pakistani government.[65] The following day, the government dispatched Menon to assess the situation.

Upon landing in Srinagar, he was met with the 'stillness of a graveyard all around. Over everything hung an atmosphere of impending calamity.' From the airfield, he drove straight to the Prime Minister's residence for a briefing on the situation before heading to the Maharaja's palace, noting the conspicuous absence of state police along the road. There he found Hari Singh 'completely unnerved by the turn of events and by his sense of lone helplessness.' With the raiders now only fifty miles from Srinagar and practically no state forces left to defend the state capital, Menon advised the Maharaja to move south into Jammu.[66]

Early in the morning of 26 October, following warnings from Mehr Chand Mahajan that raiders were on the verge of entering the capital, Menon quickly departed for New Delhi, accompanied by Kashmir's Prime Minister. Upon landing in the Indian capital, they went straight to a meeting of the Defence Committee to apprise them of conditions on the ground in Kashmir. Sheikh Abdullah was also present for the meeting, as he just so happened to be in Delhi at the time. Both Abdullah and Mahajan pressed the necessity of dispatching the Indian military at once to protect the state from the invaders and drive them out of Kashmir. It was Mountbatten who first voiced what was perhaps on the minds of the other political leaders present; the Indian government should first have the Maharaja sign the Instrument of Accession for India, which was the only legal basis the government had for sending troops to Kashmir for the state's protection. 'Otherwise,' Mountbatten argued, 'you would just be invading a valley in Pakistan.'[67] With the raiders breathing down the Kashmir government's neck, the Maharaja would have little choice but to sign the document. Mountbatten also stated that India's acceptance of Kashmir's accession should be conditional on the outcome of a plebiscite to be held once the raiders had been pushed out of the state, a condition that all the ministers present readily agreed.

Nehru was hesitant to use military force. However, Mahajan interjected in the discussion, according to his memoirs, and stressed: 'Give army, take accession and give whatever powers you want to give to the popular party [the National Conference], but the army must fly to Srinagar this evening, otherwise I will go and negotiate terms with Mr. Jinnah as the city must be saved.' An outraged Nehru told him to leave, but Patel quickly grabbed him and stressed unequivocally, 'Of course, Mahajan, you are not going to Pakistan.' It was only after Sheikh Abdullah slipped the Indian Prime Minister a note stating that he shared the sentiment expressed by Mahajan that Nehru's attitude changed. It was then decided to move forward with the military option.[68]

With the matter decided by early afternoon, Menon left the meeting and immediately departed back north to Jammu with the Instrument of

Accession in hand. Events were moving too quickly for a new Instrument of Accession to be typed up. Therefore, Menon simply grabbed a copy of the instrument, with the August date crossed out and the new October date handwritten in pen.[69] Upon his arrival at the palace where the Maharaja was now staying, Menon found it in complete disarray with valuables scattered everywhere. Hari Singh was fast asleep, fatigued from his all-night drive from Srinagar. He had reportedly given instructions that if Menon did not return as he had promised then he should simply be shot in his sleep.[70] Menon woke up the undoubtedly relieved Maharaja and briefed him on what was decided in New Delhi earlier that day. He agreed at once to sign the Instrument of Accession. Menon, with the signed Instrument of Accession and a letter from Hari Singh officially requesting military assistance in hand, was soon back abroad a flight to New Delhi, his mission to bring Jammu and Kashmir into the Indian Union a success.[71]

As dawn broke on 27 October 1947, mere hours after the Maharaja had signed the Instrument of Accession and with the raiders now in the immediate vicinity of Kashmir's capital, the first twin-engine Dakota aircraft loaded with troops and arms lifted into the sky from an airstrip on the outskirts of Delhi; twenty-eight flights bound for Srinagar departed that first day with one hundred more to follow in the coming days to deliver the First Battalion of the Indian army's First Sikh Regiment along with supplies to besieged Srinagar.[72] With military aircraft in short supply, the government requisitioned passenger aircraft, stripped clean of their luxury seating to fit as many fully armed men as they could inside. As the planes crossed into the Kashmir valley after an uneventful flight over 'long strings of refugee caravans' and 'an odd house or village still smouldering' in the killing fields of the Punjab, the men aboard looked out the windows at the snowy landscape below. 'Everything appeared so picturesque, calm and peaceful-looking out of that Dakota window,' remarked one military officer on the flight. The men had not been fully briefed on what to expect when they landed as there was little intelligence available about conditions on the ground. Yet, as they descended below the fog that covered the runway in Srinagar, 'we heard the sound of small-arms and machine-gun fire and saw one or two of our men wounded by bullets that ricocheted.' As the planes landed amid incoming fire, the soldiers aboard knew that they 'had run into it … and launched straight out into battle.'[73]

As reinforcements continued to land in Srinagar to repulse the raiders, Nehru explained that Indian military action in Kashmir was necessary due to the 'responsibility of defence that we undertook by virtue of accession' and felt that if the government had delayed the deployment of the military by even a day then Srinagar would have been left a 'smoking ruin.'[74] In an early November radio broadcast, he announced that he had before him a list of ninety-five villages in Jammu that had been destroyed by the raiders armed with modern weaponry, and if India had failed to act, it would have been 'a betrayal of trust and cowardly submission to the law of the sword with its accompaniment of arson, rapine, and slaughter.'[75]

The deployment of Indian troops into the newly acceded princely state infuriated Jinnah. After reportedly bracing himself with several brandies, the Pakistani Governor General ordered the Pakistani army into Kashmir. However, Pakistan's British Commander-in-Chief refused, and Jinnah angrily withdrew the order, leaving the tribal raiders deep within Kashmir territory without official support.[76] On 30 October, Liaquat Ali Khan wrote to Nehru: 'Your recent action of sending troops to Kashmir on pretext of accession has made things infinitely worse. The whole of the Frontier is stirring and feeling of resentment among tribes is intense. The responsibility for what is happening is entirely yours.'[77] To attempt to stop any tribal movements now, Khan stressed, 'would involve us in a major frontier war.'[78] During a Defence Committee meeting that same day, Menon recognized the difficulties faced in dealing with Kashmir as it had relations with both dominions and frontiers with other countries. He even acknowledged that 'the best solution in the end might be for Kashmir to remain independent.'[79]

Following Jammu and Kashmir's accession, the Maharaja appointed Sheikh Abdullah as the head of the state administration with the authority to deal with the current emergency, pending the establishment of an interim government. While Abdullah did not intend to overly disturb the administrative machinery given the invasion, he did appoint a number of emergency officers in the state's government departments who were largely drawn from the ranks of the National Conference and agreed to work honorarily.[80] The National Conference also filled the vacuum left by the departure of the state administration in the capital and demonstrated its capacity for governance. Srinagar residents witnessed National Conference members standing guard at street corners and bridges, generally monitoring activity within the city and working together with the Indian army as it established a protective ring around the city. One journalist coming to the city after covering the intercommunal violence within the Punjab remarked that he was 'not prepared for the incredible sights of amity and indeed fraternity that I saw in Srinagar. Hindus and Sikhs moved about with complete unself-consciousness among Muslims who constituted the vast majority of the population of the town; they marched shoulder to shoulder with them down Srinagar's streets as volunteers engaged in a common task.' In his new role, Abdullah had the backing of the highest echelons of the Indian government. On 11 November, Nehru wrote to Hari Singh that Abdullah was 'obviously the leading popular personality in Kashmir. The way he has risen to grapple with the crisis has shown the nature of the man. I have a high opinion of his integrity and balance of mind. He has striven hard and succeeded very largely in keeping communal peace. He may make any number of mistakes in minor matters, but I think he is likely to be right in regard to major decisions.'[81] In December 1947, the Maharaja agreed to the formation of an interim government with Abdullah as the head of the administration, despite his apprehensions over this selection.

On 1 November 1947, Mountbatten, accompanied by his Chief of Staff Lord Ismay, traveled to Lahore to discuss the situation with the Pakistani Prime Minister and Governor General. Jinnah reiterated the view that Kashmir's accession to India was based on 'fraud and violence' as the Maharaja was forced to sign the Instrument of Accession; he knew for a fact that the Maharaja desired independence. During the contentious meeting, he even offered to relinquish Pakistani claims to the state of Junagadh, which had acceded to Pakistan in September, in return for India giving up its claims on Kashmir (see Chapter 8). Jinnah countered Mountbatten's argument that Pakistani citizens were the cause of violence in the region by arguing that the Maharaja was to blame due to his ill treatment of Muslims, especially in Poonch, which provoked an inevitable response from the tribesmen. Jinnah also strongly rejected the idea of conducting a plebiscite while Indian troops were present in the princely state and the National Conference in power, under whose auspices 'such propaganda and pressure could be brought to bear that the average Muslim would never have the courage to vote for Pakistan.' Even when Ismay invoked world opinion as a reason to search for a path of compromise, the Pakistani Governor General was despondent, responding that he had 'lost interest in what the world thought of him since the British Commonwealth had let him down when he had asked them to come to the rescue of Pakistan.'[82] Ultimately, very little was accomplished during Mountbatten's visit with both sides remaining equally defiant to any hint of compromise.

As the tribal raiders invaded the Kashmir valley, Pashtun tribesmen also sought to secure Kashmir's western territories for Pakistan. In early November 1947, over ten thousand tribesmen from the princely state of Swat marched into the northern areas of Gilgit through Tangir and occupied it on behalf of Pakistan, with the support of the Gilgit Scouts who had rebelled against the Dogra Governor during the night of 31 October and raised the Pakistan flag to signify their new loyalties. Hunza and Nagar, despite being vassal states of Jammu and Kashmir, also unilaterally announced their accession to Pakistan.[83] While Pakistani troops were not directly involved in securing Gilgit, Hunza and Nagar, they were active in holding a defensive line against Kashmiri troops operating in the western reaches of the state. On 4 November, clashes were reported between the Pakistani army and Kashmiri troops located in Mirpur. The fighting continued until

12 November when the Indian Air Force provided reinforcements to the Kashmiri forces and conducted bombing runs against the enemy positions.

In early November, with Srinagar now secure, the Indian army took the offensive and began clearance operations against the tribal raiders. On 12 November, Indian troops took Mahuta, saving the city's power plant from destruction, and then moved toward Uri, which fell the following day. With the onset of winter, however, military operations were quickly suspended. Both Indian and Pakistani leaders now turned to the problem of finding a political resolution. If they continued to fight, Nehru was convinced this would simply mean 'grave difficulties and suffering for the people of the State,' but he maintained that Indian troops were unable to withdraw so long as the threat from the tribal raiders persisted. There were essentially four potential options being proposed. The first was to hold a plebiscite to decide which dominion the state should join. The second was to recognize an independent state of Jammu and Kashmir with defense guarantees by both India and Pakistan. The third option was to separate the Hindu-majority Jammu, which would remain with India, with the rest of the princely state being integrated into Pakistan. And the fourth was to partition the state, with Jammu and the Kashmir valley remaining within India and the remainder of the state, including Poonch and the northern areas, being ceded to Pakistan.

In assessing these proposals, the Maharaja remained committed to India—which he saw as necessary for preserving some semblance of his political authority—but feared the outcome of a plebiscite. If the vote resulted in accession to Pakistan, he would have no alternative but to abdicate and worried about the ultimate annihilation of Kashmir's Hindu and Sikh populations. Nehru, who was reluctant to give up the National Conference stronghold of the Kashmir valley, was partial to the partition of the state, particularly as he saw the majority of Poonch residents likely opposed to the Indian Union and the region was 'linguistically allied to the Punjab.'[84] But he also recognized the importance of holding a plebiscite to determine the princely state's future as a clear signal to the source of the government's legitimacy and sovereignty under a democratic state. In a 1 December 1947, letter to the Maharaja, he argued:

> It is of the most vital importance that Kashmir should remain within the Indian Union ... But however much we may want this, it cannot be done ultimately except through the goodwill of the mass of the population. Even if military forces held Kashmir for a while, a later consequence might be a strong reaction against this. Essentially, therefore, this is a problem of psychological approach to the mass of the people and of making them feel they will be benefited by being in the Indian Union. If the average Muslim feels that he has no safe or secure place in the Union, then obviously he will look elsewhere. Our basic policy must keep this in view, or else we fail.[85]

The plebiscite that never was

On 1 January 1948, under the urging of Mountbatten, India's leadership formally approached the United Nations to assist with mediation, and the Kashmir issue was admitted into the agenda of the UN Security Council five days later.[86] During January and February 1948, the eloquent Pakistani Foreign Minister Zafarullah Khan sought to connect events in Kashmir with the broader turmoil in the Subcontinent in presentations before the UN Security Council. He argued that the invasion of Kashmir was a natural reaction to the rioting across northern India in 1946 and 1947 and accused the Indian government of perpetrating a 'genocide' against Muslims in east Punjab. While the Pakistani government rejected the idea of a plebiscite in the largely Hindu state of Junagadh, Khan advocated for the full withdrawal of all armed forces from Kashmir and a plebiscite to be held under an impartial interim administration, which would exclude Sheikh Abdullah. In his testimony, Khan framed the issue not as a localized issue but unfinished business from the turmoil of Partition and representative of the broader struggles between India and Pakistan. Once the politics of this interstate rivalry was injected into the Kashmir question, it would prove difficult to disentangle it in the coming decades.

On 5 February 1948, flying in the face of Pakistani demands, it was Sheikh Abdullah who took center stage in New York City to represent Indian interests. With the full backing of the Indian government, he told the gathered diplomats: 'There is no power on earth which can displace me from the position which I have [in Kashmir]. As long as the people are behind me I will remain there.'[87] The following month, Abdullah was officially installed as Jammu and Kashmir's Prime Minister. Hari Singh, while still the ceremonial head of state, was stripped of any real governing authority and kept out of all deliberations and negotiations. The tensions between Singh and Abdullah under this arrangement would be a key point of concern for Nehru and Patel.[88] At the UN, the Indian government continued to assert that it could not withdraw its troops from Kashmir, otherwise it would leave the state vulnerable to further incursions by tribal raiders. Nor could it promise to install a neutral administration before a plebiscite could be held, as such a move would fly in the face of the country's democratic principles and was a matter of concern for the people of Kashmir.[89]

On 21 April 1948, the UN Security Council adopted Resolution 47 directing the UN Commission for India and Pakistan (UNCIP), established on 20 January 1948, to proceed at once to South Asia to take stock of the necessary measures needed to facilitate the holding of a plebiscite as soon as possible under an independent administration. Additionally, the resolution directed Pakistan to secure the withdrawal of all tribal raiders from Kashmir and, once it was confirmed that this withdrawal was taking place, direct India to begin withdrawal of its own forces, reducing them to the minimum level required to maintain law and order.[90] Yet, the following month, Pakistani forces officially entered the conflict claiming it as a defensive action to protect Pakistan's borders, further complicating efforts to end the fighting.

Through the summer and autumn of 1948, the irreconcilable positions of the two governments persisted. The Pakistani government complained to the UNCIP members that the Indian army continued to reinforce its position in Kashmir as the Indian government 'appears determined to force a military decision in Kashmir.' Zafarullah Khan wrote to the UNCIP President Dr. Alfredo Lozano that the Indian army had launched an offensive to secure control of western Kashmir. He further warned, 'Unless immediate steps are taken by Security Council to halt Indian Army offensive Pakistan Government will have no (repeat no) option but to undertake counteroffensive with all available resources to prevent over-running by Indian Army of Poonch and Mirpur Districts.' The Indian government categorically denied reports of a winter offensive, arguing that Indian military action was defensive in nature and only intended to bring relief to Indian forces in Poonch and the large civilian population taking shelter in their garrison. Nehru also argued that recent Indian military operations were a direct consequence of the continuous buildup of Pakistani positions in Poonch, Uri and Ladakh valley. 'It is Pakistan,' he stressed, 'that has been throwing in reinforcements and supplies during past few months and carrying out offensives against our forces.'[91]

Meanwhile, UNCIP continued to try and lay the groundwork for a plebiscite. While Nehru believed that 'a really fair plebiscite' would result in a majority vote for Sheikh Abdullah's government and permanent accession to India, his reservations lay with the conditions that would govern it.[92] On 14 August 1948, UNCIP provided a draft ceasefire proposal to the Indian and Pakistani governments, which had been drafted during a commission meeting in Karachi on the previous day. While India accepted the resolution as presented, Pakistan insisted on attaching several conditions before offering their acceptance of the proposal, conditions which the UNCIP members felt 'went beyond compass of resolution thereby making impossible immediate ceasefire and beginning of fruitful negotiations.'[93]

In early autumn 1948, UNCIP landed in Srinagar as part of an extensive tour of the region. During the visit, one of its members, the famed Czech diplomat and scholar Josef Korbel, spent ample time chatting with Sheikh Abdullah. 'Here was a Muslim leader who believed, as did India, in a noncommunal, secular state but who was aware of the fanatical devotion of his followers to Islam,' Korbel later wrote. 'What then should he do? Pakistan was a reactionary country, he said, and he was convinced that a union of Kashmir with Pakistan would finally work against the interests of his people. They would be better off with India—but what could he do if the sentiments of his people pushed them in a direction against his better judgment?'[94] Abdullah later described Pakistan as an 'unscrupulous and savage enemy' more interested in supporting the autocracy of the princes than the rights of the princely states' people. He also dismissed the prospect of Kashmiri independence, arguing that it would simply leave Kashmir vulnerable to being swallowed up by Pakistan at some point in the future.[95] Ultimately, Abdullah explained to Korbel: 'There is in my opinion, therefore, only one solution open. That is the division of [Kashmir]. If it is not achieved, the fighting will continue; India and Pakistan will prolong the quarrel indefinitely and our people's suffering will go on.'[96] However, Korbel found that Pakistani officials would never agree to a division that would land the Muslim-majority Kashmir valley in India.

After departing Srinagar in late September, UNCIP continued to engage with Indian and Pakistan representatives to find a compromise on a ceasefire and plebiscite. After months of deliberation, India and Pakistan approved the Karachi Agreement under which a ceasefire went into effect one minute before midnight on 31 December 1948. UNCIP returned to South Asia in February 1949 to implement the terms of the ceasefire, begin the demilitarization of Jammu and Kashmir, and begin preparations for a plebiscite. However, they failed to overcome the objections of the Indian government, and a plebiscite was never held. The Karachi Agreement also defined the boundary between Pakistani-held territory (which would become Pakistan's Azad Kashmir comprising the districts of Mirpur, Poonch and Muzaffarabad and the Northern Areas) and Indian-held territory (the Kashmir valley, Jammu and Ladakh). This ceasefire line would be redesignated the Line of Control in July 1972, and remains in place to this day.

The fallout between Sheikh Abdullah and New Delhi

On 12 October 1948, the National Conference voted unanimously to uphold Jammu and Kashmir's accession to the Indian Union. Like other princely states, it initially acceded only in matters of defense, foreign relations and communications. While other princely states would soon be fully integrated into India, Jammu and Kashmir became intimately intertwined with international politics and, as Nehru explained, 'remained where it was for a variety of reasons, among them the fact that the United Nations were seized of this problem and we did not wish to appear to by-pass them in this matter.' Faced with these unique challenges, the Indian constitution, which went into effect in January 1950, included Article 370 that enshrined Jammu and Kashmir's political autonomy and ensured that only certain parts of the constitution applied to the former princely state. However, Nehru argued this in no way diminished its status as an integral part of India. This article was intended to be a transitional measure, but given the prevailing conditions of the rivalry between India and Pakistan and the continued threat of Pakistani military action across the Line of Control, it remained in effect until the Indian government abrogated it on 5 August 2019, turning the autonomous state of Jammu and Kashmir into a Union territory.

The political autonomy granted to Jammu and Kashmir under the constitution strengthened the position of Sheikh Abdullah and the Kashmiri government. In line with Congress' broader goals of abolishing the zamindari system within the princely states, Abdullah's government pursued a policy of land redistribution, transferring some forty thousand acres of land to landless laborers and tenants within the first year and dissolving large estates without providing any compensation to the landowners for the expropriated land—a policy that New Delhi opposed.[97] Abdullah also banned absentee ownership and placed a moratorium on debt. However, following Jammu and Kashmir's accession, the state government struggled financially. In early February 1948, for example, the Defense Ministry reported that troops within the Kashmir state forces had not received any pay for a period of three months, despite engaging in combat against tribal raiders alongside the Indian army. Jammu and Kashmir's financial problems necessitated New Delhi to provide loans to the state government, which added up to approximately 2.5 crore rupees, to keep it financially solvent.[98]

Despite the political autonomy the former princely state enjoyed, and the financial support provided by New Delhi, Abdullah's relations with New Delhi began to strain, and he soon began to flirt with the prospect of Kashmiri independence. On 29 September 1950, he probed the U.S. Ambassador to India, Loy Henderson, on whether the United States would support an independent Jammu and Kashmir. Abdullah explained that his state 'should be independent; that overwhelming majority population desired their independence; that he had reason believe that some Azad Kashmir leaders desired independence and would be willing to cooperate with leaders of National Conference if there was reasonable chance such cooperation would result in independence.' He, however, recognized that independence was only possible if Jammu and Kashmir could establish friendly relations with both India and Pakistan.[99] In January 1951, Abdullah wrote to Patel concerning the framing of Jammu and Kashmir's state constitution and the matter of defining the central government's jurisdiction over the former princely state, seeming to imply that the terms of its accession to India were not a settled issued.[100]

Not all were pleased with these political developments. Some within the National Conference were dead set on protecting the accession to India and opposed any talk of independence, fearing this would result in Jammu and Kashmir eventually landing in Pakistan.[101] Hindu leaders within Jammu, where the Maharaja had drawn much of his support, also opposed Sheikh Abdullah's government and complained that the government's limited finances resulted in more attention paid to the development of the Muslim-majority Kashmir valley. Compounding the lingering problems of under-development, all trade and movement into and out of Kashmir now passed through Jammu, whereas previously it had passed through Rawalpindi now located on the Pakistan side of the border. This, alongside the large numbers of displaced persons from the conflict with Pakistan that found their way into Jammu, led to a considerable growth in the population, which put an increased strain on housing, water supplies and unemployment. Adding to the tensions with Srinagar was the perception that Hindus were being deliberately kept out of positions in the now Muslim-dominated government. Indian leaders grew concerned that Hindu nationalist groups such as the Rashtriya Swayamsevak Sangh and the Bharatiya Jana Sangh could draw this localized political struggle into the broader communal politics of India.[102]

In 1949, the Praja Parishad was formed to oppose the National Conference government and to represent the interests of Jammu's Hindu and Sikh populations. The new group advocated for the removal of Jammu and Kashmir's political autonomy as an unwanted holdover of the Maharaja's rule and its complete integration into the Indian Union, adopting the slogan 'ek vidhan, ek pradhan, ek nishan' (One constitution, one head of state, one flag).[103] In support of this position, the group's leaders advised its followers to oppose any decision 'thrust on them' by the UN, including the proposed demilitarization of the state that they feared would expose the state to further aggression from Pakistan.[104] They were also pushing for Jammu and Kashmir's representatives within the Indian parliament to be popularly elected, similar to other former princely states, rather than being nominated by the state government. The group felt that the nomination process was implemented to keep the Praja Parishad out of office (Jammu and Kashmir did not send elected representatives to the Lok Sabha until 1967). With New Delhi backing Abdullah's government, the Praja Parishad leaders argued that Congress was 'sacrificing its principles for the sake of Sheikh Abdullah,' who was granted 'a free hand' by Nehru. With the Indian government spending vast amounts of money in the state, the group further alleged that Sheikh Abdullah directed development funds toward predominantly Muslim-majority areas, while waving the banner of secularism. Under Abdullah's government, the group alleged that Hindu and Sikh communities faced 'untold hardships' while being gradually 'eliminated' as they were forced to flee the state. 'Hindus say that Kashmir is a Pakistan for them,' one Praja Parishad member argued. 'The Kashmir Muslims are happy. Why should they go to Pakistan when India is prepared to spend crores of rupees for their welfare.' Some of the group's members even spoke fondly of the days of the Maharaja's rule, during which Hindus held a favored position within the state government.[105]

During the summer of 1951, however, a lack of funds hampered the Praja Parishad's activities, with appeals to the public for subscriptions generating a poor response. Its resources were so limited that it was only nominating candidates to stand in the upcoming October elections if they were wealthy enough to cover all the expenses of their campaign. What support the group was able to generate was largely based on anti-Abdullah sentiment among Hindus, in particular stemming from his clashes with the Maharaja, his frequent references to the widespread massacring of Muslims in the province and a sense that the interests of Jammu were being ignored by the Kashmiri leadership, rather than a genuine devotion to its cause.[106]

In October 1951, elections were held for Jammu and Kashmir's Constituent Assembly. The Praja Parishad boycotted the election after the nomination papers of forty-one of its candidates, out of a total of sixty-five, were found to be invalid 'on very flimsy grounds,' including minor mistakes like misspelled names or an errant dot or dash in the printing. Not a single candidate of the National Conference had their nomination papers rejected. The group even sought to conduct separate elections financed by the Hindu nationalist political party Bharatiya Jana Sangh and form a parallel government with its own officials deputed to every village, tehsil and district.[107] Leaders of the Muslim Conference, which continued to support Jammu and Kashmir's accession to Pakistan, similarly encouraged its supporters not to cooperate in the elections, which they denounced as a 'farce.'[108] As a result, the National Conference won a resounding victory, largely without contest.

In Sheikh Abdullah's lengthy opening speech in the Constituent Assembly, he laid out in detail the options facing Jammu and Kashmir. While he had increasingly advocated for Kashmiri independence, he acknowledged that an independent Jammu and Kashmir would be unable to protect its sovereignty from invasion, as occurred in October 1947. He also maintained his opposition to Pakistan and argued that the only realistic option for the state was to find some agreeable administrative arrangement with the Indian government. He, however, stressed that this would be on their own terms in the guise of a loose federation rather than full integration into the Indian

Union, including Jammu and Kashmir keeping its own flag and retaining the office of the prime minister within the autonomous state government. As the British Foreign Office observed, 'The Sheikh is an ambitious political opportunist who wants to be master in his own house.'[109]

In July 1952, Abdullah and Nehru hammered out the Delhi Agreement, whereby Jammu and Kashmir retained its internal political autonomy, barring the matters contained within the Instrument of Accession, with Kashmiris recognized as full citizens of India.[110] On 19 August 1952, the Jammu and Kashmir Constituent Assembly unanimously approved the agreement. At this time, however, the cause of the Praja Parishad was taken up by Dr. Shyama Prasad Mukerjee and the Bharatiya Jana Sangh. Mukerjee advocated for Jammu and Kashmir to be fully integrated into India without any special concessions, giving it the same status as other princely states. However, Abdullah, strident as ever, continued to press for greater autonomy, which provoked processions and protests among the Hindus of Jammu. Through the winter of 1952/53, Abdullah's National Conference government and the Praja Parishad continued to clash. In public speeches, Abdullah denounced the activities of the Praja Parishad as fostering communal divisions that only served to weaken the country and sought to challenge the movement both politically and with the state security forces.[111] Yet, Parishad protestors persisted in ripping down the Jammu and Kashmir flag from government buildings and replacing it with the Indian tricolor, leading to their frequent arrests. This conflict came to a head when a Parishad member, Mela Ram, was shot and killed by police.

In response, Mukerjee organized street protests across Delhi in coordination with other groups, such as the Hindu Mahasabha and the Ram Rajya Parishad. By the end of April 1953, the police had arrested 1,300 people involved in the protests.[112] In the morning of 11 May, Mukerjee attempted to enter Jammu and Kashmir and was arrested after crossing the border when he refused to turn back. While still sitting in a Srinagar jail cell, he fell ill and died on 23 June from a heart attack. The following day, his body was flown back to his home of Calcutta, draped in a shawl laid by Sheikh Abdullah. However, a portion of his ashes were brought back to Jammu the following month, with large numbers of people lined up along the road as the jeep carrying the urn passed through Jammu city's main bazaar.[113]

Following Mukerjee's death, angry mobs erupted in Jammu and set fire to government buildings. Processions marched through the streets of Delhi, shouting 'Kashmir hamara hai' ('Kashmir is ours'). Abdullah was convinced that Hindu communal forces were now running rampant, even beyond Nehru's control. There were also growing divisions with the National Conference between pro-India and pro-independence camps. Rumors quickly spread that Abdullah was planning to declare Kashmiri independence on 21 August and seek the protection of the UN against 'Indian aggression.'[114] Two weeks before this date, he dismissed a member of the cabinet, which was enough for Karan Singh, Hari Singh's son and now the titular head of the state government, to dismiss him and install Bakshi Ghulam Mohammed as the new Prime Minister. Over fears that Abdullah would create 'an upheaval and civil strife on a considerable scale,' Bakshi had him arrested.[115] When the police delivered his dismissal early in the morning, Abdullah was notified that he was under arrest and had only two hours before being taken to jail.

Amid persistent international political pressure through 1953, internal political fault lines increasingly formed—within Jammu and Kashmir's government and between the state government and New Delhi. For New Delhi, Sheikh Abdullah's political position had become untenable following the dissensions within his cabinet and the National Conference. However, the Indian government was adamant that Abdullah's arrest 'followed strictly constitution lines.'[116] In 1953, Nehru wrote:

> Sheikh Abdullah's attitude became more and more bitter and he seemed to be bent on upsetting everything in Kashmir. Indeed, in the course of a conversation with a friend, he said that he would set fire to the state. I do not know what he meant by that. But it indicated the state of his mind which was almost functioning as if it was unbalanced. So we came to live under constant apprehension of an impending disaster.[117]

The new prime minister had long been involved with the National Conference; he spent a significant amount of time in Hari Singh's jails and directed the organization of volunteers in Srinagar during the tribal invasion in 1947. Having got the job, he did not intend to lose it, which required gaining New Delhi's trust and support. Shortly after assuming office, he traveled to Jammu and announced before a large audience that 'the ties between Kashmir and India are irrevocable. No power on earth can separate the two.' Returning to Srinagar, he denounced the actions of Sheikh Abdullah in 'entertaining the idea of an independent Kashmir,' which was 'a dangerous game, pregnant with disastrous consequences for Kashmir, India, and Pakistan.'[118] He used his close relationship with New Delhi to ensure development funds from the central government flowed into the state and further cement the state's future with that of the Indian Union.

In the coming decades, Kashmir settled into a precarious status quo until the region would be rocked by the eruption of an anti-government insurgency in the 1980s. Yet, the problems of Kashmir have never remained within Kashmir. The status of the former princely state has taken on a life all its own, becoming a flashpoint for a decades-long rivalry between two nations born in blood and in conflict with one another. 'The real cause of all the bitterness and bloodshed, all the venomed speech, the recalcitrance and the suspicion that have characterized the Kashmir dispute,' UNCIP member Josef Korbel wrote in the 1950s, 'is the uncompromising struggle of two ways of life, two concepts of political organization, two scales of values, two spiritual attitudes, that find themselves locked in deadly conflict in which Kashmir has become both symbol and battleground.'[119]

However, all the international-level politics, controversy and conflict over Jammu and Kashmir over the past seventy years often overshadow the origins of the dispute, stemming from the many problems and ambiguities facing the princely states over the competing visions of sovereignty in the transition from British colonial rule to independence. Within Jammu and Kashmir during this period, we see the fault lines of conflict emerging between the different visions of state sovereignty—the Maharaja and his supporters pushing for the preservation of the princely state's sovereignty as enjoyed under the umbrella of British paramountcy, even if that meant pursuing independence from the Congress-dominated Indian government, and the Congress leadership who found common cause with the National Conference representing the states' subjects as they pushed for a representative form of government that recognized the sovereignty of the Indian government. The struggles over Jammu and Kashmir's political status following the transfer of power ultimately led to the outbreak of violence. Unlike other former princely states, however, political tensions over Jammu and Kashmir's status after its accession to India were complicated by the tribal invasion in October 1947 and Pakistani claims to the princely state. These problems persisted given the unique constitutional status of the state within India, the division of its territory between India and Pakistan and continued international political pressure.

Notes

1 William Moorcraft and George Trebeck, *Travels in the Himalayan Provinces of Hindustan and the Panjab; in Ladakh and Kashmir; In Peshawar, Kabul, Kunduz, and Bokhara; From 1819 to 1825, Volume II* (London: John Murray, 1841), pp. 123–4, 248.

2 NAI, File No. 330, PR_000005002174, Brief History of the Kashmir State, Foreign Department, Government of India, 1904, p. 3.

3 Peter Hopkirk, *The Great Game: On Secret Service in High Asia* (London: John Murray, 1990).

4 NAI, File No. 1921_JUL_48, PR_000003000124, Fortnightly Reports on the Internal Political Situation for the First Half of May 1919, Home Department, Government of India, May 1919, p. 36; NAI, File No. 1921_SEP_18, PR_000003000444, Fortnightly Reports on the Political Situation in India for

the First and Second Half of September 1921, Home Department, Government of India, September 1921, p. 64.

5 NAI, File No. 15/16, PR_000005002183, Petition from the representative of the Kashmiri Mussalmans regarding the employment of Mussalmans in the Kashmir State, Foreign Department, Government of India, January 1909; NAI, File No. F-10-28, PR_000003032909, Disturbances in Srinagar and Marching of Muslims Jathas in Kashmir Territory to Secure Redress of the Alleged Grievances of Their Co-Religionists in the State, Home Department, Government of India, 1931, pp. 58, 80, 98.

6 Rai, *Hindu Rulers, Muslim Subjects,* p. 255; Prem Nath Azaz, *The History of the Struggle for Freedom in Kashmir* (New Delhi: Kashmir Publishing Company, 1954), pp. 124–5.

7 Guha, *India After Gandhi*, p. 75.

8 NAI, PP_000000005840, Kashmir very important (Miscellaneous paper on loose) in this File, Private Papers of Sardar Patel, 1947, p. 9.

9 NAI, File No. F-18-9_32, PR_00000303369, Fortnightly Reports on the Internal Political Situation for the Month of June 1932, Home Department, Government of India, 1932, p. 67; Rai, *Hindu Rulers, Muslim Subjects,* p. 271.

10 To this day, Kashmiris observe 13 July as Martyrs' Day. Luv Puri, *Across the Line of Control: Inside Pakistan-Administered Kashmir* (New York: Columbia University Press, 2012), pp. 14–15.

11 NAI, File No. F-10-28, PR_000003032909, Disturbances in Srinagar and Marching of Muslims Jathas in Kashmir Territory to Secure Redress of the Alleged Grievances of Their Co-Religionists in the State, Home Department, Government of India, 1931, p. 11.

12 NAI, File No. 25_12, PR_000003010004, Report on the internal political situation in the provinces during the month of December 1923, Home Department, Government of India, December 1923, p. 24.

13 NAI, File No. F-10-28, PR_000003032909, Disturbances in Srinagar and Marching of Muslims Jathas in Kashmir Territory to Secure Redress of the Alleged Grievances of Their Co-Religionists in the State, Home Department, Government of India, 1931, p. 18.

14 NAI, File No. 557/P, PR_000004009887, Communal disturbances in Srinagar, Kashmir, Foreign and Political Department, Government of India, 1932, p. 19; NAI, File No. 325-P, PR_000004009886, Agitation by Pandits in Kashmir and release of Political Prisoners, Foreign and Political Department, Government of India, 1932, p. 11.

15 Rai, *Hindu Rulers, Muslim Subjects,* p. 227.

16 NAI, File No. F-18–3, PR_000003034237, Fortnightly Reports From Local Governments and Administrations on the Political Situation in India, for the Month of January 1934, Home Department, Government of India, 1934, p. 75.

17 Pandit Nehru to Rear-Admiral Viscount Mountbatten of Burma, 17 June 1947, *TOP Volume XI*, p. 443.

18 'Elect Sheikh Abdullah As the President: Nehru's Advice To States' People,' *Free Press Journal* (11 March 1947).

19 M.A. Jinnah to Archibald Wavell, 27 September 1945, *Jinnah Papers Volume IX*, p. 579.

20 NAI, File No. 15(4)-H-P/47, PR_000004001180, Viceroy's visit to Kashmir, Political Department, Government of India, 17 June 1947, pp. 7–8.

21 NAI, File No. F-18-16, PR_000003016367, Fortnightly Report Received from the Residents—From July to Dec 1945, Home Department, Government of India, 1945, p. 15.

22 NAI, File No. 15(4)-H-P/47, PR_000004001180, Viceroy's visit to Kashmir, Political Department, Government of India, 17 June 1947, p. 9.

23 A Note on Kashmir, 17 June 1947, *Jinnah Papers Volume IX*, p. 165.

24 NAI, File No. 15(4)-H-P/47, PR_000004001180, Viceroy's visit to Kashmir, Political Department, Government of India, 17 June 1947, p. 11.

25 NAI, File No. F-51-2, PR_000003017378, Political Situation Reports Supplied by I & B Department, Political Department, Government of India, 1946, p. 235.

26 NAI, File No. 15(4)-H-P/47, PR_000004001180, Viceroy's visit to Kashmir, Political Department, Government of India, 17 June 1947, pp. 12–13.

27 A Note on Kashmir, 17 June 1947, *Jinnah Papers Volume IX*, pp. 166–7.

28 Campbell-Johnson, *Mission with Mountbatten*, p. 140.

29 Record of Interview between Louis Mountbatten and Jawaharlal Nehru, 24 June 1947, *Jinnah Papers Volume IX*, pp. 168–9.

30 Vallabhbhai Patel to Maharaja of Kashmir, 3 July 1947, *Jinnah Papers Volume IX*, pp. 172–3.

31 NAI, PR_000004002000, Relationship between the Dominion of Pakistan & its neighboring States, brief for H.E., States Department, Government of India, 1947, p. 3.

32 Rear-Admiral Viscount Mountbatten of Burma to Mr. Gandhi, 12 July 1947, *TOP Volume XII*, p. 78.

33 Congress Told to Keep Hands Off Kashmir, 18 July 1947, *Jinnah Papers Volume IX*, p. 182; Kashmir's Entry in Pakistan Demanded, 24 July 1947, *Jinnah Papers Volume IX*, p. 183.

34 Menon, *The Story of the Integration of the Indian States*, p. 395.

35 Press Statement by R.L. Batra, 10 October 1947, *Jinnah Papers Volume IX*, p. 243.

36 Note by All-Jammu & Kashmir Muslim Conference, 25 August 1947, *Jinnah Papers Volume IX*, p. 216.

37 Note by K.H. Khurshid, 12 October 1947, *Jinnah Papers Volume IX*, p. 248.

38 Note by All-Jammu & Kashmir Muslim Conference, 25 August 1947, *Jinnah Papers Volume V*, pp. 570–7.

39 Kashmir's Accession to Indian Dominion Regarded as a Foregone Conclusion, 14 October 1947, *Jinnah Papers Volume IX*, p. 255.

40 NAI, File No. 10(45)-K/48, PR_000004009586, Trail of Mr. Ram Chandra Kak ex. Prime Minister Jammu & Kashmir Government, Indian Ministry of States, 1948, p. 6.

41 Vallabhbhai Patel to Maharaja of Jammu & Kashmir, 21 September 1947, *Jinnah Papers Volume IX*, p. 227.

42 *Selected Works of Jawaharlal Nehru, Second Series, Volume 4* (New Delhi: Jawaharlal Nehru Memorial Fund, 1986), pp. 262–4.

43 NAI, PP_000000005840, Kashmir very important (Miscellaneous paper on loose) in this File, Private Papers of Sardar Patel, 1947, p. 79; Guha, *India After Gandhi*, p. 78.

44 'Plan to Make Kashmir Switzerland of East,' *Evening News* (13 October 1947).

45 NAI, PP_000000005095, Kashmir Junagadh & Hyderabad 27-09-49, Private Papers of Sardar Patel, 1949, p. 56.

46 Vallabhbhai Patel to Baldev Singh, 7 October 1947, *Jinnah Papers Volume IX*, p. 238; Vallabhbhai Patel to Jawaharlel Nehru, 8 October 1947, *Jinnah Papers Volume IX*, p. 240.

47 R.L. Batra to Vallabhbhai Patel, 17 October 1947, *Jinnah Papers Volume IX*, p. 262.

48 NAI, File No. F-25KW, PR_000003032281, Reports on the Internal Political Situation in India During the Month of August 1923, Home Department, Government of India, August 1923, p. 23.

49 NAI, File No. F-18-16, PR_000003016367, Fortnightly Report Received from the Residents—From July to Dec 1945, Home Department, Government of India, 1945, p. 239.

50 Puri, *Across the Line of Control*, p. 23.

51 Guha, *India After Gandhi*, p. 80.

52 NAI, File No. 11(8)-PR/47, PR_000004001178, Kashmir Affairs—Accession of Kashmir State to the Dominion of India, Indian Ministry of States, 1947, p. 1.

53 Ibid., p. 13.

54 Guha, *India After Gandhi*, p. 82.

55 Ibid.; Alastair Lamb, *Kashmir: A Disputed Legacy, 1846–1990* (Lahore: Oxford University Press, 1992), p. 143.

56 NAI, PP_000000005827, Correspondence with agent of the Govt. of India in Kashmir, Private Papers of Sardar Patel, 1947, pp. 3–4.

57 Clement Attlee to Liaquat Ali Khan, 27 October 1947, *Jinnah Papers Volume IX*, p. 291; Jawaharlal Nehru to Liaquat Ali Khan, 28 October 1947, *Jinnah Papers Volume IX*, p. 313.

58 National Archives, U.K., FO/371/63570, Transfer of power in India—relations of India with the United Kingdom (Folder 6), September–November 1947.

59 National Archives, U.K., DO/133/69, Political situation—Kashmir (Folder 2), November–December 1947.

60 Kashmir's Accession Based on Violence and Fraud, 31 October 1947, *Jinnah Papers Volume IX*, p. 322.

61 C.B. Duke to L. Grafftey-Smith, 29 October 1947, *Jinnah Papers Volume IX*, p. 328.

62 C.B. Duke to L. Grafftey-Smith, 3 November 1947, *Jinnah Papers Volume IX*, p. 360.

63 Mohamed Ali to Liaquat Ali Khan, 27 October 1947, *Jinnah Papers Volume IX*, pp. 291–2.
64 Liaquat Ali Khan to Clement Attlee, 29 October 1947, *Jinnah Papers Volume IX*, p. 318.
65 Maharaja of Kashmir to Louis Mountbatten, 26 October 1947, *Jinnah Papers Volume IX*, pp. 287–8.
66 Menon, *The Story of the Integration of the Indian States*, pp. 397–8.
67 Basu, *V.P. Menon*, p. 372.
68 Mehr Chand Mahajan, *Looking Back: The Autobiography of Mehr Chand Mahajan* (London: Asia Publishing House, 1963), p. 277.
69 Basu, *V.P. Menon*, p. 372.
70 Ibid., p. 373.
71 Menon, *The Story of the Integration of the Indian States*, pp. 399–400. There is some debate among historians about the historical accuracy of Menon's accounting of this event and its timing, with some conjecturing that the reported timing of the Maharaja signing the Instrument of Accession on 26 October was intended to ensure a historical narrative that has the Maharaja acceding to India prior to the deployment of Indian troops on 27 October. See Basu, *V.P. Menon*, pp. 374–6.
72 Guha, *India After Gandhi*, p. 83.
73 Maurice Cohen, *Thunder Over Kashmir* (Hyderabad: Orient Longman Limited, 1955), pp. 3–4.
74 Guha, *India After Gandhi*, p. 83; Madhav Khosla (ed.), *Letters for a Nation: From Jawaharlal Nehru to His Chief Ministers, 1947–1963* (New Delhi: Penguin Books, 2014), p. 217.
75 Howard Donovan to George Marshall, 4 November 1947, *Jinnah Papers Volume IX*, p. 354.
76 Claude Auchinleck to Chiefs of Staff, London, 28 October 1947, *Jinnah Papers Volume IX*, p. 314; Guha, *India After Gandhi*, p. 84.
77 Liaquat Ali Khan to Jawaharlal Nehru, 30 October 1947, *Jinnah Papers Volume IX*, p. 330.
78 Liaquat Ali Khan to Clement Attlee, 30 October 1947, *Jinnah Papers Volume IX*, p. 331.
79 Minutes of 10th Meeting of Defence Committee, 30 October 1947, *Jinnah Papers Volume VIII*, p. 371.
80 NAI, File No. 11(8)-PR/47, PR_000004001178, Kashmir Affairs—Accession of Kashmir State to the Dominion of India, Indian Ministry of States, 1947, p. 34.
81 Guha, *India After Gandhi*, pp. 84–5.
82 Note of a Discussion with Mr. Jinnah in Presence of Lord Ismay at Government House, Lahore, 1 November 1947, *Jinnah Papers Volume IX*, pp. 349, 351.
83 'Swat Tribesmen Attack Gilgit, Kashmir Troops Withdraw,' *Hindustan Times* (8 November 1947); Yaqoob Khan Bangash, 'Three Forgotten Accessions: Gilgit, Hunza, and Nagar,' *Journal of Imperial and Commonwealth History* 38:1 (2010), 117–43.

84 *Sardar Patel's Correspondence, 1945–50, Volume 1* (New Delhi: Navajivan Publishing House, 1971), pp. 103–4.
85 Ibid., p. 103.
86 Report of Security Council on Jammu and Kashmir Question, 1948, *Jinnah Papers Volume IX*, p. 486.
87 Guha, *India After Gandhi*, p. 87.
88 NAI, PP_000000006624, Correspondence Gandhiji, Pyarelal Bihar & Cabinet Mission, Private Papers of Sardar Patel, 1950, p. 276.
89 Menon, *The Story of the Integration of the Indian States*, p. 409.
90 Security Council Resolution 47, 21 April 1948, *Jinnah Papers Volume IX*, pp. 511–13.
91 NAI, File No. KS-53/48, PR_000004001185, Kashmir issue—Discussions in the security council regarding plebiscite, Indian Ministry of States, 1948, pp. 74, 76, 80–1, 83.
92 Aman M. Hingorani, *Unravelling the Kashmir Knot* (New Delhi: Sage Publications, 2016), p. 95.
93 NAI, File No. KS-53/48, PR_000004001185, Kashmir issue—Discussions in the security council regarding plebiscite, Indian Ministry of States, 1948, p. 102.
94 Josef Korbel, *Danger in Kashmir* (Princeton, NJ: Princeton University Press, 1954), pp. 146–7.
95 Guha, *India After Gandhi*, pp. 91–2.
96 Korbel, *Danger in Kashmir*, pp. 146–7.
97 NAI, File No. 11(8)-K/52, PR_000005002320, Compensation for lands taken over under the Big Landed Estates Abolition Act, Indian Ministry of States, 1952, p. 1.
98 NAI, File No. 1(4)-K/48, PR_000004009585, Formation of Jammu and Kashmir State Militia. Administration arrangements and question of the incidence of cost of this Militia, Indian Ministry of States, 1948, pp. 3–4.
99 The Ambassador in India (Henderson) to the Secretary of State, 29 September 1950, *FRUS, 1950, Volume V*, p. 1434.
100 Guha, *India After Gandhi*, p. 252.
101 NAI, PP_000000005829, Kashmir (Correspondence with H.H.S. Pandit Prime Minister & Janak singh Chief Minister & his cabinet), Private Papers of Sardar Patel, October 1950, pp. 10–1.
102 Khosla, *Letters for a Nation*, pp. 225–8.
103 Guha, *India After Gandhi*, p. 253.
104 NAI, File No. 8(6)-K/51, PR_000004008617, Reports re: Praja Parishad and Hindu and Sikh parties in Jammu Kashmir State, Indian Ministry of States, 1951, pp. 11, 24.
105 NAI, File No. 8(3)-K/52, PR_000004008618, Intelligence Reports regarding Praja Parishad Hindu and Sikh parties in Jammu and Kashmir States, Indian Ministry of States, 1952, pp. 15, 18, 36, 40, 44, 139.
106 NAI, File No. 8(25), PR_000004008992, Intelligence Reports reg. election to Constituent Assembly in Jammu Kashmir, Indian Ministry of States, 1951, pp. 40–1

107 Ibid., pp. 77, 89; NAI, File No. 8(6)-K/51, PR_000004008617, Reports re: Praja Parishad and Hindu and Sikh parties in Jammu Kashmir State, Indian Ministry of States, 1951, pp. 119, 143.

108 NAI, File No. 8(12)-K/51, PR_000004009487, Reports reg. Muslim affairs in Jammu and Kashmir State, Indian Ministry of States, 1951, p. 45.

109 National Archives, U.K., DO/134/16, Abolition of hereditary rule in Kashmir, position of Sheikh Abdullah, termination of cease-fire agreement, 1952.

110 The Delhi Agreement, 1952, accessed at: www.satp.org/satporgtp/countries/india/states/jandk/documents/papers/delhi_agreement_1952.htm [accessed 20 December 2022].

111 NAI, File No. 8(2)-K/53, PR_000004009589, Intelligence Report on National Conference in J & K State, Indian Ministry of States, 1953, pp. 1, 5.

112 Guha, *India After Gandhi*, p. 258.

113 NAI, File No. VI/6/169, PR_000005002419, Praja Parishad Agitation in Jammu, Indian Ministry of Information and Broadcasting, 1953, p. 7.

114 Guha, *India After Gandhi*, p. 262.

115 Khosla, *Letters for a Nation*, p. 231.

116 NAI, File No. P.III/53/99152/107, PR_000005003245, Instructions to Indian mission abroad regarding attitude to be adopted about the developments in Kashmir following Sheikh Abdullah's dismissal and arrest, Indian Ministry of External Affairs, 1953, p. 1.

117 Khosla, *Letters for a Nation*, pp. 229–30.

118 Guha, *India After Gandhi*, p. 263.

119 Korbel, *Danger in Kashmir*, p. 25.

7

Hyderabad: The Nizam's gambit

Alongside Jammu and Kashmir, the princely state of Hyderabad would pose one of the most serious challenges to the early territorial and political integrity of the Indian Union. Hyderabad stretched over 83,000 square miles across the Deccan Plateau of central India and served as a vital geographical and cultural link between the north and south. It had a population of over sixteen million people with a largely self-sufficient, exporting economy (though reliant on fuel imports from British India), all of which contributed to the belief of Hyderabad's autocratic ruler, known as the Nizam, that the state had the ability to maintain an independent existence after the lapse of paramountcy. Not only would this fly in the face of the Indian government's sovereign claims, but, with Hyderabad's strategic position, India's political leadership feared that allowing the princely state to assert its independence would sever the link between northern and southern India. This would further open the possibility of an independent Hyderabad allying itself with governments hostile to India, such as Pakistan, and weaken the overall internal security of the country. Patel described such a scenario as a 'cancer in the belly of India.'[1]

Following the transfer of power, the Nizam, backed by the Islamic group Majlis-e-Ittihad-ul-Muslimeen, refused to sign the Instrument of Accession in a bid to preserve his sovereignty in the face of opposition from both the Indian government and many of his subjects, including the Hyderabad State Congress. For just over a year, the princely state remained essentially an independent state in the heart of India. Despite the prolonged negotiations, New Delhi and Hyderabad were unable to find a compromise over their competing conceptions of state sovereignty. In September 1948, as law and order deteriorated within the princely state, the Indian government finally resorted to force to resolve the dispute, launching a military invasion of the state known as Operation Polo that secured control of the state and overthrew the Nizam's rule within a span of only four days. By the following year, Hyderabad was fully integrated into the Indian Union, ending over two centuries of princely rule.

Map 7.1 Map of Hyderabad (in black) in British India

Given its size, wealth and status, Hyderabad held a unique position among India's princely states, with one British official referring to the state as 'a living fragment of Moghul grandeur.'[2] Its roots date back to 1712 when the Asaf Jahi dynasty was established as a vassal state of the Mughal Empire. Beginning in 1759, its rulers signed a series of primarily military and mutual defense treaties with the East India Company; the first British Resident was appointed in 1779. In an 1803 treaty, the British provided guarantees for the recognition of Hyderabad's sovereignty. In return, the Nizam promised his loyalty to the British cause. During the 1857 uprising, the princely state did not offer any support to the rebelling sepoys, a position which earned the Nizam at the time the hereditary moniker 'Faithful Ally' from the British government. The princely state would again offer its support to the British war effort during the First World War by contributing around one hundred million dollars in cash and supplies and deploying Hyderabadi army units. At the request of the British, Hyderabad's government also issued a formal proclamation against the Ottoman sultan's November 1914 fatwa calling for a holy war against the United Kingdom and its allies, and urged his fellow Muslims to fight for the Allied forces. In the years before independence, Hyderabad was looked on as the main pillar of Islam in India, with British authorities seeking to cultivate the Nizam's continued support.[3]

In the final years of the British Raj, Hyderabad was also noteworthy for the personal wealth and character of its seventh and final Nizam, Mir Osman Ali Khan, who ascended to the throne in 1911 at the age of 25. In February 1937, a portrait of Mir Osman was featured on the cover of *Time* magazine with the tagline 'The richest man in the world.'[4] The Nizam, whose palace was called 'a show piece of the world,' earned 25 million rupees annually from his lands, plus another 5 million from the state treasury.[5] In addition to his yearly income, his jewels alone had an estimated value of $150 million, with his total capital wealth adding up to over $1.4 billion. He was even reported to have used the 185-carat Jacob diamond, the fifth largest polished diamond in the world with an estimated value today of over $120 million, as a paperweight.[6] Despite his immense wealth and his contributions to public causes, the Nizam was known as a miserly figure who rarely wore new clothes, drove an 'old, rattling, and tin-pot of a car' and once reportedly refused to pay six cents for a scoop of ice cream, rebuking the vendor for charging such a high price.[7] A 1933 issue of *John Bull* magazine referred to the Nizam as the 'Richest Miser in the World,' which caused 'very considerable excitement' in Hyderabad's court at the time.[8] While Mir Osman's personal penny-pinching was the butt of many a joke, his autocratic rule was the source of serious tensions with Hyderabad's largely Hindu subjects.

Hyderabad and the nationalist movement

Hyderabad was the mirror image of Jammu and Kashmir. While the princely state was 85 percent Hindu, it was ruled by a Muslim nizam, who owned 10 percent of the state's land with the rest predominately owned by largely Muslim landowners. Muslims were likewise dominant within the state's army, police and civil service. Much like Jammu and Kashmir's Muslim population, Hyderabad's largely Hindu population had been clamoring for increased civil rights during the early twentieth century, with political agitation within the princely state increasingly framed around the divide between Hindus and Muslims given the Muslim population's association with political power. In the mid-1920s, amid increasing political tensions between the Hindu and Muslim populations, a State Reforms Association with a largely Hindu membership was established to press for various political reforms, including the reorganization of the Nizam's Legislative Council to include a larger Hindu representation.[9] Hindu organizations complained that, despite comprising over 85 percent of the state's population, they were systematically excluded from government service, occupying only 5 percent of government posts at the time. However, the Hyderabadi officials dismissed such calls as merely attempts by outside groups to 'stir up communal feeling' that could undermine the Nizam's government, especially the Indian National Congress with the Nizam opposing Congress leaders visiting the state.[10] By the early 1930s, the status of Hyderabad's Hindu population increasingly drew the criticism of outside political groups, such as the All-India Hindu Mahasabha which highlighted various discriminations against Hyderabad's Hindu population, including restrictions on religious practices, lack of educational opportunities, lack of representation in state services and economic discrimination.[11] In 1937, the Hindu Mahasabha appointed a committee to inquire into various grievances over the treatment of Hyderabad's Hindus.[12]

During the 1930s, civil society organizations within Hyderabad increasingly played a more active role in bringing political pressure on the Nizam's government to enact various reforms and help to shape key political debates.[13] In 1938, shortly after the Indian National Congress passed the Haripura Resolution, the Hyderabad State Congress was established under the leadership of Swami Ramananda Tirtha to pursue a representative government or 'People's raj' within the princely state. The group stressed its secular credentials and made appeals to both Hindus and Muslims, but its ranks were largely filled by Hindus. The Hyderabad State Congress soon launched a satyagraha against the Nizam's rule. However, only a few months after its formation, the state government introduced a new public safety law that effectively banned the organization, with the government arresting a number of the group's members over their protest activities. The government ban on the group remained in effect until 1946, after which the State Congress became a leading voice in advocating for Hyderabad's full integration into the Indian Union and the democratization of the state in the lead up to the transfer of power.

In the late 1930s and 1940s, the Nizam announced various reforms to appease the growing political agitation against his rule. However, anti-government groups within the state saw them as largely aimed at further bolstering and legitimizing the Nizam's political authority. They argued that they did not lead to any measure of responsible government and continued to bias Muslims as the dominant population within the state administration. This included reserving 50 percent of the seats in the state legislature for Muslims, despite comprising a minority of the state's population. In August 1946, the Hyderabad State Congress announced its rejection of the reforms and passed a resolution asserting that the plan embodied neither responsible government nor civil liberties. The resolution read: 'It is based on the functional representation of vested interests, and the invidious and undemocratic principle of communal parity which converts a minority of 12% into an effective majority.'[14] The Hyderabad State Hindu Sabha also criticized the reforms scheme as 'reactionary, undemocratic, and anti-Hindu.' In particular, the group demanded the removal of the phrase 'Muslim state' to describe Hyderabad in the Nizam's firman, or administrative order, given the state's Hindu majority.[15]

Political groups were not only active in opposition to the Nizam but also in support of his continued rule and the favored position of Muslims within the state government. The pro-Nizam Majlis-e-Ittihad-ul-Muslimeen was formed as an Islamic cultural organization on 12 November 1927. It was originally intended to promote the social and educational advancement of Muslims within the state. In 1938, Bahadur Yar Jung, who spearheaded the formation of the All-India States Muslim League, was elected as its president, and increasingly politicized the group's activities. He used the Ittihad as a vehicle to advocate for Hyderabad's independence, the restoration of the state's lost territories (such as the territory of Berar, which had been leased to the British government in 1853) and protecting the political dominance of Muslims within Hyderabad's administration. By the late 1930s, Jung made no effort to conceal his farsighted plan to increase the state's Muslim population in preparation for a time when Hyderabad was a federal unit surrounded by predominantly Hindu provinces.[16] British officials feared his many fiery speeches and overt political activities exacerbated communal tensions. In response, the Hyderabad government placed a ban on his public speeches, which drew the personal intervention of Jinnah in support of Jung.[17] Upon Jung's death in 1944, Kasim Razvi, a lawyer from Osmanabad, was elected as the new leader of the group. He soon launched the organization in a more radical direction.

The combination of the Hyderabad State Congress, a more activist Ittihad and the emergence of a communist revolt in Telangana made for a volatile political environment through 1946 and 1947. The Hyderabad State Congress increased its political agitation as independence crept closer in a bid to increase the political pressure on the Nizam to accede to the Indian Union and introduce political reforms favoring their position. The group's leaders remained under constant threat of arrest and fled to organize its activities from outside the state. However, its efforts were matched by the pro-Nizam Ittihad under Razvi, who increasingly promoted the Ittihad's paramilitary body the Razakars; the group's members were known to march through the state's urban streets brandishing swords and firearms.

In rural, Telugu-speaking areas, communists also led an increasingly widespread insurrection in which large estates were occupied and the land redistributed to local peasants. In over a thousand villages across several districts, the communist movement had effectively established a parallel local government.[18]

Amid this internal turmoil, the Nizam remained disengaged from broader Indian politics as debates raged in New Delhi and London about India's constitutional future and the position of the princely states. He decided to wait and see what the ultimate outcome would be before committing Hyderabad to any path. In particular, Hyderabad's leadership was wary of Congress and the populist direction they would take the government of an independent India. In general, the Nizam and other senior Hyderabadi officials maintained that the Indian nationalist leaders, under the influence of Nehru, viewed the princely states as merely 'an inconvenient and anachronistic heritage to be pressed or cajoled, whether they wish it or not, into the pattern which British India has chosen—a pattern which no one would regard as ideal for themselves, much less for any one else.'[19]

On 11 June 1947, the Nizam issued a firman in response to the Viceroy's 3 June announcement that British India would be partitioned along communal lines. In it, he announced his decision not to send representatives of Hyderabad to either Pakistan's or India's Constituent Assemblies, explaining that he regarded the Muslims and Hindus as 'two eyes of the State and the State itself to be the indivisible asset of all the communities inhabiting it.' With the lapse of paramountcy, he asserted his legal right, as outlined within British policy, to resume the independent status of a sovereign state, while stressing that he intended to maintain friendly relations with both successor governments. He concluded: 'In these rapid changes, I am satisfied that the course of political wisdom lies in not taking sides, in concentrating on the maintenance of the integrity of my dominions and in fostering the welfare of my people. The achievement of that object depends upon the continuance of mutual goodwill between the two communities in my State and, in the unsettled conditions all around, upon ensuring for all my subjects the benefits of peace and security.'[20]

The Ittihad supported the Nizam's position. It sought primarily to maintain the privileged position of Muslims within the existing state administration, which they felt would be difficult to do under a democratic system given the state's Hindu majority. The Ittihad further laid blame for any maladministration within the Nizam's government on British interference and pushed for the recognition of Hyderabad's independent status. Bolstered by such internal support, the Nizam requested British authorities to return the Berar territory (which was denied) and to continue Hyderabad's direct relationship with the British Crown following the lapse of paramountcy, with continued recognition of the princely state's sovereignty and the granting of dominion status within the British Commonwealth. Yet, when he was made aware from press reports of Clause 7 of the Indian Independence Act, which abrogated all treaties, agreements and obligations with the princely states, he wrote straight away to Mountbatten in protest. He argued that this clause had not been discussed with him or any other representative of his state. The Nizam felt as though Hyderabad was 'being abandoned by its old ally, the British Government, and the ties which have bound me in loyal devotion to the King Emperor are being severed.'[21]

On 11 July 1947, the Viceroy met with a delegation from Hyderabad and explained that the British government was unable to grant the state dominion status. Given the fact that it was surrounded by Indian territory, Mountbatten informed the delegation that the British government would be unable to fulfill the defense commitments that dominion status carried. To remain a part of the Commonwealth, he stressed that Hyderabad must accede to either India or Pakistan. Mountbatten, of course, reiterated the difficulties that accession to Pakistan would create, especially in the event of any disputes between the two countries, and, therefore, he argued that the Nizam should consider signing the Instrument of Accession for India. Despite remaining somewhat pessimistic about the Nizam coming around, the Viceroy hoped that successfully convincing the Nizam to accede to India would set a precedent that no other prince, not even the most intransigent ones, could resist.[22]

On 28 July, Sir Walter Monckton, a noted British lawyer whose clients included former King Edward VIII during his abdication in 1936 and who the Nizam hired to represent Hyderabad to British authorities, wrote to Mountbatten that, after lengthy discussions on the topic, the Nizam had definitively decided not to sign the Instrument of Accession for India and remained committed to preserving his sovereignty through the establishment of an independent state. Monckton was confident that 'nothing—not even a visit by you—has the smallest hope of modifying this attitude.' Nevertheless, the Nizam's counsel felt that Hyderabad's association with the Indian Union in some form was inevitable and in the interests of both, even if it only took the form of a treaty relationship. Yet, he warned the Viceroy that such a relationship 'can't be rushed.'[23] That same day, Mountbatten's private secretary Sir George Abell remarked, 'I am afraid this means that there is now little chance of getting in Hyderabad.' The ever optimistic and self-assured Mountbatten retorted, 'Still a chance.'[24] Mountbatten even secured for the Nizam a two-month extension to the deadline for signing the Instrument of Accession, hoping the extra time for negotiations would allow Hyderabadi and Indian officials to resolve their differences.[25]

However, the Nizam refused to compromise, with Mountbatten referring to Hyderabad as his 'biggest headache.'[26]

Azad Hyderabad, August 1947–September 1948

As the date of the transfer of power passed, the Nizam of Hyderabad continued to refuse to sign the Instrument of Accession for India. As a result, Hyderabad effectively became an independent state surrounded by Indian territory—a status it would hold until September 1948. To express their continued opposition to the Nizam's actions, Hyderabad State Congress workers ushered in India's Independence Day by raising the Indian tricolor flag in different parts of the state. Hyderabadi authorities promptly arrested those responsible and declared the ceremonial hoisting of the Indian Union flag or the flag of any foreign state as punishable by three years' imprisonment. The Indian flag was only permitted to be raised over buildings still under control of the Indian government, such as post and telegraph offices, and only if the Nizam's flag was flown as well.[27] The Ittihad, on the other hand, doubled down on their support for the Nizam and his commitment to independence, distributing handbills reading 'Free Hyderabad for the Hyderabadis' and 'No pact with the Indian Union.'[28]

In the days that followed, celebrations of Hyderabad's independence were mixed with reports of various disturbances and shootings, in which a dozen were killed and at least a hundred more injured. The worst problems emerged in Secunderabad where communal tensions were high.[29] On several occasions, the police opened fire on gathered mobs to force them to disperse.[30] Amid worsening communal tensions, there were also reports of widespread looting and general lawlessness that further contributed to an overall panic within the state. One resident observed that heavily armed members from the state security forces 'used to go in procession through the streets, either on foot or on lorries shooting into the air.' Many people fled their homes, with portions of Hyderabad city quickly becoming 'like a city of the dead.'[31]

In an attempt to calm the situation, the Nizam announced several political reforms, such as increasing the number of public members of the Executive Council and investing the Legislative Assembly with additional powers to 'associate my people of all classes and creeds with my Government.'[32] By late November 1947, the Nizam also dissolved his Council of Ministers and established an interim government, consisting of four nominated members, four Muslim members and four Hindu members. The Nizam's reforms ultimately had little positive impact on calming the political agitation, with his critics calling them merely 'an eye-wash.'[33] The President of the Hyderabad

State Congress argued that these reforms were not nearly enough and, more importantly, failed to address the underlying autocracy of the Nizam. He instead pushed for a plebiscite to be held on the issue of accession and the establishment of representative government for the state. 'Unless the State Congress is satisfied on fundamentals,' he announced, 'it would be difficult to participate in the formation of an interim Government because that would not meet the exigencies of the situation obtaining at present.'[34] He added: 'The struggle of the State Congress is not going to be suspended or given up. Nothing short of accession to the Indian Union and establishment of responsible government will satisfy us.'[35]

In the face of growing internal and external opposition, the Nizam stuck to his guns. Patel met the Nizam's defiance with a resolve of his own. On 24 August 1947, he wrote to Mountbatten:

> I see no alternative but to insist on the Nizam's accession to the Dominion of India ... In these circumstances, I am convinced that it would neither be proper nor politic for us to agree to any arrangement other than the Instrument of Accession already settled between us and the other States ... If, however, the Nizam's Government are still unable to decide their course in the only right direction in which it lies, His Exalted Highness must agree to submit the issue to the judgment of his people and abide by their decision.[36]

The Nizam quickly rejected the possibility of any plebiscite as undermining his sovereign rule.[37] Menon tried a different approach. On 13 September, he met with Monckton and informed him that if Hyderabad acceded the Indian government would take a much more liberal position toward the trappings of the princely state's sovereignty, offering it access to a port and sharing the cost of a connecting railway, a continuation of existing currency and postage for the state and the ability to fly the Nizam's flag. However, when presented with Menon's proposal, the Nizam refused to even look at it and said, 'come what may I am not going to accede.'[38] Nearly two weeks later, Mountbatten reiterated Menon's offer, writing to the Nizam that, while the Indian government could not offer terms other than those provided to the remainder of the princely states, nevertheless they were 'prepared to go to any reasonable length to smooth away any difficulties which impede Your Exalted Highness' accession.'[39]

The negotiations were going nowhere as 'the same old arguments and the same old replies in regard to accession repeated *ad nauseam* [*sic*],' according to Menon.[40] With both sides refusing to budge, Mountbatten was getting a bit desperate for a path out of the impasse. In early October, he even recommended drawing up a document with no heading and an ambiguous opening absent the word accession; Monckton had earlier offered the phrase Article of Association to sugar-coat the document's purpose as the legal equivalent of accession. This document, Mountbatten argued, should be written on an expensive handwritten scroll in such a way that it would not be apparent that a heading was missing. In this way, he hoped that he could get both sides to sign the agreement. 'India could look upon it as Accession,' Mountbatten surmised, 'and Hyderabad upon it as Agreement.' The following day, Menon convinced a dismissive Patel to at least give this strategy a shot, which similarly failed to make any headway toward an agreement with the Nizam.[41]

By this point, the irreconcilable positions of the two sides were firmly established—a fundamental divide that no amount of bureaucratic or legal finessing would overcome. The Nizam's attitude hardened, and he would accept nothing less than Indian recognition of Hyderabad as a sovereign and independent state. The Nizam added that he would continue negotiations upon any basis short of accession but maintained his stance against signing the Instrument of Accession.[42] The Indian political leadership, on the other hand, would accept nothing less than Hyderabad's full accession to the Indian Union. New Delhi framed their opposition to the Hyderabadi government as a principled position against the autocracy of the princely states, unwanted legacies of the layered sovereignty of British rule. On 15 April 1948, Nehru explained: 'Our position has been and is that the people of Hyderabad cannot continue to live under an authoritarian and feudal regime, which is becoming increasingly violent and oppressive and which threatens the lives and property of the great majority of the population … It is manifest that Hyderabad cannot remain as it is, a feudal island in a democratic India. It is equally clear that both geographically and economically, it cannot cut itself adrift from India, nor can a small minority dominate over a large majority.'[43]

After much cajoling, Mountbatten was finally able to get Nehru and Patel to at least consider signing onto a standstill agreement with Hyderabad, but only if the document substantially contained the same terms as accession. In October, the Nizam sent a draft standstill agreement to Mountbatten, which Patel rejected straight away. The States Minister in particular objected to the document's provision that Hyderabad would manage its own foreign policy with diplomatic representation to the United Kingdom and other Commonwealth nations, an authority it had not even held under British rule and which flew in the face of the principles of accession and Indian sovereignty. When Menon met with Monckton in the early evening of 19 October to discuss the States Ministry's rejection of the draft standstill agreement, Monckton 'blew completely off the handle,' calling Patel's decision 'outrageous' and threatening to travel to London to 'expose the Government of India for their monstrous handling of this matter,' which 'had kept him out here for three months under false pretences.' But nothing

Menon said was able to calm Monckton down, and he stormed out of Government House.[44]

After Menon sent Monckton a message at once asking him to return, he arrived an hour later. Menon explained to a somewhat calmer Monckton that at no point did Patel or any other Indian official contemplate any step other than Hyderabad's complete accession. Hyderabad was landlocked and surrounded by Indian territory. Therefore, Menon explained, it was quite impossible for Hyderabad to manage its own foreign policy. This was quite unlike the situation in Jammu and Kashmir, he continued, which bordered both India and Pakistan. Monckton then waived off Menon's offer to meet Hyderabad's delegation the following day, stating, 'the later the better, for they were in such an upset condition after hearing Mr. Menon's news, that they would take some time to get back into an amenable frame of mind.'[45]

Nevertheless, upon his return to Hyderabad, Monckton secured the approval of the Executive Council, by a vote of six to three, for a draft of the standstill agreement provided by Menon that had been provisionally accepted by Nehru and Patel. The Nizam approved it on 25 October. Once word reached the Ittihad, however, they quickly acted to bring the negotiations to a halt. Around 3 a.m. in the morning of 27 October, an estimated twenty-five to thirty thousand Ittihad members, some armed with spears and swords, surrounded Shah Manzil, the house occupied by Hyderabad's negotiating committee, to protest its compromises on the standstill agreement and prevent the committee members from returning to New Delhi, as they were scheduled to depart later that day. The gathered mob demanded Hyderabad withdraw from any negotiations with New Delhi except those in pursuit of Indian recognition of the state's independence. The demonstrators shouted slogans such as 'Hyderabad shall remain independent' and 'We shall not be slaves.' Leaders of the mob informed Hyderabad's Prime Minister that they would not allow the negotiators to hand away the state's future to India. Instead, the government needed to provide assurances that Hyderabad would remain independent. 'If you want to go to Delhi to sign the agreement,' they warned, 'you will have to do it over our corpses.' After a very tense two hours, the delegation finally reached military authorities who had to send an army truck to evacuate them.[46]

Ittihad's leadership continued to criticize the negotiation committee for not taking 'a sufficiently firm and intransigent stand' in its negotiations with the Indian government. During a public meeting later that day, with some twenty thousand people present, Razvi stated of the head of the delegation that the 'strings attached to his nose are in Patel's hands.' He stressed that if he were prime minister he would have 'every member of that body shot' and added that Muslims in the state must now be prepared for any sacrifices as the Ittihad launched a direct-action campaign.[47] Around this time, the Ittihad even sent a delegation to meet with Jinnah in Karachi and beg for Pakistani intervention to ensure that the Nizam did not accede to India. Jinnah, then struggling with compounding problems in Jammu and Kashmir, remained aloof to these overtures. He explained that it was 'only a question for the Nizam and his own Government to decide.'[48] By the end of November, Razvi denounced Jinnah, accusing him of dangling false hope while showing utter disregard to the lives of Hyderabad's Muslims. Pointing to the military threat from India, the Ittihad leader urged his followers to prepare to become martyrs rather than submit to Mountbatten and Patel, predicting that Hyderabad would become 'another Karbala battlefield very shortly.'[49]

During subsequent meetings with the negotiating committee, the Nizam was firm—even described as 'violent'—in his denunciations of Razvi and the Ittihad. In private conversations and correspondences with Mountbatten, the Nizam had always been quick to stress the distance between himself and the Ittihad, referring to Razvi in a 1 September 1947 letter as a 'stupid person who is a man of low station' and 'somewhat demented' whose actions are done 'in a blind and thoughtless manner often causing complications.'[50] Monckton suspected the Nizam was playing both sides of the issue, criticizing the Razvi and the Ittihad to Indian authorities while simultaneously encouraging their actions within Hyderabad. Despite the Nizam's denunciations, he called in Razvi to join a discussion with the committee to have him explain his position, only a day after he had publicly vilified its members. The Ittihad leader stated, 'If Your Exalted Highness sign this Standstill Agreement, it will mean the death of Hyderabad.' He asked the Nizam to dissolve the existing Negotiating Committee and allow him to form a new one. He felt he could succeed where the present committee had failed, especially with India preoccupied with problems elsewhere, such as Jammu and Kashmir. Therefore, Indian officials would be in 'no position to do anything to us or refuse our demands if we insist.'[51]

After much hesitation and 'against his better judgment,' the Nizam decided 'to bow, at least temporarily, to the storm' and acquiesced to Razvi's demands. With the Nizam now backing the Ittihad, the members of the state's Negotiating Committee immediately resigned. Monckton also informed the Nizam that he could not work under these conditions and would return to England at once as 'a course is being taken of which I thoroughly and heartily disapprove'—though after his departure from Hyderabad he was convinced to return to South Asia and continued to represent Hyderabad's interests from Karachi and New Delhi. The Prime Minister, the Nawab of Chhatari, also resigned his position. In his place, the Nizam appointed Mir Laik Ali, an engineer by training and a leading Muslim industrialist in the state who had recently served as one of Pakistan's representative to the UN, on 30 November 1947 for a period of one year; his primary task was to set up a new interim government.[52] As the barrister Sir Sultan Ahmed, another member of the Negotiating Committee, departed Hyderabad following his resignation, his final words to the Nizam were, 'This will be the end of you, and your money.'[53]

By the end of October, the Nizam dispatched a new, three-member Negotiating Committee to New Delhi. Its members included Abdur Rahim and Moin Nawaz Jung (Mir Laik Ali's brother-in-law), both ministers in the Nizam's government and prominent supporters of the Ittihad movement. From Bombay, Monckton sent Mountbatten his assessment of Hyderabad's new negotiating team, souring Mountbatten's views of its members before the next round of negotiations had even begun. Rahim he 'need not describe, and cannot in printable language.' While he saw Jung as 'the ablest of the three,' the Hyderabadi official had 'given himself up entirely to the *Ittehad* [*sic*] doctrines and is much too small fry for negotiations on this level. In your shoes I should not be wasting much time with him.' As for the third member of the committee, Pingle Venkat Rama Reddy was 'a bag of lard incapable of understanding or speaking English'; he doubted he would even show up. If he did, Monckton asserted that 'he is fortunately unable to speak or understand any language intelligible to you.' Monckton further expressed his hopes that the negotiations would fail and would do so quickly, as the political control of an 'extremist minority' was no basis for a proper government.[54]

In their first meeting with an exasperated Mountbatten in the afternoon of 2 November at Government House in New Delhi, Moin Nawaz Jung communicated the Nizam's continued commitment to independence for Hyderabad. He pointed to both the Cabinet Mission's May 1946 statement and the plan for Partition as granting the princely states the right to accede to either dominion government or to stand aloof from accession and enter into suitable political arrangements with each government as an independent state, an interpretation of British policy advocated by Corfield prior to his departure from India.[55] After much wrangling and 'tortuous' discussions with the negotiating committee over the next month, with a short break so Mountbatten could attend the wedding of then Princess Elizabeth to his nephew Prince Philip in London, the Nizam finally agreed to an amended standstill agreement on 26 November 1947. He signed it three days later. This helped to calm the situation somewhat with many Hyderabad residents who had fled to neighboring provinces returning home by early 1948.[56] While speaking in the Indian parliament to cheers from its members, Patel stressed that this agreement made it quite clear that Hyderabad had no intention of acceding to Pakistan and demonstrated that Hyderabad's destiny was 'inextricably bound up with that of India.'[57] However, the standstill agreement was only to be in effect for a period of one year, with the Nizam asserting to Mountbatten that the agreement would in no way permanently prejudice his sovereign rights.[58] Both sides, however, hoped that this would offer each more time to find a path to their desired outcome: for the Nizam, independence, and, for New Delhi, accession.

Far from helping to allay suspicions on both sides, relations between India and Hyderabad only grew more strained under the auspices of the standstill agreement. Four months after signing the agreement, Menon accused the Hyderabad government of failing to carry out its obligations. These included offering a twenty-crore loan to the Pakistani government, appointing a public relations officer in Pakistan (who was recalled), making cash transactions with Indian rupees illegal within the state, increasing the strength of the Hyderabad army without the approval of the Indian government and having the state's security forces working collaboratively with the Razakars. Menon pressed the state government to ban the Ittihad and Razakars, return the state forces to its 15 August 1947 strength, repeal the ban on the use of Indian currency and fully withdraw any loans to Pakistan.[59]

The Nizam interpreted these accusations as 'an ultimatum to be regarded as a prelude to an open breach of friendly relations.' Two weeks later, the Hyderabadi Prime Minister, Mir Laik Ali, wrote to Nehru explaining that the state government had performed all its obligations under the standstill agreement 'as they understand them' and refused to ban the Ittihad and the Razakars. He then accused India of in fact violating the agreement through expanding its economic blockade of the state and increasing troop concentrations along Hyderabad's border.[60] At the same time, understanding the sensitives of Indian relations with Pakistan, the Nizam, who personally hated Jinnah, was at pains to assure New Delhi that Hyderabad was 'not a nest of Pakistan in India nor a possible source of danger to your Dominion,' including promising not to go through with his planned loan to Pakistan during the life of the standstill agreement.[61] Even with such assurances, many within New Delhi continued to perceive Hyderabad as a 'Pakistan island' in the heart of India.[62]

Senior officials in New Delhi increasingly saw the Hyderabad government as representing the interests of, and dominated by, the hardline Ittihad, and the group's leader Kasim Razvi as 'the man who really makes policy in Hyderabad.'[63] As law and order broke down amid the Ittihad's direct-action campaign, Razvi emerged as the de facto head of the state administration. Eyewitnesses reported seeing him roaming the streets taking salutes from police officers and giving them instructions as they worked hand in hand with the Razakars. At this time, Bombay's Deputy Inspector of Police received a report that the Hyderabad government had issued secret orders to the police to aid the members of the Ittihad 'when and if required.'[64] With the police working with the Razakar forces, a prominent Andhra leader in the state, K. Venkatappayya, joined the chorus of voices pressing for Indian intervention in the state, explaining that conditions in Hyderabad were like those prevailing in Junagadh and Jammu and Kashmir.[65]

The deteriorating security conditions largely impacted the Hindu population; Hindu shops were looted or burned, and Hindus attacked, often with the complicity of the police. There were reports circulating in the media of gunrunning into the state in preparation for the widespread massacre of the Hindu population.[66] The Ittihad had even made a call for Muslim refugees in India to come to Hyderabad for shelter, with the purpose of displacing Hindus and driving them out of the state. In Secunderabad, Muslim landlords were already forcing Hindu tenants out of their homes to provide shelter for the anticipated arrival of these refugees. After the 27 October demonstrations, over one hundred thousand Hindus fled the state within a span of only nine days.[67]

Patel argued that the Ittihad created 'a feeling of terror amongst the non-Muslim population, so that its agitation in favour of the independence of Hyderabad with possible alliance with Pakistan should flourish.' While Mountbatten pushed for continuing negotiations with the Nizam, Patel warned that, under the influence of Razvi, Hyderabad would use any additional time for negotiations to continue to instead prepare for open conflict.[68] It was Patel's view that the Nizam had 'mortgaged his future to his own Frankenstein.'[69] The Indian government continued to press the Hyderabad delegation to control the actions of Razvi and the Razakars and limit their influence by appointing government officials who opposed the Ittihad, alongside efforts to convince the Nizam to release political prisoners and establish a popularly elected Constituent Assembly within the state.[70] After meeting with Razvi in New Delhi in November 1947, Menon observed, 'The moment he started talking I could see that his was a fanaticism bordering on frenzy.' While Menon pressed the Indian government's case during the meeting, Razvi replied that if India insisted on a plebiscite 'the final arbiter could only be the sword.'[71]

With the two sides still at loggerheads, the Nizam continued to bristle at any perceived interference into Hyderabad's internal political matters, including any suggestions related to changes or nominations of key personnel within his government.[72] Laik Ali even defended the actions of Razakars to Mountbatten, arguing that the organization had been formed due to the apprehensions of many Hyderabadi Muslims that their lives were otherwise in danger and needed protection.[73] With Muslim dominance so closely aligned with the Nizam's rule, the Ittihad and Razakars framed their struggle through a communal clash and fed off of the broader communal conflict engendered by Partition. Even before independence, there were concerns within the state that the Indian National Congress' push for democratic governance was simply a means of pushing Hindu interests in the state as Hindus formed an electoral majority.

In early May 1948, Mountbatten, who would shortly be leaving the post of Governor General, invited the Nizam to stay with him at Government House in New Delhi for 'friendly informal conversation.' He optimistically felt that it would be possible for the two of them to sort 'all the misunderstandings and difficulties of the past months' if only given the opportunity to chat one on one. The Nizam refused this offer.[74] Mountbatten then dispatched his trusted press attaché Alan Campbell-Johnson on a three-day mission to Hyderabad for the purpose of gaining 'a personal up-to-date impression of the situation and if possible inducing a sufficient sense of urgency in the Nizam and his advisers for them to reopen negotiations and in general make the best use of Mountbatten's last few weeks here.' Just before his departure, Hyderabad's representative in New Delhi, Zain Yar Jung, stressed, 'If only the Government of India would not press too hard all would be well.'[75]

Upon his arrival in Hyderabad's capital on 15 May, Campbell-Johnson was brought to the Nizam's official residence. Within the reception room, he found the Nizam on a large settee, and thrown off by his 'threadbare appearance' initially did not realize the small figure before him was Hyderabad's ruler. Nevertheless, despite the Nizam's shabby dress and physical ailments, Campbell-Johnson found him to be 'obviously mentally alert and in full command of his faculties,' but struck by an 'aggressive fatalism.' After Campbell-Johnson presented a personal letter from Mountbatten again urging a visit to New Delhi, the Nizam explained that the Indian government had his terms, and 'he had nothing more he could say to any other party, even on a private basis.'[76]

Following his meeting with the Nizam, Campbell-Johnson met with various key players in the unfolding drama. The following day, he had a private meeting with Razvi, who he found to be a 'complete fanatic ... with eyes that bore holes into you.' The Ittihad leader reiterated that he was only acting in defense of the state's Muslims and had no expectations of a peaceable solution, especially as he felt India could not survive for more than two years. He next met with the Hyderabad army's Arab Commander-in-Chief, Major General Syed Ahmed El Edroos, who argued that pressure from India was in part to blame for the conditions within Hyderabad as it had whipped up Muslim fanaticism. 'Without this pressure,' the General remarked, 'Hyderabad in my view would have fallen like a ripe plum.' In a meeting with Laik Ali, he further informed Campbell-Johnson that

Hyderabad was not being asked to accede on only three subjects but ninety-one in all. Under these terms, the Hyderabadi identity would 'assuredly be blotted out.'[77]

While the Nizam refused Mountbatten's invitation, explaining that it was quite impossible for him to leave Hyderabad (General El Edroos claimed this was because the Nizam feared becoming stuck outside of the state), Prime Minister Ali arrived in New Delhi on 23 May 1948 for a new round of meetings with Mountbatten, Nehru and Menon. During these lengthy sessions, which often stretched into the early hours of the morning, India's leaders pushed for the introduction of a representative government within the state and a plebiscite on the issue of accession, as well as offering various exceptions with the aim of protecting the Nizam's dignity. Ali initially rejected these proposals and threatened to approach the United Nations. Following continued negotiations, the Prime Minister finally agreed to at least present these ideas to the Nizam and flew back to Hyderabad on 15 June carrying a firman drafted by Menon announcing a plebiscite on the issue of accession for the Nizam's approval. It also committed the Nizam to forming a new interim government in the lead up to the establishment of a Constituent Assembly by early 1949, fixing the strength of the state forces at no more than twenty thousand troops, allowing the Indian government to handle Hyderabad's external relations and taking progressive steps to disband the Razakars within three months.[78] Following deliberations with his Executive Council over the next several days, the Nizam decided not to accept this agreement. Hyderabad officials were now willing to consider the 17 June draft Instrument of Accession, but only with modifications, which included adding an arbitration clause, limiting the provisions for the deployment of Indian troops to the state and allowing Hyderabad more independent fiscal and trade policy.[79] The Nizam was concerned that the draft firman limited Hyderabad's fiscal freedom and the ability to control overseas trade, as well as authorizing the Indian army to station troops within the state whenever the India government should decide to declare a state of emergency.[80] By this point, however, Indian authorities were not inclined to compromise any further.

Patel's frustrations over the negotiations were palpable. Writing on 7 June from Dehra Dun in the hills north of Delhi where he was convalescing after a heart attack, he expressed to Nehru his dismay that 'after so much profitless discussion with so many Hyderabad Delegations, we are still thinking of producing formulas for their acceptance.' He asserted that the Hyderabad government never ceased to assert its sovereignty in violation of the standstill agreement and fostering and encouraging a militant group 'which is both fascist and brutal in its character and which is a serious menace to law and order not only in Hyderabad, but also in the surrounding Indian Dominion territories.' In the face of these realities, Patel argued that the negotiations had reached a stage where 'we should tell them quite frankly that nothing short of unqualified acceptance of accession and of introduction of undiluted responsible government would be acceptable to us.' In pursuing this aim, the Indian government should be prepared 'to follow whatever course of action we consider appropriate.' Any efforts to try to come up with 'devised formulas' would simply be a waste of time, and any further delays of concerted action would place India in a worse position politically and militarily.[81]

Negotiations between New Delhi and Hyderabad were finally broken off on 17 June 1948. The economic blockade of the state was subsequently intensified, an action which the Nizam's government referred to as 'legally equivalent to war.'[82] During a conference the following month, the Ittihad passed a resolution denouncing any further negotiations with the Indian government and committing the group to the pursuit of Hyderabad's independence. Given its influence over government policy, the views of the Ittihad were a key barometer for the political inclinations of the Nizam and his government.

Three days before departing the office of Governor General, Mountbatten made a final plea to the Nizam to find a compromise and become known as 'the peace-maker of South India and as the Saviour of your State, as your people.' If he remained inflexible and continued to pursue independence, Mountbatten told him that he would 'incur the universal condemnation of thinking people.'[83] He further warned the Nizam that popular opinion in India was swiftly drifting away from any moderate approach toward Hyderabad. If he hoped to avoid open conflict, he needed to come to terms with India's political leadership sooner rather than later.[84] During this period, reports continued to seep out of the state of ongoing political unrest, violence and mass conversion campaigns targeting Hindus, forcing many to flee. There were also reports of Razakars conducting periodic raids across the border into Indian territory, such as a 5 June incident in Bijapur in which five policemen and several civilians were killed.[85] These incidents further hardened India's political leaders' unwillingness to compromise.

As pressure mounted over the broader status of the princely states and their ultimate integration with India, the elephant in the room for political leaders in New Delhi was what to do about Hyderabad. There were many questions to answer about how to proceed and what kind of action to take. Nevertheless, as Nehru expressed in an early August 1948 letter to India's chief ministers: 'In no event, can we admit the right of Hyderabad to independence. There is no instance in history, so far as I am aware, when a land-locked territory, surrounded on all sides by one State, has become independent. Both in strict law, and in fact, the notion of Hyderabad's independence is a little absurd.' While Nehru stressed that India's government was not full of 'war-mongers' and remained committed to peace, he also proclaimed: 'Further action will undoubtedly be taken unless something happens which changes the situation in Hyderabad ... But events follow one another in quick succession and our patience is tried to the utmost.'[86]

Operation Polo

The question of whether to use the Indian military to force a settlement of the Hyderabad problem and assert India's sovereignty over the princely state had been debated among India's political leadership for months, initially with a great deal of hesitancy. In a 17 January 1948 press conference, Patel explained that given the unique conditions of Hyderabad, the Indian government was pursuing a 'go-slow' policy. 'Under the present atmosphere of distrust and suspicion between the two big communities,' he stated, 'if we adopt a policy of quick action, there is likely to be some misunderstanding and its repercussions would be such as would affect the people inside as well as outside the State, and may possibly disturb the peace in the Indian Union where we want to maintain peaceful conditions.'[87] Four months later, Mountbatten reassured the Nizam that the Indian government had no intention of engaging in offensive military action, though it had deployed Indian security forces to Hyderabad's borders to enforce an economic blockade of the state.[88]

Overall, Mountbatten was opposed to the use of military force. In March 1948, when he caught wind that a military plan had been recently prepared for an invasion of Hyderabad known as Operation Polo, he was incensed. He was even critical of the military's choice of name, arguing that with his known predilection for the game this name 'could hardly have been better calculated to add insult to injury for me personally.' In his next meeting with Nehru, Mountbatten criticized the plan and pointed to the potential national and international repercussions. Nehru was incredulous that Mountbatten had not heard about the plan being prepared earlier but, at any rate, assured the Governor General that there was nothing to worry about. The preparations, as was explained to Mountbatten, were only done to be ready to respond to a potential massacre of Hindus within Hyderabad, which was a circumstance 'in which the Government of India could no longer forbear from intervention.'[89]

Even with Mountbatten's public assurances, the Nizam's government also began preparing for a military assault in the coming months, such as strengthening the state's border defenses and reviving the air raids precautions organization. Hyderabad's Information and Broadcasting Secretary,

Hamiduddin Ahmed, put out a call for volunteers to fill its ranks, stating, 'We must be prepared to defend ourselves against aggression in any form.'[90] Throughout the negotiations, Hyderabad had made concerted efforts, unsuccessfully, to secure military supplies from abroad. In October 1947, General El Edroos traveled to London to attempt to buy equipment for the army, specifically tanks.[91] The British Foreign Office held suspicions that the Nizam's second son, who was in Europe at the time, had similarly been active trying to buy arms abroad, as he had been spending large amounts of money in France and Switzerland.[92] The following year, Hyderabad approached a Canadian firm to procure arms and ammunition, with the Canadian government informing Indian authorities of the attempt.[93] At the same time, there were increasing reports of arms smuggling from Pakistan through the port of Goa and by air from Karachi, actions which were denounced by British Commonwealth Secretary Philip Noel-Baker in the House of Commons.[94] Despite their supply problems, the Nizam was confident of the ability of his state forces to withstand an Indian military assault. General El Edroos did not share this confidence. Shortly after the transfer of power, he bluntly informed the Nizam that Hyderabad's forces could hold out against the Indian army for only three days, an assessment that would be proven correct some fifteen months later.[95]

Senior Indian officials also remained concerned with the activities of the Razakars and Hyderabadi security forces as they conducted raids into Indian territory, targeted civilians and clashed with India's military forces.[96] On 14 July 1948, Hyderabadi police and military personnel raided Mudkhed village in Nanded District near the border with India, suspecting it of being a stronghold of State Congress activity in the area. Upon entry into the village, state forces opened fire indiscriminately on the villagers, prompting them to offer some resistance. In the end, eighty of the villagers were killed. This followed reports of the police firing on convoys of Hindu refugees attempting to cross into Indian territory.[97] On 24 July, around fifty Razakars attacked an Indian army convoy passing through the village of Nanaj in Hyderabad territory while proceeding on routine patrol duty. The Razakars then surrounded and assaulted Nanaj, killing thirty individuals in the attack.[98] At this time, neighboring provinces were increasing their security measures along Hyderabad's frontier. In early July, the Central Provinces strengthened its defenses within border districts and implemented sections of the Public Safety Act that suspended the right of appeal and habeas corpus for detained individuals within these districts.[99] Shortly after negotiations were suspended, Nehru issued clarifying orders to Indian troops stationed along the Hyderabad frontier enforcing the economic blockade. 'In view of raids from Hyderabad territory into Indian Union territory,' he wrote, 'swift action should be taken to repel these raids and punish the raiders ... Where the raiders escape into Hyderabad territory, they should be pursued across the border and punishment inflicted and, if possible, raiders captured and brought back ... Provided also that care should be taken that our party crossing the border does not go too far beyond the border thus getting isolated from its main base and possibly entangled in the interior of Hyderabad State.'[100]

Reports of Razakar atrocities within Hyderabad were also becoming more and more common, with many Hindus fleeing the state. Earlier in the year, the president of the Hyderabad State Congress sent a letter to the Nizam complaining that '[l]oot, arson, murder, and rape have been the order of the day' with the state police and Ittihad forces having 'free play' to 'crush the people under the garb of preserving the entity of the State and perpetuating the regime of Your Exalted Highness.' He cited evidence showing that entire villages had been burnt, property looted, and women raped by the Ittihad and Razakars with the aid of the state government's administration 'which has been fully imbued with the communal virus.'[101] In early September, Indian newspapers carried sensational headlines asserting that the 1919 massacre at Jallianwala Bagh in Amritsar had been repeated at Hyderabad's Nalgonda District, where Razakar forces had reportedly shot and killed around five hundred people after driving them into a field.[102] A British general serving in the Pakistan army later reported that he had credible information from Hyderabad sources that, in the case of an Indian invasion, the Razakars intended to kill as many Hindus as possible before the Indian army took control of the state.[103]

On 31 March 1948, Razvi struck an Indian nerve by declaring in a speech that 'the forty-five million Muslims in the Indian Union would be our fifth columnists in any showdown,' compounding Indian fears.[104] As negotiations broke down in June, he further declared: 'We will see that no Razakar steps into your territory but if a single soldier of yours penetrates into our territory, five hundred thousand Razakars will march into your Union, and I cannot say where they will stop. They will not only hoist the Asafjahi flag on the Red Fort, but they might also in Masulipatam and several other places, because we cannot tolerate any violation of our territory.' He again pointed to the Muslims of India as the Razakars' allies in any war: 'We will not only make another Pakistan but free forty-five million Muslims in the Indian Dominion who are living under constant terror and oppression.'[105] By this point, the Ittihad's membership had reportedly surpassed one million, with upwards of one hundred thousand members engaged in arms training with the Razakars. Every member of the Razakar took a vow in the name of Allah that they would 'fight to the last to maintain the supremacy of Muslim power in the Deccan.'[106] There were even reports circulating in the media of Ittihad plans to invade India in conjunction with the Hyderabad Army, in particular to secure access to the Portuguese port of Goa, which media commentators feared would weaken India in the face of a potential Pakistani assault against Delhi.[107] Regardless of the impracticalities of such fears and rumors, they contributed to the growing sentiment that an independent Hyderabad posed a serious military threat.

In late July, the Nizam's commerce minister J.V. Joshi, a Hindu member of the Cabinet, created a great sensation when he resigned in protest over the actions of Razvi and the Ittihad, evoking broader fears that the communal violence sparked by Partition the previous year would be repeated and even eclipsed. In his resignation letter, he asserted:

> A complete reign of terror prevails in Parbani and Nanded districts. I have been at Loha a scene of devastation which brought tears to my eyes. Brahmins were killed and their eyes were taken out. Women were raped. Houses were burned down in larger numbers. My heart bleeds in anguish ... Instances are also not lacking in which the police joined the Razakars in their depredations of loot, arson, murder, rape and molestation of womenfolk ... War seems to be on the lips of every Muslim brother ... God forbid if the Government of Hyderabad and the Government of India have to adopt a course of armed conflict under no circumstances I will be a party to such a disaster which will lead to destruction of the entire structure of the State.[108]

The next month, the Lingayat (a Hindu sect) Public Health Minister, Mallikarjunappa, also announced his resignation over the intransigence of the Ittihad ministers in the Cabinet, arguing: 'We tried our best to co-operate with the Government. Our aim was only to have peace and tranquility in the State and to achieve it through legitimate and constitutional means. But we failed in our efforts.' On the other hand, Laik Ali asserted that these resignations were 'skillfully engineered by outside influences.'[109]

Shortly before negotiations were suspended in June 1948, Nehru wrote to Patel that India needed to 'gain definitive and positive control over ... the military situation internally in Hyderabad so that any action against us becomes quite impossible.' He felt that this was the primary concern for the Indian government and all others were secondary. While Nehru hoped to find a peaceful solution, he recognized that military measures may need to be taken. Yet, a key lesson from Jammu and Kashmir was that it was easier to launch military operations than to end them and any widespread use of the military would put a strain on India's limited resources. He felt that military force should only be used when the Hyderabad government or the Razakars made it 'impossible for us to desist from it. Of course in such circumstances we have to take action because inaction may produce worse results.' However, Nehru felt that military action should be put off for at least another two months. For the time being, the army stationed along

Hyderabad's borders would serve as a 'constant reminder of the possibility of military action.'[110]

It was now left to the Cabinet's Defence Committee to consider how to move forward after Mountbatten's efforts to find a negotiated settlement failed to deliver any results. With Mountbatten no longer in the picture, having left the post of Governor General in June 1948 and being replaced by Chakravarti Rajagopalachari, New Delhi had a freer hand in dealing with the obstinate Nizam. Some within the Defence Committee counseled against the use of the military, warning that any operation could provoke unrest among Muslims across India, provoke Pakistan to intervene on Hyderabad's behalf or lead to widespread clashes between the two militaries that could spill over into other parts of India, including Hyderabadi aircraft bombing major cities. One British general warned that, with Hyderabad's state forces under the able command of General El Edroos, India's military may not be able to quickly overwhelm Hyderabad's defenses as 'in the hands of El Edroos, even an ill-disciplined rabble could be converted into something like the famous French Foreign Legion!'[111] None of these arguments stuck. With Hyderabad surrounded by Indian forces, preparations were already underway for a military action against the state by early July 1948. The only question that remained was when. On 1 July, Nehru informed the country's chief ministers, 'We shall undoubtedly take military action when we think the time is ripe for it.'[112]

At the time, the public messaging from India's senior political leadership was clearly pointing to their willingness to resort to military force to assert Indian sovereignty and address the growing unrest in the state, in part to allay public criticism about the government's perceived inaction. On 15 July, during a visit to Patiala to inaugurate the new Patiala and East Punjab States Union, Patel explained that, while it had been his hope that Mountbatten could successfully solve the Hyderabad problem before departing India, 'that hope never materialized owing to the intransigence of the Nizam and the fanaticism of the forces at his back.' Patel did not mince his words when he announced that 'the terms and the talks which the former Governor-General had with Hyderabad have gone with him. Now the settlement with the Nizam will have to be on the lines of other settlements with the States ... There is only one way of a settlement—and that is accession. There is no other possibility of a settlement.' He struck an uncompromising tone in his speech. 'No help from outside on which [the Nizam] seems to rest his pathetic hopes would avail him,' Patel asserted. 'To those who are restless I should like to say: You must trust us; the pangs which you feel for Hyderabad are shared by me no less; but when we have to perform an operation, we have to see that as little of the limb involved is cut as possible and that the operation is performed only when the time is ripe.' Patel reminded those in the audience that when he had spoken at Junagadh he clearly stated that 'if Hyderabad did not behave properly, it would have to go the way that Junagadh did. Those words still stand and I stand by those words.'[113] Hyderabad's Prime Minister was equally uncompromising, assuring Indian authorities that Hyderabad would act to protect its sovereignty and warning them that they had miscalculated 'our strength and determination to fight to the finish.'[114]

Unlike Patel's unambiguous position, Nehru had been more cautious on the subject of a military invasion through the spring and summer of 1948, arguing that India should only pursue this path if Hyderabad and the Razakars made it impossible to do otherwise. Yet even he left open the possibility of the use of military force. As early as 24 April, he declared in front of the All-India Congress Committee in Bombay: 'There are two courses now open to Hyderabad—war or accession. War is a prolonged affair, and, if we resort to it, many problems will arise. We have therefore been trying to solve this problem by negotiations, but that does not mean that we are afraid of following the path of war.'—though he later recanted the public statement, arguing it was a product of a mistranslation of his Hindi speech.[115] However, three months later, Nehru warned during a public meeting at Island Grounds in Madras, that 'if and when it is considered necessary we shall have military operations against Hyderabad.'[116]

As the Razakars' activities intensified, Nehru was privately growing more and more inclined toward a military intervention. In an August 1948 cable to V.K. Krishna Menon, then serving as the High Commissioner in London, he wrote that the situation in Hyderabad was growing 'intolerable' as Razakars were stopping trains and looting the passengers, attacking refugees fleeing the state and abducting women. There was consequently a growing demand among the Indian public for action with fears that if the 'anarchy' prevalent in Hyderabad remained unchecked it would create a state of lawlessness in neighboring areas. 'As we have already told you,' Nehru wrote, 'this we cannot allow to happen. Police action against Razakars and their sympathizers in Hyderabad cannot, therefore, be postponed much longer.'[117] He also sent letters to the country's chief ministers explaining that the situation with Hyderabad had reached 'a stage when some kind of a positive action on our behalf may be needed.' He warned that they should 'keep wide awake about the possible reactions within their areas' and to take 'all necessary measures for internal security' in the wake of potential action taken, especially with the persistent repercussions from various communal activities that continued to plague various parts of India. He specifically highlighted the danger of 'communal trouble started by non-Muslims as a reaction to events in Hyderabad.'[118]

In early September, the Indian government was finally ready to make its move. On 7 September, Menon wrote to Laik Ali formally requesting the immediate disbanding of the Razakars and for Hyderabad to facilitate the passage of Indian troops through Hyderabad territory to Secunderabad 'for the prompt and effective restoration of law and order.' Three days later, Laik Ali asserted that the state government was perfectly capable of handling the situation and took serious exception to Menon's suggestion, which would constitute a violation of both the standstill agreement and Hyderabad's sovereignty. The next day, the Indian government responded that the only law prevalent in Hyderabad was the 'law of the jungle' and the Indian government 'regarded themselves as free to take such actions as they considered necessary,' with the responsibility for any action resting firmly on the shoulders of the Nizam and his government.[119] In anticipation of Indian military action, all British officers serving with the Hyderabad army resigned by early September.[120]

With senior officials in New Delhi feeling that no alternative remained, the Cabinet made the decision to move forward with a military intervention into Hyderabad on 9 September, even before receiving a response from Laik Ali. This was a difficult decision to make. During the Cabinet meetings leading up to this decision, Rajagopalachari was 'very cynical' and argued that to consider the use of military force against Hyderabad only a few months after Gandhi's assassination 'strikes me as something very wrong,' according to Home Secretary H.V.R. Iyengar who was present at the meeting. Nehru also expressed extreme apprehension over the police action. At one point, he even lost his temper and shouted at the hawkish Patel and Menon, with Patel simply getting up and leaving the meeting and Menon on the verge of resigning his position.[121] However, Patel's forceful arguments for military action, supported by Defense Minister Baldev Singh, ultimately swayed the Cabinet.[122] With the decision made, General K.S. Rajindrasinhji, the commanding general of the army's Southern Command, who was himself a member of the ruling family of the Nawanagar State, soon departed New Delhi for Madras, carrying with him the detailed plans for Operation Polo.[123] It was the government's intention to bring the fighting to a speedy conclusion to avoid violent reprisals and manage the spread of the conflict. Military planners asserted that the operation should last no longer than three weeks to achieve this effect.[124]

Early in the morning of 13 September, the Indian army's First Armored Division under the command of Major General Jayanto Nath Chaudhuri moved into Hyderabad territory in a two-pronged advance. A Ministry of Defense communique read: 'The Government of Hyderabad having declined to accede to the Government of India's request to disband the Razakars and to facilitate the return of Indian troops to Secunderabad for restoration of law and in the State. Indian troops crossed the State border at 4 am today.'[125] The poorly equipped Hyderabadi army and Razakars were quickly overwhelmed. While the Indian advance initially met stiff resistance, this waned over the next two days of the campaign, with Hyderabadi troops withdrawing rather than engaging with the Indian forces. By 15 September, Indian troops captured Aurangabad after Hyderabad's forces were evacuated from the second largest city in the state. Indian armored units, supported by the Indian air force conducting bombing runs against Hyderabad's airfields, continued their advance toward Secunderabad and Hyderabad city from five directions.

Laik Ali had ordered that the bridges leading to Hyderabad city be destroyed to slow the Indian army until the government could rouse international support.[126] However, this failed to have any measurable effect as Indian forces soon reached the outskirts of the capital city. With Hyderabad's forces unable to stop the Indian advance, General El Edroos took a jeep to the Indian lines and surrendered to General Chaudhuri in the middle of a road outside of Secunderabad. He stated: 'The men under my command were called upon to perform a superhuman task and against very heavy odds. There was no alternative for me left but to surrender.'[127] Aware of his forces' deficiencies, El Edroos had earlier ordered his men to either fall back on the capital city or surrender in the face of the superior Indian forces.[128] In only four and a half days, Indian forces had taken control of the state. In total, the Indian government counted 42 Indian soldiers, 490 soldiers of the Hyderabad army, and 2,727 Razakars killed in the fighting.[129] Following India's invasion, thousands of refugees returned to their homes, the economic blockade of the state was lifted and around eleven thousand Congress workers held as political prisoners were released.[130] Many of Hyderabad's residents treated the Indian troops as conquering heroes, with newsreels showing tanks rumbling down roads lined with cheering crowds waving the Indian tricolor flag.

The Indian government was sensitive to the international implications of their actions. Indian officials treated the military invasion as an internal police action, a phrase originally suggested by V.K. Krishna Menon, intended to restore law and order within the state. Nehru was adamant that 'our action was supposed to be a "police action" against a recalcitrant State. We did not call it war and we must not therefore do anything now which might indicate that we consider it as a foreign state, whatever its strict legal position might have been since August 15.'[131] He further explained the action taken to assert Indian sovereignty over Hyderabad was not a 'reversion to the old paramountcy of the British power, because such paramountcy can only be exercised by an alien authority or an autocratic regime.'[132] This was also the view of the States Ministry. Patel asserted that 'once we enter Hyderabad, it is no longer an international affair. It is a States Ministry function.'[133] On 16 September, with Indian troops advancing deeper into Hyderabadi territory, Menon called the U.S. Charge d'Affaires, Howard Donovan, to his office and reiterated that Hyderabad was a purely internal matter for India to handle as Hyderabad had 'no international *locus standi* [*sic*].' The princely state was in an 'identical position as other Indian states.' During this meeting, Menon further expressed the fear that if the principle of UN intervention into India's relations with its princely states was broadly accepted in the international community, then it was possible that the 'whole structure of accession states to India would collapse,' as other princely states that had resisted accession, such as Jodhpur, might again challenge Indian authority.[134]

Soon after the military surrender, the Nizam announced over the radio a ban on the Razakars and urged his subjects to 'live in peace and harmony with the rest of the people in India,' ending Hyderabad's bid for independence.[135] Six days after his initial radio announcement, the Nizam once again took to the radio waves to denounce Razvi and the Razakars who had taken 'possession of the State' using 'Hitlerite' methods to 'spread terror.' In the wake of Indian military action, he now lay the blame entirely at the feet of the Razakars, claiming that he was rendered completely helpless as a mere puppet of the conspirators. He was, in fact, 'anxious to come to an honourable settlement with India but this group ... got me to reject the offers made by the Government of India from time to time.'[136] Of course, the Indian press lambasted the Nizam's sudden change of heart as a 'face-saving device.'[137] Indian authorities immediately disbanded the Razakars and arrested around twelve thousands of its members, including Razvi who was put on trial for murder charges. (In 1957, he was released from prison and migrated to Pakistan.) In the days after Hyderabad's surrender, Indian troops continued to engage with roving bands of Razakars in different parts of the state.[138] In addition, the military and police authorities indiscriminately arrested many Muslims under suspicion of being Razakars or complicit in some way with the atrocities committed by the Razakars.[139]

The military administration of Hyderabad

In the evening of 20 September 1948, the Nizam officially relinquished control of the state government to an interim military administration and issued a proclamation to his subjects to 'render faithful and unflinching obedience to the Military Governor.' The Indian government installed General Chaudhuri as the military governor, a position he stayed in until December 1949, with the Nizam retained as the constitutional head of the state. Menon argued that the Nizam's removal could have a 'very unsettling effect on the Muslims.'[140] By late November 1948, the U.S. Charge d'Affaires reported back to Washington, DC: 'Nizam is powerless, has lost much prestige with former ruling class; heir apparent not impressive; Asaf Jahi dynasty seems finished.'[141] Yet, the weakened Nizam was slow to cooperate with the governor. In one January 1949 meeting to discuss proposals regarding the administration of the Sarf-i-Khas, or Crown lands, and his privy purse (which was set at five million rupees per year), the Nizam 'pretended to be extremely dense as to what was meant by anything I said,' Chaudhuri reported. At one point in the meeting, the Nizam became 'extremely heated' and complained that the Indian government was being 'very unjust to him and if this injustice continued, though the Indian Government could do anything they like to him, he would announce his illtreatment to the world at large.'[142]

Following the installation of the military government, it took several weeks for it to re-establish semi-functioning administrative structures in large parts of the state. In the administrative vacuum, communal violence became a problem, including retaliatory attacks against Muslims and violence perpetrated by members of the Indian army.[143] Between 29 November and 21 December 1948, the Indian government dispatched Pandit Sundarlal, Kasi Abdul Ghaffar and Moulana Abdulla Misri to travel throughout the state on a goodwill mission to attempt to restore better communal relations. While the delegation asserted that they were not an official commission of investigation and enquiry, the confidential report they submitted to Nehru and Patel, known as the Sundarlal Report,[144] recounted the details and scope of various atrocities committed during and after Operation Polo. In their travels, they found that only three out of the state's sixteen districts were free from communal disturbances connected to the activities of the Razakars and the reprisals following its disbanding. They found the worst violence to have occurred in the Razakar strongholds of Osmanabad, Gulburga, Bider and Nander districts, where the number of people killed was reportedly at least eighteen thousand. The reprisals included murder, rape, the abduction of women, loot, arson, forced conversions, desecration of mosques and seizure of property. The reprisal attacks against Muslims for Razakar atrocities were not limited to residents of Hyderabad, the delegation asserted, but also included groups of armed men 'belonging to a well known Hindu communal organization' that had crossed into Hyderabad in the wake of the Indian army. This was most likely referring to the Arya Samaj headquartered in neighboring Sholapur District, a group that had strong links with the Hyderabad State Congress, which was also involved in actions against the Nizam's government.[145] In total, the delegation estimated that between twenty-seven thousand and forty thousand people were killed during and after the 'police action,' figures which they call a 'very conservative estimate.'[146]

The delegation also reported that Hindu mobs looted Muslim shops and houses under the encouragement, and sometimes even with the participation, of members of the Indian army. Though the delegation's report was careful to clarify they did not intend to 'imply a slur on the Indian army,' and despite the actions of a few of its members, the army overall maintained 'a high standard of discipline and sense of duty,' with General Chaudhari winning accolades for his impartial handling of disruptive elements within the state. The committee provided a number of recommendations to improve communal relations, including providing relief to the victims of the violence, restoring mosques, declaring forced conversions null and void in law, pressing the Nizam to contribute financial assistance to his 'suffering subjects' from his private purse, accelerating and supplementing the efforts of the military governor to arrest responsible parties, increasing Muslim representation in the government and ensuring that all arrested individuals who 'publicly recant and repent' be pardoned and released with as few exceptions as possible.[147]

Six months after India's annexation of Hyderabad, the state government released a pamphlet titled *Hyderabad Reborn: First Six Months of Freedom* detailing its efforts to re-establish law and order and introduce responsible government within the state. In it, the government asserted:

> At dawn on September 13, 1948—a day that will live in history—the Government of India moved Indian forces into Hyderabad State in response to the call of the people. They found a population stricken by fear and a State empty of all beneficent activity. Six months later, the State is pulsating with new life, and its 170 lakhs of inhabitants are breathing the air of freedom and confidence. They are well on the way to the fulfilment of their declared desire—the establishment of democratic government leading to a popular decision on the future of the State, and the progressive elimination of political and economic autocracy.[148]

On 23 November 1949, the Nizam issued a firman announcing that the new Constitution of India adopted by the Constituent Assembly in New Delhi would become the Constitution of Hyderabad, subject to ratification by the state's Constituent Assembly. When the new constitution went into effect in January 1950, Hyderabad formally became a part of the Republic of India. As a gesture of reconciliation, the Nizam was made the rajpramukh, or governor, of the now Indian state of Hyderabad, a role he served in until 1956, when the state was dismantled as part of the linguistically based reorganization of the Indian states and split between Andhra Pradesh, Mysore and Bombay State.

Following the transfer of power, the Nizam had been seduced by Hyderabad's size and wealth and believed that the state would be able to survive as an independent country with continued relations with the British Commonwealth. He argued that this right was granted to the princes under British policy. Moreover, he feared that acceding to India would force democratic reforms within the state that would ultimately undermine his political authority and the dominant position of the state's Muslim population. Yet, Indian political leaders made it clear that they could not abide an independent Hyderabad in the heart of India, which would set a dangerous precedent among the princely order and threaten the unity of the new country. Nehru compared the situation in Hyderabad with the emergency in Malaya in defense of the actions taken by the Indian government. He explained: 'In Hyderabad, there was something in the nature of open insurrection, and I doubt very much if any Government anywhere would have dealt with such insurrectionary activities under the normal civil law.' While he acknowledged that excesses by Indian security forces had occurred in Hyderabad, which 'distressed' him, Nehru was quick to point out that the actions taken in Malaya were much harsher than anything done in Hyderabad and people should remember 'the terrible excesses on the other side and the difficulties that the police had to experience.'[149] In the face of an intractable Nizam who had fallen under the influence of the increasingly militant Ittihad, Indian leaders came to believe that military force was the only viable option to break the impasse and assert Indian sovereignty over Hyderabad.

Notes

1 Guha, *India After Gandhi*, p. 67.
2 Fitze, *Twilight of the Maharajas*, p. 82.
3 Copland, *The Princes of India in the Endgame of Empire*, p. 33; NAI, File No. F-18-8_41, PR_000003012028, Fortnightly Report on the Political Situation In India For the Month of August 1941, Home Department, Government of India, 1941, p. 66; Purushotham, *From Raj to Republic*, pp. 46–52.
4 'The Nizam of Hyderabad,' *Time* magazine.
5 'Hyderabad Has Still To Settle Its Future 1947,' News Reel, British Pathe (15 December 1947).
6 Yunus Y. Lasania, '"The last Nizam of Hyderabad was not a miser",' *The Hindu* (25 February 2017).
7 'The Nizam of Hyderabad,' *Time* magazine; Guha, *India After Gandhi*, p. 66.
8 NAI, File No. F-18-6_33, PR_000003033814, Fortnightly Report on the Internal Political Situation in India for the Month of May 1933, Home Department, Government of India, 1933, p. 72.

9 NAI, File No. F112_Apr_P-2, PR_000003031238, Fortnightly Reports on the Internal Political Situation in India for April 1925, Home Department, Government of India, 1925, p. 55.

10 NAI, File No. 17_29_29, PR_000003010043, Reports on the political situation in India for the month of August 1929, Home Department, Government of India, August 1929, p. 28; NAI, File No. 17_1, PR_000003010038, Reports on the political situation in India for the month of October 1929, Home Department, Government of India, October 1929, p. 71.

11 NAI, PP_000000010466, Hindu Maha Sabha- (i) Papers regarding the condition of Hindus in Hyderabad state, Private Papers of M.R. Jayakar, 1932, pp. 5, 24, 46, 71.

12 NAI, File No. F-18-7, PR_000003036700, Fortnightly Reports on the Political Situation in India for the Month of July 1937, Home Department, Government of India, 1937, p. 63.

13 Rama Sundari Mantena, 'Publicity, Civil Liberties, and Political Life in Princely Hyderabad,' *Modern Asian Studies* 53:4 (2019), 1248–77.

14 NAI, PP_000000005336, States July 1946–Nov 1946, Private Papers of Sardar Patel, 1946, p. 20.

15 NAI, File No. F-18-16, PR_000003016367, Fortnightly Report Received from the Residents—From July to Dec 1945, Home Department, Government of India, 1945, p. 379.

16 NAI, File No. F-18-8, PR_000003036662, Fortnightly Reports on the Political Situation in India for the Month of August 1937, Home Department, Government of India, 1937, p. 71.

17 NAI, File No. F-3-16_42, PR_000003013652, Miscellaneous Reports on the Congress Movement (Military, DIB Etc), Home Department, Government of India, 1942, p. 240; NAI, File No. F-34-2, PR_000003015885, DIB Bi Monthly Review of the Indian States, Home Department, Government of India, 1943, pp. 4, 27.

18 Guha, *India After Gandhi*, p. 67.

19 Note on the Position of Hyderabad, 7 June 1947, *Jinnah Papers Volume IX*, p. 4.

20 Firman, 11 June 1947, *Jinnah Papers Volume IX,* pp. 9–10.

21 Nizam of Hyderabad to Louis Mountbatten, 9 July 1947, *Jinnah Papers Volume IX*, p. 16.

22 Cabinet, India and Burma Committee Paper 1.B.(47)146, 25 July 1947, *Jinnah Papers Volume IX*, pp. 17–19.

23 Sir W. Monckton to Rear-Admiral Viscount Mountbatten of Burma, 28 July 1947, *TOP Volume XII*, p. 377.

24 The Nawab of Chhatari to Rear-Admiral Viscount Mountbatten of Burma, notes of Abell and Mountbatten on the letter, 26 July 1947, *TOP Volume XII*, p. 359.

25 Louis Mountbatten to Nizam of Hyderabad, 12 August 1947, *Jinnah Papers Volume IX*, p. 33.

26 Viceroy's Personal Report No. 16, 8 August 1947, *TOP Volume XII*, p. 593.

27 NAI, PP_000000005898, Acquiring of the Praga Tools Corporation in Hyderabad, Private Papers of Sardar Patel, 1947, p. 124; R.E.B. Bower to George Marshall, 23 August 1947, *Jinnah Papers Volume V*, p. 559.

28 Guha, *India After Gandhi*, p. 67.

29 R.E.B. Bower to George Marshall, 23 August 1947, *Jinnah Papers Volume V*, p. 559.

30 Ibid., p. 560.

31 NAI, PP_000000005898, Acquiring of the Praga Tools Corporation in Hyderabad, Private Papers of Sardar Patel, 1947, pp. 12–13.

32 R.E.B. Bower to George Marshall, 23 August 1947, *Jinnah Papers Volume V*, p. 560.

33 'An Eye-Wash,' *Indian Express* (18 December 1947).

34 'Plebiscite to Decide Accession to India, Swami Ramanand States Demand Of Hyderabad Congress,' *Indian Express* (2 December 1947).

35 'Hyderabad Struggle Not To Be Suspended Or Given Up, "Nothing Short of Accession And Full Responsible Govt.",' *Indian Express* (5 December 1947).

36 Vallabhbhai Patel to Louis Mountbatten, 24 August 1947, *Jinnah Papers Volume IX*, pp. 39–40.

37 Nizam of Hyderabad to Louis Mountbatten, 28 August 1947, *Jinnah Papers Volume IX*, p. 42.

38 Extract from a letter from Hyderabad, 13 September 1947, *Jinnah Papers Volume IX*, p. 54.

39 Louis Mountbatten to Nizam of Hyderabad, 24 September 1947, *Jinnah Papers Volume IX*, p. 57.

40 Menon, *The Story of the Integration of the Indian States*, p. 323.

41 Note by Louis Mountbatten of his meeting with Walter Monckton, Sultan Ahmed and V.P. Menon, 3 October 1947, *Jinnah Papers Volume IX*, pp. 62–3; Campbell-Johnson, *Mission with Mountbatten*, p. 202.

42 Nizam of Hyderabad to Louis Mountbatten, 15 October 1947, *Jinnah Papers Volume IX*, p. 63.

43 Khosla, *Letters for a Nation*, pp. 201–2.

44 Note by Louis Mountbatten of an interview with V.P. Menon, 20 October 1947, *Jinnah Papers Volume IX*, p. 68.

45 Ibid., pp. 68–70.

46 'Muslim Demonstration at Chhatari's House, Hyderabad Delegates Postpone Departures for Delhi,' *Hindustan Times* (28 October 1947); 'Draft Dictated by Patel, Says Majlis Leader,' *Statesman* (2 November 1947).

47 Nizam of Hyderabad to Louis Mountbatten, 1 September 1947, *Jinnah Papers Volume IX*, pp. 43–4; 'Muslim Demonstration at Chhatari's House.'

48 Note of Discussion by Louis Mountbatten with M.A. Jinnah, 1 November 1947, *Jinnah Papers Volume IX*, p. 92.

49 'Jinnah Has Let Down Hyderabad Muslims,' *Indian Express* (24 November 1947).

50 Nizam of Hyderabad to Louis Mountbatten, 1 September 1947, *Jinnah Papers Volume IX*, pp. 43–4.

51 Note by Louis Mountbatten of Interview with Sultan Ahmed and V.P. Menon, 31 October 1947, *Jinnah Papers Volume IX*, pp. 81–3; Main points of Qasim Rizvi's Speech at a Public Meeting, 27 October 1947, *Jinnah Papers Volume IX*, pp. 85–6.

52 'Nizam's Council Dissolved, New Interim Govt. To Be Formed,' *Bombay Chronicle* (11 December 1947); National Archives, U.K., FO/371/63572, Transfer of power in India—relations of India with the United Kingdom (Folder 8), November 1947–January 1948.

53 Walter Monckton to H.L. Ismay, 28 October 1947, *Jinnah Papers Volume IX*, p. 72; Main points of Qasim Rizvi's Speech at a Public Meeting, 27 October 1947, *Jinnah Papers Volume IX*, p. 85.

54 Walter Monckton to H.L. Ismay, 28 October 1947, *Jinnah Papers Volume IX*, p. 72; Walter Monckton to Louis Mountbatten, 30 October 1947, *Jinnah Papers Volume IX*, pp. 74–5.

55 NAI, PP_000000005898, Acquiring of the Praga Tools Corporation in Hyderabad, Private Papers of Sardar Patel, 1947, pp. 19–20.

56 Ibid., pp. 12, 54; Menon, *The Story of the Integration of the Indian States*, p. 334.

57 'India and Hyderabad Agreement, Patel Explains Terms,' *Evening News* (29 November 1947).

58 Standstill Agreement between India and Hyderabad, 29 November 1947, *Jinnah Papers Volume IX*, pp. 106–7; NAI, File No. F-117-21_47, PR_000003041988, Stand Still Agreements Between India Union and Hyderabad State Copy of Agreement, Indian Ministry of Education, 1947, pp. 9–10.

59 V.P. Menon to Mir Laik Ali, 23 March 1948, *Jinnah Papers Volume IX*, pp. 112–13.

60 Mir Laik Ali to Jawaharlal Nehru, 5 April 1948, *Jinnah Papers Volume IX*, pp. 116–18.

61 Nizam of Hyderabad to Louis Mountbatten, 9 March 1948, *Jinnah Papers Volume IX*, p. 111; NAI, PP_00000000607683, Dr. M. Munshi 1948 Hyderabad, Private Papers of Sardar Patel, 1948, p. 83.

62 Noorani, *The Destruction of Hyderabad*, p. 183.

63 NAI, File No. 1(4)-H/48, PR_000004009706, Negotiations with the Hyderabad Delegation regarding the accession of the Hyderabad State to the Indian Dominion, Indian Ministry of States, 1948, p. 11.

64 NAI, PP_000000005898, Acquiring of the Praga Tools Corporation in Hyderabad, Private Papers of Sardar Patel, 1947, pp. 80–2, 85, 87.

65 'Crisis in Hyderabad Similar to Kashmir, Andhra Leader's Warning,' *Hindustan Times* (23 November 1947).

66 'Plan for Massacre of Hyderabad Hindus,' *Indian Express* (4 October 1947).

67 'One Lakh Hindus Leave Hyderabad In 9 Days, Panic Following Muslim Demonstrations on Oct. 27,' *Indian Express* (6 November 1947).

68 Vallabhbhai Patel to Louis Mountbatten, 24 August 1947, *Jinnah Papers Volume IX*, p. 40.

69 Vallabhbhai Patel to Louis Mountbatten, 19 September 1947, *Jinnah Papers Volume IX*, p. 53.

70 NAI, File No. 1(4)-H/48, PR_000004009706, Negotiations with the Hyderabad Delegation regarding the accession of the Hyderabad State to the Indian Dominion, Indian Ministry of States, 1948, pp. 11–12.
71 Menon, *The Story of the Integration of the Indian States*, p. 334.
72 NAI, File No. 1(4)-H/48, PR_000004009706, Negotiations with the Hyderabad Delegation regarding the accession of the Hyderabad State to the Indian Dominion, Indian Ministry of States, 1948, p. 30.
73 Menon, *The Story of the Integration of the Indian States*, p. 344.
74 NAI, File No. 1(4)-H/48, PR_000004009706, Negotiations with the Hyderabad Delegation regarding the accession of the Hyderabad State to the Indian Dominion, Indian Ministry of States, 1948, pp. 6–9.
75 Campbell-Johnson, *Mission with Mountbatten*, pp. 371–2.
76 Ibid., pp. 375, 377.
77 Ibid., pp. 379–85.
78 Louis Mountbatten to Nizam of Hyderabad, 15 June 1948, *Jinnah Papers Volume IX*, pp. 132–4.
79 'Hyderabad Attitude Clarified, Only Result of Recent Negotiations, Nawab Zain Yar Jung Returns to Delhi,' *Statesman* (8 August 1948).
80 Nizam of Hyderabad to Louis Mountbatten, 17 June 1948, *Jinnah Papers Volume IX*, pp. 137–8.
81 NAI, File No. 1(4)-H/48, PR_000004009706, Negotiations with the Hyderabad Delegation regarding the accession of the Hyderabad State to the Indian Dominion, Indian Ministry of States, 1948, p. 39.
82 'Nizam Revives A.R.P. Organisation, "Keep Alert", Says Minister,' *Free Press Journal* (1 July 1948).
83 Guha, *India After Gandhi*, p. 70.
84 NAI, File No. 1(4)-H/48, PR_000004009706, Negotiations with the Hyderabad Delegation regarding the accession of the Hyderabad State to the Indian Dominion, Indian Ministry of States, 1948, pp. 14–15.
85 Ibid., p. 52.
86 Khosla, *Letters for a Nation*, p. 203.
87 NAI, PP_000000005108, Reports from Deputy High Commissioner in Pakistan, Private Papers of Sardar Patel, 1948, p. 25.
88 M. Vanderman to Jawaharlal Nehru (Copy to M.A. Jinnah), 9 April 1948, *Jinnah Papers Volume IX*, p. 125.
89 Noorani, *The Destruction of Hyderabad*, p. 186.
90 'Nizam Revives A.R.P. Organisation, "Keep Alert", Says Minister.'
91 NAI, PP_00000006062, Hyderabad General, Private Papers of Sardar Patel, 1947, p. 31.
92 National Archives, U.K., FO/371/63571, Transfer of power in India—relations of India with the United Kingdom (Folder 7), November 1947.
93 NAI, PP_000000005819, Fortnightly letters of the hon'ble Prime minister to the Provincial Premiers from 1948 to 1949, Private Papers of Sardar Patel, 1949, p. 148.
94 'Suspension of Air Service, Nizam Govt.'s Protest,' *The Hindu* (5 July 1948);

'Britain Strongly Disapproves Arms Smuggling Into Hyderabad,' *India News Chronicle* (9 July 1948).

95 Mason, *A Shaft of Sunlight*, p. 212.

96 Khosla, *Letters for a Nation*, p. 201.

97 '80 Villagers Die in Encounter, Razakar Vandalism,' *Free Press Journal* (21 July 1948).

98 'Razakar Attack at Nanaj, Union Govt. Explain Incident, "Pre-Planned" Ambush,' *The Hindu* (28 July 1948).

99 'Nizam Revives A.R.P. Organisation, "Keep Alert", Says Minister.'

100 Pakistan High Commission, London to Foreign Office, Karachi, 20 June 1948, *Jinnah Papers Volume IX*, p. 139.

101 NAI, PP_000000005873, Letter of Swami Ramanand Tirth president, State Congress 1948, regarding atrocities in state, Private Papers of Sardar Patel, 1948, pp. 2–3.

102 'Jallianwallabagh Repeated At Nalgonda, Razakars Kill 500, Villagers Driven Into Fields, Surrounded & Shot With Bren Guns,' *National Standard* (3 September 1948).

103 National Archives, U.K., DO/134/22, Indian invasion of Hyderabad, 1948.

104 Menon, *The Story of the Integration of the Indian States*, p. 351.

105 Noorani, *The Destruction of Hyderabad*, p. 194.

106 Guha, *India After Gandhi*, p. 68.

107 'Ittehad's Plan to "Invade" India!,' *Free Press Journal* (23 April 1948).

108 'Genocide & Reign of Terror in Hyderabad, Nizam's Forces and Razakars Indulge in Devil Dance, War Preparations: Minister Resigns in Protest,' *Hindustan Times* (24 July 1948).

109 'Co-Operation With Nizam's Govt. Impossible, Colleagues Conniving At Lawlessness: Lingayat Minister's Statement,' *Evening News*, 11 August 1948; 'Hyderabad Determined to Be Independent, Laik Ali's Declaration in State Assembly,' *Hindustan Times* (5 November 1948).

110 NAI, PP_000000006624, Correspondence Gandhiji, Pyarelal Bihar & Cabinet Mission, Private Papers of Sardar Patel, 1950, pp. 272–3.

111 Menon, *The Story of the Integration of the Indian States*, pp. 371–2.

112 NAI, PP_000000005819, Fortnightly letters of the hon'ble Prime minister to the Provincial Premiers from 1948 to 1949, Private Papers of Sardar Patel, 1949, p. 133.

113 'Terms to Nizam Withdrawn, Sardar's Announcement,' *Indian Express* (16 July 1948); 'No Special Terms for Hyderabad Now,' *Hindustan Times* (16 July 1948).

114 'Will Remain Independent, Says Laik Ali,' *Indian Express* (16 July 1948).

115 Noorani, *The Destruction of Hyderabad*, p. 194.

116 'Nehru Warns Hyderabad, No Alternative to Accession, "Military Action If Necessary",' *The Hindu* (26 July 1948).

117 Noorani, *The Destruction of Hyderabad*, p. 197.

118 Khosla, *Letters for a Nation*, pp. 39–40, 92.

119 Menon, *The Story of the Integration of the Indian States*, pp. 374–5.

120 The Charge in India (Donovan) to the Secretary of State, 12 September 1948, *FRUS, 1948, Volume V, Part 1*, p. 385.

121 Basu, *V.P. Menon*, pp. 353–4.

122 Noorani, *The Destruction of Hyderabad*, pp. 212–13.

123 NAI, PP_000000006192, Miscellaneous Correspondence with HE the Governor General, Private Papers of Sardar Patel, 1947, p. 93; Menon, *The Story of the Integration of the Indian States*, p. 376.

124 Menon, *The Story of the Integration of the Indian States*, p. 376.

125 Noorani, *The Destruction of Hyderabad*, p. 199.

126 Purushotham, *From Raj to Republic*, p. 76.

127 'Hyderabad Surrenders 1948,' News Reel, British Pathe (24 September 1948).

128 Syed Ahmed El Edroos and L.R. Naik, *Hyderabad of the 'Seven Loaves'* (Hyderabad: Laser Prints, 1994), p. 140.

129 NAI, PP_000000005577, Hyderabad, 1947, Private Papers of Sardar Patel, p. 31.

130 '11,000 Congress Workers Released in Hyderabad,' *National Call* (3 October 1948).

131 Noorani, *The Destruction of Hyderabad*, p. 197; *Selected Works of Jawaharlal Nehru, Second Series, Volume 7* (New Delhi: Jawaharlal Nehru Memorial Fund, 1988), p. 247.

132 Khosla, *Letters for a Nation*, pp. 92–3.

133 Purushotham, *From Raj to Republic*, p. 78.

134 The Charge in India (Donovan) to the Secretary of State, 17 September 1948, *FRUS, 1948, Volume V, Part 1*, p. 394.

135 'Menon Leaves Hyderabad With Nizam's Reported Accession to Indian Union,' *Hindustan Standard* (22 September 1948).

136 Guha, *India After Gandhi*, p. 70.

137 'Spotlight on Hyderabad: Nizam's Turnface—A Face-saving Device,' *National Call* (5 October 1948).

138 'Razakars Continue Hostile Activity, Roving Bands Engaged By Indian Troops,' *Statesman* (22 September 1948).

139 NAI, PP_000000005813, Hyderabad 1950–1, 1951, Private Papers of Sardar Patel, pp. 126, 213–14.

140 'Nizam Informs Hyderabad of End of Control,' *New York Herald Tribune* (22 September 1948); Menon, *The Story of the Integration of the Indian States*, p. 378.

141 The Charge in India (Donovan) to the Secretary of State, 29 November 1948, *FRUS, 1948, Volume V, Part 1*, p. 464.

142 NAI, File No. 159-H, PR_000001667279, Matters relating to the administration, revenue, etc. of the Sarf-i-Khas areas of the Nizam, Indian Ministry of States, 1948, p. 40.

143 Purushotham, *From Raj to Republic*, pp. 85–93.

144 Historian Sunil Purushotham notes that the Sundarlal Report was not publicly released and was long considered lost, destroyed or officially suppressed. Yet, Purushotham located a copy in the Nehru Memorial Museum and Library

in 2010, which was later publicly released. See Mike Thomson, 'Hyderabad 1948: India's hidden massacre,' *BBC News* (24 September 2013). For my analysis, I located a copy of the report's findings within the Private Papers of Sardar Patel held at the National Archives of India in Delhi.

145 Purushotham, *From Raj to Republic*, pp. 91–2, 104–11.

146 NAI, PP_000000005813, Hyderabad 1950–1, 1951, Private Papers of Sardar Patel, p. 140.

147 Ibid., pp. 140–8, 213–14.

148 *Hyderabad Reborn: First Six Months of Freedom [September 18, 1948–March 17, 1949]* (Hyderabad: Director of Information, Government of Hyderabad, 1949), pp. 13–14.

149 Khosla, *Letters for a Nation*, p. 136.

8

Junagadh: Between the sea and a hard place

Before the violence in Jammu and Kashmir and Hyderabad flared up, India had to deal with Junagadh in Gujarat's Kathiawar Peninsula. One month before the tribal invasion of Kashmir, the dispute over the minor princely state of Junagadh was already bringing India and Pakistan dangerously close to war and provoking serious disagreements within the Indian Cabinet that threatened to break it apart. Even though Junagadh did not share a border with Pakistan, had a majority Hindu population and was surrounded by Indian territory, the state's Muslim Nawab signed the Instrument of Accession for Pakistan to preserve his rule and the privileged position of Muslims within the state. This provoked a storm of consternation among Indian leadership fearing this could have a domino effect on other princely states within India's sphere of influence. As a result, the Indian government deployed its military to the region to blockade Junagadh and force its various vassals to accede to India to apply pressure to Junagadh's government. At the same time, the Provisional Government of Junagadh, formed from among Junagadh's subjects, launched a campaign to retake state territory and push for the full integration of Junagadh into India, demonstrating the same clashing ideas of sovereignty at play as in other princely states. As tensions mounted between India and Pakistan, the resulting turmoil within the region eventually led to the flight of the Nawab to Pakistan, the annexation of Junagadh by Indian forces and the integration of the princely state into the Indian Union.

The British first advanced into the Kathiawar region in 1807 at the invitation of several local talukdars, or landowners. These local landowners opposed the tribute system under the ruling Maratha forces that had replaced Mughal suzerainty in the latter half of the eighteenth century and hoped an alliance with the British would help to improve their status. In 1821, the Nawab of Junagadh signed a treaty with the East India Company, authorizing it to collect revenues within Junagadh territory on behalf of the Nawab and retain one-fourth of the total amount. Junagadh, formed in 1748 during the decline of the Mughal Empire, was the largest

Map 8.1 Map of Junagadh (in black) in British India

(at approximately 3,500 square miles) and premier state of the Kathiawar region, receiving tribute from 134 subsidiary states. While Junagadh was surrounded on three sides by Hindu states and British-ruled districts, what distinguished it from many other princely states was its lengthy coastline and access to international trading networks. The state possessed sixteen ports in total, with the principal one based at Veraval, only 325 nautical miles from the port city of Karachi, Pakistan's future capital. The Veraval port not only supplied grain, timber and other necessities for Junagadh proper, but also the broader Kathiawar region—as well as facilitating various illicit activities such as opium smuggling.[1]

Junagadh did not have the political standing of major princely states in India. It was described as a 'little-regarded' and 'over-looked patchwork quilt' of territory scattered throughout the hills and forests of Gujarat's Kathiawar peninsula on the Arabian Sea, some of which were pockets of villages surrounded by neighboring princely states.[2] One member of the IPS remarked, '[T]o people at home who did not know India, it was the easiest way to explain where Kathiawar was by referring to the big bulge on the map above Bombay.'[3] The broader Kathiawar region was a landscape of intertwined and overlapping princely states—14 salute states plus another 191 small, non-salute states (many of which were included in the British government's short-lived attachment scheme introduced in 1943, during which many small states were combined with Junagadh[4]) with varying levels of authority, revenues and state capacity. This resulted in frequent disputes between the states over the limits of their jurisdiction and legal claims to various sources of revenue.

The British colonial official William Lee-Warner described the region as 'full of anomalies and apparently insoluble problems.' He was, of course, quick to add that these were brought into 'harmonious working order by the magic of His Majesty's protection.'[5] While traveling by car through Kathiawar in September 1947, Menon also noted the practical effects of the intertwined borders of the many princely states within the region. He wrote:

> As we proceeded on our way, I could feel the interlacing of jurisdiction which made Kathiawar such a veritable jig-saw puzzle. For a few miles, because we were in the territory of some progressive ruler like Gondal, who kept his State roads in good condition, it would be a comfortable ride, but then the car would plough through bumpy stretches and one gathered at once that this must be the territory of some other ruler who had neglected his roads.[6]

Besides its curious geography, Junagadh was noteworthy for a variety of reasons. The state possessed the dense Girnar forests, the only remaining sanctuary for the Asiatic lion, and was the site of the historic Somnath Temple, a Hindu temple that had been plundered and destroyed by the Afghan ruler Mahmud Ghazni in the early eleventh century. The temple was rebuilt and destroyed several times before its final desecration by the Mughal Emperor Aurangzeb in the seventeenth century. In the centuries after its destruction, the site became an important pilgrimage site for Hindus. As Shah Nawaz Bhutto, the last Diwan of Junagadh, explained, 'in the estimation of our non-Muslim people, Junagadh is considered the most sacred place after Kashi [Varanasi].'[7]

Junagadh and the march to independence

Like Jammu and Kashmir and Hyderabad, Junagadh's dynasty of Muslim rulers—the ninth and final of which was Nawab Mahabat Khan who had been placed on the throne in 1920 (described as 'an eccentric of rare vintage' who was noted for his all-encompassing and costly obsession with his over two thousand dogs)—possessed a different faith than most of their subjects. Over 80 percent were Hindu and approximately 16 percent Muslim.[8] Despite forming a minority of the population, Muslims were dominant within the state administration, especially officials from nearby Sindh. Through the late nineteenth and early twentieth centuries, communal tensions were a problem as competition between Hindu and Muslim elites for access to power within Junagadh's administration became colored by their religious divide and intertwined with the broader political grievances of the state's subjects. In July 1893, for instance, communal rioting erupted in Prabhas Patan. Shortly before the riots, tensions between Hindus and Muslims ran high. Hindu pilgrims in the area protested their perceived mistreatment at the hands of largely Muslim state officials. Conversely, many Muslims in the area felt that the Nawab's government was too lenient in allowing Hindus to serve in the state's administration. Following an attack on Hindus during Muharram, influential Hindu representatives of the state traveled to Bombay to seek British intervention within Junagadh on their behalf.[9]

Through the 1930s, members of the Hindu majority continued to agitate against the state government and advocate for democratic reforms within the princely state. In 1938, several residents in Junagadh had worked to recruit members to set up a local Praja Mandal in the state to press for such reforms. However, the Junagadh State Council blocked the formation of the group since its membership almost exclusively consisted of members of the Hindu population.[10] At the time, no public or political meeting could be held without the permission of state government authorities. On the other hand, a number of Muslims were vocal opponents of these reform efforts, arguing that they were detrimental to their interests, and sought to preserve Muslims' privileged access to political power.[11]

In the years leading up to independence, like so many other parts of India, communal tensions between Hindus and Muslims became more and more prevalent and frequently led to clashes between the two communities, with Hindus frequently leveling charges of anti-Hindu bias against the Muslim-dominated government. In June 1946, for instance, a clash erupted between Hindu and Muslim sailors in Veraval that provoked escalating violence between the two populations in the port, during which a Muslim mob attempted to burn down a Hindu temple. In response, Hindu shopkeepers soon declared a hartal, or strike, as they claimed their lives were in danger and blamed the police officials investigating the matter as siding with the Muslim perpetrators of the attack. The following month, a protest meeting attended by a number of Hindus passed a resolution warning the Nawab that 'if assurance of justice and satisfactory pacification to Hindu subjects will not be given within a week, appeal shall have to be made to Hindus of India.' Reports circulated that outside groups, such as the Arya Samaj, continued to play a role in keeping alive communal tensions and instigating further distrust of the Nawab's government.[12]

In April 1947, a Hindu daily, *Nav Saurashtra*, declared that the Junagadh administration had the goal of 'spreading communal poison in Kathiawar' and asserting supremacy over the region. The British Resident for the Western India States Agency, L.G. Coke Wallis, remarked that the communal problems prevalent in Junagadh created 'something like a panic in the country-side.'[13] Given Junagadh's status as a Muslim-ruled state with a Hindu majority and surrounded by Hindu-ruled territory, the Nawab was overly sensitive to external criticisms leveled at him and his state within the Hindu press from the surrounding territory and nearby Bombay Province. Ahead of the transfer of power, the prevailing tensions between the Muslim-dominated government and Junagadh's Hindu majority was the foundation of a broader fear among the state's political elite of the repercussions of the accession to India and the introduction of democratic institutions, which they saw as threatening the Nawab's rule and the privileged position of Muslims within the state administration.

While the future of the princely states after the British withdrawal was being debated, Junagadh authorities made repeated declarations that their primary intention was to promote the unity of the Kathiawar states, rather than Junagadh pursuing independence, and alluded to their desire to find common cause to maintain security in the region. An 11 April 1947 press statement from the Junagadh government affirmed: 'What Junagadh pre-eminently stands for is the solidarity of Kathiawar and would welcome the formation of a self-contained group of Kathiawar States. Such a group while providing for the autonomy and entity of individual States and their subjects would be a suitable basis for co-operation in matters of common concern generally and co-ordination where necessary.' As Menon noted, 'This clear statement had set all doubts at rest.'[14] Yet, the state's political leadership was clear in its concerns that broader political and constitutional changes in India could lead to the loss of both its status as the region's premier state and its territory, some of which were islands surrounded by other princely states. Junagadh officials blamed Congress leadership for encouraging Hindu-ruled states within Kathiawar and Junagadh's own Hindu population to take actions that would undermine the integrity of the Muslim-governed state. They, therefore, feared the repercussions of acceding to India with a government controlled by the Indian National Congress.

Following the announcement of Partition, rumors abounded that the Nawab and his key advisers were considering acceding to Pakistan in a bid to protect the Nawab's authority, despite assurances to the contrary by Junagadh's Diwan. As a demonstration of the state's interest in joining the

Indian Union, Junagadh's Constitutional Adviser, Nabi Baksh, attended the special session of the Chamber of Princes in July 1947 and participated in several follow-up discussions about the princely states' future status within India. During the proceedings, Baksh even met privately with Mountbatten and informed him that he intended to advise the Nawab to accede to India.[15] While there were several questions regarding Junagadh's position, especially as it was the only salute state within the Kathiawar region not to have joined India's Constituent Assembly, Baksh's personal assurances to Mountbatten helped to calm the concerns of India's political leadership for the time being.

By early August 1947, Junagadh's future remained unclear. Nevertheless, the Nawab chose this sensitive time to take a vacation in Europe. In his absence, a group led by the Nawab's private secretary schemed to replace the state's Diwan, Abdul Kadir, with a leading Muslim League figure from nearby Sindh, Sir Shah Nawaz Bhutto, who had a close relationship with Jinnah (as well as being the father and grandfather to the future prime ministers of Pakistan, Zulfiqar Ali Bhutto and Benazir Bhutto). After Bhutto was installed as Diwan while Kadir was abroad for medical treatment, this group similarly ousted Nabi Baksh, who had been inclined toward accession to India, and helped establish a bias toward acceding to Pakistan within the state government. British authorities described these measures as 'a virtual coup d'etat.'[16] After assuming power, there were reports that Bhutto's control over the Nawab was total. He even reportedly put a cordon of Sindhi troops around the Nawab's palace to limit and control his contact with the outside world.[17]

At the time, there was some debate about the various influences over the Nawab's decision making. K.S. Digvijaysinhji, the Jam Saheb of the princely state of Nawanagar within the Kathiawar region, argued that the Nawab had originally agreed to accede to India, but was persuaded to instead accede to Pakistan under pressure from Bhutto and other Sindhi officials within the Junagadh government.[18] However, the U.S. Vice Consul in Bombay, Albert Rabida, reported that Kadir had actually made the decision to accede to Pakistan, with its leadership at the time taking a more laissez-faire approach to the princely states, as the surest means of protecting Muslim interests and the sovereignty of the state before being removed from office, a decision that was then enforced by his successor Bhutto.[19] Nevertheless, Mountbatten was dismissive of such a move by Junagadh authorities. He privately remarked, 'I mean, the idea that Junagadh could join with Pakistan across all the other Kathiawar states was just stupid.'[20]

At the time, Junagadh's leadership was under mounting internal and external pressure to announce its intention to accede to India. In the days leading up to the transfer of power, Menon reached out several times to

Bhutto reminding him of the impending deadline for submitting the signed Instrument of Accession, which had not yet been received in New Delhi. On 13 August, Bhutto stalled by stating that the issue was still under consideration, while publicly alluding to the government's growing inclination toward Pakistan. That same day, representatives of Junagadh's Hindu population submitted a memorandum to the Diwan arguing for the necessity of accession to India based on the principles of geographic and economic connectivity.[21] Unknown to them, Bhutto had reached out to Jinnah two days earlier over fears that if he acquiesced to pressure to accede to India, Junagadh would have its neck 'put under the guillotine,' which 'shall be cut and finished.' In acceding to Pakistan, the state government argued that it only sought to preserve the Nawab's sovereignty and territorial integrity of the state while protecting the Muslims of Kathiawar. Bhutto and other state officials were 'full of apprehensions when Baroda threatens to claim Somnath. Jamnagar is encouraging particularly our petty Muslim states attached to Junagadh who in turn receive messages of encouragement and help from Hon'ble Pandit Nehru and Sardar Patel.' Bhutto warned of potential fifth columnists backed by India seeking to undermine the state government from within. 'Our opponents,' he stated, 'want to play the same game and repeat the same tactics as were adopted by the East India Company.' Jinnah assured him that Pakistan would not allow the Indian government to starve or tyrannize the state.[22]

Junagadh's accession to Pakistan

On 15 August 1947, the Junagadh government formally announced it was acceding to Pakistan, certain of its legal right to do so under British policy. Nawab Mahabat Khan had already written to Jinnah to inform him of his decision.[23] The state government's press announcement read:

> Its main preoccupation has been to adopt a course that would in the long run make the largest contribution towards the permanent welfare and prosperity of the people of Junagadh and help to preserve the integrity of the State and to safeguard its independence and autonomy over the largest possible field. After anxious consideration and a careful balancing of all factors the Government of the State has decided to accede to Pakistan and hereby announces its decision to that effect.[24]

Junagadh did not directly communicate its decision to the Indian government, and the announcement was overlooked by Indian officials wholly absorbed by the communal violence in the Punjab. It was only when Menon wired the Diwan after reading about the state's accession in the press on 17 August that the Indian government received confirmation from Junagadh authorities on the state's accession to Pakistan, a move that caught New Delhi by surprise.[25] Other princes within Kathiawar who had acceded to India, such as the Maharaja of Dhrangadhra, reached out to the Nawab and asked him to reconsider his decision, which they argued flew in the face not only of the geographical basis of accession but the wishes of his largely Hindu subjects. The Nawab stood firm and dismissed such arguments. He asserted: 'The Indian Independence Act did not and does not require a ruler to consult his people before deciding on Accession. I think we are making an unnecessary fetish of the argument of geographical contiguity. Even then, this is sufficiently provided by Junagadh's sea coast with several ports which can keep connection with Pakistan.'[26]

Yet, Pakistani authorities were slow to accept Junagadh's accession. In the coming weeks, the largely one-way communications from Junagadh's leaders to the Pakistani government show their desperation for recognition of their accession and support in the face of growing Indian political pressure. The day after receiving the Nawab's 11 August letter, Jinnah acknowledged its receipt and informed him that Pakistan had appointed a Negotiating Committee for handling the various princely states falling within Pakistan's sphere of influence. He advised the Nawab to send his representative to Karachi after 15 August to settle the terms of Junagadh's accession. On the day of the Nawab's formal announcement, the Nawab wrote once again to Jinnah stating Junagadh's decision. When a confirmation from Jinnah was not immediately forthcoming, Bhutto wrote an urgent letter to Liaquat Ali Khan four days later, stating that his government was 'awaiting the formal acceptance of Junagadh's accession to the Pakistan Dominion and I should be glad if you would kindly arrange to convey it as soon as possible.' Not content to wait long for a reply, he wrote the following day to M.W. Abbasi, the Secretary of the Ministry of Refugees and Reconciliation, requesting him to remind Jinnah to 'give directions for an early answer.' He informed Abbasi that the state government was facing 'immense difficulties' and felt that 'some kind of official announcement or answer from Pakistan Dominion is sure to smoothen matters for us here.'[27] On 31 August, as Junagadh's leaders were losing patience, the Nawab wrote directly to Jinnah, 'The reports in the press must have given you an idea that Junagadh is showered with criticism all over. Thanks to Almighty we are firm. We expect an early announcement of the Pakistan Government regarding Junagadh's accession to it.' He then dispatched his private secretary, H.M. Abrahani, to Pakistan to expedite the process.[28]

On 4 September, Bhutto again wrote a lengthy letter to Jinnah stressing the difficult situation the princely state faced. He stressed: 'The events of the last few weeks seem to show that the beginning of the tyranny is already being felt. Most venomous propaganda has been stated by the Congress folk; senior officers have been sent by the States Department of the Indian Government to Kathiawar and these with the help of the Police and other machinery still left of the old Residency have bullied into submission most of the States and Estates.' He pointed out that the Indian government had instituted an economic blockade of the state, stopping food shipments and other needed supplies. He further feared that the Indian government was contributing to the spread of communal violence. While Junagadh remained peaceful at the moment, he warned, 'Congress activities may result in orgy of destruction of life and property of innocent people.' He further pressed: 'I submit that it is time for Pakistan to lodge a strong protest with the Indian Government to end such mischievous activities ... It is, therefore, important that Your Excellency should kindly extend your powerful protection to this premier State of Kathiawar ... Your Excellency's strong hand, which has organised and built the greatest Muslim State in the world, will, I am sure, not abandon Junagadh and its people to be devoured by the wolves.' Bhutto concluded his letter with a reminder of what Jinnah had told him during an earlier meeting in Delhi: 'Pakistan will not allow Junagadh to be stormed and tyrannized.'[29]

Two days later, Bhutto sent a police report by special messenger (as the 'Post and Telegraph Department cannot be trusted') to Abrahani, now ensconced in Karachi's Bristol Hotel, asking him to personally explain the worsening situation to the Pakistani Prime Minister, or Jinnah himself if necessary. He instructed the Nawab's private secretary to press 'for immediate action regarding the kind of help we need from Pakistan.'[30]

A long-awaited response from Jinnah finally arrived on 8 September. Jinnah reassured Bhutto that he had received his previous letters, and Abrahani had discussed various matters concerning Junagadh with both the Prime Minister and Foreign Secretary. He then promised that the Pakistani government would soon provide a 'report with regard to the arrangements that have been arrived at ... Tomorrow there is going to be a Cabinet meeting when the matter will be further discussed and a definite policy will be laid down.'[31] The Pakistani government accepted Junagadh's Instrument of Accession on 15 September, seemingly under the assumption that it would be able to use it as leverage to secure control over Jammu and Kashmir. This recognition, however, did not produce the salutary effects for which Bhutto had hoped.

Junagadh's actions enraged India's political leadership who saw it as the arbitrary decision of an autocratic ruler opposed by his largely Hindu subjects and flew in the face of India's sovereign claims. This was 'a clear attempt to cause disruption in integrity of India' and 'inconsistent with friendly relations that should exist between two Dominions.'[32] Campbell-Johnson described Patel as having a 'militant frame of mind' at the time.[33] Indian officials were especially concerned with the potential of a Pakistani island within India that could be exploited to instigate anti-government activities and communal unrest in Kathiawar and further encourage 'intractable elements' in other princely states, such as Hyderabad.[34] Menon, who shared Patel's perspective, also expressed worry that Pakistan would begin importing arms into Junagadh, despite India's naval chief Rear Admiral J.T.S. Hall downplaying the seriousness of such a development. In late August 1947, Menon wrote:

> Import into Junagadh of large quantities of arms without the knowledge of [New Delhi] will be a direct threat to the ... whole Kathiawar ... We may justifiably claim that the question of self-preservation is involved in the proper restriction of arms traffic between Junagadh and foreign countries. On the question of how best to take preventive action, I would only emphasis that our measures should not be half-hearted.[35]

On 12 September, Nehru wrote to Liaquat Ali Khan arguing that a plebiscite needed to be held under the joint supervision of India and Junagadh to decide the issue of accession, as the state was not contiguous to Pakistan and contained a Hindu majority with a clear desire to join India. If the 'democratic will' of the people was ignored and Junagadh joined Pakistan, Nehru affirmed that the Indian government would not accept such a political arrangement pushed by the autocratic Nawab.[36] Jinnah, on the other hand, complained that India's objections were 'totally misconceived and untenable.' The princely states' position within British policy, he maintained, 'is very clearly defined and it has been repeatedly accepted that after the lapse of paramountcy, every Indian state is independent and sovereign and free to join Pakistan or India Dominion.' Therefore, Jinnah claimed that the Indian government 'by their policy and action are infringing the sovereignty of Pakistan.'[37]

Patel's first move to counteract the Nawab's accession to Pakistan was to push two of Junagadh's tributary states, Mangrol and Babariawad, to accede to India to pressure the Nawab. Liaquat Ali Khan dismissed their accession as invalid given their vassal status in relation to Junagadh.[38] The Junagadh authorities also argued that as the state's subsidiaries they required the Nawab's consent to sign the accession paperwork. The day after signing the Instrument of Accession for India the Sheikh of Mangrol began to have second thoughts, arguing that Menon forced his signature without even giving him one hour to consider the matter. He had already alluded to his desire to accede to Pakistan. On 3 August 1947, Shri Mohammad Nasiruddin of Mangrol State told Jinnah: 'I shall certainly like to join Pakistan even at the cost of some sacrifice provided I can possibly do so. The present ambiguous political status of Mangrol is the result of the compulsory mediation of the British Govt.'[39] After signing the Instrument of Accession, the Sheikh concluded that acceding to India 'might lead to some serious and grave consequences.' He went so far as to write to the States Ministry formally renouncing Mangrol's accession and requesting that it be withdrawn.[40] Nevertheless, the Indian government accepted Mangrol's instrument, claiming that his request was made under duress from Junagadh authorities.[41]

Other princes in the region remained firmly within the Indian camp. The Jam Saheb of Nawanagar, a leading figure in the princely order who had served as the Chancellor of the Chamber of Princes from 1933–43, issued several statements condemning Junagadh's actions (which he referred to as 'a danger to the peace of India'), pressed the Indian government to defend the integrity of the Indian nation and urged the Nawab of Junagadh to hold a plebiscite on the issue of accession.[42] He also traveled to New Delhi to affirm his staunch support of the Indian Union. In a meeting at the States Ministry, the Jam Saheb presented numerous stories about the harassment of Junagadh's Hindu population and acts of aggression against its neighboring princely states. He argued that the Indian government needed to take immediate steps to counter Junagadh's actions before the Kathiawar states lost their faith in the government to carry out its responsibilities of security as outlined in the Instrument of Accession. Two of Junagadh's neighboring states, Gondal and Jetpur, likewise appealed to the Indian government to send troops to protect them against any potential military action from Junagadh.[43] By early September 1947, the Indian government had moved up additional forces of Gurkhas and Sikhs from Delhi to Junagadh's frontier. Upon receiving reports of these troop movements, Jinnah asked Mountbatten to block their deployment and to ensure that no Indian troops violated Junagadh territory, 'under any pretext whatsoever.' He warned that 'any encroachment on Junagadh sovereignty or its territory would amount to hostile act.'[44]

The States Ministry soon dispatched its officials, including Menon, to apply pressure to the princes of regional princely states 'still clinging' to Junagadh, including Manavadar, Sardargadh, Bantwa and Majmu, and secure their accession to India. On 19 September, Menon met with the Nawab of Manavadar. Just before the meeting, the Nawab had received a call from Karachi advising him to stand firm in the face of Indian pressure. Nevertheless, Menon made his case, telling him it would be intolerable to have pockets of foreign soil within the Indian Union. Despite promising to meet again with Menon the following day, the Nawab never showed at the appointed time and instead signed the Instrument of Accession for Pakistan the same day, placing his 'personal services and all the resources of my State at the disposal of the Government of Pakistan.'[45] Jinnah accepted the document three days later.

During his visit to the region, Menon also attempted to meet with the Nawab of Junagadh and convince him to reverse course. Menon, accompanied by the Jam Saheb of Nawanagar and the Regional Commissioner N.M. Buch, arrived in Rajkot in the evening of 18 September and immediately wrote a telegram to the Nawab requesting a meeting the following morning to personally deliver a message from the Indian government. However, when Menon arrived in Junagadh the next day, the Nawab feigned an illness and refused to see him. The state's heir apparent was also unavailable, though in his case it was due to a cricket match. Meeting instead with the state's Diwan, Menon argued that Junagadh's accession to Pakistan was an ill fit for the state given various cultural and geographical factors. While he agreed with Menon's logic and even said he would be personally open to deciding the issue by referendum, he defended the Nawab's actions, which were made under the advice of the state's constitutional adviser and Pakistani Foreign Minister Zafarullah Khan. He also explained that he was certain that the Congress government would be unable to resist the growing inroads of communist influence, which threatened the wellbeing and integrity of the princely order and the princely states' political elites.[46] Menon feared that 'the whole of Kathiawar will disintegrate if we yield on this issue' and urged Mountbatten for a decisive military and naval demonstration.[47]

In the face of various Indian military and political maneuvers within Kathiawar, Bhutto wrote to Liaquat Ali Khan concerning the 'life and death struggle' his government faced and appealed to the Pakistani government for immediate assistance; at the time, Bhutto was 'frightened out of his life.' He argued that the Indian government's military preparations, including the deployment of Indian forces to occupy Mangrol and Babariawad, 'indicate definite plans of organized attack on all sides.' There were also reports that the heads of various estates within Junagadh territory opposed to its accession to Pakistan were organizing their own small forces to support any imminent Indian invasion. Under pressure from the States Ministry and the threat of Indian military action, even the vassal states that had supported Junagadh's decision were becoming nervous and wavered in their resolve. The Indian strategy was 'plain,' Bhutto explained. 'Having set up our feudatories to accede, Indian Union will come to their aid with armed strength, the moment Junagadh interferes and asserts its rights over them.' Bhutto asked the Pakistani government to lodge a strong protest with the Indian government to help prevent any potential invasion and, as a further show of support, requested the deployment of a Pakistani battalion to the port city of Veraval and the landing of fighters and bombers within the state. Bhutto warned the Pakistani Prime Minister that Junagadh, with its small and poorly equipped force of irregular troops and policemen, 'would be powerless to stop any invasion of this kind.' He concluded the letter by asking the Pakistani leader to 'please send wire telling us in code "yes" or "no."'[48]

As the situation in Junagadh deteriorated, India and Pakistan exchanged a series of tense communications. India's political leadership argued that Junagadh's claims of large troop concentrations along Junagadh's frontier were patently false. Mountbatten informed Jinnah on 22 September that India had deployed only a small force on Indian territory as a 'very natural counter-measure' to the 'large scale military preparations of Junagadh and supply of arms and ammunition to its Muslim subjects.' The Indian government pressed Pakistan to reconsider their acceptance of Junagadh's accession and accept the outcome of a plebiscite as the democratic will of Junagadh's subject. If the Pakistani government persisted in its present course, Mountbatten stated, 'responsibility of consequences must, I am compelled to inform you, rest squarely on shoulders of the Pakistan Government.'[49]

In reply, Jinnah forcefully repeated the legalistic argument that the princely states held the right to accede to either dominion with the lapse of paramountcy, denied the reports of Junagadh's military preparations and dismissed the idea of a plebiscite overseen by Indian authorities.[50] Mountbatten retorted, 'The Government of India take strong exception to tone of message.' He pointed to Jinnah's claims on the peaceful intentions on the part of Junagadh as 'totally incorrect,' citing the fact that large numbers of non-Muslims had been forced to leave the state due to insecurity and state-backed oppression.[51] On 25 September, the States Ministry publicly announced that although theoretically the lapse of paramountcy left the princely states free to accede to either dominion government, it was recognized that 'in practice this freedom will be exercised with regard to the facts of geography' and the accession of Junagadh to Pakistan would only serve as a 'source of strained friction between Junagadh and [its neighboring] States, between Junagadh and the Dominion of India, and ultimately between the Dominions of India and Pakistan.'[52] Liaquat Ali Khan warned Nehru that India's military action in Kathiawar was 'tantamount to invasion of Junagadh which forms now part of Pakistan' and bluntly told Mountbatten, 'All right, let India go ahead and commit an act of war and see what happens.'[53] As tensions mounted between Indian and Pakistani leaders, the U.S. Charge d'Affaires in Karachi, Charles W. Lewis, Jr., observed that Junagadh's accession to Pakistan presented 'one more bone of contention and strain upon the relationship of the two Dominions.'[54]

A month before the tribal invasion of Kashmir, it was Junagadh that was of foremost concern to India's political leaders as a potential flashpoint for war between the two countries. Mountbatten warned Nehru that if India continued its aggressive actions against Junagadh they would bring outright conflict 'immeasurably nearer, and with it, the extinction of Indian culture for at least a generation. What would happen to the four and a half crores of Muslims in India if there were to be a war between the communities, as exemplified by India and Pakistan?'[55] However, he also recognized the demands of defense that the Instrument of Accession committed the Indian government to provide the princely states in the region. Within Kathiawar, this presented some difficulties as some of the smaller princely states that acceded to India could only be reached by passing through Junagadh territory, given the idiosyncrasies of the borders in the region. Mountbatten eventually agreed with the continuation of military preparations, including the movement of troops through Junagadh territory to reach the smaller states, so long as the columns did so under a flag of truce and following the due notification of Pakistani and Junagadh authorities.[56] Yet, he was reticent to do so and advised Patel to seek some method, such as an impartial tribunal, to settle the matter of the legal relationship between Junagadh and its vassal states and their right to accede to India—a suggestion that Patel dismissed. 'I feel that if we are going to put troops into either of the disputed areas,' Mountbatten appealed to the States Minister, 'we must be sure that in doing so we are acting with unchallengeable correctitude.'[57]

Not all in New Delhi were so understanding or supportive of India's military preparations. In late September 1947, as the Indian government moved troops into Kathiawar, India's three defense chiefs (all British officers) submitted a letter to Defense Minister Baldev Singh warning that military deployments in Kathiawar carried with them the danger of clashes with Junagadh forces, with any escalating violence in the region potentially pulling in the Pakistani military. With the high demand for troops elsewhere in India, they advised against large-scale military operations. 'In brief,' they wrote, 'military action in Kathiawar may lead to war between the two Dominions and, with the bulk of the Army involved on internal security, the Army is no position to wage war.' As British officers belonging to the British Fighting Services, the defense chiefs also added that in no way could they or any other British officer serving in the Indian military take part in a war between two Dominion governments.[58] Only days earlier Field Marshal Claude Auchinleck, the Supreme Commander of all British forces serving in India and Pakistan, had already made it clear to the six commanders of the armed forces of India and Pakistan that the approximately 2,700 British officers who had volunteered to serve in the dominion forces were deputed to them for a period of one year solely for the reconstitution of the forces and advising on their future organization. Should war between the two dominion governments appear to be inevitable, Auchinleck was adamant that he would entertain no alternative course except the complete withdrawal of all British officers in the Subcontinent. It would be 'inconceivable,' he argued, to have British officers fighting against one another on opposing sides of a war.[59]

In the evening of 28 September 1947, the Indian Cabinet held a three and a half hour meeting to discuss Junagadh, which provoked 'considerable feeling' among its members. Foremost among their concerns was the 'very extraordinary' joint letter from the defense chiefs that, in effect, announced that they would be unable to carry out government policy. While Nehru was not an advocate of the use of military force and favored a diplomatic approach, he was insistent that this was 'a position which hardly any Government can accept' and promptly called in the British officers to explain themselves the following evening. Under pressure from Mountbatten and Lord Ismay, the Army Commander-in-Chief withdrew the letter and called the Cabinet's concerns a misinterpretation of their original intent.[60]

Despite the withdrawal of the letter, it produced a dangerous divide within the Cabinet, especially between Nehru and Patel. While some members, including Defense Minister Singh, supported the position of the Defense chiefs, others saw the necessity of an aggressive, militaristic approach. Patel, who as a Gujarati was especially sensitive to developments in Kathiawar, even threatened to resign unless the Cabinet backed the military preparations underway. He was prepared to risk war, which he thought a slight risk at any rate, to protect India's sovereignty and was categorically opposed to approaching any outside authority, including the UN, on the matter. Patel's position was supported by Menon, who was also on the verge of resigning as he personally handled the Kathiawar states' accession and felt the 'honour of those who had negotiated the Instruments of Accession with Indian States was at stake.' He explained that 'we have accepted the Instruments of Accession from Mangrol, Babariawad and some of the small States inside Junagadh. When they came to me for advice as to whether it was safe for them to accede, I naturally told them that the Dominion of India would protect them. Now you tell me that I cannot use troops to protect them, and we are going to let them down.' Menon even threatened to leave New Delhi and volunteer to fight with lathi in hand on behalf of the 'wronged States inside Junagadh against their oppressors,' before Mountbatten was able to calm him down. Menon told Mountbatten that unless he was able to 'pull off another miracle,' the government would break apart within the next twenty-four hours and 'disaster would overtake the country.'[61]

Mountbatten called in Nehru and Patel to discuss their disagreement that threatened the unity of the new government. After much 'fencing and maneuvering and gradually pulling the position round,' in which Mountbatten laid out the broader repercussions of India and Pakistan drifting into a war, the three were able to reach a compromise. It was agreed that, as an intermediate course, military forces up to a full brigade should be sent to Kathiawar to surround the Junagadh frontier as a show of force. But these forces should remain on Indian territory and no additional forces should be sent to Mangrol or Babariawad. In the meantime, they would 'pin their hopes' on the activities of the Provisional Government of Junagadh, which had been established from among the state's subject a few days prior, to stoke a popular uprising in the state, for which 'funds, arms and volunteers were not likely to be lacking.' While the impasse had been resolved for the moment, Mountbatten felt 'the price we had had to pay was to bring appreciably nearer the danger of war' with tensions remaining between the Prime Minister and Deputy Prime Minister. Nehru maintained that if Mountbatten's advice was ever overridden by the Cabinet, he would resign. On the other hand, Mountbatten recounted Patel's comment that 'he had eaten out of my hand from the day I had arrived, and that, if I wished him to continue to do so, I must appreciate how seriously his honour was involved over the question of Junagadh.'[62]

While debates continued within the Cabinet, events on the ground worsened. During a 1 October lunch in New Delhi between Mountbatten and the Indian and Pakistani Prime Ministers to discuss recent events in Kathiawar, Nehru was coincidentally passed a telegram stating that Junagadh troops had entered Mangrol. Nehru immediately turned to Liaquat Ali Khan and demanded a full withdrawal of Junagadh troops from both Mangrol and Babariawad. In return, he promised that no Indian troops would be sent into the two princely states, or into Junagadh, until their legal position was clearly delineated through a fair and proper general election, referendum, or plebiscite. Khan 'rather bitterly' stated that Indian troop movements along Junagadh's frontier 'savours of pressure and the intent to commit a hostile act.' Nehru vehemently replied, 'Not at all, we have no intention of committing a hostile act, but we are protecting all peoples of this State whom Junagadh's action had frightened so much.' However, when Mountbatten explained that Nehru's push for a plebiscite could be taken as a 'statement of Government policy' applicable to any other princely state, 'Pandit Nehru nodded his head sadly; Mr Liaquat Ali Khan's eyes sparkled; and there is no doubt that the same thought was in each of their minds "Kashmir."'[63] Khan later remarked to Mountbatten that he would consider the issue of a plebiscite 'if the same general principle was to apply in other cases.'[64]

The Provisional Government of Junagadh

As part of Menon's September 1947 trip to Kathiawar, he traveled to Rajkot to confer with various regional political leaders, including the Jam Saheb of Nawanagar, about setting up a Provisional Government of Junagadh under the leadership of Mahatma Gandhi's nephew Samaldas Gandhi, a Junagadh native. This populist organization was intended to serve as an alternative political authority challenging the Nawab's sovereignty. During a lengthy conversation on 18 September, Menon directed them to renounce the actions of the Nawab in front of the largest possible gathering and proclaim the formation of the provisional government consisting of the 'true representatives of the people.' Menon promised moral and material support, though the movement should maintain the appearance of having been an organically formed and spontaneous uprising against the Nawab and autonomous from the Indian government. While its headquarters would be initially based on Indian soil, he advised them that it should shift to Junagadh territory as soon as possible to become a vehicle for generating popular opposition against the Nawab's government.[65]

On 25 September 1947, a day after Mahatma Gandhi condemned the Nawab's actions during a prayer meeting in Delhi, the formation of the Provisional Government of Junagadh was announced at a large public meeting in Bombay. The organization issued a proclamation declaring:

> [B]y transferring the allegiance of his subjects against their will to Pakistan and preparing for a reign of terror to coerce them to acquiesce in such trans- fer, the Nawab has forfeited his claim to the allegiance of his subjects … the Dominion of Pakistan in accepting the said Instrument of Accession has violated the principle of self-determination as also the forestated understand- ing on which Pakistan was agreed to be formed and that therefore the said Instrument of Accession is null and void and not binding on the subjects of the State or the territories.[66]

Four days later, as members of India's Cabinet debated the use of military force in Junagadh, Mountbatten argued instead that India's political leaders rest 'their hope' on the provisional government, 'which Mr. Menon had so ably formed in Bombay under the leadership of Mr. Gandhi's nephew.' Nehru quickly agreed with this suggestion and pressed that this group, as the representative of Junagadh's people, 'should quickly establish their reign over those "island" territories in Junagadh within the Dominion of India,' according to a top secret note by Mountbatten.[67]

The Indian government was careful to squash any suspicion that it was providing any support or encouragement, or was in any way connected, to Samaldas Gandhi and the provisional government. In early October 1947, when Buch informed Menon that Gandhi wanted to come to New Delhi to discuss events in Kathiawar, Menon refused this request, arguing that 'any official recognition on our part [of the provisional government] would be unwise as it would derogate from the character of the movement as a spontaneous rising of the Junagadh people.'[68] Nehru also informed Liaquat Ali Khan that the Indian government played no role in the establishment of this group or encouraged its activities. He affirmed that it 'appears to be the spontaneous expression of popular resentment against Junagadh's accession.'[69] Samaldas Gandhi later echoed this position to a *Daily Telegraph* correspondent, explaining that it was his 'inner voice' that told him that he must liberate Junagadh from 'the yoke' of the Nawab's rule and began recruiting supporters and purchasing firearms to accomplish this self-appointed mission.[70] In his 1956 memoir, Menon alluded to this perspective and omitted his promise of Indian support for the establishment of the group. He wrote: 'Samaldas Gandhi was determined to set up a parallel government for the State and to organize an intensive agitation throughout Kathiawar. All I could do in the circumstances was to counsel restraint on the leaders, and to warn Buch, the Regional Commissioner, to keep a watch over developments and report to me, if necessary, daily.'[71]

Soon after its formation, the provisional government moved from Bombay to Rajkot. In the afternoon of 31 September, armed volunteers from the group scaled the outside walls of Junagadh House in Rajkot city and forced their way in, occupying the building as its new headquarters—though, at the time of its occupation, there were only around ten servants within the house acting as caretakers. Later that evening they ceremoniously raised the Indian tricolor flag to mark the occasion and renamed the building Azad Junagadh House. Pakistani officials condemned this as a subversive and criminal act against Pakistani territory encouraged by Indian authorities.[72] From this base, the provisional government became the principal instigator of popular agitation against the Nawab and his government. The provisional government's supporters within Kathiawar were encouraging the region's residents to provide the group their full moral and material support while also emphasizing that the fight was against the Nawab and his government and not directed against Junagadh's Muslim population.[73] The actions of the provisional government were paired with the Indian government enforcing an economic boycott and suspending air, postal and telegraph services to the state. In Samaldas Gandhi's first speech in Rajkot, he warned that any violations of the economic boycott would be 'punished in a drastic manner.'[74]

Forces under the provisional government soon expanded their reach as they marched ever closer to the Junagadh frontier in the coming weeks, occupying villages along the way. On 25 October, Indian media reported that the group's members had seized twelve villages within a pocket of Junagadh state territory, with all state servants and policemen taken prisoner. Their early morning advance into these villages was met with little local resistance. In Amrapur village, the provisional government troops even stumbled upon twelve sleeping policemen with loaded rifles under their pillows. Soon after this occupation, the villagers held a meeting to announce their accession to India and request protection and supplies from the Indian government. By 1 November, the number of occupied villages had increased to thirty-three with a total population of thirty thousand; the provisional government forces were now only around twenty miles from Junagadh proper.[75] As the group continued its quick advance from village to village, Samaldas Gandhi announced, 'Not a sparrow from the Junagadh Nawab appeared to offer resistance to our forces in any of the villages captured by our advancing army.' Nevertheless, he warned, 'we cannot rule out the possibility of a counterattack by the Nawab's forces, as this is, after all, a war. But let it be understood that we are thoroughly prepared for any such contingency.' In late October, Kalidas Shelat, president of the Junagadh Aid Committee, claimed that the provisional government had secured enough arms for a thousand-man battalion to serve as the nucleus of its army.[76]

As pockets of Junagadh territory increasingly slipped out of the state government's control, the security situation rapidly worsened. Indian authorities received widespread reports of 'a reign of terrorism' against Junagadh's Hindu population, with many 'panicky and fleeing.' These included mass conversions of Hindus, the desecration of Hindu temples and dacoits being released from prison and then armed and set loose in Hindu communities. It was even claimed that the Begum of Junagadh took a vow that she would refrain from eating her dinner each day unless she had converted six Hindu girls. By the end of September, over sixty thousand Hindus, or around 10 percent of the state's total population, had fled the state.[77] Adding to the government's problems, its primary sources of revenue (railways and customs) had completely dried up over the previous two months due to India's economic blockade. Despite Pakistan providing some assistance, many residents faced severe food shortages. If the anti-Hindu actions within Junagadh were not checked, Indian authorities feared a repetition of the violence in the Punjab as Muslim communities were targeted within Gujarat and Bombay as retribution.[78] In the face of pressure from India and growing unrest within the state, the Nawab and the Royal Family, along with the Nawab's dogs, the family jewels and the entire cash balance of the state treasury, were evacuated by air to Karachi on 24 October, leaving the state's Diwan to handle any fallout from his actions. Shortly after, a seven thousand person gathering at Junagadh House in Rajkot, largely consisting of Junagadh subjects who had fled the state, passed a resolution that the

Nawab's flight was an abdication of his political authority and called on the Indian government to assist the provisional government in taking control of the state, a move that was even supported by some Islamic organizations in the state, including the influential Jamiat organization.[79]

India's annexation of Junagadh

On 4 October 1947, the Indian Defence Committee (established the previous month in response to disagreements within the Cabinet over Junagadh) continued to debate how to handle the situation, but directed the defense chiefs to prepare plans for the military occupation of Babariawad and Mangrol.[80] Nehru ordered India's naval ships and aircraft to be available 'for such use as may be necessary in Kathiawar.' Above all, he felt India should deploy sufficient forces in the region to 'exercise a strangling pressure on Junagadh' and 'make people in Kathiawar and elsewhere realize that we are actively dealing with the situation,' while also taking steps to ensure these actions did not lead to war with Pakistan by continually framing the military deployments as a defensive action.[81]

In the morning of 5 October, six Indian naval ships docked in the nearby Porbandar State and deposited a company group with engineering, signals and medical support along with a troop of light tanks and a squadron of Tempest fighter aircraft. The forces belonging to other princely states within the region were also requisitioned by the Indian government for guarding Junagadh's frontier. The purpose of this deployment, according to an Indian government press communique, was 'to reassure the people of the States which have acceded to the Dominion of India and to convince them that the Government of India will do all that lies in their power to protect their legitimate interests.'[82] Other princes in Kathiawar who had already acceded to India supported such military movements. Two days after troops landed in Porbandar, the Maharaja of Gondal State, which had sovereignty over villages surrounded by Junagadh territory, publicly announced his opposition to Junagadh's accession to Pakistan and hoped that all possible efforts would be made 'to restore Junagadh to its proper and legitimate place as an integral part of Kathiawar.'[83]

For the princely states within the region that had not yet acceded, senior Indian officials were no longer in a waiting mood. The Nawab of Manavadar, Ghulam Moinuddin Khan, reported to the Pakistani government that a States Ministry official had passed through his territory accompanied by around three hundred Indian troops in lorries to reach the taluka, or hereditary estate, of Bantwa and take over its management. That same day, Bantwa's talukdar, Himat Khan, was driven away under armed escort to Rajkot to sign the Instrument of Accession for India and where his wife claimed he was being forcibly confined by Indian authorities. Moinuddin Khan interpreted this as imminent preparations for Indian military action against his state and requested military assistance from Pakistan.[84] The Nawab was right. On the morning of 23 October, over one thousand Indian troops entered Manavadar and took control of the state, with one Arab soldier of the Manavadar state forces killed in the operation.[85] The troops placed the Nawab and royal family under house arrest in the palace at Sonagadh. Following an extensive search of the palace, the troops reported finding an underground arms factory for making muzzle-loading guns, which they claimed were being distributed among the Muslims to terrorize the state's Hindu population.[86]

With Indian forces increasingly surrounding Junagadh, the state government attempted to consolidate its own limited forces into defensive positions at the state's frontier. Bhutto also reached out to Jinnah and the Pakistani Foreign Secretary to request military assistance before the state was 'overwhelmed by superior forces hanging over us.' However, Prime Minister Khan had intimated to Nehru that he had no intention of dispatching Pakistani troops to the state.[87] With both Indian and Pakistani attention increasingly occupied by events in Kashmir, Pakistani officials were growing impatient with the situation in Junagadh and the intransigence of state authorities. During a lengthy meeting with Mountbatten in Lahore on 1 November, Jinnah bent to his counterpart's arguments and acknowledged that he had been 'most averse' to accepting Junagadh's accession. In the discussion, he explained that he had 'demurred for a long time' but finally gave in to the desperate appeals from the Nawab and other Junagadh officials. Jinnah also stated that Mangrol's accession was forced on him and withdrawn 'almost before the ink was dry.'[88] Junagadh's political leadership was sensitive to this declining interest. Bhutto complained to Jinnah that while 'immediately after accession [to Pakistan], His Highness and myself received hundreds of messages chiefly from Muslims congratulating us on the decision, today our brethren are indifferent and cold. Muslims of Kathiawar seem to have lost all their enthusiasm for Pakistan.'[89]

Despite the assurances of the Pakistani government, an exasperated Nehru wrote to Mountbatten on 15 October that not only had Junagadh's troops not been withdrawn but they had crossed through the territory of Jetpur State, which had acceded to India. He asserted that this was 'not only a further act of aggression, but also, in the circumstances, appears to be a deliberate flouting of our proposals.' Nehru continued: 'All this is rather difficult to swallow and we can hardly sit by watching these developments. The smaller States of Kathiawar are getting nervous and rather frightened and have appealed to us for help. None of them is safe from this kind of aggression.'[90] At that time, reports were circulating in the Indian media about hundreds of 'visitors,' the majority of whom were alleged to be ex-servicemen, arriving in Junagadh from Pakistan, and armed by the state government along with a general release of criminals from prisons to aid in the state's defense.[91]

Patel was also losing his patience. In a 21 October Defence Committee meeting, he argued that the prolonged delay in taking any positive action put other states who had acceded to India in a difficult position as the government was giving a general impression of weakness and inability to act decisively. Patel explained that princes in the region were informing him that unless the Indian government provided them with protection, they would return their Instruments of Accession. He pushed for sending troops into Mangrol and Babariawad, which would enable a plebiscite to be held in both states on the issue of accession. Nehru concurred that any further delay was to Pakistan's advantage. It was finally agreed that troops should be sent into the two states without delay under a flag of truce but with overwhelming force to dissuade any resistance.[92] By early November, the Indian government had taken over the administration of both princely states.[93]

Nehru pushed that military action in Junagadh must now be considered in the context of the invasion of Kashmir as military operations in Kathiawar could affect the Indian position along the northern frontier. Patel was quick to offer his support for maintaining the course in Junagadh as other princely states in the region had already been informed of India's intentions. He further argued that 'the longer the Junagadh situation was prolonged, the bigger an issue and the more insoluble it would become.' However, he stated that if Pakistan accepted an immediate plebiscite in Junagadh the military action, now planned for 1 November, could be safely canceled. The other members of the committee echoed Patel's arguments. At any rate, General Rob Lockhart, the army Commander-in-Chief, explained that troops were not yet able to move out of the region and redeploy to Kashmir. Ultimately, it was decided to move forward with the military operation.[94]

At this point, Junagadh's administrative structures had essentially collapsed. Bhutto finally came to recognize the disastrous consequences of the decision to accede to Pakistan, which demanded a reorientation of state policy. On 8 November, Bhutto informed the Indian government through N.M. Buch that he was prepared to hand over the Junagadh's administration to avoid a complete breakdown within the state, to which Indian authorities agreed with immediate effect.[95] The Indian government acted without delay to secure control of the state under the authority of Buch; Mountbatten was angry that the decision was made without consulting him beforehand.[96] The following day, an Indian battalion accompanied by tanks crossed into Junagadh territory. They were met at the state's frontier by a crowd of senior Junagadh officials including Major Harvey Jones, the head of the Junagadh state forces and senior member of the Junagadh State Council, who escorted the Indian troops into the state. Bhutto was not present as he had flown to Karachi the previous day to meet with the Nawab.

Indian forces quickly took control of Veraval airport and the city's port facilities and met no opposition from the state forces as Major Jones had already disarmed them as a precaution. While Buch reported that Major Jones was fully cooperative, he found many of the Muslim officers within the state forces to be 'sullen' about the turn of events, and 'some mischief makers' burnt several railway carriages and the Saradiya railway station and severed some telegraph wires.[97] By 6 p.m. on 9 November, Indian forces reached Junagadh City.[98] Media reports stated that the local population, who had been under duress amid the deteriorating security conditions, welcomed the advancing Indian troops with large crowds lining the road and giving them an ovation as they marched through the city.[99] Hot on the heels of the Indian advance was the Provisional Government of Junagadh. After hearing news of the capitulation of the Nawab's government, the group's leadership decided to relocate its operations to Junagadh proper immediately and announced that it would be celebrating victory in Junagadh's capital on Diwali (12 November 1947).[100]

The Nawab and Bhutto insisted that this arrangement was only a temporary measure to protect law and order in the state and did not mean that all issues between India and Junagadh had been resolved or that the Junagadh government had agreed to accede to the Indian Union. Nevertheless, with the Junagadh authorities now painfully aware that help from Pakistan was not forthcoming, it was reported that Major Jones had concluded negotiations with Samaldas Gandhi and the provisional government on the same day that Indian troops entered the state, with the result that Junagadh had effectively joined India. The Indian troop presence within the princely state made this a fait accompli. Once India had Junagadh firmly in their grasp, they would not let it out again, citing the need for India's steadying hand to avoid further disorder and potential bloodshed that could spread beyond Junagadh's border.[101] Indian authorities dissolved Junagadh's State Council, disbanded the state forces and began to set up an interim executive council to run the state administration. Under an ordinance issued by Mountbatten, the administrator of the state also seized control of the Nawab's existing assets, including bank deposits, government securities and shares in various companies.[102] After India took control of Junagadh, Bhutto attempted to rationalize his action by explaining that the state's original accession to Pakistan was motivated by fear of the communist movement, which he argued was much stronger in India than in Pakistan.[103]

Despite previously expressing private apprehensions about supporting Junagadh, the Pakistani government registered its strong protest with New Delhi, referring to the military action as an 'unwarranted violation' of Pakistani territory.[104] In a December 1947 meeting in Lahore, Liaquat Ali Khan drew explicit parallels between Indian action in Kashmir and Junagadh. He pointed to the fact that the Provisional Government of Junagadh had been set up on Indian territory and provided with arms before invading and capturing territory belonging to Junagadh. While Nehru openly admitted that India had in fact been 'in the wrong' about certain issues in Junagadh, he argued that drawing this kind of parallel was untenable given the vast differences in scale between the situations.[105] Nevertheless, Khan continued to highlight the hypocrisy inherent in the Indian position toward the two princely states, arguing that its acceptance of Jammu and Kashmir's accession was a 'repudiation of the very principles on which it had only one month before opposed Junagadh's accession to Pakistan.' India's military actions within Kathiawar, Khan further argued, 'lend further support to the contention of the Pakistan Government that the Government of India intend by all possible means at their disposal to destroy Pakistan.'[106]

With Junagadh now firmly in the hands of the Indian government and Pakistani officials only lodging complaints, Patel was triumphant, hoping the assertion of India's sovereignty over Junagadh would have a mollifying effect on other princely states, in particular Hyderabad. On 12 November, he flew into Rajkot where he was met by a large crowd at the airport. In a speech at a public meeting later that day, Patel stated: 'Despite the attempts of Pakistan to avoid commitment in the case of Hyderabad, and despite their attempts to avoid facing facts in Junagadh, the will of people will have its way. If Hyderabad does not see the writing on the wall, it goes the way Junagadh has gone.' He continued: 'I assure you that we are not going to let the grass grow under our feet. Even if all these troubles come at the same time we have got resources which would enable us to stand up to all them at the same time.' He then asked the crowd to indicate by a show of hands who favored accession to India and who Pakistan. Menon recounted that over ten thousand hands immediately shot up in the air in favor of accession to India. Afterwards, Patel completed his tour by visiting the Somnath Temple, finding it 'dilapidated, neglected and forlorn,' and pledged to rebuild it to its original glory.[107] Journalists reported a festive spirit spreading throughout the state's capital city, with signs posted stating 'Jai Hind' and 'Sardar Patel Zindabad.' Almost overnight, twenty thousand people who had fled their homes over the previous two months had returned.[108] On 22 November, the leaders of the Muslim Jamiat even declared their intention to dissolve the organization and join forces with the local Praja Mandal, despite a backlash against Muslims in the state that included mobs looting Muslim-owned shops. Following the prevailing winds of political opinion, they urged Muslims in Junagadh to forget past events and align themselves with the popular forces within the state while pledging loyalty to the Indian Union and expressing their willingness to fight Pakistan if the two dominions should go to war.[109]

While the Nawab's actions provoked fears within India of Muslim-ruled princely states joining Pakistan, events progressed rapidly after the Indian military took control of the state. In early January 1948, the Provisional Government of Junagadh was dissolved as the primary purpose for which it was formed was fulfilled, according to an announcement by Samaldas Gandhi. Junagadh's Praja Mandal, with Gandhi now serving as its President, assumed the provisional government's role as the political representative of the state's subjects. In September of that year, Gandhi was elected unopposed as a representative to the Constituent Assembly.[110] On 20 February 1948, the Indian government held the promised plebiscite under the supervision of the Judicial Commissioner of Western India and the Gujarat States Region, C.B. Nagarkar. This was the first popular election in the history of the state. In the days leading up to the vote, a correspondent from the *Daily Telegraph* reported seeing lorries with loudspeakers and covered in placards exhorting the people to vote for India, with the Praja Mandal active in generating support for India. However, some Muslims within the state reportedly told foreign journalists that their vote for India was out of fear rather than conviction, as attacks continued against the Muslim population. The resulting vote was an overwhelming majority in favor of India. Among Junagadh's electorate, 190,779 voted for accession to India against only 91 for Pakistan, a final rebuke of the Nawab's actions.[111] New Delhi maintained control of Junagadh to reorganize its administration and work to democratize the state until 20 February 1949, when the administrator of Junagadh handed control of the state over to the Chief Secretary of the Saurashtra Union, an amalgamation of the former princely states within Kathiawar. In 1956, the Saurashtra Union was dissolved, with its territory joined with Bombay State. Four years later, the political boundaries would again be reorganized, with the former princely state of Junagadh becoming a part of the state of Gujarat.

The problems with Junagadh were soon eclipsed by events in Jammu and Kashmir and Hyderabad. Yet, before international attention was drawn to India's two largest princely states, Junagadh's accession to Pakistan served as a curtain raiser to the ongoing political tensions and conflict between India and Pakistan in relation to the status of the former princely states and an example of the underlying tensions between the princely states and the Indian government.[112] It served as a demonstration of India's uncompromising position toward the political status of the princely states as it found common cause with the state's subject to assert Indian leaders' conception of state sovereignty, regardless of what the various princes and their supporters argued about the princely states' position under the layered sovereignty of the British Raj and their legal rights under the terms of the British withdrawal. Junagadh was an early test of the government's ultimate willingness to deploy the military to challenge the political authority of the princes, undo the layered sovereignty of the British Raj and force the issue of the princely states' political integration into the Indian Union.

The situation in Junagadh also exposed dangerous cracks within the Indian government—in particular, between Nehru and Patel. There were markedly different ideas among the Cabinet members about how best to handle Junagadh to ensure its integration with India and to what extent military force should be deployed within India's claimed territory, divisions that would persist in the handling of Jammu and Kashmir and Hyderabad. Regardless of this debate, all within New Delhi agreed that acquiescing to Junagadh's accession to Pakistan would create a dangerous precedent for the other princely states and give legitimacy to the princes' claims that they held the right to abstain from acceding to the Indian Union—whether by acceding to Pakistan or declaring independence—to protect their sovereignty. Ultimately, the Indian government felt that a show of military force within the region was necessary to demonstrate its commitment to the territorial integrity of India and to assert its political control within Junagadh and the broader Kathiawar region.

Notes

1 Colonel J.W. Watson, *Statistical Account of Junagadh; Being the Junagadh Contribution to the Kathiawar Portion of the Bombay Gazette* (Bombay: Bombay Gazette Steam Press, 1884), p. 11.
2 Rakesh Ankit, 'The accession of Junagadh, 1947–48: Colonial sovereignty, state violence and post-independence India,' *Indian Economic and Social History Review* 53:3 (2017), 371–404.
3 Corfield, *The Princely India I Knew*, p. 33.
4 McLeod, *Sovereignty, Power, Control*, pp. 115–65.
5 Sir William Lee-Warner, 'Kathiawar,' *Journal of the Royal Society of Arts* 61:3145 (1913), 391–405.
6 Menon, *The Story of the Integration of the Indian States*, p. 131.

7 Shah Nawaz Bhutto to M.A. Jinnah, 11 August 1947, *Jinnah Papers Volume VIII*, p. 257.
8 Campbell-Johnson, *Mission with Mountbatten*, p. 223.
9 McLane, *Indian Nationalism and the Early Congress*, pp. 319–20.
10 'Junagadh "Praja Mandal", No State Recognition,' *Times of India*, 5 December 1938.
11 NAI, PP_000000005420, Rajkot Agreement & Breach, Private Papers of Sardar Patel, 1938, p. 204.
12 Rakesh Ankit, 'Junagadh, India and the Logic of Occupation and Appropriation, 1947–49,' *Studies in History* 34:2 (2018), 113–14.
13 Ibid.
14 Menon, *The Story of the Integration of the Indian States*, p. 125.
15 NAI, PP_000000005926, Kathiawar state (Junagadh) 1947–1948, Private Papers of Sardar Patel, 1948, p. 32; Menon, *The Story of the Integration of the Indian States*, p. 125.
16 Guha, *India After Gandhi*, p. 64; Note by Alan Campbell-Johnson on Junagadh, 19 September 1948, *Jinnah Papers Volume VIII*, p. 275.
17 NAI, PP_000000005926, Kathiawar state (Junagadh) 1947–1948, Private Papers of Sardar Patel, 1948, p. 32.
18 National Archives, U.K., FO/371/63569, Transfer of power in India—relations of India with the United Kingdom (Folder 5), September 1947.
19 Note by Albert A. Rabida, 15 October 1947, *Jinnah Papers Volume VIII*, p. 286.
20 Copland, 'The Princely States, the Muslim League, and the Partition of India in 1947,' p. 41.
21 Ankit, 'Junagadh, India and the Logic of Occupation and Appropriation, 1947–49,' pp. 114–15; Menon, *The Story of the Integration of the Indian States*, p. 126.
22 Shah Nawaz Bhutto to M.A. Jinnah, 11 August 1947, *Jinnah Papers Volume VIII*, p. 257.
23 Ruler of Junagadh to M.A. Jinnah, 11 August 1947, *Jinnah Papers Volume VIII*, p. 259.
24 Press Communique, 15 August 1947, *Jinnah Papers Volume V*, p. 550.
25 Campbell-Johnson, *Mission with Mountbatten*, p. 222; Menon, *The Story of the Integration of the Indian States*, p. 127.
26 Menon, *The Story of the Integration of the Indian States*, p. 129.
27 Ruler of Junagadh to M.A. Jinnah, 15 August 1947, *Jinnah Papers Volume VIII*, pp. 260–1; Shah Nawaz Bhutto to M.W. Abbasi, 20 August 1947, *Jinnah Papers Volume V*, p. 548.
28 Ruler of Junagadh to M.A. Jinnah, 31 August 1947, *Jinnah Papers Volume V*, p. 573.
29 S.N. Bhutto to M.A. Jinnah, 4 September 1947, *Jinnah Papers Volume V*, pp. 578–9.
30 Shah Nawaz Bhutto to I.H.M. Abrahani, 6 September 1947, *Jinnah Papers Volume V*, pp. 584–5.

31 M.A. Jinnah to S.N. Bhutto, 8 September 1947, *Jinnah Papers Volume V*, p. 586.
32 Louis Mountbatten to M.A. Jinnah, 22 September 1947, *Jinnah Papers Volume V*, p. 608.
33 Note by Alan Campbell-Johnson on Junagdah, 19 September 1947, *Jinnah Papers Volume VIII*, p. 277.
34 Menon, *The Story of the Integration of the Indian States*, p. 127.
35 Ankit, 'The accession of Junagadh, 1947–48,' p. 375.
36 Jawaharlal Nehru to Liaquat Ali Khan, 12 September 1947, *Jinnah Papers Volume VIII*, pp. 269–70.
37 M.A. Jinnah to Louis Mountbatten, 25 September 1947, *Jinnah Papers Volume VIII*, pp, 287–8.
38 Liaquat Ali Khan to Jawaharlal Nehru, 25 September 1947, *Jinnah Papers Volume V*, p. 614.
39 S.M. Nasiruddin to M.A. Jinnah, 3 August 1947, *Jinnah Papers Volume VIII*, p. 256.
40 Regional Commissioner, Rajkot to Ministry of States, 21 September 1947, *Jinnah Papers Volume VIII*, p. 278; NAI, PP_000000005926, Kathiawar state (Junagadh) 1947–1948, Private Papers of Sardar Patel, 1948, pp. 30, 53.
41 NAI, PP_000000005926, Kathiawar state (Junagadh) 1947–1948, Private Papers of Sardar Patel, 1948, p. 53.
42 '"Hold Plebiscite In Junagadh", Jam Saheb's Appeal to Nawab,' *Times of India* (23 September 1947); '"Danger To Peace Of India", Jam Saheb on Issue of Junagadh,' *Times of India* (24 September 1947).
43 Charles W. Lewis, Jr. to George Marshall, 27 October 1947, *Jinnah Papers Volume V*, p. 612; Menon, *The Story of the Integration of the Indian States*, pp. 129–30.
44 M.A. Jinnah to Louis Mountbatten, 18 September 1947, *Jinnah Papers Volume V*, p. 604.
45 Ruler of Manavadar to M.A. Jinnah, 21 September 1947, *Jinnah Papers Volume V*, pp. 606–7; NAI, PP_000000005926, Kathiawar state (Junagadh) 1947–1948, Private Papers of Sardar Patel, 1948, p. 52.
46 NAI, PP_000000005926, Kathiawar state (Junagadh) 1947–1948, Private Papers of Sardar Patel, 1948, pp. 47–50.
47 Ankit, 'Junagadh, India and the Logic of Occupation and Appropriation, 1947–49,' p. 117; Campbell-Johnson, *Mission with Mountbatten*, p. 224.
48 Shah Nawaz Bhutto to I.H.M. Abrahani, 6 September 1947, *Jinnah Papers Volume V*, p. 584; S.N. Bhutto to Liaquat Ali Khan, 16 September 1947, *Jinnah Papers Volume V*, pp. 600–2.
49 Louis Mountbatten to M.A. Jinnah, 22 September 1947, *Jinnah Papers Volume V*, pp. 607–8.
50 M.A. Jinnah to Louis Mountbatten, 25 September 1947, *Jinnah Papers Volume V*, p. 610.
51 Louis Mountbatten to M.A. Jinnah, 29 September 1947, *Jinnah Papers Volume VIII*, p. 306.

52 Charles W. Lewis, Jr. to George Marshall, 27 October 1947, *Jinnah Papers Volume V*, p. 613.
53 Ibid., p. 614; Campbell-Johnson, *Mission with Mountbatten*, p. 244.
54 Charles W. Lewis, Jr. to George Marshall, 27 October 947, *Jinnah Papers Volume V*, p 614.
55 Louis Mountbatten to Jawaharlal Nehru, 28 September 1947, *Jinnah Papers Volume VIII*, p. 300.
56 Louis Mountbatten to Jawaharlal Nehru, 28 September 1947, *Jinnah Papers Volume VIII*, p. 304–5.
57 NAI, PP_000000005282, Accession to Junagadh to Pakistan Dominion, Private Papers of Sardar Patel, 1947, pp. 1–2, 5.
58 Projected Operations in Kathiawar, 27 September 1947, *Jinnah Papers Volume VIII*, pp. 298–9.
59 National Archives, U.K., FO/371/63570, Transfer of power in India—relations of India with the United Kingdom (Folder 6), September–November 1947.
60 Jawaharlal Nehru to Louis Mountbatten, 28 September 1947, *Jinnah Papers Volume VIII*, pp. 302–3; R.M.M. Lockhart to Jawaharlal Nehru, 29 September 1947, *Jinnah Papers Volume VIII*, pp. 307–8.
61 Notes by Louis Mountbatten on Junagadh Crisis, 29 September 1947, *Jinnah Papers Volume VIII*, pp. 309–11.
62 Ibid., p. 313–14, 316.
63 Note by Louis Mountbatten, 1 October 1947, *Jinnah Papers Volume VIII*, pp. 320–2.
64 Louis Mountbatten to Jawaharlal Nehru, 18 October 1947, *Jinnah Papers Volume VIII*, p. 354.
65 NAI, PP_000000006644, Confidential Report about States 1947, Private Papers of Sardar Patel, 1947, p. 1; National Archives, U.K., FO/371/63570, Transfer of power in India—relations of India with the United Kingdom (Folder 6), September–November 1947.
66 Declaration by the Subjects of Junagadh State, Formation of Provisional Government, 25 September 1947, *Jinnah Papers Volume VIII*, p. 294.
67 Notes by Louis Mountbatten on Junagadh Crisis, 29 September 1947, *Jinnah Papers Volume VIII*, pp. 313–14.
68 Ankit, 'Junagadh, India and the Logic of Occupation and Appropriation, 1947–49,' pp. 118–19.
69 Jawaharlal Nehru to Liaquat Ali Khan, 5 October 1947, *Jinnah Papers Volume VIII*, p. 341.
70 A.S.B. Shah to S.M. Yusuf, 24 February 1948, *Jinnah Papers Volume VIII*, p. 399.
71 Menon, *The Story of the Integration of the Indian States*, p. 135.
72 Charles W. Lewis, Jr. to George Marshall, 27 October 1947, *Jinnah Papers Volume V*, p. 613; M. Ikramullah to G.S. Bajpai, 2 October 1947, *Jinnah Papers Volume VIII*, p. 325; 'Provisional Government Occupy Junagadh House in Rajkot,' *Evening News* (1 October 1947).
73 'No Quarrel with Junagadh Muslims,' *Hindustan Times* (5 October 1947).

74 Charles W. Lewis, Jr. to George Marshall, 27 October 1947, *Jinnah Papers Volume V*, pp. 613–14.

75 '12 Junagadh Villages Occupied by Émigré Government,' *India News Chronicle* (26 October 1947); 'India Takes Control in Junagadh,' *Statesman* (10 November 1947); 'Four More Junagadh Villages Occupied,' *Hindustan Times* (27 October 1947); 'Three More Junagadh Villages Occupied,' *Hindustan Times* (2 November 1947); 'India's Seizure of Manavadar, Pakistan's Protest,' *Times of India* (4 November 1947).

76 'Pakistan Troop Movement Near Kathiawar,' *Free Press Journal* (30 October 1947); 'Ready to Meet Counterattack,' *Free Press Journal* (30 October 1947).

77 'Junagadh Encroaches on Union Territory,' *Hindustan Times* (23 September 1947); Menon, *The Story of the Integration of the Indian States*, pp. 138, 142.

78 NAI, PP_000000005926, Kathiawar state (Junagadh) 1947–1948, Private Papers of Sardar Patel, 1948, p. 37.

79 'Plea of Junagadh Residents, "Occupy All Territory",' *Times of India* (1 November 1947); 'Junagadh Muslims, Talks with "Provisional Government" Head,' *Times of India* (3 November 1947).

80 Notes by Louis Mountbatten on Junagadh Crisis, 29 September 1947, *Jinnah Papers Volume VIII*, p. 315; Minutes of Second Defense Committee meeting, 4 October 1947, *Jinnah Papers Volume VIII*, p. 334.

81 A Note on Junagadh by the Prime Minister of India, 3 October 1947, *Jinnah Papers Volume VIII*, pp. 339–40.

82 'Indian Land, Air And Naval Units Move to Porbandar,' *Hindustan Times* (5 October 1947); 'India Demands Plebiscite on Junagadh Issue,' *Hindustan Times* (6 October 1947).

83 'Junagadh Must Return To Its Place As Integral Part of Kathiawar, Accession To Pakistan Is Danger to Peace Says Gondal Maharaja,' *National Call* (7 October 1947).

84 Ruler of Mandavar to M.A. Jinnah & Others, 3 October 1947, *Jinnah Papers Volume VIII*, p. 412; Ruler of Mandavar to M.A. Jinnah, 4 October 1947, *Jinnah Papers Volume VIII*, p. 413; Begum Himat Khan to M.A. Jinnah, 9 October 1947, *Jinnah Papers Volume VIII*, p. 414.

85 A.K. Quraishi to M.A. Jinnah, 24 October 1947, *Jinnah Papers Volume VIII*, p. 415.

86 'Gun-Making Factory in Manavadar, Search of Ruler's Palace,' *Evening News*, 3 November 1947.

87 S.N. Bhutto to M. Ikramullah (Copy to M.A. Jinnah), 3 October 1947, *Jinnah Papers Volume VIII*, p. 327; Minutes of Second Defence Committee meeting, 4 October 1947, *Jinnah Papers Volume VIII*, p. 331.

88 Note of Discussion of Mountbatten with M.A. Jinnah, 1 November 1947, *Jinnah Papers Volume VIII*, pp. 373–4.

89 Guha, *India After Gandhi*, p. 65.

90 Jawaharlal Nehru to Louis Mountbatten, 15 October 1947, *Jinnah Papers Volume VIII*, pp. 351–2.

91 'Junagadh Arms "Visitors" From Pakistan, General Release of Criminals,' *Hindustan Times* (15 October 1947); 'Situation in Junagadh Worsens, Arms and Ammunition Pour In,' *Free Press Journal* (25 October 1947).

92 Minutes of Sixth Meeting of Defence Committee, 21 October 1947, *Jinnah Papers Volume VIII*, pp. 357–8; Note by Conference Secretary to Commander-in-Chief, Indian Army, 20 October 1947, *Jinnah Papers Volume VIII*, p. 360; Jawaharlal Nehru to Liaquat Ali Khan, 22 October 1947, *Jinnah Papers Volume VIII*, pp. 361–2; Minutes of Seventh Meeting of Defence Committee, 23 October 1947, *Jinnah Papers Volume VIII*, p. 365.

93 'Peaceful Occupation of Babariawad and Mangrol,' *Statesman* (2 November 1947).

94 Minutes of 10th Meeting of Defence Committee, 30 October 1947, *Jinnah Papers Volume VIII*, pp. 368–72.

95 Jawaharlal Nehru to Liaquat Ali Khan, 9 November 1947, *Jinnah Papers Volume VIII*, p. 376.

96 Guha, *India After Gandhi*, p. 65.

97 NAI, PP_000000005926, Kathiawar state (Junagadh) 1947–1948, Private Papers of Sardar Patel, 1948, p. 16.

98 'India Takes Over, Troops Sent at Ruler's Request,' *Hindustan Times* (10 November 1947).

99 'India Takes Control in Junagadh.'

100 'Sardar Patel to Visit Junagadh,' *Hindustan Times* (10 November 1947).

101 'India Takes Control in Junagadh'; 'Junagadh Administration Handed Over to India; Accession Issue to Be Settled Through Further Talks,' *Pakistan Times* (11 November 1947); Faiz Muhamad Khan and Others to Louis Mountbatten, 28 November 1947, *Jinnah Papers Volume VIII*, pp. 390–1; G.S. Bajpai to M. Ikramullah, 6 January 1948, *Jinnah Papers Volume VIII*, p. 394.

102 'Junagadh Council Dissolved, Ban on Bombay Daily,' *Free Press Journal* (21 November 1947); 'Junagadh State Forces Disbanded,' *Hindustan Times* (27 November 1947); 'Junagadh Nawab's Assets Taken Over By Administrator,' *Hindustan Times* (26 December 1947).

103 'Taking Over Govt. In Junagadh,' *Hindustan Times* (11 November 1947).

104 M. Ikramullah to Liaquat Ali Khan, 2 November 1947, *Jinnah Papers Volume VIII*, p. 375.

105 Minutes of Inter-Dominion Conference on Kashmir, 8 December 1947, *Jinnah Papers Volume IX*, p. 434.

106 Liaquat Ali Khan to Jawaharlal Nehru, 30 December 1947, *Jinnah Papers Volume IX*, pp. 456, 458.

107 'Final Arbiters are the People, Sardar Warns Pakistan,' *Free Press Journal* (14 November 1947); Menon, *The Story of the Integration of the Indian States*, pp. 147–8.

108 'Junagadh People Vote for India,' *Times of India* (14 November 1947).

109 'Junagadh Muslims Join Mandal, Decision at Public Meeting,' *Times of India* (24 November 1947); NAI, PP_000000005826, Privy Purse Payments to Rulers safeguarding, Private Papers of Sardar Patel, 1949, p. 134.

110 'Junagadh Provisional Govt. Dissolved,' *Hindustan Times* (4 January 1948); 'Samaldas Gandhi Elected to Constituent Assembly,' *Hindustan Times* (22 September 1948).

111 A.S.B. Shah to S.M. Yusuf, 24 February 1948, *Jinnah Papers Volume VIII*, pp. 399–402.

112 Campbell-Johnson, *Mission with Mountbatten*, p. 9.

9

Kalat: Pakistan's frontier challenge

Just as India struggled to integrate the many princely states within its borders, Pakistan faced a similar challenge with the Muslim-majority princely states that fell within its sphere of influence. Pakistani officials initially took a more relaxed position than the Indian government regarding the ten princely states that landed within Pakistan, the most developed of which was Bahawalpur, a sizable state in the western Punjab covering an area of over sixteen thousand square miles (though, even with their small numbers, the princely states constituted half of the landmass of west Pakistan in 1947.) On the eve of the transfer of power, Jinnah maintained his legalistic position that the lapse of British paramountcy meant that every princely state would be sovereign and free to decide which domain to join, especially regarding Pakistani engagement with princely states within India. Therefore, within Pakistan, it was not only the ambiguities of British policy but the policies and promises of the Muslim League's leadership that contributed to some princes' belief in their right to maintain their sovereignty as enjoyed under the British Raj, which even attracted the interest of princely states like Junagadh and Jodhpur that would eventually accede to India. On the day Pakistan's States Negotiating Committee was established (11 August 1947), Jinnah maintained his contrasting position to Indian leadership and reiterated:

> I do not think that any of the states should be hustled into giving a definite reply immediately on or before the 15th of August. In my opinion the various states must have sufficient time to carefully consider their respective positions before they go into one constituent assembly or the other, or remain independent and enter into such arrangements as may be beneficial to both.[1]

Despite this legalistic argument, Pakistani officials were hesitant to recognize the outright independence of princely states within their sphere of influence and even less willing to entertain any of these state's interest in joining India. In the weeks before the transfer of power, Sardar Nishtar, a leading Muslim League figure from the North-West Frontier Province (NWFP), admitted to Mountbatten, 'Pakistan had no wish to coerce any State, but they would be embarrassed if States within their sphere of influence wished to join the Indian Union, and would have to consider their attitude.'[2] However, India had little interest in pursuing the accession of the princely states on the Pakistani side of the Radcliffe Line, as all were Muslim-ruled states with Muslim-majority populations. In July 1947, Menon advised Mountbatten and his assistant private secretary Peter Scott that India's principle toward these princely states should be: 'Render unto Caesar that which is Caesar's and unto God that which is God's,' without which there would 'bound to be serious trouble ahead.'[3] Apart from the circumstances in Jammu and Kashmir, this helped to relieve the pressure of quick action by Pakistani authorities. Jinnah's later attitude toward the situation in Kalat, however, reflected the pragmatism of Pakistan's state-building efforts and challenged the sincerity of his initial laissez-faire approach and respect for the princes' sovereignty, as Pakistan initially did not have the necessary administrative machinery or capacity to force the issue of accession. In the early days and weeks after the transfer of power, Pakistan's skeletal government was consumed with establishing an administrative structure and handling the chaotic aftermath of Partition.

For most princely states, Pakistani officials were also not too concerned to rush the issue of accession given many of the princes' enthusiastic support for the new Muslim state, which made clear that they would in no way challenge Pakistan's sovereignty. In the days after Pakistan's creation, letters of congratulation from the princely states poured into Karachi. On 15 August 1947, the Ruler of Amb, M. Farid Khan, wrote to Jinnah that 'for the first time we are living under the Pakistan Flag. May God bless both the Flag and the State of which it is a symbol.'[4] Amb was an early supporter of Pakistan, and, during the previous month, its ruler had placed all his personal and state resources at the disposal of the Pakistani government. His enthusiasm for joining Pakistan was such that on 1 September, after hearing the name of Amb left out of a radio announcement on the planned accession of the frontier states to Pakistan, he wrote straight away to Jinnah to have the error corrected and an announcement made that Amb was the first among the princely states in NWFP to agree to a standstill agreement and accession as clear signs of its allegiance to Pakistan.[5] Even with his enthusiastic support of the new Muslim state, he expressed his concerns over the weakness of the Pakistani government on the frontier and, once the British departed, 'there will be no power to restrain [the tribes] from flying at each other's throats.'[6]

In early August 1947, the Mehtar of Chitral, Muzaffar ul-Mulk, communicated to Jinnah his intention of shaking off Jammu and Kashmir's suzerainty, which he claimed was forced upon the state by the British government, and acceding to Pakistan.[7] In late September 1947, though he had not yet signed the Instrument of Accession, the Mehtar expressed his anxiety 'to contribute our due share towards the success and consolidation of Pakistan.' He offered up a portion of his state's timber resources, adding up to approximately twenty-five thousand logs free of cost to Pakistan, to support the country's building program, in addition to offering a special concession to the Pakistani government for the exploitation of the state's mineral resources.[8] In the next month, the Mehtar also contributed thirty thousand rupees to the Quaid-i-Azam's Relief Fund and collected warm clothing for refugees from India.[9] The Wali of Swat, an early and enthusiastic supporter of the Muslim League and Pakistan, also told Jinnah that he had no wish to continue drawing his ten thousand rupee annual allowance from the Pakistani government, as authorized under the standstill agreement he signed, and desired that this amount should instead be used by the government for expanding educational opportunities.[10]

Amid these assurances, the incoming Pakistani leadership did not pressure the princely states to sign the Instrument of Accession by the date of the transfer of power, as Indian leaders did. The negotiations over the princely states' accession were only taken up by the Pakistani government after independence with Jinnah's intention that formal accession could be finalized once these negotiations were concluded.[11] In fact, the first princely states to accede to Pakistan were Junagadh (on 15 September) and Manavadar (on 24 September), which India later annexed. The remaining of Pakistan's princely states gradually acceded between October 1947 and March 1948. For Dir and Chitral on the northwestern frontier, their rulers signed the Instrument of Accession in November 1947. Yet, the Pakistani government did not formally accept the instruments until February 1948.

Several of the princely states within Pakistan were strategically positioned—Kalat abutting the Iranian border in Balochistan and the several frontier states occupying a key part of the northwestern frontier near the border with Afghanistan. The small princely states in the mountainous and difficult to reach frontier lacked the jewels, marble palaces and other luxuries of their counterparts in the heart of India, not to mention the absence of many administrative structures or social services. The rulers of these princely states were essentially local tribal chiefs who had earned the recognition of British authorities as sovereign princes within their sections of the frontier. While these frontier states were comparatively poor and mostly running on the subsidies the British government provided, their importance far outweighed their lack of size or wealth due to their strategic positions. For the British government, it was only necessary that the princes of the frontier 'keep a firm hold' over the tribesmen within their territory and maintain law and order.[12] Beyond this imperative, they cared little for the bureaucratic efficiency and reach of the frontier states' governments. Thus, frontier states had their own rationale, distinct from the wealthier princely states in the heart of India. One British official recognized that 'Practice elsewhere is of course not always a suitable guide for dealing with these frontier "States."'[13] Olaf Caroe, who served as British Governor of NWFP from 1946–47, similarly observed that the frontier states occupied a unique place within the pantheon of princely states. 'They cannot be considered from the same aspects as other Indian states,' he wrote in 1946. '[T]hey are developments of tribal organisms among tribes to whom the tradition of chiefdom has a certain appeal as among the Arabs ... All these states are in what might be described a state of monarchical tribalism, not unlike that of the Arab Sheikhdoms.'[14]

Despite several princes' enthusiastic support for Pakistan, not all was rosy in the relationship between the Pakistani government and the princely states. The Muslim-ruled and Muslim-majority state of Bahawalpur, which occupied an important position in the Punjab along Pakistan's border with India, only acceded after a period of some hesitation. Following the lapse of paramountcy, Bahawalpur's Nawab asserted that the princely states had become fully independent with the lapse of paramountcy and that he would retain his sovereignty. On 15 August 1947, the Nawab declared himself the ruler of an independent and sovereign state, but still expressed his desire to cooperate with Pakistan. In discussions with Pakistan's first Commander-in-Chief, General Frank Messervy, Bahawalpur provided early assurances that its state forces were available to Pakistan for internal defense anywhere in the country or for shared action with the Pakistan army in face of external aggression. To support their readiness to serve Pakistan, the state's premier also expressed his desire to improve the training and equipment of the state forces along modern lines, which General Messervy strongly recommended given the advantages it provided to Pakistan's defense as it struggled to scale up its military forces.[15] Under pressure from Pakistani officials, and amid the communal violence of Partition that affected the state (though not nearly to the extent within East Punjab), the Nawab eventually agreed to join Pakistan, signing the Instrument of Accession for Pakistan in early October 1947.

There were also lingering questions about some of the frontier states' rulers and their position toward Pakistan. In September 1947, for instance, the Pakistani Minister of Communications received reports that the Nawab of Dir was not friendly toward Pakistan. He conjectured that his apathetic position was due to the fact that his rival, the Wali of Swat, was a staunch supporter of the Muslim League and the Pakistani government.[16] Only the previous month, the ruler of Amb had warned Jinnah that the Nawab of Dir still persisted in his belief that the British would never leave India, and if such a thing did come to pass he would be free to do what he wished as the sovereign ruler of his state, which had the danger of creating unrest on the frontier.[17] Pakistan's first NWFP Governor, George Cunningham, further cautioned that the Nawab was 'very suspicious by nature and it will be difficult to get him to play any intelligent part in the general setup of Pakistan.'[18] The Nawab eventually came around and signed the Instrument of Accession for Pakistan, which the government accepted on 18 February 1948.

Through the transfer of power, the princes of the frontier states also faced growing opposition from among their subjects, who looked to Pakistan as their savior. In the months before Partition was announced, members of Chitral's state forces wrote directly to Jinnah complaining that the Nawab, a leading member of the Muslim League, was 'a cruel and dishonest man' and requesting Jinnah's help 'to prevent the cruel Ruler from bad actions.' They warned that due to 'his cruelness, all the people of the State hate the Muslim League Party.'[19] The ruler of Amb also faced opposition to his continued rule. In February 1948, he wrote to Liaquat Ali Khan warning that the opposition within his state had been originally instigated by Hindus prior to Partition, and now the 'anti-landlord elements are obviously guided by nefarious motives of self-interest, designed to uproot the established social order.' He pressed the Prime Minister to curb the movement with the 'iron hand under emergency laws or promulgation of an ordinance.'[20] Ultimately, the Pakistani government's main priority along the northwestern frontier, much like the British government before them, was to take what it saw as necessary actions to maintain law and order, even if that meant maintaining colonial institutions, such as the Frontier Crimes Regulation within the Tribal Areas and the rule of the princely states, to avoid disruptions that could result in tribal unrest and political turmoil challenging the writ of the state.[21]

Pakistan's frontier challenge

Nine of the princely states within Pakistan's sphere of influence informed Pakistani authorities of their intention to accede shortly before or after the transfer of power and frequently provided a range of assistance to the new Muslim state, not only through words of encouragement and political support to the Muslim League's cause but also through various financial and logistical assistance. However, the tenth state, Kalat, made a bid to assert its independence following the lapse of paramountcy to preserve the state's sovereignty. Before and after the transfer of power, the Khan of Kalat made clear to the Pakistani government that Kalat would seek to retain its full sovereignty and refused to accede to Pakistan. After the violence and immediate aftermath of Partition, this would prove to be one of the most serious internal challenges facing Pakistan within its first year of existence, much like the challenges the Indian government faced in asserting its sovereignty within Jammu and Kashmir, Hyderabad and Junagadh.

Kalat was a frontier state that comprised the majority of the sparsely populated but vast periphery of Balochistan, which constituted 40 percent of West Pakistan's territory. The prospect of losing so large a chunk of its claimed territory so soon after its creation threatened to have a ripple effect throughout Pakistan's disparate ethnic and social groups. If the Khan of Kalat could successfully claim independence, this could invite others to question and challenge the writ of the new Pakistani government. Kalat also held a strategic position on the frontier, whose separation could lead to various law and order problems among its tribes and negatively influence Pakistan's relations with its western neighbors—Afghanistan and Iran.

Map 9.1 Map of Kalat and its subsidiary states (in black) in British India

A February 1948 *New York Times* article observed that the 'lost land' of Kalat was:

> about the size of Nebraska but sparsely settled by roving nomads and solitary farmers. There is not much there that anybody would want. To Pakistan, however, it is of vital importance. The new state cannot protect itself against aggression from the west unless it holds the Bolan Pass, the only feasible route of eastward invasion and the path through which the Mongols overran India. Above the mud huts of Quetta rises the frowning citadel that guards the pass.[22]

Understanding the strategic necessity of holding onto this frontier state, Jinnah and other Pakistani leaders could not allow the Khan of Kalat to succeed in his bid for independence.

The princely state of Kalat was originally established in 1666 primarily as a tribal confederacy, with the khans maintaining only limited control over the various Baloch tribes within his territory. Never strictly an independent kingdom, the ruling khans had paid tribute to Persian rulers before recognizing the suzerainty of Afghanistan's emirs in Kabul in the mid-eighteenth century under whom it enjoyed internal political autonomy; the Khan's niece wed the Afghan Emir Ahmed Shah Abdali.[23] Britain's engagement with Kalat originated with the events of the Anglo-Afghan War beginning in the late 1830s. The first British troops to enter Balochistan sought to secure the region's Bolan Pass as an alternative entry point to Afghanistan for the invading British forces. To secure this route, the British government signed an agreement with the Khan of the Kalat at the time, Mir Mehrab Khan, that ensured protection for the British troops as they moved through the Bolan Pass in exchange for a payment of 150,000 rupees.

With the Khan's limited control over the region's tribes, British movement through the Bolan Pass during the 1839 invasion of Afghanistan did not go as planned. Despite the agreement with the Khan, the tribes surrounding the pass attacked the advancing British army column. In retaliation, British forces assaulted Kalat, perceiving the Khan as violating the original agreement and stirring up tribal resistance against the British advance. Following Mir Mehrab Khan's death in 1840, British forces occupied the frontier state and installed a pro-British Khan in his place, Mir Nasir Khan II. Relations between the British and Kalat were defined by a new agreement, signed in October 1841. Under this agreement, the Khan would permit British troops to be stationed on his territory, a British resident would be dispatched to the state's capital to oversee Kalat's internal affairs and the British would be responsible for Kalat's foreign affairs.[24]

Through the 1840s, 1850s and 1860s, the region was rocked by persistent conflict between the Khan and various tribes within his domain, as well as broader political disorder and raiding into British territory. In particular, the Marri and Bugti tribes nestled in the eastern hills of Kalat and nominally owing allegiance to the Khan took advantage of the weakness of the Khan's government, with the British military invasion sparking an intense conflict with the Bugti that lasted until 1847. The British government felt that it was impossible to allow a 'state of anarchy' to persist given the state's strategic position on the frontier. Kalat's primary importance ultimately stemmed from its position bordering Afghanistan and Persia (as Iran was then known), which could give Imperial Russia an easier route to invade India. Calcutta intended to use Kalat as a buffer state as part of its forward policy for the defense of the frontier, signing a new treaty with the Khan in 1876 that brought the frontier state firmly within the fold of the British Indian government.

The position of the Khan of Kalat was unique within the princely order, given his position on the frontier and the strength of local tribal leaders, known as sardars. He was simultaneously the ruler of Kalat proper, territory known as the Niabats where he exercised complete authority, and the head of a tribal confederacy of tribal sardars within Balochistan, in which the khans' fluid role was essentially *primus inter pares* among the tribal chieftains. While the confederacy consisted of all the territory under the control of the hereditary sardars, they contributed no revenues to the Kalat government and were essentially autonomous in governing their territory. The khans exercised little practical authority over the sardars, with several of the more difficult and isolated tribes remaining completely outside of their influence and having never sworn allegiance to Kalat's rulers or the tribal confederacy. As part of the Treaty of 1876, the British officials acted as mediators between the Khan and sardars, with British political officers serving in Balochistan exercising most of the powers officially reserved for the Khan.

The role of the British served to further weaken the position of the Khan in relation to the sardars, with his position maintained by British recognition and support. Even in the Niabats, Kalat's administration was 'far from satisfactory' with almost 'no administrative machinery' and a lack of security forces. In this way, British officials in Balochistan observed that Kalat possessed 'not even the semblance' of a princely state.[25] By 1893, when the Durand Line was demarcated between British India and Afghanistan, Balochistan was separated into the princely state of Kalat and its feudal territories, areas that Kalat had leased to the British government (including Quetta, Bolan and Chaghi), different tribal agencies through which the British government indirectly ruled through engagement with local tribal leaders and British-ruled Balochistan, which consisted of territory ceded to the British government by Afghanistan under the terms of the 1879 Treaty of Gandamak signed during the Second Anglo-Afghan War.

Kalat and the transfer of power

By virtue of Kalat's position on India's frontier, Kalat had little in the way of direct relations with the imperial capital, a distance that fostered a certain level of detachment from British colonial affairs. Therefore, the final Khan of Kalat, Ahmad Yar Khan, who had inherited his title in September 1933, maintained that his state had never been properly a part of the British Raj and was therefore, legally speaking, not strictly a princely state, a position stoutly opposed by the British government. In addition to its geographical position, he asserted that Kalat's customs, social institutions, language and cultures were completely distinct from both British and Princely India.[26] He argued that Kalat was, for all intents and purposes, a sovereign state whose political autonomy was recognized by past Afghan and Persian kings and predated its first contact with the British in the nineteenth century. The 1876 treaty concluded with British authorities, the Khan further understood, was between two independent and sovereign governments, with the wording of the treaty describing the Khan as 'a firm ally' of the British government and 'Ruler of the Sovereign State of Kalat,' with promises that the British 'would respect the sovereignty and the independence of Kalat.'[27] When British paramountcy ended, thereby dissolving the state's treaty obligations, the Khan insisted that Kalat would simply revert to its original status held prior to the 1876 treaty, with no intention of acceding to any successor government in the Subcontinent.

In December 1946, Kalat's Prime Minister, Nawabzada Mohammed Aslam Khan, informed the Nawab of Bhopal, then serving as Chancellor of the Chamber of Princes, 'Kalat state being an independent State, His Highness can never agree to its being included in any form of an Indian Union.'[28] British officials rejected the Khan's argument, having earlier recognized Kalat as a princely state of India that did not hold a status distinct from any other princely state. The India Office in London was further concerned that Kalat's decision would encourage other princely states to pursue the same path, particularly on the frontier where it might prove easier to maintain independence from the distant capitals of the successor governments.[29] Following the announcement of Partition, Mountbatten explained to a Kalat delegation that, while princely states would, *de jure*, become independent following the transfer of power, few would benefit from it. He, therefore, advised the delegation members that Kalat had no other choice than to find some kind of association with Pakistan.[30]

In the run up to the transfer of power, Kalat's political leadership also clashed with Indian leaders over its status following the British withdrawal. Earlier that year, Nehru wrote to the Baloch leader Khan Abdus Samad Khan that under no circumstances would India agree to Kalat independence, given its position on the frontier. 'Because these areas are frontier areas, their importance is heightened from many additional points of view, including that of defence,' Nehru reasoned. 'The fact that Kalat is a border State adds to its importance from our point of view, as frontier areas are always strategic areas. An independent India cannot permit foreign forces and foreign footholds such as Kalat might afford near its own territories.'[31]

Given the geographical and cultural differences, the Muslim League generally found it difficult to develop connections into Balochistan. Nevertheless, Ahmad Yar Khan announced his general support for the creation of Pakistan in April 1947, in part to allay the restlessness increasingly prevalent among his Muslim subjects. He assured them that his government was 'ready to render any sacrifice for establishing Pakistan.'[32] After Mountbatten's 3 June announcement on Partition, he wrote to Jinnah offering 'his sincere thanks to God Who through His kindness has crowned with success your efforts in respect of *Pakistan* [*sic*]. You will very kindly accept my heartfelt congratulations on it.'[33] The Khan was later 'extremely complimentary' to Mountbatten on his role in the negotiations with Jinnah that led to Pakistan's creation.[34] On 29 June 1947, a referendum was held among the members of the Baloch Shahi Jirga (excluding the sardars from Kalat) and the elected members of the Quetta Municipal Committee, who voted unanimously to join the Pakistan Constituent Assembly. However, the electorate consisted of only a handful of individuals within British Balochistan, many of whom had been appointed to their positions by British authorities and were hardly a representative sample of Baloch public opinion at the time.[35] The Khan, on the other hand, stressed that his support for Pakistan in no way undermined Kalat's status as a sovereign state in complete control of its external and internal affairs. Its future relationship with Pakistan, he asserted, would be no different than its relationship with other neighboring Muslim states, such as Afghanistan and Iran.[36]

Shortly before the transfer of power, Mountbatten met with Ahmad Yar Khan in New Delhi to discuss the future relationship between Kalat and Pakistan. Mountbatten believed it would be most appropriate for Kalat to either accede to Pakistan or develop some mutually agreeable working relationship with the new Muslim state, given that Kalat was a Muslim-majority and Muslim-ruled princely state on the Pakistan side of the Radcliffe Line. Khan informed Mountbatten that Jinnah had already reached out to him to inquire whether Kalat would be willing to send representatives to the Pakistani Constituent Assembly and replied that this would not be possible given Kalat's independent status.[37] Toward the end of the meeting, Mountbatten stepped out of the room and pulled in Jinnah and Liaquat Ali Khan, as they had just happened to have arrived at the Viceroy's House for a Partition Council meeting. Immediately after the tense and ultimately unproductive discussion, Jinnah privately told Mountbatten that the Khan was being difficult because 'the other side' (Congress leadership) was encouraging him to create trouble for Pakistan.[38]

In negotiations with British and Pakistani authorities, the Khan was not only adamant that Kalat's independent status be recognized, but that the leased territories be returned to Kalat control after the lapse of paramountcy, a matter which he made little headway on. During an early August meeting, Jinnah asked him to first sign the Instrument of Accession for Pakistan and then they could discuss the status of the leased territories afterwards. The Khan refused.[39] Following haggling between both sides over the exact wording, a communique was released on 11 August announcing that Pakistan recognized Kalat 'as an independent sovereign State' and the two parties had entered into a standstill agreement with future discussions to take place on the terms of Kalat's accession.[40] However, Mountbatten refused to affix his name to the communique, signaling a lack of acceptance on the part of the British government and undermining its credibility.[41]

Jinnah's definitive recognition of Kalat as an independent sovereign state, different than other princely states, was not a final position on Kalat's future political status but, rather, the terms by which he was prepared to negotiate regarding Kalat's relationship with Pakistan.[42] This move was emblematic of Jinnah's pragmatic approach to the creation of Pakistan and the handling of the princely states, in contrast to Nehru and Patel's immovable position on the issue of accession. While Jinnah had officially announced a noninterference policy for the princely states, he still pushed for Kalat to accede to Pakistan. From the Pakistani leadership's perspective, all the political posturing over Kalat's independence prior to the transfer of power was in many ways simply a technical debate with little practical application. As Pakistani Foreign Secretary Mohammed Ikramullah wrote to the Chief Commissioner of Balochistan and Agent to the Governor General Ambrose Dundas in November 1947, 'During his last visit the Khan was told quite clearly that the fact of independence was immaterial because according to our interpretation all states became independent and sovereign on the lapse of Paramountcy. Therefore, even if there was a difference in the position of Kalat in the pre-partition days ... after the partition the position changed completely.'[43] While the Kalat representatives attempted to persuade their Pakistani counterparts to agree to a treaty that recognized Kalat's independence, Jinnah directed that the Pakistani government was not willing to enter into any such treaty relationship with Kalat. The only compromise the Pakistani government was willing to accept was to provide the Khan with a modified Instrument of Accession that removed references to the Government of India Act of 1935.

On the eve of the transfer of power, Pakistan's leadership was keenly aware of the problems that an independent Kalat could create. In July 1947, M. Zia-ud-Din, a Peshawar-based lawyer handling a case in Quetta, wrote to Jinnah about his observations from his eight months traveling through Balochistan and his assessment of challenges that Pakistan would face in the region if Kalat was able to assert its independence. With Kalat remaining independent, Pakistan would retain neither Quetta with its key military installations nor Nasirabad, a key food- and revenue-producing area, and would lose strategic trade routes with Iran and Afghanistan and the majority of the region's mineral wealth. On the other hand, British Balochistan, which would automatically become part of Pakistan, would become isolated from the rest of Pakistan and was 'in reality mountain areas and quite useless.' These isolated districts would then become 'hotbeds of intrigue for the neighbouring countries and ambitious tribesmen.' While Balochistan in any form could be a liability for Pakistan, Zia-ud-Din argued, 'it will become a millstone around its neck' if the region was carved up in this way.[44]

On 15 August 1947, Ahmad Yar Khan gave a speech at the Jama Masjid in Kalat following Friday prayers, announcing Kalat's independence. He maintained his position of defiance against acceding to Pakistan and argued that Pakistani leaders had recognized Kalat's sovereignty in their negotiations prior to the transfer of power. Now that the 'constraints of alien rule' had been lifted, he affirmed his desire that 'the Baluch people be united on one platform where this freedom-loving and vibrant people should have its own government and distinct system so that, like all free peoples, they should be united and progressive. I thank God that one aspiration, that is independence, has been achieved.'[45] Following this announcement, the Khan introduced several political and administrative reforms in the state, most notably the creation of a bicameral legislature, with its first session held in December 1947. This body included the Lower House (Dar-ul-Awam) consisting of fifty elected members and five members appointed by the Khan to represent minority groups, and the Upper House (Dar-ul-Umara) comprised of Kalat's thirty-six hereditary sardars.

The Khan's announcement and subsequent efforts to generate international support did not receive a warm welcome as he had hoped. On 24 August 1947, Kalat's Prime Minister reached out to the Indian government in a bid for recognition of Kalat independence and to establish a trade relationship, including dispatching a Kalat trade representative to New Delhi. His note argued that his overture was based on the Pakistani government's purported recognition of Kalat as an independent sovereign state with a distinct status from that of other princely states. Kalat was hoping to find markets in India for the state's raw goods, as well as gaining Indian assistance in developing two ports on its Arabian coastline and in exploiting the region's oil resources. However, it was the opinion of India's States Ministry that Kalat's status was the same as that of any other princely state and therefore India would be unable to recognize its independence. States Ministry officials further argued that any recognition of Kalat independence would strengthen the claims of Hyderabad and weaken the Indian position, as well as potentially instigating Pakistani intervention. Thus, they recommended that the question of any potential relations between India and Kalat should be avoided, at least until India's relationship with all other princely states, in particular Hyderabad and Jammu and Kashmir, were settled. By December 1947, the Khan of Kalat's political adviser, Sir Sultan Ahmed, had spoken personally with Menon who explained the situation to him and, in deference to the Indian position, made the decision not to press this request any further.[46] The British Minister of State for Commonwealth Relations Arthur Henderson also rejected the possibility of the British government maintaining direct relations with Kalat given the state's inability 'to undertake the international responsibilities of an independent State,' a position communicated to Pakistani authorities.[47]

With little progress on the international front, Ahmad Yar Khan again met with Jinnah in Karachi on 14 October 1947 to discuss Kalat's relationship with Pakistan. He was stunned to find that Jinnah's conciliatory position had vanished. He now forcefully pushed the Kalat leader to integrate his state into Pakistan.[48] Seeking to delay Jinnah and hoping to buy more time for negotiations, he promised to inform him of his final decision regarding accession within a month or two. The position of Kalat continued to stew for the time being, with the only positive upshot of the meeting being that the two agreed to meet again.

Kalat's leadership not only confronted external political pressure, but also pressure from within the state. Since the 1920s, a political movement known as the Anjuman-e-Ittihad-e-Balochan wa Baluchistan had emerged to agitate for representative government in a unified Balochistan and formed the early foundations for modern Baloch nationalism. In 1937, the Anjuman established the first political party in Kalat, the Kalat State National Party (KSNP), dedicated to an independent and democratic Balochistan.[49] With its calls for democratic reforms, the Khan banned the party in 1939. Nevertheless, the party continued to work toward its goal, increasingly in concert with the Indian National Congress—the Kalat political party joined the All-India States' People's Conference in 1945.[50] The following year, the mouthpiece of the KSNP, the newspaper *Al Hanif*, had been at pains to demonstrate the impracticability of the Khan's efforts to secure the return of the leased territories and expressed its opposition to any plans for the separation of Kalat from the Indian Union, which would lead to the Khan being 'crowned king' of Balochistan following the transfer of power. Editorials argued that this would not be in the interest of Kalat's subjects and instead advocated for constitutional reforms to make Kalat's government more representative.[51]

Following the creation of Pakistan, Kalat's internal politics on accession shifted. While the Congress-aligned KSNP had not been an enthusiastic supporter of Kalat independence prior to the transfer of power, its opposition to the Muslim League now manifested in its opposition to Kalat joining Pakistan. The Khan was now under increasing pressure from the KSNP against signing the Instrument of Accession for Pakistan, as the group advocated for full independence with relations with Pakistan defined by a treaty based on equal status between the two sovereign states. In December 1947, the leader of the party, Ghaus Bakhsh Bizinjo, announced in the opening session of Lower House debates,

> We have a distinct civilization. We have a separate culture like that of Iran and Afghanistan. We are Muslims but it is not necessary that by virtue of our being Muslims we should lose our freedom and merge with others. If the mere fact that we are Muslims requires us to join Pakistan then Afghanistan and Iran, both Muslim countries, should also amalgamate with Pakistan ... We are ready to have friendship with that country on the basis of sovereign equality but by no means [are we] ready to merge with Pakistan ... We can survive without Pakistan.[52]

Another member of the Lower House called Bizinjo's declaration 'the representation of the aspirations of all the Baloch who live in the mountains.'[53]

Douglas Fell, then serving as Kalat's Foreign Minister but who would soon take over as Prime Minister, noted an increase in the KSNP's political influence within Kalat at this time. The KSNP was even able to force out Kalat's pro-accession Prime Minister Muhammad Aslam Khan, whose resignation they had been calling for, in early 1948. With a rise in its political influence, the group's critics became more vocal, denouncing the party as merely a tool of India and the Indian National Congress. By late 1947, rumors circulated within the Pakistani government that Kalat nationalists had approached the Indian and Afghan governments for assistance.[54] Nevertheless, the Khan appointed several KSNP members as 'so-called secretaries to the Ministers' within the Kalat government even though 'none of them was in any way qualified to hold an administrative post.' With the numerous challenges facing the state, these officials proved to be 'mischievous nuisances.' Fell felt the appointment of the KSNP officials was a conscious effort on the part of the Khan to create an alternative political base if 'Pakistan started making active trouble in the State.'[55] After lengthy discussions with Pakistani officials, during which he realized Jinnah's uncompromising position, Fell (who was perceived as 'Pakistan's man' within Kalat) came to the conclusion that Kalat 'would be well advised to come to terms as soon as possible with Mr. Jinnah on the basis of accession and to pursue plans of local independence and development within the framework of Pakistan.'[56] He pushed the Khan to ignore the activities of the KSNP and accede to Pakistan.

As delays further complicated negotiations and strengthened the sentiment within Kalat against accession to Pakistan, the terminally ill Jinnah, who would succumb to tuberculosis within seven months, took the extraordinary move of making the long and difficult trip to Balochistan in February 1948 to attend the Sibi Durbar, a ceremonial gathering of influential Baloch tribal leaders. In his speech in front of the gathered political elite, many of whom were wary of accession to Pakistan, Jinnah spoke of his personal connection to Balochistan in their joint struggle for freedom and apologized for not traveling to the region sooner. He explained that he had been occupied with setting up the new Pakistani government, handling the arrival of millions of refugees from India and dealing with the war in Kashmir. 'You will, therefore, forgive me if I was not able to attend to the affairs of Balochistan as speedily as I would have wished,' he stated. 'Let me assure you, however, that I have not for one moment allowed the affairs of Balochistan to slip out of my mind.' He further promised as Pakistan's Governor General that he would protect Baloch autonomy within Pakistan and wished to learn 'the way and means of improving the lot of our people in this Province.'[57]

In conversations with Jinnah during this trip, the Khan privately agreed to accede to Pakistan but argued that he was hampered by opposition within his state. He even claimed that 'the sardars were totally against accession but I tried hard to convince them and shared with them the advantages of acceding to Pakistan.'[58] On the evening of 14 February, the indecisive Khan changed his mind at the last minute and feigned an illness to avoid meeting Jinnah at the Residency where he was expected to sign the Instrument of Accession.[59] Owing to the Khan's absence, Jinnah immediately dispatched A.S.B. Shah, a former member of the IPS who now served as the Joint Secretary of the Pakistani Foreign Ministry, to the Khan's residence at Dhadar to check on his health and to confer with him on the draft instrument. Following a back and forth, the Khan gave his verbal consent to accession but would not agree to sign the instrument immediately as he would first need to get the assent of the tribal sardars and the newly created state legislature. But he promised, once again, that he would provide his final decision by the end of the month. He sent Shah to Jinnah that evening with a verbal message, which Shah recounted in a letter back to the Khan the following day,

[A]fter discussions and consideration of all the pros and cons, Your Highness has definitely come to the conclusion that it is in the best interests of the State and the people of Kalat to accede to Pakistan and that Your Highness has decided to do so. That Your Highness has examined the terms of the draft Instrument of Accession, and after discussion of the various terms and examination, Your Highness was fully satisfied and approved of it. That, as Your Highness has already summoned the two Houses of your Advisory Legislature to meet on the 21st, you will, after consultation with them, communicate your final answer before the end of this month.[60]

Jinnah's presence at the Sibi Durbar did not have the desired effect. On 25 February, the KSNP-dominated Lower House unanimously adopted a resolution against accession and proclaimed that future relations between Kalat and Pakistan should be decided by treaty. In the deliberations, one member of the house openly wondered 'why Kalat, where *Shariat* [*sic*] was the Law, was being subjugated to Pakistan where *Shariat* [*sic*] was not in force and where liquor shops, brothels and many other vices were flourishing. Pakistan should first purify itself and then seek union with the State.'[61] Bizinjo further warned: 'Pakistan's real intention is only to enslave us and nothing else.'[62] Within Kalat's Upper House, outspoken sardars, sensitive to protecting the political status quo that favored their status, opposed accession to Pakistan and passed a resolution stating: 'We want that both the Muslim governments of Pakistan and Kalat establish cordial relations. But these relations should be on a treaty basis and not on the basis of an accession through which our separate national existence and honour is extinguished forever.'[63] Despite passing this resolution, the legislative body still had not held a vote for a final decision on accession, claiming that the short amount of time did not allow its members to consult with their tribes.

Reports circulated that some of the Upper House members did not agree with the resolution, signaling the sardars' potential opposition to the Khan's position. Whether or not these reports were accurate, Pakistani leadership felt that the sardars were on their side. Foreign Secretary Ikramullah noted in September 1947 that if the Khan chose not to accede, 'his sardars would turn him out, as they were determined to join Pakistan anyhow and were only waiting to be assured of their own rights.'[64] By February 1948, a deputation of tribal sardars, many of whom were members of the Upper House, did meet with Jinnah to express their support and loyalty to Pakistan. Faced with doubts about how the Upper House would ultimately vote and seeking to buy time, the Khan informed Jinnah that he had granted the Upper House an additional three months to make their decision, which necessarily delayed his own final decision on the issue of accession.

While the Khan had reportedly intended to come to some agreement with Jinnah, he succumbed to last-minute pressure from his family, in particular his brother Abdul Karim, and failed to arrive at a decision on Kalat's relationship with Pakistan within the promised time frame. His appeals to the state legislature were merely a delaying tactic.[65] By this point, Jinnah had lost all patience with the prevaricating Khan and his conflicting positions, whose actions made the Pakistani Governor General look 'foolish' within Balochistan.[66] The Khan even reportedly told Jinnah during his visit that he had received tempting offers from the Afghan government and contemplated accepting them if Kalat and Pakistan were not able to bring their negotiations to a satisfactory conclusion.[67] Whether or not his claims about an offer from Afghanistan were true, such a statement was calculated to put pressure on Jinnah given the tense relationship at the time between the Afghan and Pakistani governments over the disputed Durand Line. But this only served to further anger Jinnah.

The endgame of Kalat's independence

With Ahmad Yar Khan continuing to dissemble over Kalat's accession, a furious Jinnah moved to undermine the Khan's position by securing the accession of his subsidiary states, Las Bela, Kharan and Mekran, similar to the Indian government's approach to Junagadh. Jinnah accepted their Instruments of Accession on 17 March 1948. The Pakistani government had already been in contact with their rulers about their interest in acceding to Pakistan but, up to this point, Pakistani authorities had remained largely evasive on the matter of accepting their accession in the hopes of first settling Kalat's status.[68] Throughout the negotiations, the Khan of Kalat maintained the position that these states had no right of self-determination and therefore could not independently accede to Pakistan.

The ruler of Kharan, Mir Mohammad Habibullah Khan, who had a tense relationship with the Khan, had already signaled his state's intention to repudiate the supremacy of Kalat with the lapse of paramountcy and to join Pakistan. In August 1947, shortly after the transfer of power, Mir Mohammad held a conference of various local political leaders to discuss the issue of accession and to take their advice on the future of Kharan. Two days later, he wrote to Jinnah to inform him of his decision to accede to Pakistan.[69] In November 1947, as Pakistan restarted food supplies to Kharan, he wrote to Jinnah:

> I may submit that during this difficult period, the Kalat State unsuccessfully tried to drive a wedge in our relations with Pakistan Government. I would like to make it clear that my State will never submit to the dictates of the Kalat State and will continue to oppose any moves aimed at an interference in the

State's freedom to act. *Insha Allah* [*sic*], my state will accede to Pakistan independently and will be prepared to offer all sacrifices for the cause of Pakistan.

Mir Mohammad also claimed that Kalat was arming 'mischief-mongers' to
create law and order problems and multiply the difficulties for Pakistan's
engagement with the region.[70]

The ruler of Las Bela, Ghulam Qadir Khan, had some initial doubts
about acceding to Pakistan due to the Khan's declaration of independence
for Kalat. Only a few days after sending his congratulations to Jinnah on
the creation of Pakistan, Ghulam Qadir wrote again to Jinnah requesting a meeting to 'elucidate any controversial points,' telling the Governor
General that he was 'constrained to feel vitally concerned regarding my
own political position as a ruler [of] virtually independent state "Las Bela
State" in Baluchistan.'[71] The following day, Jinnah wrote back that he not
yet studied the relationship of Las Bela to Kalat and the implications of the
Khan's actions, but assured him that the government, through the States
Negotiating Committee, would 'soon tackle the question of Indian States
and other cognate matters relating to the various problems that we have to
solve.' He waved off the request for a meeting, saying that it would not be
productive until he had an opportunity to examine and study the problems
Las Bela faced.[72] In early September 1947, Ghulam Qadir wrote to Liaquat
Ali Khan and, once again, to Jinnah to explain the rapidly evolving situation and to offer Las Bela's accession to Pakistan as his people were 'yet
determined not to accept Kalat's subordination.' Moreover, he requested
immediate aid from Pakistan for his subjects, who were experiencing
famine conditions. He explained that 'we are told that we must bend knees
before the Khan of Kalat or our people—men, women and children—shall
die of hunger and remain naked. We are deprived of rights of drawing our
supplies direct, and are compelled to apply to the *Wazir-i-Azam* [*sic*] of
Kalat for our means of supply.' He stressed to Jinnah that he was prepared
to sign the Instrument of Accession 'when called upon to do so.'[73]

The accession of Kalat's subsidiary states reduced the state's size by half,
cut off its access to the sea and left the state even further isolated—both
geographically and politically. The Khan of Kalat was furious and considered Pakistan's acceptance of the accession of what he considered his
feudal territories a direct violation of the standstill agreement and the state's
sovereignty. He immediately directed Fell to write to Foreign Minister
Zafarullah Khan, stating, 'The Kalat Government strongly request you to
take steps to ensure that no illegal or hostile action should be taken against
Kalat State by the Foreign Office.'[74] He even considered a military response
against what he saw as an illegal act. Mindful of the limitations of Kalat's
forces, Fell advised the Khan on 'the fallacy of contemplating any kind of

resistance of a military sort to Pakistan. Such a campaign could only have one ending and that quickly, the complete extinction of the State.' If he was not prepared to recognize Pakistan's sovereignty over the princely states, Fell further argued that the only realistic option was to send representatives of the state abroad to plead Kalat's case and find international supporters, such as Afghanistan and India, or through appeals to the United Nations. However, such international support would not be forthcoming from any quarter.[75]

Pakistan's political leaders were unmoved by the Khan's protests. On 20 March, the Foreign Ministry issued a press statement explaining that the timing of the government's decision was driven by the 'rapidly deteriorating' administrative situation.[76] With the accession of Mekran, the Foreign Ministry's A.S.B. Shah wired Kalat's Prime Minister requesting him to withdraw Kalat's governor, the Khan's brother Abdul Karim. He also pushed Pakistan's Foreign Secretary to send reinforcements to Mekran at once, including dispatching senior Pakistani officers to take command of the Mekran Levy Corps. He saw Mekran, with its strategic position along the Arabian coast, as the key to forcing Kalat's accession. Yet, officials loyal to the Khan were already working against Pakistan in the coastal region, such as ordering all private lorries to depart the region, thereby depriving the Mekran Levy Corps of available transport. Following Mekran's accession, the Khan also instructed Abdul Karim to continue his administration without any change. (On 26 March, Fell agreed to withdraw Abdul Karim and assured the Pakistani government the Khan would not interfere with Pakistan's control of Mekran.) Due to the machinations of Kalat's leadership, Pakistani authorities felt that they did not have the luxury of time in taking over Mekran's administrative machinery and organizing its security forces. Shah argued, 'It is essential now to show force in Mekran to deter Khan and his officials from taking any precipitate action and to enable change-over in administration to take place peacefully.'[77]

The Pakistani government made the decision to deploy its troops to take over the administration of the region's ports and secure lines of communication within the acceding feudatory states. Troops were also dispatched to Quetta, with the Khan now fearing Pakistani military action against Kalat.[78] Liaquat Ali Khan soon met with the service chiefs of Pakistan's military to discuss the situation in Balochistan. At the meeting, General Douglas Gracey (who succeeded General Messervy as Pakistan's Commander-in-Chief in February 1948) explained that an entire brigade was already being sent to the province due to accommodation issues elsewhere, and this movement was not connected with local political or security conditions. However, given the present situation, it was decided that a single battalion would be redeployed for various security details within the area, with a portion of the forces allocated for deployment to Mekran by way of Las Bela.[79] Shah, however, continued to push for more immediate action, including sending the Zhob Militia to Mekran, given that the dangers of conflict with 'local mischief-makers' was increasing daily.[80] With Kalat's feudal territories now under Pakistani control, Jinnah gave instructions on 27 March that no further negotiations, discussions or any other actions should be taken that might give the 'slightest impression' that any course other than accession to Pakistan and full recognition of Pakistani sovereignty was possible.[81]

That very evening, the Khan's position would be drastically undermined by an entirely unexpected source. All-India Radio (AIR) reported that Kalat officials had approached the Indian government earlier in the year to offer the princely state's accession to India. Referencing a States Ministry press conference, the broadcast stated that Indian leaders had not agreed, and refused to have anything to do with Kalat as the Indian government had no intention to interfere with any princely state that rightly belonged to Pakistan—no doubt with India's relations with its own princely states in mind. Menon reportedly stated in the press conference: 'We do not want accession to India of any area which is contiguous to Pakistan. It is not worth the candle.'[82]

When he heard about the broadcast, the Khan wrote straight away to Mountbatten concerning 'this mischievous news which I emphatically deny.'[83] Three days later, Nehru issued a correction in response to a question in the Constituent Assembly, explaining that the story was based on incorrect information and a misrepresentation of Menon's references to Kalat during the press conference. He recounted that Kalat had only approached the Indian government to request recognition of Kalat's independence and for permission to post a trade agent in New Delhi.[84] However, Nehru's explanation came too late. The announcement had already placed increased pressure on Ahmad Yar Khan to demonstrate his loyalty to Pakistan, fearful of the repercussions both from his Muslim subjects and the Pakistani government if he did not take immediate action to allay their suspicions. There were even reports that the Pakistani army's leadership had ordered the local commander to march straight into the state and threaten to arrest the Khan unless he agreed to accede to Pakistan immediately.[85]

Whatever the intentions behind the Indian broadcast, it did help to break the impasse between Kalat and Pakistan. Ahmad Yar Khan sent a telegram to Jinnah explaining that Kalat had made no such approach to India. He portrayed the report as 'false propaganda' by India, intended to spoil negotiations between Kalat and Pakistan and 'give the false impression to the world that they are right in their policy in respect of Kashmir, Junagadh and Hyderabad.' He continued,

It is therefore declared from that from 9 p.m. on 27th March the time I heard the false news from the A.I.R. I forthwith decided to accede to the Dominion of Pakistan whatever difference of view point exists between Kalat and Pakistan shall be placed in writing before the Quaid-i-Azam, whose decision I shall accept. I trust that by grace of God my *Sardars* [*sic*] and people will welcome the decision taken by me.[86]

On 30 March, the Khan affixed his signature to the Instrument of Accession without first gaining formal sanction or agreement from the sardars. He felt immense pressure to immediately accede or face potentially disastrous consequences for his state, with his hopes of a viable independent Kalat state already dashed by the accession of Kharan, Las Bela and Mekran.[87] The following day, Kalat's signed instrument was presented to Jinnah, which he promptly accepted.

The Pakistani government quickly dissolved Kalat's Council of Ministers and appointed new secretaries to run the state's administration under the direction of the state's Prime Minister. Within days of Kalat's accession, Pakistani officials came face to face with the many challenges of integrating Kalat, particularly with the unsatisfactory state of Kalat's finances and concerns of capital flight out of the state. Government efforts to improve the state's economy, including introducing a small savings scheme in 1950, had a limited impact. Regarding the savings scheme, local officials noted that 'the public are generally poor and cannot afford to contribute to the scheme and being mostly illiterate do not understand the advantages of the scheme.'[88] There were also various groups within Kalat opposed to Pakistani plans for further integration of Kalat, including members of the KSNP who rescinded their support for the Khan following accession and several tribal chiefs who feared losing their political influence within Balochistan. In June 1948, the Pakistani government banned the KSNP and arrested its leadership.

The most serious challenge came from Abdul Karim, who refused to recognize his brother's decision. Not only did he feel slighted from his removal as Governor of Mekran, but he saw the Pakistani government as a vehicle for the Punjabi domination of the Baloch people and other groups within Pakistan. In a letter to his brother, he wrote: 'From whatever angle we look at the present Government of Pakistan, we will see nothing but Punjabi Fascism. The people have no say in it. It is the army and arms that rule ... There is no place for any other community in this government, be it the Baloch, the Sindhis, the Afghans or the Bengalis, unless they make themselves equally powerful.'[89] When Fell ordered Karim out of Mekran and replaced him as governor with the Kalat Revenue Minister Sardar Behram Khan Lahri, Karim took it upon himself to take with him much of the contents of the Mekran treasury. Abdul Karim and around 700 of his followers soon fled into Afghanistan's Shorawak District, taking with them a truckload of arms, ammunition and food rations. They settled within around three miles of Afghanistan's border with Balochistan, from where Karim and his followers formed a 'free' Baloch government and did their best 'to stir up mischief' among the Baloch tribes. In May 1948, he officially launched a rebellion against the Pakistani state.[90]

While Abdul Karim hoped to gain the backing of the Afghan government, Afghan political leaders refused to side with the exiled prince. Sitting in the desert without encouragement or support from within Afghanistan, Karim was dependent on what supplies he could smuggle across the border. Rumors circulated in Quetta and Karachi that the prince was covertly supported by his brother, seeing the rebellion as a potential point of leverage to reassert his political authority in Kalat—though Fell later refuted these rumors.[91] With the Pakistani government unable to secure the cooperation of the Afghan government, it moved two platoons of the Zhob Militia along the border nearest Karim's encampment to at least cut off his supply lines.[92] The presence of the militia along the border, however, provoked unrest among the area's tribes. In response to this deployment, Karim's forces began to launch guerilla attacks against Pakistani forces in Jhalawan District beginning in late May.[93]

On 24 May 1948, the Khan publicly denounced the actions of his brother and prohibited any Baloch from supporting Karim's rebellion. He affirmed,

> This action on the part of the Prince is without my knowledge and is wholly unauthorized, being against the State's interest and policy. Except for impairing the State's interests it will serve no useful purpose. The State subjects are directed to keep away from him, have no truck with him, and desist to help him in any manner. Those found in league with him should be arrested forthwith and produced before the Prime Minister of Kalat.[94]

The Pakistan army's Seventh Regiment, under the command of General Akbar Khan, was dispatched to track down Karim's forces. Following military engagements in June, Abdul Karim agreed to surrender, reportedly under pressure from the Khan who was threatened with reprisals from the Pakistani government. He did so on the promise of safe conduct and amnesty. Karim and a number of his followers were disarmed and taken under escort to Kalat. There Pakistani authorities arrested him, and a jirga sentenced him to ten years' imprisonment.[95]

Pakistan's initial showdown with the Khan of Kalat proved to be only the opening salvo of over seven decades of political tensions and conflict between the Pakistani government and various Baloch groups, with four subsequent tribal rebellions breaking out within the underdeveloped and sparsely populated province.[96] Despite Jinnah's assurances that he sought to learn ways to improve conditions within Balochistan, it has consistently lagged behind Pakistan's other provinces in terms of economic and social development. The high levels of poverty that plagued the region and the lack of development, combined with strong local identities, instilled the idea among the region's inhabitants that 'deep down the Baloch don't consider themselves Pakistanis,' having 'nothing common between the Baloch and Pakistanis,' according to one Baloch journalist.[97] Following its accession to Pakistan, the Khan's nascent bid for Kalat independence soon became a rallying cry for an emergent Baloch nationalism that challenged the writ of the Pakistani state in Balochistan over the next seventy years.[98]

Pakistan's handling of Kalat demonstrates several aspects of the Pakistani position toward its princely states. Bogged down by the many demands for the creation of Pakistan before the transfer of power, the Muslim League leadership had a laissez-faire approach toward political activities within the princely states. In contrast to the Indian government, the Pakistani government initially maintained this approach regarding the states' accession to Pakistan. So long as the princes offered their support and signified their intention to accede to Pakistan, Pakistani authorities were satisfied to take things slowly, especially as they were fearful of disrupting the status quo within the frontier states. Yet, after the transfer of power, Pakistan confronted a vast mosaic of different ethnicities, cultures and political units, and struggled to form them into a new Muslim state. Any opposition to Pakistan had the potential to quickly spread to other parts of the country eager to protect their political interests against the new government. Therefore, in the face of challenges to Pakistani sovereignty such as the Khan of Kalat's bid for independence and his brother's rebellion, the Pakistani government was quick to discard their laissez-faire approach and take an uncompromising position toward its relationship with the princely states, including the deployment of its military. In addition, while the political tensions and conflict between the Indian government and the princely states after the transfer of power were exacerbated by communal problems, these communal pressures were largely absent from the situation in Kalat. Kalat was a Muslim-ruled and Muslim-majority princely state within the boundaries of Pakistani-claimed territory. Yet there were still clashes between the princely state and the Pakistani government on the issue of accession. This further helps to demonstrate that the underlying problem driving these conflicts was the competing conceptions of sovereignty at play leading up to and following the transfer of power.

Notes

1 Yaqoob Khan Bangash, *A Princely Affair: The Accession and Integration of the Princely States of Pakistan, 1947–1955* (Karachi: Oxford University Press, 2015), p. 103.

2 Record of Interview between Rear-Admiral Viscount Mountbatten of Burma and Sardar Nishtar and Mr. Akhtar Hussain, 18 July 1947, *TOP Volume XII*, p. 221.

3 NAI, PR_000004002000, Relationship between the Dominion of Pakistan & its neighboring States, brief for H.E., States Department, Government of India, 1947, p. 3.

4 Ruler of Amb to M.A. Jinnah, 15 August 1946, *Jinnah Papers Volume V*, p. 541.

5 Ruler of Amb to M.A. Jinnah, 1 September 1947, *Jinnah Papers Volume V*, p. 577.

6 Ruler of Amb to M.A. Jinnah, 3 August 1947, *Jinnah Papers Volume VIII*, p. 63.

7 Ruler of Chitral to M.A. Jinnah, 3 August 1947, *Jinnah Papers Volume VIII*, pp. 96–7.

8 Ruler of Chitral to M.A. Jinnah, 20 September 1947, *Jinnah Papers Volume V*, pp. 604–5.

9 Ruler of Chitral to M.A. Jinnah, 29 October 1947, *Jinnah Papers Volume VIII*, p. 100.

10 F. Amin to M. Ikramullah, 24 May 1948, *Jinnah Papers Volume VIII*, p. 247; Ruler of Swat to Ambrose Dundas, 4 June 1948, *Jinnah Papers Volume VIII*, p. 248.

11 M. Ikramullah to George Cunningham, 8 October 1947, *Jinnah Papers Volume VIII*, p. 99.

12 NAI, File No. 250_973, PR_000003009656, Frontier disturbances from the Malakand to Kurram, and measures taken by Government for suppressing them, Foreign Department, Government of India, 1897, p. 32.

13 NAI, File No. 286-C.A., PR_000004001966, Proposals for deposition of Mir of Hunza on grounds of Kashimir misrule in favour of his and capable heir Mirzada Jamal Khan, External Affairs Department, Government of India, 1945, p. 8.

14 Bangash, *A Princely Affair*, p. 69.

15 Frank Messervy to A.D.F. Dundas, 19 August 1947, *Jinnah Papers Volume V*, p. 546.

16 Note by Abdur Rab Nishtar, September 1947, *Jinnah Papers Volume V*, p. 300.

17 Ruler of Amb to M.A. Jinnah, 3 August 1947, *Jinnah Papers Volume VIII*, p. 63.

18 Bangash, *A Princely Affair*, p. 129.

19 Muslims of Chitral state to M.A. Jinnah, 22 March 1947, *Jinnah Papers Volume VIII*, p. 95.

20 Ruler of Amb to Liaquat Ali Khan, 17 February 1948, *Jinnah Papers Volume VIII*, p. 65–6.
21 Akins, 'Mashar versus Kashar in Pakistan's FATA,' pp. 1142–3; Bangash, *A Princely Affair*.
22 'Kalat, A Lost Land,' *New York Times* (14 February 1948).
23 Selig S. Harrison, *In Afghanistan's Shadow: Baloch Nationalism and Soviet Temptations* (Washington, DC: Carnegie Endowment for International Peace, 1981), pp. 16–17; Rizwan Zeb, *Ethno-Political Conflict in Pakistan: The Baloch Movement* (Abingdon: Routledge, 2020), pp. 24–31.
24 Zeb, *Ethno-Political Conflict in Pakistan*, p. 42.
25 NAI, File No. 537-F/39, PR_000004002110, Question of the accession of the Kalat State to the Federation, External Affairs Department, Government of India, 1939, pp. 1–2.
26 Note By a Legal Adviser, 19 March 1947, *Jinnah Papers Volume VIII*, p. 124.
27 Record of Interview Between Mountbatten and Ruler of Kalat, 28 July 1947, *Jinnah Papers Volume VIII*, p. 139.
28 Muhamed Aslam to Lancelot Griffin, 26 December 1946, *Jinnah Papers Volume VIII*, pp. 118–20, 123.
29 India Office Note on Minutes of Viceroy's Meeting of 19 July 1947, 28 July 1947, *Jinnah Papers Volume VIII*, pp. 138–9.
30 Minutes of Viceroy's Twentieth Miscellaneous Meeting, 19 July 1947, *TOP Volume XII*, p. 265.
31 NAI, File No. F-51-2, PR_000003017378, Political Situation Reports Supplied by I & B Department, Political Department, Government of India, 1946, p. 275.
32 Government of Kalat's Announcement About Ceded Territories, 11 April 1947, *Jinnah Papers Volume VIII*, p. 129.
33 Khan of Kalat to M.A. Jinnah, 9 June 1947, *Jinnah Papers Volume II*, p. 124.
34 Record of Interview Between Mountbatten and Ruler of Kalat, 28 July 1947, *Jinnah Papers Volume VIII*, p. 139.
35 Louis Mountbatten to Earl of Listowel, 27 June 1947, *Jinnah Papers Volume II*, p. 950; M. Zia-ud-Din to M.A. Jinnah, 8 July 1947, *Jinnah Papers Volume VIII*, p. 133; Harrison, *In Afghanistan's Shadow*, p. 24.
36 Government of Kalat's Announcement About Ceded Territories, 11 April 1947, *Jinnah Papers Volume VIII*, pp. 129–31.
37 Minutes of Viceroy's Twenty Fifth Miscellaneous Meeting, 4 August 1947, *Jinnah Papers Volume IV*, p. 192.
38 Louis Mountbatten to Earl of Listowel, Viceroy's Personal Report No. 16, 8 August 1947, *Jinnah Papers Volume VIII*, p. 149.
39 The Khan of Kalat to Rear-Admiral Viscount Mountbatten of Burma, 1 August 1947, *TOP Volume XII*, p. 457.
40 Press Communique on Situation between Pakistan and Kalat State, 12 September 1947, *Jinnah Papers Volume VIII*, p. 154.
41 Bangash, *A Princely Affair*, p. 168.
42 Minutes of Viceroy's Twenty-Fifth Miscellaneous Meeting, 4 August 1947, *TOP Volume XII*, p. 498.

43 Bangash, *A Princely Affair*, pp. 169–70.
44 M. Zia-ud-Din to M.A. Jinnah, 8 July 1947, *Jinnah Papers Volume VIII*, pp. 132–3.
45 Speech by the Ruler of Kalat, 15 August 1947, *Jinnah Papers Volume VIII*, p. 156.
46 NAI, File No. 14-IA/47, PR_000004002002, Request from the Wazir-E-Azam Kalat State regarding recognition of the Independent Sovereign Status at Kalat State by the Government of India, Indian Ministry of External Affairs, 1947, pp. 4–5, 11–13, 47.
47 Memorandum by the Minister of State for Commonwealth Relations, 12 September 1947, *Jinnah Papers Volume V*, pp. 591–2.
48 Mir Ahmad Yar Khan, *Inside Baluchistan: A Political Autobiography of Khan-e-Azam* (Karachi: Royal Book Company, 1975), p. 153.
49 Harrison, *In Afghanistan's Shadow*, p. 23.
50 Bangash, *A Princely Affair*, pp. 173–4.
51 NAI, File No. 18/8/46-Pol(i), PR_000004001839, Fortnightly Report for the First half of August 1946, Home Department, Government of India, 1946, p. 76.
52 Bangash, *A Princely Affair*, pp. 176–7.
53 Ibid., p. 177.
54 Ibid., p. 180.
55 'Kalat Accession Issue: Premier May Resign,' 5 March 1948, *Jinnah Papers Volume VIII*, p. 168, n. 2.
56 Bangash, *A Princely Affair*, p. 179.
57 Ahmed, *The Thistle and the Drone*, pp. 138–9.
58 Zeb, *Ethno-Political Conflict in Pakistan*, p. 73.
59 Ruler of Kalat to M.A. Jinnah, 14 February 1948, *Jinnah Papers Volume VIII*, p. 160.
60 A.S.B. Shah to Ruler of Kalat, 15 February 1948, *Jinnah Papers Volume VIII*, pp. 161–2.
61 G. Ahmed to Mohamad Ali, 10 March 1948, *Jinnah Papers Volume VIII*, p. 171.
62 Bangash, *A Princely Affair*, p. 182.
63 Ibid., p. 178.
64 Ibid., pp. 170–1.
65 S.M. Yusuf to Ruler of Kalat, 4 March 1948, *Jinnah Papers Volume VIII*, p. 167.
66 Summary of Note by D.Y. Fell on Consultations between M.A. Jinnah and Khan of Kalat at Dhadar, March 1948, *Jinnah Papers Volume VIII*, p. 165.
67 Ruler of Kalat to M.A. Jinnah, 2 March 1948, *Jinnah Papers Volume VIII*, 163; Summary of Note by D.Y. Fell on Consultations between M.A. Jinnah and Khan of Kalat at Dhadar, March 1948, *Jinnah Papers Volume VIII*, p. 165.
68 Zeb, *Ethno-Political Conflict in Pakistan*, p. 74.
69 Ruler of Las Bela to M.A. Jinnah, 5 September 1947, *Jinnah Papers Volume VIII*, p. 240.

70 Ruler of Kharan to M.A. Jinnah, 12 November 1947, *Jinnah Papers Volume VIII*, p. 224; Ruler of Kharan to M.A. Jinnah, 18 November 1947, *Jinnah Papers Volume VIII*, p. 225.

71 Ruler of Les Bela to M.A. Jinnah, 20 August 1947, *Jinnah Papers Volume V*, pp. 550–1.

72 M.A. Jinnah to Ruler of Les Bela, 21 August 1947, *Jinnah Papers Volume V*, p. 552.

73 Ruler of Les Bela to M.A. Jinnah, 5 September 1947, *Jinnah Papers Volume V*, p. 580.

74 Bangash, *A Princely Affair*, p. 186.

75 A.S.B. Shah to M. Ikramullah, 27 March 1948, *Jinnah Papers Volume VIII*, p. 187, n. 1.

76 Paul H. Alling to George Marshall, 23 March 1948, *Jinnah Papers Volume VIII*, p. 230.

77 A.S.B. Shah to M. Ikramullah, 24 March 1948, *Jinnah Papers Volume VIII*, pp. 175–6; A.S.B. Shah to M. Ikramullah, 25 March 1948, *Jinnah Papers Volume VIII*, p. 176; M. Ikramullah to A.S.B. Shah, 25 March 1948, *Jinnah Papers Volume VIII*, p. 179; A.S.B. Shah to M. Ikramullah, 26 March 1948, *Jinnah Papers Volume VIII*, p. 181; A.S.B. Shah to M. Ikramullah, 27 March 1948, *Jinnah Papers Volume VIII*, p. 185.

78 Khan, *Inside Baluchistan*, p. 161.

79 M. Ikramullah to A.S.B. Shah, 26 March 1948, *Jinnah Papers Volume VIII*, p. 182.

80 A.S.B. Shah to M. Ikramullah, 27 March 1948, *Jinnah Papers Volume VIII*, p. 185.

81 M.A. Jinnah to M. Ikramullah, 27 March 1948, *Jinnah Papers Volume VIII*, p. 184.

82 NAI, File No. 14-IA/47, PR_000004002002, Request from the Wazir-E-Azam Kalat State regarding recognition of the Independent Sovereign Status at Kalat State by the Government of India, Indian Ministry of External Affairs, 1947, pp. 23–4.

83 Ruler of Kalat to Louis Mountbatten, 27 March 1948, *Jinnah Papers Volume VIII*, p. 189.

84 Press Information Bureau, Government of India, 30 March 1948, *Jinnah Papers Volume VIII*, pp. 189–90; NAI, File No. 14-IA/47, PR_000004002002, Request from the Wazir-E-Azam Kalat State regarding recognition of the Independent Sovereign Status at Kalat State by the Government of India, Indian Ministry of External Affairs, 1947, p. 56.

85 Harrison, *In Afghanistan's Shadow*, p. 25.

86 D.Y. Fell to M.A. Jinnah, 30 March 1948, *Jinnah Papers Volume VIII*, pp. 191–2.

87 Khan, *Inside Baluchistan*, p. 162.

88 Chughtai Library, 2325, *Administration Report of the Baluchistan Agency for 1949–50*, Government of Pakistan, 1953, p. 49; M. Ikramullah to C.A.G. Savidge, 5 April 1948, *Jinnah Papers Volume VIII*, p. 198.

89 Farhan Hanif Siddiqi, *The Politics of Ethnicity in Pakistan: The Baloch, Sindhi, and Mohajir Ethnic Movements* (Abingdon: Routledge, 2012), p. 61.

90 Harrison, *In Afghanistan's Shadow,* p. 26.

91 Zeb, *Ethno-Political Conflict in Pakistan,* p. 80.

92 Summary of anti-Pakistan Activities of Prince Abdul Karim, Narrated by D.Y. Fell, Prime Minister, Kalat, 24 May 1948, *Jinnah Papers Volume VIII,* pp. 210–11; A.S.B. Shah to M. Ikramullah, 7 July 1948, *Jinnah Papers Volume VIII,* p. 214.

93 Harrison, *In Afghanistan's Shadow,* p. 26.

94 Announcement by the Ruler of Kalat, Kalat Papers, 24 May 1948, *Jinnah Papers Volume VIII,* p. 210.

95 A.S.B. Shah to M. Ikramullah, 7 July 1948, *Jinnah Papers Volume VIII,* p. 214, n. 2; Harrison, *In Afghanistan's Shadow,* p. 26.

96 Zeb, *Ethno-Political Conflict in Pakistan.*

97 Author interview with Malik Siraj Akbar, Baloch journalist, Washington, DC, 22 October 2018.

98 Martin Axmann, *Back to the Future: The Khanate of Kalat and the Genesis of Baluch Nationalism 1915–1955* (New York: Oxford University Press, 2008); Zeb, *Ethno-Political Conflict in Pakistan.*

Conclusion: The false promise of autonomy

We were the princes; no one mourned our passing. We were a jest of history, a tribe that had lived long beyond its day because it had been carefully preserved in the strong chemicals of British protection. And when that protection was withdrawn and all of us were exposed to the harsh glare of the sun like frogs under an overturned slab, it was inevitable that we should perish. I realize that it could not have been otherwise, and yet I cannot rid myself of a purely selfish sense of loss; and above all, I cannot help wondering at the suddenness of it all: one day we were ruling princes, the next we were frogs shriveling under a burning sun.

Manohar Malgonkar, *The Princes*

The opening passage of Manohar Malgonkar's 1963 novel *The Princes* captures the melancholy of India's princely order as its members sought to find a place within an independent and democratic India; some were successful, others were not. Almost eighteen years after signing the Instrument of Accession for India, the former Maharaja of Maihar State, Brijnath Singh Ju Deo Bahadur, lived a life of quiet retirement in the town of Jabalpur in Madhya Pradesh, some hundred miles distant from the seat of his former government. The elderly prince spent his twilight years steeped in nostalgia. His modest home was full of mementos from his past reign over 60,000 souls and 400 square miles of sovereign territory. In retirement, his income was primarily derived from the privy purse provided by the Indian government, but supplemented by two local cinemas he owned. He recognized that the princes, an anachronism of British colonial rule, increasingly had no place within an independent, democratic India. 'We all sleep under our beds instead of on them, and with cotton in our ears, we are so frightened of the government,' he recounted to a journalist. 'When the British departed, the Viceroy, Lord Mountbatten, said that we maharajas could choose whether or not to join independent India. But did we actually have such a choice? Had any of us not joined, we would have been dealt with as the Nizam of Hyderabad was.' He further lamented, 'I can't have much longer to live. I can't even play polo or go on a *shikar* [*sic*] anymore, because of a bad knee. The world I knew has passed.'[1]

On the first anniversary of the formation of the States Department, the Indian government published a white paper celebrating the integration of the hundreds of princely states—'a sealed book, so far as the leaders of public opinion in British India were concerned.' In it, Indian authorities asserted that the process of establishing the government's sovereignty over the entirety of its claimed territory was 'a momentous event in India's history.' The princely states, the white paper read, had been separated by '[h]igh walls of political isolation' under the layered sovereignty of British rule and 'reared up and buttressed to prevent the infiltration of the urge for freedom and democracy.' Adding to these difficulties was the presence of many inside and outside the princely states 'who nursed the hope that, overwhelmed by the combined weight of the partition of India and the disruption of the States, the Government of India would go under,' and the princes would be able to maintain their sovereign and autocratic rule. Despite many challenges, New Delhi now stood triumphant due to Indian officials' tireless efforts over the previous year leading to the creation of a sovereign India comprising both the provinces and the princely states. 'For the first time, after hundreds of years,' the white paper read, 'India became welded into a constitutional entity.'[2] In contrast to the government's triumphant narrative focusing on the role of India's political leaders, the socialist leader Ram Manohar Lohia highlighted the key influence of the political agitation by the princely states' subjects in helping to push the recalcitrant princes into the Indian Union, which he stressed had been far from a smooth process. Moreover, he pointed out that the process of fully integrating the princely states into the Indian Union was not yet complete as several princes continued to cling onto political authority and stood in the way of the development of democratic institutions within their states.[3]

Even before India had completed the annexation of Hyderabad and the complete accession of Princely India, the question on the minds of many in New Delhi was what to do with the numerous princely states now that they were part of the Indian Union. While the princes were assured that, besides the issues of defense, foreign affairs and communications, their political autonomy would be respected, the ruling Indian National Congress soon reversed its position. Indian officials saw an inherent tension between the princes' continued political authority and India's democratic principles, a tension that they would not abide. Even before the transfer of power, Nehru saw the absence of any measurable democratic reforms within the princely states as a key impediment to overcome. 'In view of basic changes that are going to take place in India within the next two months resulting from the complete transfer of power to Indian hands,' he stated in June 1947, 'it is of vital importance that progress leading to responsible government should take place rapidly in the States.'[4] After independence, Menon explained,

> What they failed to realize at the time was that the new Government of India could not possibly uphold the idea of autocracy in the States and that for their very existence the rulers had to have either the support of their people, or the protection of the Government of India. The former the rulers generally lacked; the latter had automatically terminated with the lapse of paramountcy … Gradually the realization dawned on them that after the advent of independence they would have no choice but to grant responsible government to their people.[5]

The Indian government's policy toward the princely states was soon marked by the twin forces of integration and democratization—key aspects of the decolonization process to remove the last vestiges of the British Empire, including the abolishment of princely rule that had been maintained by the umbrella of British paramountcy. The princes were now under immense pressure, both top-down and bottom-up, to relinquish their political authority to pave the way for democratic governance throughout Princely India. In November 1947, the All-India Congress Committee expressed its concerns that several princes continued to suppress states' people's organizations and demonstrated 'an unpatriotic attitude' in their commitment to remaining in power. The committee unequivocally stated,

> Whatever may be the legal implications of accession and lapse of British paramountcy, the moral result of the independence of India was undoubtedly the establishment and recognition of the power of the people, as distinguished from that of Princes and feudal or other interests hostile to natural popular aspirations. Therefore, all such interests, and especially the Princes, should know that the Congress cannot uphold them unless they are demonstrably in favour of regarding the voice of the people as the supreme law.

The princes were being asked to 'read the signs of the times' and cooperate with the establishment of democratic institutions within their states.[6] At its fifty-fifth session in Jaipur in December 1948, the Indian National Congress approved a resolution, stating:

> The Congress welcomes the developments that have taken place in regard to the States in India, resulting in the ending of the Indian States system which the British Government had built up early in the 19th century. While welcoming this process of integration, merger and union, so as to make the States approximate to the provinces, the Congress trusts that all feudal relics and impediments to the free development of the people will be removed.[7]

Even before Operation Polo was launched in Hyderabad, some princes saw the shift in India's prevailing political winds and understood the necessity of adapting to them. On 7 December 1947, Mountbatten and Menon met with leading representatives of several major princely states, including the Nawab of Bhopal and the Maharajas of Gwalior, Indore, Jaipur, Patiala, Bikaner and Alwar, to discuss the establishment of a Committee of Privileges to represent the interests of the princes to the States Ministry following their accession. It was clear from the discussion that the princes still viewed their interests as distinct from the Indian Union and were apprehensive about their status within India. Under pressure from New Delhi, the princes present agreed to implement several political reforms in the hopes of preserving their rule in some form, even within a democratic government, and made the decision to bring the princes and their subjects closer than ever before.[8]

Following the meeting with Mountbatten and Menon, the Maharaja of Indore stressed that 'the ultimate goal of constitutional development in my State is full responsible Government under my aegis.'[9] The Maharaja of Bikaner, who had been a leading proponent of accession before the transfer of power, argued that princes should now share power with the states' subjects, in a compromising bid to ensure the survival of the princely order. In a December 1947 broadcast, he stressed the role that the princes played in forming the Indian Union. 'There was never a time in the history of India when the position of the States was more important or more significant than it is today,' the Maharaja argued, continuing,

> It was by their accession that the Indian Dominion was converted from an area of 680,000 square miles to a Union of 1,200,000 square miles. How important they are in maintaining the stability and upholding the integrity of India has been amply proved in the four months of crisis through which we have passed. The way the Princes of India rallied to the aide of their mother country and gave every kind of assistance to enable her to surmount what seemed to be insuperable difficulties, will always be a memorable chapter in the history of new India.[10]

Supporting the Maharaja's position, Bikaner's Prime Minister, K.M. Panikkar, recognized the impossibility of having two distinct political structures within India—one democratic and one authoritarian. Nevertheless, he advised a 'go-slow policy' for the introduction of democratically elected governments in the princely states to allow the proper administrative machinery to be built up first.[11] As an intermediate step, nearly one hundred ruling princes and ministers met with Mountbatten in New Delhi the following month to discuss aggregating the princely states together into the new political units of states' unions. Mountbatten even argued that in the present stage of political development that India had reached, 'an ever-progressive monarchy was as good a form of Government as could be found,' which he felt had the advantage of contributing to broader political stability, in contrast to potentially chaotic populist forces that could be given voice within a democracy.[12] However, Indian leaders remained committed to the removal of the layered sovereignty of British rule and were not receptive to such arguments from the Governor General.

Regarding the princely states' transition to democratic rule, Nehru felt that one of the greatest obstacles India faced was the administrative vacuum created within the states after the transfer of power, with few having the appropriate administrative structure or experience to handle the new demands of democratization. At this point in time, many of the princely states still lacked any semblance of democracy, with political authority concentrated within the hands of the princes and their key advisers. Under the system of paramountcy, the British government maintained the states' administration to ensure the perpetuity of the princes' rule, rather than focusing on building up an efficient and comprehensive government, which, at any rate, had little in the way of democratic representation for the states' subjects. The British were able, to an extent, to deal with any discontent or disorder that emerged from princes' maladministration, often through pressuring rulers to alter their actions, intervening to restructure states' governing institutions or simply removing princes whose sins were too egregious to maintain in power. Within the provinces of British India, on the other hand, the institutional transition from British domination to democratic self-governance was a gradual process conducted over three decades. At Indian independence, the provinces had held democratic elections, possessed provincial legislatures, and had established political parties and experience in engaging in democratic politics.

Before and after the transfer of power, many princely states were busy in instituting various political reforms. However, most of these reforms were criticized as only going far enough to temporarily constrain political agitation within the states. Dissatisfaction among states' subjects persisted following the accession to the Indian Union as they saw little improvement in the overall political conditions within many princely states, with some princes continuing to point fingers at Congress as inspiring such unrest.[13] The princely states' accession provided an opportunity for the unleashing of popular movements in opposition to the princes' rule, often finding common cause with various political groups within the provinces who increasingly sought to integrate the problems of the princely states into their broader struggles. Many political groups representing the states' subjects, encouraged by the support of the Indian government, continued to be active in advocating for the abolishment of any remains of princely rule and the establishment of representative government.

In December 1947, for instance, Praja Mandals in the Gujarat region issued ultimatums to several princes demanding the introduction of responsible government by the end of the year, after which they would begin a satyagraha against their rule.[14] In Mysore State, thousands faced arrest for launching a movement for full democratic government, while protestors occupied government offices, courts and prisons in a number of Kathiawar and Orissa states.[15] The Praja Mandal in Indore State called for New Delhi to take control of the state administration after the Maharaja dismissed the Diwan, who was appointed to the post in August 1947 on the recommendation of the States Ministry.[16] In early 1948, Jodhpur's subjects reached out to Nehru to alert him to the 'reign of terror' they were living under due to the 'inexperienced young Ruler,' describing him as 'loose charactered' and a 'drunkard' whose Prime Minister (his uncle) was 'almost illiterate.' Due to the ruler's wasting of money 'like water,' the state budget was suffering a deficit of one crore rupees, even as the public was burdened with over-taxation by state authorities.[17] During a 28 February 1948 procession in the Sikh-ruled Patiala Stata, Praja Mandal members marched through Sirhimdi Basar shouting slogans such as 'Sikh raj khatam kare' (end Sikh rule), which infuriated the Sikh crowds observing the procession. The protestors made their way to the Arya Samaj Park where several speeches were given in which the Maharaja of Patiala was given a quit notice of two months before the Praja Mandal would resort to direct action.[18] In November 1947, the Praja Parishad in Bikaner State even spread false rumors that the state's ruler had entered into a trade agreement with Bahawalpur State and Pakistan in an attempt to undermine the state government.[19] On 1 January 1948, the Praja Parishad in Akalkot, a Maratha state within the Deccan States Agency, launched a satyagraha to force the introduction of a democratic government in the state, arguing that the current state government was corrupt and harmful to the people. The group alleged that Akalkot's Raja attempted to suppress the movement through inciting and aiding hired criminals to attack the protestors and commit looting and arson. Two days later, the unrest had spiraled out of control, resulting in the state government handing over responsibility for law and order to New Delhi. The next day, the Raja sent a telegram to Patel announcing his willingness to merge his state with the Bombay Province 'owing to the awakening of political consciousness amongst the subjects of the Indian states and since there does not seem to be any other alternative.'[20]

While the princes had acceded to the Indian Union under promises of political autonomy, they were now being asked to relinquish their authority and integrate their states by forming blocs of several princely states together as a single political unit with democratic institutions. Nehru argued that it was 'of the utmost importance to create in the states an administrative apparatus that will deal efficiently and sympathetically with the urgent needs of the population. The need for creating such an apparatus becomes all the greater when unions are formed, because the conception of a union is a new conception involving a new loyalty.'[21] While the princes understood the Instrument of Accession to be a binding document protecting their internal autonomy—apart from those matters outlined within the instrument as the responsibility of the central government—Indian political leadership privately understood it to be an expedient step to ensure the princely states' entry into the Indian Union and that it would be subject to renegotiation following independence. Menon referred to the Instrument of Accession as essentially a stopgap measure.[22] While accession had largely been framed within a scope to which the individual princes would agree at the time, India's political leadership understood that the clash between India's sovereignty based in democratic principle and the perpetuity of the princely states' political autonomy was unsustainable, necessitating the political integration and democratization of the princely states.

Soon after Indian independence, the princely states began to be amalgamated into several states' unions under a presidentially appointed rajpramukh (several of the rajpramukhs were former princes), such as Madhya Bharat, Patiala and East Punjab States Union, Rajasthan, Saurashtra and Travancore-Cochin, or were integrated into neighboring provinces. Seven princely states (Hyderabad, Mysore, Bhopal, Tripura, Manipur, Cooch-Behar and Jammu and Kashmir) transitioned into their own governor-ruled states within the Indian Union. Not all were pleased with this development. For instance, supporters of the Maharaja of Patiala State, which joined the Patiala and East Punjab States Union, had rejected such a merger, arguing: 'By merging with the East Punjab, all chances of prosperity for us will disappear, and our Exchequer will go to feed the people of a deficit province ... During the ten eventful months of the Interim Government, not a day passed when the Ministers were not "ordered by S. Patel" or the "Rajpramukh" to return their cars and vacate their kothies.'[23]

After acceding to India, the princely state of Bilaspur was grouped together with Himachal Pradesh. But, in October 1950, the Raja of Bilaspur expressed his concern to V.P. Menon that his state would not be properly represented by the single seat allocated to this political grouping within the Rajya Sabha (Council of States), given that its population was only one-eighth of that of Himachal Pradesh. He wrote that 'owing to disparity in population of the two units, as well as the basis of joint representation being repugnant to the established fundamental of Federation, I have all along been saying that a system should be devised whereby the States of Bilaspur and Himachal Pradesh elect their representatives to the Council of States in rotation.'[24] Nevertheless, in April 1948, Menon presented to the Cabinet a plan for a further transfer of powers away from the states' governments, with New Delhi using the spreading unrest among the states' subjects to force the issue of integration. The following month, a meeting was held in New Delhi in which the governors of Rajasthan, Madhya Bharat, Saurashtra, Vindhya Pradesh and Matsya ceded additional authorities to the central government to pass laws within their territory.[25]

By November 1948, all the princely states had been amalgamated into states' unions, absorbed into neighboring provinces or transitioned into governor-ruled states within the Indian Union, marking the effective end of Princely India. Menon later recalled the shock felt by the princes with the rapid transitions leading to the end of their reign, writing,

> No ruler had thought even a month previously that he would have so soon to part with his State and rulership. Something which had been in their families for generations and which they had regarded as sacrosanct had disappeared as it were in the twinkling of an eye. Though all of them put up a bold front, the mental anguish they were going through was writ large on their faces.[26]

Nehru treated the rapid decline and fall of the archaic and autocratic princely order as an inevitable part of the modern political development of India. In July 1948, he wrote to the Nawab of Bhopal that the end of the princely states was 'bound to happen whether we wanted it or not. All we could do was to see that the changes that were inevitable took place in as reasonable and amicable way as possible.'[27] On 15 October 1948, Nehru also wrote to the country's chief ministers that an important landmark had been reached with the integration of Hyderabad into the Indian Union. 'The removal of the Hyderabad sore,' he argued, 'has attained a measure of unity which India had never attained during the last so many centuries ... by the elimination of all pretence to independence from the biggest of the States, the Indian polity is now in a position to be shaped according to a common pattern.' But he acknowledged that several outstanding issues with the princely states remained. The government now needed to turn to settling problems of consolidating and administratively reorganizing the states to further integrate them into the Indian Union and introduce democratic government for the states' subjects. 'Without a satisfactory solution of those,' he warned the chief ministers, 'the gains which we have so far registered will become largely illusory.'[28]

With the integration of the princely states, the States Ministry undertook the careful accounting of all the princes' properties to divide them between personal property, which could be retained by the princes and their families, and state property, which was taken over by the government. In return for relinquishing their authority, the princes were provided an annual allowance, known as a privy purse, and were able to retain their recognized titles, which they could pass to their heirs. The princes' privy purses were set at a certain percentage of the value of their states' revenues, and were initially provided tax-free and in perpetuity throughout the princes' lifetimes. In 1949, the Indian government's total annual privy purse commitment was 46,673,535 rupees.[29] These payments, Patel felt, were 'comparatively an insignificant price to pay for the consolidation and unity of India which we have achieved.'[30] The government also provided allowances to other members of the princely families, which varied in size based upon the average expenditures of the states, the duties of the family members prior to accession and the size of the families. These allowances, however, were only intended to be paid during the lifetime of the existing members of the princely families and were nontransferable to future generations. These payments quickly became an endless source of complaint for the former princes and their families. Some argued the amounts were too small and did not cover all their expenses. Others complained that they were not being paid the amount owed to them.[31]

Overall, there were feelings of bitterness and sadness among many of the princes over New Delhi's treatment of the princely states. They struggled to adapt to life as private citizens while their princely states were handed over to popularly elected governments. The Maharani of Jaipur later recalled in her memoirs, 'Although I accepted the idea that we would, in some way, be part of independent India, it never really occurred to me that our lives would change so radically once our states lost their special identities. Somehow I imagined that we would always maintain our particular relationship to the people of our states and would continue to have a public role to play.' When Jaipur was merged into the Greater Rajasthan Union, she explained, 'Sadly I realized, at long last, that the identity of Jaipur as a separate state had really gone forever and that Jai [the Maharaja of Jaipur] had ceased to be responsible for the welfare of the people he loved and had been destined to rule.'[32] After being reprimanded by Patel for his absence from the opening session of the Rajasthan legislature in 1949, the ruler of Bikaner complained that the 'ties of blood extending over the last five centuries have been severed by a stroke.'[33]

In a lengthy Farewell Memorandum, which Mountbatten sent to Patel on 19 June 1948, the departing Governor General lingered on the issue of the princes. He congratulated the States Minister for his 'miracle,' arguing that 'by far the most important achievement of the present Government is the unification of the States into the Dominion of India. Had you failed in this, the results would have been disastrous. But since you succeeded, no one can see the disastrous results that have been avoided.' But what was to happen to the princes now that their states were transitioning to democracy and being integrated into the Indian Union? This question was at the forefront of Mountbatten's mind. He recalled the fate of the aristocracy after the French Revolution and argued that the animosity toward France's aristocratic class was 'undoubtedly bad not only for the aristocratic families, but what was very much more important, for France herself, as she lost the potential services of a class who were rich enough to ensure the best education for their children, and who had had a tradition and background of service up to the revolution.' He stated his hope that India would avoid any similar trend regarding its own princely class. Mountbatten concluded, 'Unless the Princes, particularly of the merged States, can be made to feel that their services are wanted by the country as a whole and that they are not merely political pensioners, the Princes will become a liability instead of an asset.'[34]

Several of the leading princes were appointed as rajpramukhs of the reorganized states' unions. Some members of the princely class settled abroad following independence, whether retiring to Europe or being given largely ceremonial diplomatic postings. Other princes and their families engaged in various political activities, through contesting state and national elections or providing financial support to political parties.[35] The descendants of other princely dynasties continued to be leading members of Indian society, serving as the heads of large businesses, noted athletes and movie stars, or simply wealthy socialites. Yet many lived a life of quiet retirement, like the former Maharaja of Maihar. On 20 June 1949, Jammu and Kashmir's Maharaja Hari Singh boarded a train for Bombay, where he would remain in exile until his death on 26 April 1961. Although he was still nominally the state's Maharaja, he named his 18-year-old son, Yuvraj Karan Singh, as Prince Regent under pressure from Nehru and Patel. Under the constitutional changes introduced in 1952, Hari Singh's status as titular head of state was terminated, and he was replaced by Karan Singh as the head of state, known as the sadr-i-riyasat. He served in this role until 1965 when the post was replaced by a centrally nominated governor (Karan Singh served as the first governor). The last Nizam of the princely state of Hyderabad, Mir Osman Ali Khan, was made the rajpramukh of the now Indian state of Hyderabad. He served in this role until 1956 when the position was abolished following Hyderabad's dismemberment as part of the linguistically based reorganization of the Indian states; Hyderabad was split between the states of Andhra Pradesh, Mysore and Bombay. Mir Osman died at Hyderabad's King Koti Palace on 24 February 1967. The last Nawab of Junagadh, Mahabat Khan, settled with his family in Karachi after fleeing his state, with his property within Junagadh seized by the Indian government.[36] He remained in Karachi until his death on 7 November 1959.

In April 1951, only four months after Patel's death, the States Ministry was shut down as its primary role had been fulfilled with all the princely states now integrated into the Indian Union, leaving Menon without a job in government for the first time in three decades (though he was briefly made Governor of Orissa before retiring). Then, in July 1971, Prime Minister Indira Gandhi introduced the twenty-sixth amendment to the Indian Constitution, which abolished all remaining official symbols of the princely order, including stripping the princes of their titles, privileges and privy purses. The amendment read,

> The concept of rulership, with privy purses and special privileges unrelated to any current functions and social purposes, is incompatible with an egalitarian social order. Government have, therefore, decided to terminate ... expressly the recognition already granted to such Rulers and to abolish privy purses and extinguish all rights, liabilities and obligations.[37]

In the lead-up to the parliamentary approval of this amendment, the former princes resisted the Prime Minister's efforts to abolish their privy purses and relinquish their status, even taking the matter before India's Supreme Court in 1970.[38] Three years earlier, Mountbatten even wrote a private letter to the Indian Prime Minister from London expressing his opposition to the proposed abolishment of the princes' privy purses—some former princes reportedly met with him, urging him to intervene on their behalf.[39] However, the former princes found little public support for their campaign. During parliamentary debates on the issue, Home Minister Y.B. Chavan explained that the position of the government was not intended to target the princely order as such, but was necessary given 'certain compulsions of time and history.' He continued: 'Things are moving in a particular direction in this country and possibly it requires that the decisions that we took at a certain time should be reviewed, re-considered and re-shaped.'[40]

Regarding the administration of Pakistan's princely states, tensions with Afghanistan and concerns to maintain law and order among the tribes on the frontier slowed efforts to introduce political reforms and further integrate the princely states beyond the issues outlined in the Instrument of Accession over the next two decades. In March 1951, Dr. Mahmud Hussain, the head of the States and Frontier Regions Ministry (formed in July 1948), observed of Karachi's relations with the frontier states, 'We have dealings with one single individual who looks after law and order and who practically does exactly the same thing in the states which all the maliks do in the tribal regions. So here at the moment we are not thinking in terms of establishing a parliamentary system of government on western lines.'[41] In 1969, however, President Yahya Khan introduced the Dir, Chitral and Swat (Administration) Regulation that removed the princes from the administration of the princely states and established Pakistani government control over them. The populist Sindhi political leader Zulfiqar Ali Bhutto, who succeeded Yahya Khan as the President and Chief Martial Law Administrator before becoming Prime Minister, similarly sought to undo Pakistan's existing princely order. At the end of 1971, only days after being installed as President, Bhutto used his wide-ranging powers and implemented the Abolition of Privy Purses and Privileges Orders, which stripped the princes of their titles, rights and privileges. They were offered a maintenance allowance in place of their privy purse, though this was not transferable to their heirs.[42] While the smaller number of princely families in Pakistan eventually lost hold of their states, they have integrated themselves into the country's ruling elite. In May 1962, for instance, the son of the last Wali of Swat married the daughter of Pakistani President Mohammed Ayub Khan. The heir to the title of Nawab of Bahawalpur, Mohammad Abbas Khan Abbasi, served as the Governor of Punjab from 1975 to 1977 (the princely state had been integrated into the Punjab Province in 1970), with several other members of the Bahawalpur royal family holding senior positions within Pakistan's government.

The Khan of Kalat had a more tumultuous political career following the integration of his state. In 1952, Kalat and its former feudal territories were combined into the Balochistan States Union (BSU). Ahmad Yar Khan was appointed as its head with the title Khan-i-Azam, a conciliatory gesture by the Pakistani government. In October 1955, the BSU was dissolved and joined together with the remainder of West Pakistan as a single administrative unit as part of Pakistan's One Unit scheme, a means of establishing a political counterweight to the numerical superiority of Bengalis in East Pakistan. The One Unit scheme lasted until 1970 when Balochistan became its own province. Nevertheless, Ahmad Yar Khan continued to be a significant but controversial political actor in Balochistan, including a period of imprisonment on sedition charges that helped to stoke an anti-state uprising among the Baloch in the late 1950s and a three-year tenure as Balochistan's Governor beginning in January 1974. He died in Kalat in 1979. Many of the other individuals active in the debates and conflict over Kalat's accession continued to play leading roles in the politics—and rebellions—of Balochistan in the coming decades.

The legacy of indirect rule in India

The divide between Princely and British India had varying and long-term effects following independence, such as on economic and social development in different parts of India and the varying patterns of ethnic and inter-religious conflict, areas that have attracted scholarly attention.[43] However, at its core, the trajectory of the princely states through the end of empire in South Asia is a story of the evolving understanding of state sovereignty and the resulting debates and clashes over it. As the British withdrawal inched closer and closer, the princes feared the repercussions of independence on their rule—especially under an Indian government controlled by the Indian National Congress—and worked to protect their sovereignty as it existed under British paramountcy. Yet, the autocracy of the princes was an ill fit with Indian authorities' conception of a modern democratic government. The struggle between these two positions lies at the heart of the political and military conflicts involving the princely states leading up to and following the transfer of power, with the Indian government's idea of sovereignty ultimately winning out.

The princely states were not the only territory in which India and Pakistan faced the legacy of British indirect rule and struggled to establish political control. For instance, India also worked to assert the writ of the central government within the northeastern frontier bordering China, Burma and East Pakistan (later Bangladesh). By 1947, large swathes of this frontier area remained effectively unadministered by British authorities. Further complicating the situation, a number of political leaders in the region clamored for greater political autonomy within the Indian Union, or even opposed joining the Indian Union at all and sought to either maintain their relationship with the British government or assert independence for the region's various ethnic groups. After China's October 1950 invasion of Tibet, across the international border, New Delhi's precarious hold over the northeastern frontier was understood to be a strategic vulnerability. As a result, New Delhi expanded its administrative reach, implemented several development projects and increased the presence of security forces in the underdeveloped northeastern frontier to bolster its political control. A series of separatist insurgencies erupted in the region in the 1950s and 1960s that fought against the expanding presence of the central government. Concerned with the broader ramifications of the potential loss of its border territory, Indian officials increased efforts to extend the government's administrative hold and military presence within the restive border region. To this day, India continues to deal with the legacy of British colonial rule within the northeaster frontier and of the decades of insurgent violence.[44] The efforts to assert the writ of the state in the northeastern frontier were not always as successful as the process of integrating the princely states generally turned out to be. As political scientist Sanjib Baruah sums up, northeastern India 'stands as an example of the shortcomings and failures of the territorially circumscribed postcolonial nation-state as an institutional complex.'[45]

Many today take for granted the inevitability of the princely states' integration into India and Pakistan, and ignore the unique position of the princely states under British colonial rule. By January 1955, as one editorial remarked, the Indian population had 'come to take integrated India so much for granted that it requires a mental effort today even to imagine that it could be different.'[46] But to indulge in a hypothesized counterfactual, what would have happened if Patel and Menon had failed in their monumental task of uniting over 500 disparate political units, or if the Indian government had been unwilling to resort to military measures to support its territorial integrity; if Jinnah had been less willing to apply pressure to the Khan of Kalat and balked at the use of force against fellow Muslims in Balochistan, or if he had been willing to use force to back the accession of Junagadh or intervene on behalf of Hyderabad? Could India and Pakistan have survived a scenario in which several princely states successfully asserted their independence, or would this have resulted in the further splintering of both countries as more and more princes were encouraged to push for independence to protect their sovereignty? In the minds of many in New Delhi and Karachi on the date of the transfer of power, this 'balkanization' of South Asia was indeed a very real possibility. In August 1947, one former British official predicted that, with the opposition of the princely states to the Indian Union and many other fault lines of conflict dividing Indians, a unified India was not likely to survive. The 'ultimate pattern of India,' he argued, 'is likely to consist of three or four countries in place of British India, together with a Federation of South Indian States. This will be, approximately speaking, a return to the pattern of sixteenth century India.'[47]

The transition from colonial rule to independence involved numerous false starts, debates and conflicts in relation to the hundreds of princely states that dotted the political landscape of South Asia. The rulers of the princely states had to be cajoled, convinced and, in some cases, outright forced to accede to either India or Pakistan. This was no easy task among the many recalcitrant princes, whose main aim was to protect their sovereignty and their personal status and privileges. As this book has demonstrated, the problems of integrating the princely states following the transfer of power derived from the ambiguity of British colonial policy toward the princely states and the clashing conceptions of state sovereignty. Through the first half of the twentieth century, British authorities took a laissez-faire approach to the princely states' internal affairs. As a result, they failed to make a definitive determination about what status the princely states should have after the British withdrawal from the Subcontinent and even alluded to the possibility of the princely states becoming independent. As the Indian writer Nirad Chaudhuri describes it, 'If in dividing British India the British Government was guilty of a wrong act of commission, in *not* [sic] dividing the Princely States between India and Pakistan they were guilty of a wrong act of omission ... This British sin of omission in regard to the Indian States has left a legacy of many injuries.'[48] Amid this ambiguity, some princes rejected the successor governments' sovereignty over their states and asserted their right to declare independence, goaded on by past British positions in support of their sovereignty and the ongoing encouragement of some British officials. This set the stage for the coming clashes with Indian and Pakistani authorities, who saw these declarations as a threat to the sovereignty of the newly independent countries, and for the eruption of violence, including the use of the military to force the accession and integration of the most recalcitrant princely states—Jammu and Kashmir, Hyderabad, Junagadh and Kalat.

Looking back at the efforts to integrate the princely states under a constitutional polity during the 1930s and 1940s, Francis Wylie, a member of the IPS and political adviser to the Viceroy from 1943 to 1945, argued that the failure of the federation scheme can be chalked up to the British approach to the princely states and their failure to adopt an uncompromising course. India's leadership, on the other hand, did take just such an approach, which was necessary to maintain the territorial integrity of the country in the face of princely demands. Over two decades after Indian independence, Wylie concluded,

> [I]f left to their own devices, there was never the slightest chance of getting rulers representing fifty percent of the population of the princely states to sign instruments of accession before the second world war broke out in September 1939. The only way, so far as the British government were concerned, if they genuinely wanted to expedite the creation of federation, would have been to take the princes by the neck and compel them to come. This is what Patel and V.P. Menon did later on.[49]

If the princes had been more enthusiastic about acceding to an All-India Federation, or British officials had taken a different approach to bring the requisite number of princes into the federation, the implementation of the federation scheme in the latter half of the 1930s could have changed the course of history in the Subcontinent. This would have put a unified India on a path toward dominion status in a way that could have potentially bypassed the necessity of Partition in 1947, as Menon felt. During the 1930s and 1940s, the position of the princely states thus played a key role in the historical trajectory of both India and Pakistan. To ignore or gloss over their role in the development of events leading up to the transfer of power and in its aftermath provides an incomplete understanding of how the British withdrawal from India played out and the key challenges facing India and Pakistan as part of their efforts to assert the two governments' sovereignty and build up political control throughout their claimed territory. V.P. Menon later described his task:

> To have dissolved 554 States by integrating them into the pattern of the Republic; to have brought order out of the nightmare of chaos whence we

started, and to have democratized the administration in all the erstwhile States, should steel us to the attainment of equal success in other spheres. For the first time India has become an integrated whole in the real sense of the term.[50]

Notes

1 Ved Mehta, *Portrait of India* (New Haven, CT: Yale University Press, 1967), pp. 40–5.
2 'Princes' Co-Operation Helped in Smooth and Peaceful Transfer of Power, Indian Government's White Paper on States Policy,' *Statesman* (7 July 1948).
3 'States Problem Not Solved, Says Lohia,' *National Call* (11 July 1948).
4 National Archives, U.K., FO/371/63538, Situation in India—preparations for the transfer of power (Folder 11), June 1947.
5 Menon, *The Story of the Integration of the Indian States*, pp. 485–6.
6 National Archives, U.K., FO/371/63572, Transfer of power in India—relations of India with the United Kingdom (Folder 8), November 1947–January 1948.
7 NAI, PP_000000005369, Indian National Congress, Jaipur, Private Papers of Sardar Patel, 1949, p. 4.
8 NAI, PP_000000005832, Minutes of meeting between H.E., The Governor General and the Ruling Princes & representatives of states held on 7-12-1947, Private Papers of Sardar Patel, 1947, p. 3.
9 'Full Responsible Govt. In State, Indore Ruler Reiterates Assurance,' *Hindustan Times* (18 December 1947).
10 'Power Must Be Shared With People, Bikaner Ruler's Appeal to Princes,' *Statesman* (13 December 1947).
11 'Demand for Popular Govts. In States, Panikkar Advocates "Go-Slow Policy",' *Hindustan Times* (22 December 1947).
12 'Princes' Relations with Union Govt., Conference to Meet in Delhi To-Day,' *The Hindu* (7 January 1948); Campbell-Johnson, *Mission with Mountbatten*, pp. 303–5.
13 Campbell-Johnson, *Mission with Mountbatten*, p. 305.
14 'Demand for Responsible Govt. in Gujarat States, Praja Mandal Negotiations With Rulers,' *National Call* (25 December 1947).
15 Guha, *India After Gandhi*, p. 58.
16 'Indore's Hostility Calls For Drastic Action, Praja Mandal Workers Suggest Taking Over Administration,' *Evening News* (2 January 1948).
17 NAI, PP_000000005335, States General File 1948, Private Papers of Sardar Patel, 1948, pp. 64–5.
18 NAI, PP_000000005543, Patiala 1947 to 1948, Private Papers of Sardar Patel, 1948, p. 7.
19 NAI, PP_000000005817, Copies of telegrams etc. issued or received by the Ministry of States, 1947, Private Papers of Sardar Patel, pp. 8–9.

20 NAI, PP_000000005335, States General File, Private Papers of Sardar Patel, 1948, pp. 130–1; NAI, PP_000000005817, Copies of telegrams etc. issued or received by the Ministry of States, 1947, Private Papers of Sardar Patel, p. 33.
21 Khosla, *Letters for a Nation*, pp. 86–7.
22 Menon, *The Story of the Integration of the Indian States*, p. 94.
23 NAI, PP_000000005543, Patiala 1947 to 1948, Private Papers of Sardar Patel, 1948, pp. 216–17.
24 NAI, PP_000000005547, Representation of the State of Bilaspur in the Council of States, Private Papers of Sardar Patel, 1950, p. 5.
25 Copland, *The Princes of India in the Endgame of Empire*, pp. 264–5; Guha, *India After Gandhi*, p. 58.
26 Ibid., p. 193.
27 Copland, *The Princes of India in the Endgame of Empire*, p. 270.
28 NAI, PP_000000005819, Fortnightly letters of the hon'ble Prime minister to the Provincial Premiers from 1948 to 1949, Private Papers of Sardar Patel, 1949, p. 95.
29 The privy purse for princes was calculated on the basis of 15 percent of the first 100,000 rupees of the average annual revenue of their State, 10 percent of the next 400,000 rupees and 7.5 percent of revenue above 500,000 rupees, subject to a maximum of 1,000,000 rupees. NAI, File No 87-P, PR_000001652932, Securities and Cash balances surrendered by the various states. Allowance drawn by the Rulers and their relatives of States, Indian Ministry of States, 1949, p. 80.
30 NAI, PP_000000005826, Privy Purse Payments to Rulers safeguarding, Private Papers of Sardar Patel, 1949, p. 12.
31 NAI, File No. 3(21)-P, PR_000001652459, Payment of privy purse to H.H. the Nabha and his private properties, Indian Ministry of States, 1949, p. 12.
32 Gayatri Devi, *A Princess Remembers: The Memoirs of the Maharani of Jaipur* (New Delhi: Rupa Publications, 1995), pp. 205, 218.
33 Copland, *The Princes of India in the Endgame of Empire*, p. 266.
34 NAI, PP_000000006192, Miscellaneous Correspondence with HE the Governor General, Private Papers of Sardar Patel, 1947, pp. 111, 145–6.
35 NAI, File No. 5(37)-P/50, PR_000005014104, Participation of the members of the Cochin Ruling family in Communist activities, Indian Ministry of States, 1950; Copland, *The Princes of India in the Endgame of Empire,* p. 268.
36 'Junagadh Nawab's Property Transferred To State, India's Governor-General Issues Ordinance,' *Times of India* (25 December 1947).
37 The Constitution (Twenty-Sixth Amendment) Act, 1971, accessed at: https://constitution.org/1-Constitution/cons/india/tamnd26.htm [accessed 20 December 2022].
38 National Archives, U.K., FCO/37/599, India—Abolition of Privy Purses of Princes leading to their derecognition, 1970.
39 National Archives, U.K., FCO/37/364, Abolition of Privy Purses and recommendation for Lord Mountbatten, 1968–1969. Though Mountbatten's letter was private, its existence was later leaked to the Indian press. This caused some

consternation within the British Foreign Office, which pressed him to avoid publicly raising his views on the matter and the appearance of intervening in India's internal government affairs. Following his departure as Governor General of India in 1948, Mountbatten had maintained his links with India and remained involved to varying degrees in Indian politics, with Indian officials frequently seeking his views on different matters; though, his links were weakened following the death of Nehru in 1964. See Rakesh Ankit, 'Mountbatten and India, 1948–64,' *International History Review* 37:2 (2015), 240–61.

40 National Archives, U.K., FCO/37/364, Abolition of Privy Purses and recommendation for Lord Mountbatten, 1968–1969.
41 Bangash, *A Princely Affair*, p. 235.
42 Barth, *The Last Wali of Swat*, pp. 136–7.
43 Lakshmi Iyer, 'Direct versus Indirect Colonial Rule in India: Long-Term Consequences,' *The Review of Economics and Statistics* 92:4 (2010), 693–713; Shivaji Mukherjee, 'Historical legacies of colonial indirect rule: Princely states and Maoist insurgency in central India,' *World Development* 111 (2018), 113–29; Ashutosh Varshney, *Ethnic Conflict and Civic Life: Hindus and Muslims in India* (New Haven, CT: Yale University Press, 2002); Ajay Verghese, *The Colonial Origins of Ethnic Violence in India* (Stanford, CA: Stanford University Press, 2016).
44 Harrison Akins, 'The Assam Rifles and India's North-East frontier policy,' *Small Wars & Insurgencies* 31:6 (2020), 1373–94; Bertil Lintner, *Great Game East: India, China, and the Struggle for Asia's Most Volatile Frontier* (New Haven, CT: Yale University Press, 2015).
45 Sanjib Baruah, *In the Name of the Nation: India and Its Northeast* (Stanford, CA: Stanford University Press, 2020), p. 3.
46 Guha, *India After Gandhi*, p. 72.
47 Ibid., p. 71.
48 Nirad C. Chaudhuri, *Thy Hand, Great Anarch! India: 1921–1952* (London: Chatto & Windus, 1987), p. 831.
49 Francis Wylie, 'Federal Negotiations in India 1935–9, and After,' in C.H. Philips and Mary Doreen Wainwright (eds), *The Partition of India: Policies and Perspectives, 1935–1947* (London: Geo. Allen & Unwin, 1970), pp. 517–26, at 521.
50 Menon, *The Story of the Integration of the Indian States*, p. 493.

Bibliography

Archives

British Library
  India Office Records (IOR)
Chughtai Library, Lahore, Pakistan
  Reports Archive
Library of Congress
  Princely States Papers
National Archives of India (NAI)
  External Affairs Ministry Papers
  Home Department Papers
  Political Department Papers
  Private Papers of M.R. Jayakar
  Private Papers of Sardar Patel
  States Ministry Papers
National Archives, U.K.
  Dominion Office Files (DO)
  Foreign Office Files (FCO)
National Library of Scotland (NLS)
  Records of the Governor General: The Indian Papers of the Fourth Earl of Minto
U.K. Parliament
  House of Commons Hansard Archives

Primary Source Collections

Foreign Relations of the United States (FRUS), 1948, The Near East, South Asia, and Africa, Volume V, Part 1 (Washington, DC: US Government Printing Office, 1975).

Foreign Relations of the United States (FRUS), 1950, The Near East, South Asia, and Africa, Volume V (Washington, DC: US Government Printing Office, 1978).

Hingorani, Anand (ed.). *To the Princes and Their People, Gandhi Series, Volume IV* (Karachi: Anand T. Hingorani, 1942).

Keith, A. Berriedale. *Speeches & Documents on Indian Policy, 1750–1921, Volume I* (London: Oxford University Press, 1929).

Mansergh, Nicholas and Penderel Moon (eds). *Constitutional Relations Between Britain and India: The Transfer of Power, 1942–7 (TOP), Volumes I–XII* (London: Her Majesty's Stationery Office, 1970–83).

Papers Relating to The Treaty Concluded Between the Government of India and the Khan of Khelat, on the 8th December 1876 (London: Her Majesty's Stationery Office, 1877).

Sardar Patel's Correspondence, 1945–50, Volume 1 (New Delhi: Navajivan Publishing House, 1971).

Selected Works of Jawaharlal Nehru, Second Series, Volume 4 (New Delhi: Jawaharlal Nehru Memorial Fund, 1986).

Selected Works of Jawaharlal Nehru, Second Series, Volume 7 (New Delhi: Jawaharlal Nehru Memorial Fund, 1988).

Speeches by Lord Curzon of Kedleston, Viceroy and Governor-General of India, Volume IV, 1904–1905 (Calcutta: Office of the Superintendent of Government Printing, 1906).

Zaidi, Z.H. (ed.). *Quaid-i-Azam Mohammad Ali Jinnah Papers (Jinnah Papers), Volumes I–XVIII* (Islamabad: Quaid-i-Azam Papers Project, National Archives of Pakistan, 1993–2012).

Newspaper/Media Sources

Amrita Bazar Patrika, BBC News, Bombay Chronicle, British Pathe, Civil & Military Gazette, Daily Telegraph, Dawn, Evening News, Free Press Journal, GQ India magazine, The Hindu, Hindustan Standard, Hindustan Times, Indian Daily Mail, Indian Express, India News Chronicle, The Leader, National Standard, National Call, New York Herald Tribune, New York Times, Pakistan Times, Statesman, Time magazine, Times of India, United Press International

Secondary Sources

Abhyankar, G.R. *Problem of Indian States* (Poona, India: Aryabhushan Press, 1928).

Ahmed, Akbar. *The Thistle and the Drone: How America's War on Terror Became a Global War on Tribal Islam* (Washington, DC: Brookings Institution Press, 2013).

Aitchison, Charles Umpherston. *The Native States of India: An Attempt to Elucidate a Few of the Principles which Underlie Their Relations with the British Government* (Calcutta: Office of the Superintendent of Government Printing, 1881).

Akins, Harrison. 'Mashar versus Kashar in Pakistan's FATA: Intra-tribal Conflict and the Obstacles to Reform,' *Asian Survey* 58:6 (2018), 1136–59.

Akins, Harrison. 'The Assam Rifles and India's North-East frontier policy,' *Small Wars & Insurgencies* 31:6 (2020), 1373–94.

Amselle, Jean-Loup. *Affirmative Exclusion: Cultural Pluralism and the Rule of Custom in France*, translated from the French by Jane Marie Todd (Ithaca, N.Y.: Cornell University Press, 2003).

Ankit, Rakesh. 'Mountbatten and India, 1948–64,' *International History Review* 37:2 (2015), 240–61.

Ankit, Rakesh. 'The accession of Junagadh, 1947–48: Colonial sovereignty, state violence and post-independence India,' *Indian Economic and Social History Review* 53:3 (2017), 371–404.

Ankit, Rakesh. 'Junagadh, India and the Logic of Occupation and Appropriation, 1947–49,' *Studies in History* 34:2 (2018), 109–40.

Axmann, Martin. *Back to the Future: The Khanate of Kalat and the Genesis of Baluch Nationalism 1915–1955* (New York: Oxford University Press, 2008).

Azaz, Prem Nath. *The History of the Struggle for Freedom in Kashmir* (New Delhi: Kashmir Publishing Company, 1954).

Balasubramaniam, Uma. *Sayajirao Gaekwad III: The Maharaja of Baroda* (New Delhi: Rupa Publications, 2019).

Banerjee, Milinda. *The Mortal God: Imagining the Sovereign in Colonial India* (Cambridge: Cambridge University Press, 2018).

Bangash, Yaqoob Khan. 'Three Forgotten Accessions: Gilgit, Hunza, and Nagar,' *Journal of Imperial and Commonwealth History* 38:1 (2010), 117–43.

Bangash, Yaqoob Khan. *A Princely Affair: The Accession and Integration of the Princely States of Pakistan, 1947–1955* (Karachi: Oxford University Press, 2015).

Barth, Fredrik. *The Last Wali of Swat: An Autobiography as told to Fredrik Barth* (New York: Columbia University Press, 1985).

Baruah, Sanjib. *In the Name of the Nation: India and Its Northeast* (Stanford, CA: Stanford University Press, 2020).

Basu, Narayani. *V.P. Menon: The Unsung Architect of Modern India* (New Delhi: Simon & Schuster, 2020).

Benton, Lauren. 'Colonial Law and Cultural Differences: Jurisdictional Politics and the Formation of the Colonial State,' *Comparative Studies in Society and History* 41:3 (1999), 563–88.

Beverley, Eric Lewis. *Hyderabad, British India, and the World, c. 1850–1950* (Cambridge: Cambridge University Press, 2015).

Beverley, Eric Lewis. 'Frontier as Resource: Law, Crime, and Sovereignty on the Margins of Empire,' *Comparative Studies in Society and History* 55:2 (2013), 241–72.

Bhagavan, Manu. 'Demystifying the "Ideal Progressive": Resistance through Mimicked Modernity in Princely Baroda, 1900–1913,' *Modern Asian Studies* 35:2 (2001), 385–409.

Bhagavan, Manu. *Sovereign Spheres: Princes, Education and Empire in Colonial India* (New Delhi: Oxford University Press, 2004).

Bhagavan, Manu. 'Princely States and the Hindu Imaginary: Exploring the Cartography of Hindu Nationalism in Colonial India,' *Journal of Asian Studies* 67:3 (2008), 881–915.

Campbell-Johnson, Alan. *Mission with Mountbatten* (Bombay: Aico Publishing House, 1951).

Chaudhuri, Nirad C. *Thy Hand, Great Anarch! India: 1921–1952* (London: Chatto & Windus, 1987).

Cohen, Maurice. *Thunder Over Kashmir* (Hyderabad: Orient Longman Limited, 1955).

Cohn, Bernard S. 'Representing Authority in Victorian India,' in Eric Hobsbawm and Terence Ranger (eds), *The Invention of Tradition* (Cambridge: Cambridge University Press, 1992), pp. 165–209.

Condos, Mark. *The Insecurity State: Punjab and the Making of Colonial Power in British India* (Cambridge: Cambridge University Press, 2017).

Copland, Ian. 'The Princely States, the Muslim League and the Partition of India in 1947,' *International History Review* 13:1 (1991), 38–69.

Copland, Ian. *The Princes of India in the Endgame of Empire, 1917–1947* (Cambridge: Cambridge University Press, 1997).

Copland, Ian. 'Crucibles of *Hindutva?* V.D. Savarkar, the Hindu Mahasabha, and the Indian princely states,' *South Asia: Journal of South Asian Studies* 25:3 (2002), 211–34.

Copland, Ian. *State, Community and Neighbourhood in Princely North India, c. 1900–1950* (Basingstoke: Palgrave Macmillan, 2005).

Corfield, Sir Conrad. *The Princely India I Knew: From Reading to Mountbatten* (Madras: Indo-British Historical Society, 1975).

Davies, Norman. *Vanished Kingdoms: The Rise and Fall of States and Nations* (London: Penguin Books, 2011).

Dalrymple, William. *The Anarchy: The East India Company, Corporate Violence, and the Pillage of an Empire* (New York: Bloomsbury, 2019).

Devi, Gayatri. *A Princess Remembers: The Memoirs of the Maharani of Jaipur* (New Delhi: Rupa Publications, 1995).

Dutt, Romesh. *The Economic History of India in the Victorian Age, From the Accession of Queen Victoria in 1837 to the Commencement of the Twentieth Century* (London: Kegan Paul, Trench, and Trubner, 1903).

El Edroos, Syed Ahmed and L.R. Naik. *Hyderabad of the 'Seven Loaves'* (Hyderabad: Laser Prints, 1994).

Ernst, Waltraud and Biswamoy Pati (eds). *India's Princely States: People, princes and colonialism* (Abingdon: Routledge, 2007).

Ernst, Waltraud, Biswamoy Pati, and T.V. Sekher. *Health and Medicine in the Indian Princely States, 1850–1950* (Abingdon: Routledge, 2017).

Fitze, Sir Kenneth. *Twilight of the Maharajas* (London: John Murray, 1956).

Gerth, H.H. and C. Wright Mills (eds). *From Max Weber: Essays in Sociology* (Abingdon: Routledge, 1991).

Guerin, Adam. 'Racial myth, colonial reform, and the invention of customary law in Morocco, 1912–1930,' *Journal of North African Studies* 16:3 (2011), 361–80.

Guha, Ramachandra. *India After Gandhi: The History of the World's Largest Democracy* (New York: Ecco, 2007).

Hansen, Thomas Blom and Finn Stepputat (eds). *Sovereign Bodies: Citizens, Migrants, and States in the Postcolonial World* (Princeton, NJ: Princeton University Press, 2005).

Harrison, Selig S. *In Afghanistan's Shadow: Baloch Nationalism and Soviet Temptations* (Washington, DC: Carnegie Endowment for International Peace, 1981).

Hingorani, Aman M. *Unravelling the Kashmir Knot* (New Delhi: Sage Publications, 2016).

Holdich, Colonel Sir Thomas Hungerford. *India* (London: Henry Frowde, 1904).

Hopkins, Benjamin D. *Ruling the Savage Periphery: Frontier Governance and the Making of the Modern State* (Cambridge, MA: Harvard University Press, 2020).

Hopkirk, Peter. *The Great Game: On Secret Service in High Asia* (London: John Murray, 1990).

Hussain, Shahla. *Kashmir in the Aftermath of Partition* (Cambridge: Cambridge University Press, 2021).

Hyder, Mohammed. *October Coup: A Memoir of the Struggle for Hyderabad* (New Delhi: Roli Books, 2012).

Hyderabad Reborn: First Six Months of Freedom [September 18, 1948–March 17, 1949] (Hyderabad: Director of Information, Government of Hyderabad, 1949).

Ikegame, Aya. *Princely India Re-imagined: A Historical Anthropology of Mysore from 1799 to the Present* (Abingdon: Routledge, 2013).

Iyer, Lakshmi. 'Direct versus Indirect Colonial Rule in India: Long-Term Consequences,' *Review of Economics and Statistics* 92:4 (2010), 693–713.

Keen, Caroline. *Princely India and the British: Political Development and the Operation of Empire* (London: Bloomsbury Academic, 2012).

Khan, Mir Ahmad Yar. *Inside Baluchistan: A Political Autobiography of Khan-e-Azam* (Karachi: Royal Book Company, 1975).

Khan, Yasmin. *The Great Partition: The Making of India and Pakistan* (New Haven, CT: Yale University Press, 2007).

Khan, Yasmin. *India at War: The Subcontinent and the Second World War* (New York: Oxford University Press, 2015).

Khilnani, Sunil. *The Idea of India* (New York: Farrar, Straus and Giroux, 1997).

Khosla, Madhav (ed.). *Letters for a Nation: From Jawaharlal Nehru to His Chief Ministers, 1947–1963* (New Delhi: Penguin Books, 2014).

Kooiman, Dick. 'Invention of Tradition in Travancore: A Maharaja's Quest for Political Security,' *Journal of the Royal Asiatic Society* 15:2 (2005), 151–64.

Korbel, Josef. *Danger in Kashmir* (Princeton, NJ: Princeton University Press, 1954).

Lamb, Alastair. *Kashmir: A Disputed Legacy, 1846–1990* (Lahore: Oxford University Press, 1992).

Lee-Warner, Sir William. *The Native States of India* (London: Macmillan and Co., 1910).

Lee-Warner, Sir William. 'Kathiawar,' *Journal of the Royal Society of Arts* 61:3145 (1913), 391–405.

Lewis, Mary Dewhurst. *Divided Rule: Sovereignty and Empire in French Tunisia, 1881–1938* (Berkeley, CA: University of California Press, 2014).

Lintner, Bertil. *Great Game East: India, China, and the Struggle for Asia's Most Volatile Frontier* (New Haven, CT: Yale University Press, 2015).

Lugard, Frederick. *The Dual Mandate in British Tropical Africa* (London: William Blackwood and Sons, 1922).

Mantena, Rama Sundari. 'Publicity, Civil Liberties, and Political Life in Princely Hyderabad,' *Modern Asian Studies* 53:4 (2019), 1248–77.

Mason, Philip. *A Shaft of Sunlight: Memories of a Varied Life* (London: Andre Deutsch, 1978).

McLane, John R. *Indian Nationalism and the Early Congress* (Princeton, NJ: Princeton University Press, 1978).

Menon, A. Sreedhara. *Triumph and Tragedy in Travancore: Annals of Sir CP's Sixteen Years* (Kottayam, India: Current Books, 2001).

Mahajan, Mehr Chand. *Looking Back: The Autobiography of Mehr Chand Mahajan* (London: Asia Publishing House, 1963).

McLeod, John. *Sovereignty, Power, Control: Politics in the States of Western India* (Leiden: Brill, 1999).

Mehta, Ved. *Portrait of India* (New Haven, CT: Yale University Press, 1967).

Menon, V.P. *The Story of the Integration of the Indian States* (Bombay, India: Orient Longmans Ltd., 1956).

Minto, Mary. *India: Minto and Morley, 1905–1910, Compiled from the Correspondence Between the Viceroy and the Secretary of State* (London: Macmillan and Co., 1934).

Moorcraft, William and George Trebeck. *Travels in the Himalayan Provinces of Hindustan and the Panjab; in Ladakh and Kashmir; In Peshawar, Kabul, Kunduz, and Bokhara; From 1819 to 1825, Volume II* (London: John Murray, 1841).

Morris-Jones, W.H. 'The Transfer of Power, 1947: A View from the Sidelines,' *Modern Asian Studies* 16:1 (1982), 1–32.

Muldoon, Andrew. *Empire, Politics and the Creation of the 1935 India Act: Last Act of the Raj* (Surrey: Ashgate, 2009).

Mukherjee, Shivaji. 'Historical legacies of colonial indirect rule: Princely states and Maoist insurgency in central India,' *World Development* 111 (2018), 113–29.

Narasimhan, Sakuntala. *Sati: Widow Burning in India* (New York: Anchor Books, 1990).

Naseemullah, Adnan and Paul Staniland. 'Indirect Rule and Varieties of Governance,' *Governance* 29:1 (2016), 13–30.

Noorani, A.G. *The Destruction of Hyderabad* (New Delhi: Tulika Books, 2013).

Overstreet, William C. *The Geologic Occurrence of Monazite* (Washington, DC: U.S. Government Printing Office, 1967).

Panikkar, K.M. *An Autobiography*, Translated from the Malayalam by K. Krishnamurthy (Madras: Oxford University Press, 1977).

Parel, Anthony J. (ed.). *Gandhi: Hind Swaraj and Other Writings* (Cambridge: Cambridge University Press, 1997).

Patil, S.H. *The Congress Party and the Princely States* (Bombay: Himalaya Publishing House, 1981).

Pernau, Margrit. *The Passing of Patrimonialism: Politics and Political Culture in Hyderabad, 1911–1948* (Delhi: Manohar, 2000).

Puri, Luv. *Across the Line of Control: Inside Pakistan-Administered Kashmir* (New York: Columbia University Press, 2012).

Purushotham, Sunil. 'Sovereignty, Federation, and Constituent Power in Interwar India, ca. 1917–39,' *Comparative Studies of South Asia, Africa and the Middle East* 40:3 (2020), 421–33.

Purushotham, Sunil. *From Raj to Republic: Sovereignty, Violence, and Democracy in India* (Palo Alto, CA: Stanford University Press, 2021).

Raghavan, Srinath. *War and Peace in Modern India* (Basingstoke: Palgrave Macmillan, 2010).

Raghavan, Srinath. *India's War: World War II and the Making of Modern South Asia* (New York: Basic Books, 2016).

Rai, Mridu. *Hindu Rulers, Muslim Subjects: Islam, Rights, and the History of Kashmir* (Princeton, NJ: Princeton University Press, 2004).

Ramusack, Barbara N. *The Princes of India In the Twilight of Empire: Dissolution of a Patron–Client System, 1914–1939* (Columbus, OH: Ohio State University Press, 1978).

Ramusack, Barbara N. *The New Cambridge History of India: The Indian Princes and Their States, Volume III, No. 6* (Cambridge: Cambridge University Press, 2004).

Reid, Anthony. 'Colonial Transformation: A Bitter Legacy,' in Anthony Reid (ed.), *Verandah of Violence: The Background to the Aceh Problem* (Singapore: University of Singapore Press, 2006), pp. 96–108.

Report of the Committee on FATA Reforms (Islamabad: Ministry of States and Frontier Regions, Government of Pakistan, 2016).

Report of the Indian States Committee, 1928–1929 (London: His Majesty's Stationery Office, 1929).

Roy, Surendra Nath. *A History of the Native States of India, Volume 1, Gwalior* (Calcutta: Thacker Spink & Co., 1888).

Rudolph, Susanne Hoeber, Lloyd I. Rudolph and Mohan Singh. 'A Bureaucratic Lineage in Princely India: Elite Formation and Conflict in a Patrimonial System,' *Journal of Asian Studies* 34:3 (1975), 717–53.

Sachdev, Vibhuti. 'Negotiating Modernity in the Princely State of Jaipur,' *South Asian Studies* 28:2 (2012), 171–81.

Saksena, Priyasha, 'Jousting Over Jurisdiction: Sovereignty and International Law in Late Nineteenth-Century South Asia,' *Law and History Review* 38:2 (2020), 409–57.

Sherman, Taylor. *Muslim Belonging in Secular India: Negotiating Citizenship in Postcolonial Hyderabad* (Cambridge: Cambridge University Press, 2015).

Siddiqi, Farhan Hanif. *The Politics of Ethnicity in Pakistan: The Baloch, Sindhi, and Mohajir Ethnic Movements* (Abingdon: Routledge, 2012).

Talbot, Ian. 'The Punjab Under Colonialism: Order and Transformation in British India,' *Journal of Punjab Studies* 14:1 (2007), 3–10.

Tilly, Charles. 'War Making and State Making as Organized Crime,' in Peter Evans, Dietrich Rueschemeyer, and Theda Skocpol (eds), *Bringing the State Back In* (Cambridge: Cambridge University Press, 1985), pp. 169–87.

Verghese, Ajay. *The Colonial Origins of Ethnic Violence in India* (Stanford, CA: Stanford University Press, 2016).

Wagner, Kim A. *Amritsar 1919: An Empire of Fear and the Making of a Massacre* (New Haven, CT: Yale University Press, 2019).

Watson, Colonel J.W. *Statistical Account of Junagadh; Being the Junagadh Contribution to the Kathiawar Portion of the Bombay Gazette* (Bombay: Bombay Gazette Steam Press, 1884).

Wylie, Francis. 'Federal Negotiations in India 1935–9, and After,' in C.H. Philips and Mary Doreen Wainwright (eds), *The Partition of India: Policies and Perspectives, 1935–1947* (London: Geo. Allen & Unwin, 1970), pp. 517–26.

Zeb, Rizwan. *Ethno-Political Conflict in Pakistan: The Baloch Movement* (Abingdon: Routledge, 2020).

Zutshi, Chitralekha. 'Re-visioning princely states in South Asian historiography: A review,' *Indian Economic and Social History Review* 46:3 (2009), 301–13.

Index

Milton Keynes UK
Ingram Content Group UK Ltd.
UKHW022223170124
436215UK00004B/40